Dramatic Extracts
in Seventeenth-Century
English Manuscripts

Dramatic Extracts in Seventeenth-Century English Manuscripts

Watching, Reading, Changing Plays

Laura Estill

UNIVERSITY OF DELAWARE PRESS
Newark

University of Delaware Press
© 2015 by Laura Estill
All rights reserved
Printed in the United States of America on acid-free paper
Distributed by the University of Virginia Press

ISBN 978-1-64453-046-7 (paper)
ISBN 978-1-64453-047-4 (ebook)

British Library Cataloguing-in-Publication Information Available

Library of Congress Cataloging-in-Publication Data

Estill, Laura.
　Dramatic extracts in seventeenth-century English manuscripts : watching, reading, changing plays / Laura Estill.
　　　pages cm
　Includes bibliographical references and index.
　1. English drama—17th century—History and criticism. I. Title.
　PR655.E88 2014
　822'.309—dc23
　2014040029

Contents

List of Figures — vii

List of Tables — ix

List of Abbreviations — xi

Note on Transcription and Editorial Practice — xiii

Acknowledgments — xv

Introduction — xvii

1 The Rise of Dramatic Extracting: Extracting from English Plays, 1590–1642 — 1

2 Dramatic Extracts from Elizabethan and Stuart Masques and Entertainments — 43

3 Theatrical Nostalgia: Dramatic Miscellanies and the Closure of the Theatres, 1642–1660 — 77

4 Re-Presenting and Re-Reading the Renaissance: Restoration Extracts from Renaissance Plays, 1660–1700 — 115

5 Archbishop Sancroft, Play-Reader and Collector of Dramatic Extracts — 161

6 Proverbial Shakespeare: The Print and Manuscript Circulation of Extracts from *Love's Labour's Lost* — 201

Conclusion	225
Bibliography	229
Manuscript Index	233
Subject Index	237
About the Author	255

List of Figures

Figure 1.1	BL MS Add. 61822, f. 90v–91.	15
Figure 2.1	Milton's autograph. Harvard MS Fr. 487, p. 110.	52
Figure 3.1	BL MS Add. 22608, f. 111, Wright's table of contents.	82
Figure 3.2	Folger MS V.a.87, f. 4v–5.	100
Figure 4.1	BL MS Sloane 161, f. 18.	129
Figure 5.1	Shakespeare, Folio 3 (1664 edition), sig. Cccc5, detail. "Hark, hark, the Lark" and surrounding text.	171
Figure 5.2	Shakespeare, Folio 3 (1664 edition), sig. Xxx5, detail. "She that was ever fair" and surrounding text.	173
Figure 5.3	Bodleian MS Sancroft 29, f. i, Sancroft's list of plays.	180
Figure 5.4	Bodleian MS Sancroft 29, p. 1. Sancroft's initial extracts from plays sorted by commonplace heading.	181
Figure 5.5	Title page and frontispiece of the first Beaumont and Fletcher folio (1647).	185

List of Tables

Table 3.1	Transcription, BL MS Add. 22608, f. 111, Wright's table of contents.	83
Table 3.2	The contents of Folger MS V.a.87.	102
Table 4.1	Shakespearean Extracts in BL MS Lansdowne 1185.	144
Table 5.1	Non-Shakespearean dramatic extracts from Bodleian MS Sancroft 29.	182
Table 5.2	Shakespearean and apocryphal extracts in Bodleian MS Sancroft 29.	186
Table 6.1	Some Non-Shakespearean print versions of Jerome's proverb.	205
Table 6.2	Transmission of the "Fat Paunches" couplet in print sources.	206
Table 6.3	Print sources that contain the "Fat Paunches" couplet arranged by variants.	209
Table 6.4	Transmission of the "Fat Paunches" couplet in manuscript sources.	214

List of Abbreviations

Add.	Additional
Adv.	Advocates
BL	British Library, London
CELM	*Catalogue of English Literary Manuscripts*
DLB	*Dictionary of Literary Biography*
Don.	Donation
EEBO	*Early English Books Online*
Eng. Misc.	English Miscellaneous
Eng. Poet.	English Poetry
ESTC	*English Short Title Catalogue*
Fr.	French
MS	manuscript
NLS	National Library of Scotland, Edinburgh
NYPL	New York Public Library
ODNB	*Oxford Dictionary of National Biography*
OED	*Oxford English Dictionary*
PMLA	*Publications of the Modern Language Association of America*
Rawl.	Rawlinson
TLN	through line number

Note on Transcription and Editorial Practice

In quotations from early sources, I have normalized i/j, u/v/w, long s, and ff for F. I have silently expanded common abbreviations (such as "y^e" for "the" and macrons indicating dropped m or n). I use square brackets to show my additions. I mark intralinear insertions in the manuscript with ^carets^. Spelling is normalized when discussing multiple early sources for texts.

To clarify page, folio, and signature, I use p., f., and sig. for early sources. The recto of folios is unmarked except when citing both sides as r–v.

Unless otherwise noted, early modern printed texts were consulted using *Early English Books Online* (*EEBO*) or *Eighteenth-Century Collections Online* (*ECCO*).

Line numbers for Shakespeare's plays are taken from the *The Riverside Shakespeare*, 2nd ed., ed. G. Blakemore Evans et al., (Boston: Houghton Mifflin, 1997). Line numbers for Jonson's plays are taken from *The Cambridge Edition of the Works of Ben Jonson*, ed. David Bevington, Martin Butler, and Ian Donaldson, et al., 7 vols. (Cambridge: Cambridge UP, 2012).

Acknowledgments

I would like to thank the many people whose patience and support have made this book possible. Especial thanks to Arthur Marotti and Ken Jackson for encouraging me to undertake this project and to Ray Siemens and Erin Kelly for helping me see it through. Thanks also to Jaime Goodrich and James Purkis for their valuable insights. I'm grateful to all whose suggestions helped shape and improve this material, including Kailin Wright, Sarah Milligan, Andie Silva, Renuka Gusain, and J. Matthew Huculak. Thanks also to Claire Bryony Williams, Joel Swann, Megan Heffernan, Heidi Craig, Miranda Lewis, Katie Will, and John Heggelund.

This book would not have been possible without funding from multiple sources, including the Banting Postdoctoral Fellowship Program, the Social Sciences and Humanities Research Council of Canada, the Electronic Textual Cultures Lab at the University of Victoria, the Wayne State University Graduate School, Wayne State's College of Liberal Arts and Sciences, the English Department at Wayne State, the Renaissance Society of America, and the Glasscock Humanities Centre at Texas A&M University. The fellowships, research awards, and grants from these sources allowed me to undertake archival research that was critical to this project. I would also like to thank the archivists and librarians at the British Library, the Bodleian Library, University College London, Queen's College, the Houghton Library, Lambeth Palace Library, the National Library of Scotland, the University of Edinburgh, the Folger Shakespeare Library, the Newberry Library, the Shakespeare Birthplace Trust Record Office, University College London, William Salt Library, and the National Archives in Kew for their helpful and thoughtful assistance. Thanks also to Liesbeth Vijfhuizen and Jaime Goodrich for the assistance with translations from Dutch and Latin, respectively.

I would like to thank the editors of *Shakespeare*, *Early Theatre*, and *New Ways of Looking at Old Texts* for their permission to publish revisions of previous essays. An earlier version of chapter six, "Proverbial Shakespeare: The print and manuscript circulation of extracts from *Love's Labour's Lost*" appeared in *Shakespeare* 7.1 (2011): 35–55; sections in Chapter 1 have been adapted from "New Contexts for Early Tudor Plays: William Briton, and Early Reader of *Gorboduc*" *Early Theatre* 16.2 (2013): 197–210 and "'All the Adulteries of Art': Margaret Bellasys's BL MS Add. 10309" in *New Ways of Looking at Old Texts V: Papers of the Renaissance English Texts Society* ed. Michael Denbo (Arizona Center for Medieval and Renaissance Studies, forthcoming). Thanks also to the Bodleian Library at Oxford University, the Houghton Library and Harry Elkins Widener Collection at Harvard University, the British Library, and the Folger Shakespeare Library for their permission to print images.

Introduction

A Christ Church reader turned to William Cartwright's 1651 collected works to copy pages of poetry and selections from *The Royal Slave* and *The Ordinary*. In Scotland, William Drummond read some recently published plays from the London stage and gathered *bons mots*. William Lilly, the astrologer, wrote pseudoscientific notes in a volume that also contains extracts from James Shirley's *Changes*, Thomas Nabbes's *Hannibal and Scipio*, and Thomas Heywood's *The Royal King*.[1] We have long imagined early modern bookworms—but this university man, Drummond, and Lilly are actual readers who left tangible evidence of their interaction with plays. Early modern readers were not passive audiences: they were often themselves compilers, transcribers, revisers, and writers.

Throughout the seventeenth century, early modern play-readers and playgoers copied dramatic extracts, that is, selections from plays and masques, into their notebooks. These records provide information that is not available in other forms about the popularity and importance of early modern plays, the reasons plays appealed to their audiences, and the ideas in plays that most interested audiences. As this under-examined archival evidence reveals, play-readers and playgoers viewed plays as malleable and modular texts to be altered, appropriated, and most importantly, used.

With early modern plays, scholars often focus on how the original performance brings the text to life. Book historians have examined early modern print and manuscript plays to show the material circumstances under which these plays were written and published. As D. F. McKenzie famously asserts, however, "different readers [bring] the text to life in different ways."[2] When we analyze dramatic extracts as a record of early modern responses to plays, we can incorporate a consideration of both print and performance, while also reconsidering the plays' reception. This book is the first sustained study of dramatic extracts in manuscript, and the cultural, political, and literary forces of the early modern period that affect how we should approach and interpret both plays and their extracts. Dramatic extracts reveal what early modern audiences and readers took, literally and figuratively, from plays.

Dramatic excerpting (or extracting) is the practice of copying selections from a play, either at a performance or from a print or manuscript source. These extracts appear in many types of manuscripts, including miscellanies, composite volumes, commonplace books, and diaries. While dramatic excerpting is easily defined, it can be more of a challenge to articulate what constitutes a dramatic extract.[3] In some cases, a dramatic extract is easy to identify: it is a group of lines copied from a play. For the purpose of this study, I differentiate between extracts and abridgments or adaptations, although at times, they can overlap. For instance, George Bannatyne's manuscript copy of David Lindsay's *Ane Satyre of the Thrie Estaits* and Edward Dering's telescoped version of both parts of William Shakespeare's *Henry IV* are abridgments or adaptations. While these adaptations involve making a selection from a larger source text, they still present the final version as a play by including speech prefixes and maintaining the integrity of the plot.[4] Not all cases, however, are as clear-cut as Bannatyne's or Dering's textual interventions, especially in those manuscripts that contain extensive extracts.[5] If a manuscript contains the majority of a play or masque, I consider it an abridgment and only discuss these abridgments in their relation to shorter dramatic extracts.

Dramatic extracts are not abridgments or adaptations, but neither are they play fragments. A fragment is part of a once-complete version of a play that has been damaged, whereas manuscript compilers conceptualized dramatic extracts as separate from the plays. A dramatic excerpt is part of a larger play that a compiler selects and copies, deliberately omitting the rest of the play. For instance, the single leaf of Christopher Marlowe's from *The Massacre at Paris* (Folger MS J.b.8) was once part of a complete text of the play, and therefore beyond the scope of this study. Similarly, handwritten additions meant to supplement imperfect print copies are not extracts.[6] Acting parts, those manuscripts created for a player to rehearse his role, are not dramatic extracts because they do not indicate selectivity on the part of the compiler.[7] Dramatic extracts are valuable for the study of early modern play reception because they provide a glimpse into early readers' and playgoers' reactions through their choices.

Although book-lists, allusions, and literary appropriations provide valuable insight into theatre history and early modern reception, they are not dramatic extracts either. Dramatic extracts involve copying selections from a play, whereas book-lists and allusions mention a title, playwright, character, or even moment in a play without offering any lines from the play. For instance, one gentleman, Henry Oxinden, copied a list of early modern plays in his commonplace book, Folger MS V.b.110 (p. 93). Gabriel Harvey famously pointed to *Hamlet* in a list of works enjoyed by "The younger sort" in his manuscript additions to Thomas Speght's *Chaucer* (BL MS Add. 42518, f. 422v). Authors themselves would often refer to existing plays by title or character; *The Shakspere Allusion-Book* is chock-full of examples.[8] Charles Whitney's *Early Responses to Renaissance Drama* shows the value of exploring early modern reception history through these allusions.[9] A mention of a play, however, is not the same as copying lines from that play. And although authors and playwrights would often recycle lines from other texts, literary appropriations or allusions (what William N. West calls "play scraps") are not in the same vein as dramatic extracts because they intentionally repurpose parts of plays into other complete works.[10]

After reading what a dramatic extract is not (an abridgment, an adaptation, a fragment, a mention, or a literary appropriation), you might be left wondering about how much there is to say about those rare occasions where we find actual dramatic extracts. Except that dramatic extracts are not rare. Peter Beal's *Catalogue of English Literary Manuscripts* (*CELM*) lists hundreds of manuscripts compiled before 1700 that contain dramatic extracts from early modern plays written before the closure of the theatres in 1642.[11] The hundreds of manuscripts that Beal cites, however, provides only a sample of those that contain seventeenth-century dramatic extracts. Although *CELM* catalogues an extensive set of manuscripts that contain literary works from 1450–1700 and expands the coverage of Beal's printed *Index*, it nevertheless focus on particular authors, thereby excluding lesser-known playwrights (such as Peter Hausted and William Peaps) and anonymous dramatic works (such as *The Tragedy of Nero* and *The Mountebank's Masque*) that were also excerpted in seventeenth-century manuscripts.[12] Dramatic extracts reveal that early modern readers and audiences did not make the same assumptions about canon and authorship as modern scholars, but instead enjoyed plays by anonymous authors and playwrights who are almost entirely forgotten today. Many manuscript compilers copied dramatic extracts without ascribing the selection to its author, or even, at times, its play—though, as the examples in this book will show, others avidly followed the works of a particular playwright or scrupulously noted play titles, authors, and even page numbers. As *CELM* shows, there are thousands of known dramatic extracts, and many more to be discovered—these will certainly contribute even more to our understanding of early modern tastes, responses, and attitudes.

Just as there are certainly numerous manuscripts to be catalogued and copious extracts to be uncovered—even in catalogued material—many dramatic extracts have been lost because of their potentially ephemeral nature.

Published dramatic extracts, which were printed in multiple copies, survive at a higher rate than those that were copied by hand. Most of the manuscripts discussed here are bound volumes: some readers copied extracts into empty notebooks that were pre-bound; other notebooks were bound after they were composed; and still other volumes, called aggregate or composite volumes, gather a variety of loose papers, such as letters and poems. In a few rare cases, we have evidence of a reader jotting a selection from a play onto a single leaf of paper—but these fragile documents rarely survive.[13] It is likely that many readers who copied dramatic extracts never intended them to survive for centuries, but rather saw them as personal texts of value to themselves and perhaps a few friends. The low survival rate suggests that the evidence in extant manuscripts, such as dramatic extracts, needs to be considered as part of larger practices of reading and writing, instead of anomalous or rare.

Because of their changeable, adaptable, and useful nature, dramatic extracts are valuable pieces of archival evidence that should influence our understanding of early modern reading habits, textuality, and theatre. The examples discussed in this book prove that readers viewed early modern plays, like other texts, as works to be broken into fragments for personal use. Reconsidering plays as works that are malleable and divisible changes our understanding of how to evaluate early modern plays: we can consider them not as complete artistic units but as compendia of smaller pieces to be taken apart. For many early modern readers, the wit and value of a playwright lay in his or her use of *sententiae*, those pithy and often moral phrases that retain their value even when removed from the context of the play. Current scholarship on early modern drama explores multiple versions of texts (consider *King Lear*) and recognizes that many plays were the result of collaborative authorship. Valuing drama for its extracts and extractable nature further distances us from the idea of a Renaissance play as a single unit created by one author.

This examination of dramatic extracts in seventeenth-century manuscripts functions, in part, as a corrective to author-centric and Shakespeare-centric scholarship by returning to lesser-known plays as well as anonymous or relatively unknown compilers, which better captures early modern thinking about plays. This method of examination furthers our understanding beyond both the stage and the page by looking at how audiences and readers divided, changed, and used the plays as part of their daily lives. Dramatic extracts are evidence of the interpretive relationship that play-readers and playgoers had to plays—and the extracts themselves are often yet to be interpreted by scholars. The study of dramatic extracts is the study of particulars: particular readers, particular manuscripts, particular plays or masques, particular historic moments. Although no beautifully coherent history of dramatic extracts can (or, perhaps, should) be written, it is nevertheless important to attend to the historic patterns of dramatic extracting.

The study of dramatic extracts has its roots in literary studies, textual scholarship, and book history. Another valuable context for researching dramatic extracts can be found in analyses of manuscript poetry, just as manuscript poetry itself is often a context for the extracts themselves.[14] Scholarship on commonplacing, print commonplace books and miscellanies, manuscript commonplace books, and scribal publication provides a framework for understanding the culture of extracting and anthologizing.[15] Even with the scholarly work on full-text plays, playhouse documents, and acting parts, dramatic extracts are often ignored—though recent editors of Shakespeare and Thomas Middleton have begun to gesture toward this archival evidence.[16] Examining dramatic extracts combines elements of all of these areas of research, while also making a distinct contribution by analyzing overlooked texts that change how we understand the reception of early modern plays.

To date, any discussion of dramatic extracts has been focused on primarily Shakespearean extracts, while research on non-Shakespearean extracts generally takes a music history approach to songs from plays.[17] This Shakespearean focus points more to our modern preoccupation with Shakespeare than to early modern reading practices; the archival evidence suggests that there are more manuscripts with extracts from plays by Jonson, Francis Beaumont & John Fletcher, James Shirley, or even Sir John Suckling than Shakespeare.[18] Shakespearean extracts, furthermore, are more frequently identified and catalogued than their non-Shakespearean counterparts. It used to be that when faced with an unidentified stanza in a commonplace book or verse miscellany, a scholar could only determine its origins through intuition and extensive searching—and even that might have yielded no results. With digitized and searchable online play-texts, however, we can now identify the sources of extracts more easily, which provides a fuller picture of early modern textual culture.

Considering dramatic extracts complements previous research done on parts of plays, such as songs, epilogues, and prologues. Tiffany Stern's *Documents of Performance in Early Modern England* casts early modern playwrights as "play-patchers" who brought together many disparate texts into one play.[19] Her landmark book is important to the study of dramatic extracts because it shows how parts of plays, particularly songs, prologues, and epilogues, were frequently written and circulated separately from plays. Where Stern focuses on how plays are created from various separate texts, this book reveals how readers and audiences took plays apart after they were performed and published as complete texts. Both before and after their inclusion in a complete play, smaller sections circulated separately.

The practice of dramatic extracting was undertaken for centuries. This book focuses on extracts from English plays and masques first performed or published before 1642; the wealth of extracts from Restoration plays deserves in-depth consideration on their own. To show how extracts from dramatic works circulated beyond the moments of their play's initial publication or performance, this examination considers dramatic extracts that were copied in manuscripts until 1700. Creating a narrative of dramatic extracts requires maintaining multiple historical points of focus: the original circumstances when the play was written, performed, and published and the later moment(s) when a playgoer or reader encountered the text or performance and copied selections into manuscript. As a series of microhistories, the study of dramatic excerpting can more accurately gauge the "fierce particularities" of these manuscripts, their individual compilers, and the changing cultural and literary contexts in which plays were seen and read.[20] Extracting from both plays and other literary works continued into the eighteenth century and beyond, which would be an area for further research that could concentrate on the changing literary and theatrical landscapes.

Chapter 1 demonstrates that dramatic extracting evolved from the long tradition of copying pithy and wise sayings from classical and religious sources, a practice known as commonplacing. In this chapter, I address the related questions of when dramatic excerpting began in England, why manuscript compilers began selecting dramatic extracts in the 1590s, and how dramatic extracting evolved over the early seventeenth century. I describe individual manuscripts and instances of dramatic excerpting, while also offering patterns and connections. This chapter includes an analysis of William Briton's extracts from *Gorboduc*, a new way of considering the selections from *Titus Andronicus* in the Longleat manuscript, as well as a discussion of the newly rediscovered writing guide, "The Modell of Poesye" (BL MS Add. 81083). I show how changing attitudes toward vernacular literature and popular theatre led to the appearance of dramatic extracts in print and manuscript. This chapter also investigates the material contexts of dramatic extracting by considering the increase in play publication, typographical conventions such as commonplace markers, and writing technologies such as the table-book. Chapter 1 outlines multiple ways dramatic extracts circulated: for instance, they could be copied from full-text plays or print miscellanies, transmitted orally, or jotted down during a performance. As this chapter shows, early modern audiences and readers did not consider plays as unified artistic wholes, but as sources to be dismantled, changed, and mined for wit, wisdom, and song. This exploration of early extracts sets up how and why readers copied extracts (from performance, full-text plays, print miscellanies, other manuscripts, and memory) in order to provide contexts for the analysis in later chapters.

The over-arching argument of Chapter 2 is that the act of excerpting from a masque or entertainment creates meanings distinct from both the moment of performance and from the complete print or manuscript version. In Chapter 2,

I argue that we can no longer consider masques as purely performed or occasional texts, but instead need to recognize them as cultural and literary currency whose meaning and value changed over time. I show how masque extracts were decontextualized from their full-text sources and recontextualized, in, for instance, state papers, to highlight their status as political texts, or alongside classical authors to add literary gravitas. I do not dispute the historical readings of performed masques as cultural and political texts, but instead offer an examination of excerpts from masques as embedded in new manuscript and print contexts. To put it another way, this chapter looks at the occasions of excerpting and the circulation of those extracts rather than the occasions of performance. I investigate the popularity of Nicholas Breton's "In the Merry Month of May," examine John Milton's not-yet-discussed self-quotation from *Comus* ("—if Vertue feeble were / Heaven it selfe would stoope to her"), and consider Jonson's *The Gypsies Metamorphosed* in relation to a scandal that involved adultery, cross-dressing, and expatriation. The study of dramatic extracts reveals that the cultural value of masques and entertainments extends beyond the initial moments of performance and publication.

Chapter 3 establishes dramatic extracting as a key way that theatrical activity persisted after the closure of the theatres. This chapter introduces a major development in seventeenth-century dramatic extracting: the dramatic miscellany, a book or manuscript primarily comprising dramatic extracts. Some well-known examples of dramatic miscellanies are John Cotgrave's print *English Treasury of Wit and Language*—which contains extracts from plays by Samuel Daniel, John Ford, and William Davenant—and Abraham Wright's commonplace book, BL MS Add. 22608. Wright, for instance, noted that *Hamlet* was "but an indifferent play" (f. 85v) and preferred the works of James Shirley to Shakespeare; Wright also copied selections from less popular plays, including Henry Shirley's *The Martyred Soldier* and Philip Massinger's *A New Way to Pay Old Debts*. Taking into account the complicated political valences of the mid-seventeenth century, I show that early modern responses to drama were personalized and contingent. This chapter demonstrates the importance of attending to each manuscript and extract carefully; for instance, my research uncovers hitherto overlooked extracts in Wright's dramatic miscellany that require scholars to re-date and reconsider both his manuscript and his attitudes toward plays. Many studies of early modern theatre take 1642 as a seemingly natural end-date. Dramatic miscellanies, one of the apogees of dramatic extracting, force us to consider the afterlives of plays beyond the closure of the theatres.

Attending to individuals and their manuscripts encourages us to rethink traditional periodization of theatrical and literary history. Chapter 4 explores how revivals, adaptations, and republications contributed to the continued extracting from Renaissance plays during the Restoration. The reopening of the theatres was a momentous event that in many cases altered how readers and playgoers perceived earlier plays by juxtaposing them with new drama predicated on different aesthetic values. This chapter shows how songs from Shakespeare's *The Tempest* (most prominently "Where the bee sucks") circulated alongside songs from the John Dryden-William Davenant and Thomas Shadwell adaptations. Extracts from *The Tempest* elicited both response poems and additional verses with topical references—in one case, to King Charles II's notorious womanizing. In other cases, however, dramatic extracts from Renaissance plays continued to circulate as they had in the earlier seventeenth century, in verse miscellanies and commonplace books without reference to new productions and publications. Along with other primary sources, this chapter analyzes John Muddyclift's diary entries (BL MS Sloane 161) about play reading and dramatic extracting that were bound with his dramatic extracts from an Elizabethan masque (Sir Philip Sidney's *Lady of May*), a recently revived tragedy (Jonson's *Catiline*), and a contemporary adaptation (Shadwell's *The Miser*). The manuscripts discussed in this chapter offer concrete evidence of Restoration attitudes toward earlier plays.

Though William Sancroft is best known as the Archbishop of Canterbury during the nonjuring schism, he was also a prolific manuscript compiler who, as Chapter 5 reveals, copied hundreds of extracts from Renaissance plays. Sancroft's manuscripts include previously unnoted dramatic extracts that exemplify many of the trends in dramatic extracting: the circulation of extracts in separates (short, contained manuscripts that were passed from person to person), their inclusion as poems in verse miscellanies, the appreciation of them as rhetorical utterances, the construction of dramatic miscellanies replete with selections from plays, the recontextualizing and decontextualizing of dramatic material, and the Restoration expression of nostalgia for Renaissance theatre. Sancroft is a significant example of dramatic extracting not only because of his high-profile standing but also because of his wide-ranging scholarship and his prolific extracting. The varied purposes and range of Sancroft's extracts offer evidence of one educated man's tastes, his views of authorship, and his conceptions of the canon, while also showcasing the multiple ways snippets from drama were part of quotidian seventeenth-century textual culture.

While previous chapters establish the importance of attending to one manuscript or one compiler, Chapter 6 demonstrates the value of studying the transmission of a single extract by tracing the path of one particular dramatic extract that appeared in multiple print and manuscript sources over the seventeenth century: Shakespeare's "fat paunches have lean pates" from *Love's Labour's Lost*. This chapter investigates the proverbial nature of commonplaces in relation both to playwriting and to dramatic extracting.

The "fat paunches" extract is a prime example of how dramatic extracts were not always taken from the plays themselves and could be copied from intermediate sources. The diverse intermediate sources show how extracts were not just parts of plays; they were parts of early modern textual culture. The widely varied contexts for this couplet (from a print physiognomical tract to a collaboratively written University miscellany) reveal how dramatic extracts circulated beyond their source texts, accruing new meanings in new contexts.

The conclusion of *Dramatic Extracts in Seventeenth-Century English Manuscripts: Watching, Reading, Changing Plays* reinforces the importance of archival research on dramatic extracts as a means of understanding the circulation and textuality of early modern plays, reader and audience responses, and the historically changing meaning of dramatic texts. I suggest that the multiple ways of approaching dramatic extracts (by play, by playwright, by manuscript, by compiler, and, indeed, by extract) will deepen our understanding of particular plays and historic moments. This book offers a foundation for the study of dramatic extracts and highlights the importance of further work on these significant, although rarely analyzed, texts.

Dramatic extracts show how theatrical texts circulated in everyday life, not as full-text artistic works, but as phrases to be used in conversation, as songs and poems, and as snippets of wisdom and advice. The act of watching a performance or reading a play was not passive: audience members scribbled notes into table-books just as readers jotted down their impressions or copied lengthy passages. In our classrooms and on our stages, twenty-first-century teachers and directors have treated Renaissance plays as unified works of art, but recent scholarship calls this treatment into question by pointing out that plays were cobbled from various sources, written collaboratively, and revised extensively. The evidence provided by dramatic extracts confirms this challenge to the received perception of plays as whole artistic units by proving that early modern reading and viewing audiences did not see plays solely as cohesive wholes, but rather, as texts that could be fragmented and changed.

Centuries have passed since the works of Shakespeare and his contemporaries were first performed and read, leaving scholars to lament the lack of evidence, but dramatic extracts in print and manuscript provide one often-overlooked form of archival documentation that presents a glimpse into how early modern readers and audiences approached the plays. As more dramatic extracts are uncovered, and as the known dramatic extracts can be examined more fully, further research will undoubtedly reveal valuable information about early responses to plays, early modern reading, writing, playgoing, and ultimately, the plays themselves.

Dramatic extracts are tangible evidence of what the plays themselves have told us: early modern plays were written for you to make of "what you will" and to take "as you like it."

NOTES

1. The William Cartwright extracts are from Bodleian MS Rawl. D. 951; William Drummond's extracts can be found in NLS MS 2059 (discussed in Chapter 1); William Lilly's notes, which are "in a hand-writing not unlike" the dramatic extracts, can be found in Bodleian MS Ashmole 420. The handwriting observation is taken from William Henry Black, Bodleian Library Quarto Catalogue (Ashmole collection).
2. D. F. McKenzie, *Bibliography and the Sociology of Texts*, The Panizzi Lectures, 1985 (London: The British Library, 1986), 17.
3. I use the terms "extract" and "excerpt" (both as nouns and verbs) interchangeably.
4. Bannatyne's manuscript, NLS Adv. MS 1.1.6; Dering's manuscript, Folger MS V.b.34.
5. For instance, Arbury Hall MS 414 could be considered an abridgment or a series of extensive extracts taken from the 1617/18 Gray's Inn Revels (sometimes called *Gesta Grayorum Part 2* or *The Masque of Mountebanks*).
6. One of example of this is the Globe's first folio (sometimes called West 172, formerly owned by John Wolfson), which has a handwritten page to supplement an incomplete version of *Cymbeline*. See Peter Beal, comp., *Catalogue of English Literary Manuscripts 1450–1700 (CELM)*, King's College London, celm2.dighum.kcl.ac.uk, entry ShW41.8.
7. See Simon Palfrey and Tiffany Stern, *Shakespeare in Parts* (Oxford: Oxford University Press, 2007).
8. C. M. Ingleby et al., eds., *The Shakspere Allusion-Book: A Collection of Allusions to Shakspere From 1591 to 1700*, 2 vols. (London: Chatto & Windus and Duffield & Company, 1909).
9. Charles Whitney, *Early Responses to Renaissance Drama* (Cambridge: Cambridge University Press, 2006). For more on allusions to Shakespeare and documentary evidence, see Catherine Loomis, *Shakespeare: A Documentary Volume*, *Dictionary of Literary Biography*, vol. 263 (Detroit: Gale, 2002).
10. William N. West, "'Go By!': Intertheatrical Passages Between Early Modern Playhouses" (paper presented at the annual meeting of the Shakespeare Association of America, Toronto, Ontario, March 28–30 2013). Douglas Bruster explores "Shakespeare both quoting and quoted" (3), but similarly does not look at the "quotation" of Shakespeare or other dramatists in manuscript. Bruster, *Quoting Shakespeare: Form and Culture in Early Modern Drama* (Lincoln: University of Nebraska Press, 2000).
11. *CELM* expands the information previously available in his print *Index*: Beal, comp., *Index of English Literary Manuscripts,* vol. 1, 1450–1625 (New York: Mansell, 1980); vol. 2, 1625–1700 (New York: Mansell, 1993).
12. Excerpts from Hausted's *The Rival Friends* are found in Folger MS V.a.87 (ff. 24v–26) along with excerpts from the anonymous play *The Tragedy of Nero* (ff. 10–11). Excerpts from Peaps's *Love in it's Extasie* appear in BL MS Add. 22608, ff. 114–15. For more on these manuscripts, see Chapter 3. For a list the multiple manuscripts that contain excerpts from *The Mountebank's Masque*, see Alan H. Nelson and John R. Elliott, Jr., eds, *Records of Early English Drama: Inns of Court*, 3 vols. (Cambridge: D.S. Brewer, 2011).

13. Steven May and Heather Wolfe suggest that the survival rate of small, unbound manuscripts could be comparable to that of broadside ballads at around one in one thousand. See "Manuscripts in Tudor England," in *A Companion to Tudor Literature*, ed. Kent Cartwright (Malden, MA: Blackwell, 2010), 133.

14. Important work in this field includes Mary Hobbs, *Early Seventeenth-Century Verse Miscellany Manuscripts* (Aldershot, UK: Scolar, 1992); Harold Love, *Scribal Publication in Seventeenth-Century England* (Oxford: Oxford University Press, 1993); Arthur F. Marotti, *Manuscript, Print, and the English Renaissance Lyric* (Ithaca: Cornell University Press, 1993); Henry Woudhuysen, *Sir Philip Sidney and the Circulation of Manuscripts 1558–1640* (Oxford: Clarendon, 1996); Joshua Eckhardt, *Manuscript Verse Collectors and the Politics of Anti-Courtly Love Poetry* (Oxford: Oxford University Press, 2009); and Matthew Zarnowiecki, *Fair Copies: Reproducing the English Lyrics from Tottel to Shakespeare* (Toronto: University of Toronto Press, 2014).

15. See, for instance, Joan Marie Lechner, *Renaissance Concepts of the Commonplaces* (New York: Pageant, 1962); Beal, "Notions in Garrison: The Seventeenth-Century Commonplace Book," in *New Ways of Looking at Old Texts: Papers of the Renaissance English Text Society, 1985–1991*, ed. W. Speed Hill (Binghamton: Renaissance English Text Society, 1993), 131–47; Ann Moss, *Printed Commonplace-Books and the Structuring of Renaissance Thought* (Oxford: Clarendon, 1996); Mary Thomas Crane, *Framing Authority: Sayings, Self, and Society in Sixteenth-Century England* (Princeton: Princeton University Press, 1997); and Adam Smyth, *"Profit and Delight": Printed Miscellanies in England, 1640–1682* (Detroit: Wayne State University Press, 2004).

16. Work on full-text plays, playhouse documents, and acting parts includes multiple contributions by G. B. Evans; T. H. Howard-Hill, "'Nor Stage, Nor Stationers Stall Can Showe': The Circulation of Plays in Manuscript in the Early Seventeenth Century," *Book History* 2 (1999): 28–41; Grace Ioppolo, *Dramatists and Their Manuscripts in the Age of Shakespeare, Jonson, and Middleton* (New York: Routledge, 2002); Palfrey and Stern, *Shakespeare in Parts*; and Paul Werstine, *Early Modern Playhouse Manuscripts and the Editing of Shakespeare* (Cambridge: Cambridge University Press, 2012). Some of the forward-looking editions that mention dramatic extracts include Juliet Dusinberre, *As You Like It* (London: Arden, 2006); E. A. J. Honigmann *Othello* (London: Arden, 1997); and Gary Taylor and John Lavagnino's companion to the Oxford collected works of Thomas Middleton, *Thomas Middleton and Early Modern Textual Culture* (Oxford: Clarendon, 2007).

17. Articles that focus on Shakespearean extracts include Evans, "A Seventeenth-Century Reader of Shakespeare," *Review of English Studies* 21 (1945): 271–79; James C. McManaway, "Excerpta Quaedam per A.W. Adolescentem," in *Studies in Honor of DeWitt T. Starnes*, ed. Thomas P. Harrison et al. (Austin: University of Texas Press, 1967), 117–29; Sasha Roberts, "Reading Shakespeare's Tragedies of Love: *Romeo and Juliet*, *Othello*, and *Antony and Cleopatra* in Early Modern England," in *A Companion to Shakespeare's Works: The Tragedies*, ed. Richard Dutton and Jean Elizabeth Howard (Malden, MA: Blackwell, 2003), 108–33; and Guillaume Coatalen, "Shakespeare and other 'Tragicall Discourses' in an Early-Seventeenth-Century

Commonplace Book from Oriel College, Oxford," *English Manuscript Studies 1100–1700* 13 (2007): 120–64. Articles that focus on non-Shakespearean extracts and take a musicological approach to songs from plays include many works by John P. Cutts, such as "The Original Music to Middleton's *The Witch*," *Shakespeare Quarterly* 7 (1956): 203–9 and "Henry Shirley's 'The Martyred Soldier,'" *Renaissance News* 12 (1959): 251–53; as well as research by Mary Chan, including *Music in the Theatre of Ben Jonson* (Oxford: Oxford University Press, 2002).

18. This figure is based on the entries in *CELM*.

19. Tiffany Stern, *Documents of Performance in Early Modern England* (Cambridge: Cambridge University Press, 2009).

20. Werstine advocates attending to the "fierce particularities" of early modern manuscripts, although his purview is primarily full-text plays and playhouse documents. See "Plays in Manuscript," in *A New History of Early English Drama*, ed. John D. Cox and David Scott Kastan (New York: Columbia University Press, 1997), 492.

Chapter 1

The Rise of Dramatic Extracting

Extracting from English Plays, 1590–1642

"Whose horse is white & wife is faire / His head is never vouid [void] of care," reads some marginalia in a 1602 copy of Ben Jonson's *Poetaster*.[1] During the seventeenth century, readers and audience members jotted short sayings into their playbooks and also selected passages from plays to copy into other books and manuscripts. This chapter traces the roots of dramatic extracting from classical commonplacing through early modern printing practices. While we might not know who that first industrious person was to put pen to paper (or stylus to table-book, as the case may be) and copy lines from a play, we do know that the earliest documented extant dramatic extracts from English professional plays date to the 1590s.

In this chapter, I seek to answer the related questions of when dramatic excerpting from professional plays began in England, why manuscript compilers began including dramatic extracts, and how dramatic extracting evolved over the early seventeenth century, by describing both individual manuscripts and larger trends in extracting. Each manuscript reveals a different approach to extracting and offers varied motivations for copying dramatic extracts. Documented dramatic extracts—and there are certainly more to be discovered—exhibit a clear trend: the practice of dramatic excerpting from English plays was sporadic during the middle ages, but extracts from the 1590s signal the growing movement to extract from plays that burgeoned throughout the seventeenth century. Ultimately, I contend that a confluence of related cultural, literary, and theatrical changes precipitated extracting from English plays in both print and manuscript, including the legitimization of vernacular literature, the rise of popular theatre, the increase in play publication, and the increased use of commonplace markers in plays.

These manuscripts reveal the varied ways people copied dramatic extracts: while attending the theatre, from print sources, from other manuscripts, from memorial reconstruction, from friends. Although for some extracts, we do not have definitive proof of the source, other sources can be ascertained. As this chapter will discuss, for instance, we know that Edward Pudsey copied extracts from *Othello* before the play was published. In an early modern letter, Stephen Powle described a dramatic extract being passed (perhaps orally, perhaps in writing) from person to person. Sometimes, readers copied page numbers with extracts, making it possible to trace the particular print edition of a play they were reading. The multiplicity of ways people copied dramatic extracts shows, importantly, how plays came to be seen not as unified artistic wholes, but as sources to be mined for wit, wisdom, and song.

Before we discuss the extracts themselves, I would like to highlight the importance of the classical commonplacing tradition that informed Tudor education practices. I trace the roots of dramatic extracting through the Tudor culture of excerpting and the *flores poetarum*, miscellanies, and commonplace books that circulated during the sixteenth century. Certain medieval texts, often called "fragments," can be reconsidered as forerunners to the widespread trend of copying extracts from plays that flourished in the seventeenth century. I then turn to the earliest manuscripts that include dramatic extracts, those copied before 1600. Because there are so few manuscripts known to contain dramatic extracts from the sixteenth century, this chapter treats each one individually. Rather than discussing every manuscript from 1600–1620 known to contain dramatic extracts, however, I point to some representative manuscripts as examples of how early dramatic extracts functioned. The manuscripts examined tie extracting to related cultural phenomena such as the increased publication of plays and the publication of plays with commonplace markers. The final part of this chapter surveys certain manuscripts from the prolific period of the 1620s and 1630s until the closure of the theatres in 1642, with a focus on the generic indeterminacy of dramatic extracts.

A BRIEF HISTORY OF COMMONPLACING AND EXTRACTING

Aristotle called them *koinoi topoi*, Cicero called them *communes loci*, and English speakers call them commonplaces or sentences (*sententiae*).[2] Commonplaces are rhetorically well-phrased sayings that express an accepted insight. In an often-appropriated passage, Seneca expressed the value of copying and learning commonplaces:

> We should imitate bees and we should keep in separate compartments whatever we have collected from our diverse reading, for things conserved separately keep better. Then, diligently applying all the resources of our native talent, we should mingle all the various nectars we have tasted, and turn them into a

single sweet substance, in a way that, even if it is apparent where it originated, it appears quite different from what it was in its original state.[3]

For Seneca, copying commonplaces allows an individual to create new ideas by harvesting the best of what one has read. This floral metaphor extended into the middle ages, when manuscript writers would compile *florilegia* (literally, a gathering of flowers), anthologies comprising primarily extracts from other works. In the middle ages, *florilegia* were mainly composed of selections from works by classical authors and church fathers such as Augustine.

Seneca himself demonstrates the value of gathering "nectar" from other works—he has borrowed this bee metaphor.[4] Early modern writers often employed this familiar metaphor, as Peter Stallybrass and Roger Chartier point out: "the analogy between the reader and the bee is, in the positive sense that the Renaissance reserved for the term, the commonplace of commonplacing."[5] A 1681 tract on commonplacing by an unknown W. H. echoes Seneca but changes the emphasis of commonplacing to the importance of memorization: "what you would *willingly remember* be sure to refer or enter, and then you are sure of it on all occasions. And when you have thus, like the bee, sucked honey out of every flower and safely laid it up in these hives, you are stocked for a winter season when health, age, or opportunity are gone and you cannot so well further improve. And so, we have done with *common places*."[6] For both Seneca and W. H., copying commonplaces provides a way to improve the self. The bee-as-reader metaphor functioned in three ways beyond memorization: the bee chooses the nectar from the best flowers (selection); the bee sorts the nectar into different cells (organization/classification); and the bee transforms the nectar(s) into honey (elaboration/alteration).[7] Commonplacing offered a concrete way to internalize the canons of rhetoric, from finding phrases to copy (*inventio*), arranging them under headings (*dipositio*), mimicking their style (*elocutio*), memorizing them (*memoria*), and presenting them (*actio*). Although the acts of gathering, copying, classifying, and elaborating are not much lauded in today's pedagogy, in the early modern period they were considered crucial tools for developing a person's writing, speech, cognitive ability, and creativity.[8]

And so, the practice of commonplacing and extracting began with the impulse toward self-improvement through education. In Tudor England, grammar school pupils were encouraged to keep their own commonplace books to help with learning Latin and composition. Early modern educators hoped that students would assimilate the values of the books they read, which would make them morally upstanding; William Kempe, for instance, in *The Education of Children in Learning* (1588), pointed out that learning *sententiae* would "teach . . . all things, framing [the student] to eloquence in talke, and vertue in deedes."[9] Tudor students were encouraged to copy both beautiful and moral phrases from the great humanist writers, most notably Desiderius Erasmus. From schoolroom practice and pedagogical theory to printed miscellanies, extracting was an important part of becoming literate and participating in written and literary culture.

Like their manuscript counterparts, the earliest English printed commonplace books often focused on serious materials, that is, religion and the classics. For instance, Richard Taverner's translation of Erasmus Sarcerius's *Common places of scripture ordrely and after a compendious forme of teachyng, set forth with no litle labour, to the gret profit and help of all such studentes in gods worde as have not had longe excercyse in the same* (1538) was followed by Thomas Paynell's *The Piththy and moost notable sayinges of al Scripture. . . very necessary for al those that Delite in the consolacions of the Scriptures* (1550, reprinted 1552, 1560, 1562). The titles alone demonstrate the important work of commonplacing: these pieces of wisdom are "necessary" for faith; these are books made for the "gret profit and help of all." Early English commonplace books were regularly translated from Latin, such as Thomas Blague's *A Schole of wise conceytes . . . Translated out of divers Greke and Latine Wryters* (1569), which contained a series of animal fables each summed up by a "moral" (*sententia*).[10] Although Sarcerius, Paynell, and Blague did not present short sentences organized according to commonplace headings, they offered readers brief, edifying texts advertised for their commonplaces and pithy sayings. Even the printed verse miscellanies of the Elizabethan period focused on the moral improvements of the reader and approached their texts with a certain seriousness.[11]

In the sixteenth century, extracting was serious business in two senses: it was undertaken with gravitas and printers, editors, and booksellers alike cashed in on the ubiquitous phenomenon. John Foxe first published *Locorum Communium Tituli* in 1557, which he later revised and expanded as *Pandectae Locorum Communium* in 1572 and 1585. This mostly blank commonplace book of more than a thousand pages included pre-printed headings so that readers could fill in appropriate selections. As Foxe explains in his preface to the reader, the act of gathering and arranging extracts by topic would help readers improve their memorization and reasoning abilities. Foxe's book is, of course, in Latin, the language of scholarly pursuits in Tudor England; commonplacing itself was a learned activity.

Foxe's blank commonplace book reveals his bias through its headings and allotment of space. For instance, when Foxe offers the heading "Antichristus," he clarifies and lets his readers know that he means the Roman Catholic pope, clearly demonstrating his Protestant leanings.[12] In the 1585 edition, most subjects are given one page, quite a few are given two pages and some, like "Pain, Suffering, Tribulation, Vexation, Crucifixion, Difficulties / Considering the Reputation of Martyrs" are given three pages.[13] This allotted space reflects Foxe's own interest in martyrology. Even the most mundane commonplace headings signal a particular focus, and Foxe's book includes some far-from-mundane headings, such as "Lent. Abstinence. Fasting. Delicious Food. Self-Control."[14] Foxe's *Pandectae Locorum Communium* shows the serious and scholarly side of commonplacing and extracting, while also underscoring its popularity. Furthermore, the *Pandectae Locorum Communium* demonstrates that even a blank commonplace book offers interpretive possibilities. When dramatic extracts are found in print or manuscript commonplace books, there are yet more avenues of investigation to be explored including how those parts of plays are titled and placed.

The English interest in commonplacing from classical and religious sources eventually led to extracts from vernacular poetry, which in turn prompted extracts from vernacular plays. One popular Latin *flores poetarum* (an anthology of passages from poems, often arranged by subject heading), Octavianus Mirandula's *Illustrium Poetarum Flores* (1538), was reprinted for more than a century.[15] Terence's classical comedies were mined for quotations as early as the fifteenth century (*Vulgaria quedam abs Terencio in Anglicam linguam traducta*, 1483); collections of Latin extracts from his plays were published throughout the sixteenth century.[16] John Bodenham was instrumental in publishing many of these anthologies of poetic excerpts, including *Politeuphuia: Wits Commonwealth* (1597), *Palladis Tamia: Wits Treasury* (1598), *Wits Theater of the Little World* (1599), *Bel-vedére or the Garden of Muses* (1600) and *Englands Helicon* (1600).[17] Vernacular collections of poetic extracts began to be published in the 1590s, just as the first dramatic extracts began to appear in manuscript.

The increase of dramatic excerpting in manuscript is both evident in and partly accounted for by the inclusion of excerpts from drama in print miscellanies. For instance, *Palladis Tamia* famously includes extracts from Shakespeare's plays, *Englands Parnassus* contains selections from plays by Kyd and Shakespeare, and *Bel-vedére* has excerpts from Jonson, Shakespeare, and the anonymous *Arden of Feversham*, among others.[18] Robert Allott billed his miscellany, *Englands Parnassus*, as "the choysest Flowers of our Moderne Poets," showing the rising status of vernacular writers.[19] In *Englands Parnassus*, Allott extracted primarily from Shakespeare's poems, *Venus and Adonis* and *The Rape of Lucrece*, although he also included some selections from his dramatic works. At the same time as Allott and others began turning to the English stage for snippets worth publishing for a wide audience, individual manuscript compilers similarly turned to English theatre to fill their own personal commonplace books and miscellanies.

As the seventeenth century progressed, printed miscellanies and commonplace books included an increasing number of extracts from drama, mirroring the rise in dramatic excerpts found in manuscript.[20] The publication of dramatic excerpts in print not only paralleled manuscript dramatic excerpting, but could at times lead to manuscript extracting, as Chapter 6 demonstrates. It is not surprising that print dramatic extracts gained popularity at the same time as their manuscript counterparts: they were born of the same cultural moments and social attitudes. The inclusion of vernacular dramatic excerpts in both print and manuscript commonplace books and miscellanies indicates the literate public's acceptance of vernacular authors as equal to their classical forebears and of the genre of drama as a worthwhile literary endeavor.[21]

Printed commonplace books and miscellanies did not, of course, supplant their manuscript counterparts. In fact, the rise of printed commonplace books and miscellanies led some purists to decry these pre-arranged, pre-packaged versions. Sir Francis Bacon, for instance, insisted on the importance of each scholar's creating his own commonplace books, as the notes of others would be of no benefit.[22] For Bacon, and other detractors of printed commonplace books, the value lay in each person's reading, gathering, and arranging the *sententiae*, not in absorbing other people's selections. In *Belvédere*, Bodenham printed a prefatory poem by R. Hathway that anticipated this type of criticism by presenting the volume as "The hive where many Bees their honey bring, /. . . / The garden where survives continuall spring, /. . . / Abstract of knowledge, Briefe of Eloquence /. . . / How-ever ignorance presume to scoffe."[23] Similarly, Allott's "To the Reader" begins, "I Hang no Ivie out to sell my Wine, / The *Nectar* of good witts will sell it selfe; / I feare not, what detraction can define, / I saile secure from *Envies* storme or shelf."[24] Some critics attacked not only using print commonplace books but also the practice of keeping personal commonplace books. Bacon repudiated those who believed that "the transferring of the things we read and learn into common-place books is. . .detrimental to learning. . .and inviting the memory to take holiday" by arguing that the act of copying improved one's memory.[25]

Over the course of the seventeenth century, both print and manuscript commonplace books and miscellanies began including "lighter" materials. Commonplaces became more than a repository of moral knowledge: some readers turned to commonplaces and dramatic extracts to learn pithy phrases that could be used in social situations. I contend that the printing of vernacular *flores poetarum*, and miscellanies and commonplaces more generally, contributed to the trend of excerpting from English plays. In the rest of this chapter, I turn to the extracts themselves in order to show how the publication of full-length plays, the inclusion of dramatic extracts in printed commonplace books, and the changing attitudes toward theatre in the late Elizabethan period all influenced (and were, in turn, influenced by) dramatic extracting in manuscripts.

THE EARLIEST KNOWN ENGLISH DRAMATIC EXTRACTS (PRE-1600)

Despite the centuries-old tradition of commonplacing and the prevalence of extracting in Tudor schools, there is a paucity of catalogued dramatic extracts in manuscript from the middle ages and sixteenth century. The advent of English dramatic excerpting in both print and manuscript predictably follows the rise of professional English theatre. Even when plays began to be produced in English during the middle ages, these plays were not excerpted in manuscript. It was not until the professionalization of English theatre that manuscript compilers turned to dramatic extracts as a source of beautiful phrases and knowledge. Appropriately, the earliest English dramatic extracts both rely on and support the larger history of English theatre. Moreover, extracts require that we rethink our narratives of theatre history by considering plays not as monolithic units, but as divisible works.

While there are multiple fragments from medieval plays, that is, unfinished or damaged manuscripts, there are relatively few known extracts. Some medieval theatrical texts, often referred to as "fragments," are best characterized as actors' parts, such as *Dux Moraud* and the Shrewsbury fragments.[26] In other cases, we have manuscripts that include only a prologue from a medieval play, like the Durham Prologue and the Cambridge Prologue;[27] both anticipate the later circulation of prologues from plays and masques. Many of the problems associated with early modern dramatic extracts (identifying the source, dating the manuscript, gathering clues about the copyist) are exacerbated with medieval manuscript evidence.[28]

The Reynes extracts (late fifteenth century, in Bodleian MS Tanner 407) are perhaps the most similar to later dramatic extracts because they are found in a miscellany—they were gathered with other texts that reflect one person's interest.[29] In this case, the compiler was Robert Reynes of Acle, Norfolk, who copied the extracts in the late fifteenth century. Reynes collected three potential dramatic extracts from unknown source texts. The first is three stanzas about the Worthies that might have been taken from a pageant (or two separate pageants).[30] The second, and perhaps the best known, is a speech spoken by the character Delight, which was likely taken from a now-lost morality play. The speech of Delight is one example that shows how extracts are valuable for what they can reveal about lost plays—this speech is also a rare example of a non-Shakespearean extract that has received critical attention. The final possibly dramatic text Reynes collected is an epilogue that was performed following a church play. These three potential dramatic extracts are gathered with disparate texts, in both Latin and English, including accounts, obituaries, religious readings, and proverbs. Although Reynes's manuscript is often called a commonplace book, it is by the strictest definition a miscellany, with its miscellaneous contents and lack of commonplace headings. These extracts are not presented as commonplaces, but rather, as longer self-contained texts that can be taken without the context of their full-text sources. The presentation of the Reynes extracts anticipates the later circulation of songs, speeches, epilogues, and prologues, which, in the seventeenth century, would all appear regularly in both manuscript and print verse miscellanies.

As Chapter 2 explains, there are more sixteenth-century manuscripts with extracts from masques and entertainments than from plays; this chapter focuses on plays. From the beginning of the sixteenth century until 1590, we have no examples of manuscript extracts from English plays. Throughout the early modern period, readers often overlooked early- to mid-Tudor plays (those written before 1590). *CELM* lists only one other manuscript containing extracts from an early play: Bodleian MS Rawl. poet. 26 (compiled c. 1620–1630) includes Custance's letter from *Ralph Roister Doister* (written c. 1553).[31] While scholars could yet find manuscripts that include extracts from works by John Bale or Richard Edwards, extant and catalogued manuscripts show that readers extracted more from plays written after 1590.

Only a handful of surviving manuscripts contain excerpts from professional or published plays that could have been copied before 1600.[32] In brief, the earliest known extracts from Renaissance plays in manuscript are as follows: (1) Henry Peacham's excerpts and famous drawing from *Titus Andronicus* in the Longleat manuscript, (2) William Scott's quotations from *Richard II* in the newly rediscovered BL MS Add. 81083, (3) anonymous selections from *1 Henry IV* in BL MS Add. 64078, and (4) William Briton's extracts from *Gorboduc* in BL MS Add. 61822, also known as the Houghton manuscript. Although further research is bound to reveal other sixteenth-century manuscripts with dramatic extracts, they are still far outnumbered by later instances. Of these four manuscripts, however, only the Houghton manuscript and BL MS Add. 64078 reflect the trends in dramatic extracting that were to continue throughout the seventeenth century (that is, extracting as commonplacing, extracts found in a miscellany, and extracts taken seriatim from one play).

Perhaps the most famous dramatic extract is also the most unusual: Peacham's drawing and extracts from *Titus Andronicus* in the Longleat manuscript.[33] This manuscript was copied by Henry Peacham the younger (1578–c. 1644), author of the handbook *The Compleat Gentleman* (1622). Although many scholars have discussed this manuscript, there is still little consensus regarding the subject and meaning of the drawing, the handwriting, and even the date.[34] I include the Longleat manuscript in my discussion of the earliest dramatic extracts because there is a possibility that it was copied before 1600. To consider the Longleat manuscript as an early dramatic extract, we must first discuss the contentious issue of its date before turning to the text itself.

For a single leaf that contains one drawing and two passages from *Titus Andronicus*, Tamora's speech pleading for her son's life (1.1.104–20) and Aaron reveling in his wickedness (5.1.124–44), the Longleat manuscript has spurred much scholarly speculation. It begins with a stage direction that does not appear in any of the early print versions of the play: "Enter Tamora pleadinge for her sonnes going to execution" and ends with a speech prefix for Alarbus, who does not have any lines in the play. The drawing at the top of the manuscript, as many scholars point out, does not dramatize an actual moment that would have occurred on stage during a performance of *Titus*. The oft-reproduced drawing depicts two guards in Roman garb on the left: these are sometimes identified as two of Titus's sons. In the middle stands a man, normally identified as Titus, wearing laurels and holding a large staff, facing a woman on her knees with her hands clasped, Tamora, "pleadinge" for Alarbus. On the right are two men, bound and on their knees, probably Chiron and Demetrius. On the far right stands Aaron the Moor holding a sword.

Peacham signed the Longleat manuscript with the date (in code) of 1594, the year *Titus* was published.[35] The signature may have been added after the text, however, and may not reflect the date of composition; the current tentative scholarly consensus is that the drawing and image were created at the same time.[36] Similarly, some scholars assert that the image was drawn first and the text added after, although I agree with Alan Hughes and Richard Levin that it is unlikely that an artist with a whole page would leave so much empty space.[37] The signature and drawing do not shed light on the date of this leaf; unfortunately, the text is equally void of clues. The Peacham text cannot be accurately associated with a single print edition of the play. Although the orthography of each print edition varies, Peacham's spelling does not coincide with a single edition. Peacham's individual spelling is not unusual, as manuscript compilers (like compositors) often used their personal spelling preferences instead of accurately representing the words they copied. The most compelling textual argument that this manuscript was copied from a later quarto is the use of "Tut" instead of "But" at the beginning of Aaron's line, "Tut I have done a thousand dreadfull thynges."[38] The first quarto (1594) reads "But I have done" while later editions (Q2, 1600; Q3, 1611; F1, 1623) include "Tut." If Peacham wrote this manuscript between 1604 and 1615, as Bate suggests, it is still a fairly early example of dramatic extracting.[39]

The Longleat manuscript is atypical because it is the only known instance of an illustrated dramatic excerpt—though, as Katherine Duncan-Jones points out, Peacham's interest in the text itself, as a source of commonplaces, is not unusual.[40] The lack of illustrated dramatic excerpts perhaps points to the literary roots and commonplacing history of dramatic excerpting. Further archival research may reveal more illustrated dramatic extracts, although they would still be rare. While other scholars have discussed the Longleat manuscript at length, it bears mention in this study as an anomaly: the only known illustrated dramatic extract.

If the Peacham drawing cannot be taken as representative of most early modern dramatic extracts, neither can William Scott's selections from *Richard II* (found in BL MS Add. 81083). Scott (c. 1579–after 1611) likely matriculated at Cambridge in 1593, was admitted to the Inner Temple in 1595, and returned to Cambridge to earn his LLB from Trinity College in 1600.[41] Scott probably wrote the main section of BL MS Add. 81083, "The Modell of Poesye," in summer 1599.[42] In "The Modell of Poesye," an early work of literary criticism, Scott responds to Sir Philip Sidney's *The Defense of Poesie* and cites multiple examples from literary works to prove his points. These examples are taken from a number of sources, including Sidney's *Astrophil and Stella*, and *The Arcadia*, Spenser's *The Faerie Queene*, and Daniel's *Rosamund*. Scott at times names the poets he discusses, and although he does not name Shakespeare, he cites passages from both *The Rape of Lucrece* and *Richard II*.

Scott's treatise on how to write well uses dramatic extracts to illustrate his points. Stanley Wells, who announced the "discovery" of this manuscript in 2003, gives the following example:

> Sometyme the person shall be so plunged into the passion of sorrowe,
> that he will euen forgett his sorrow and seeme to enterteine his
> hardest fortune with dalliance and sporte, as in the very well-pend
> Tragedy of Rich. the 2ᵈ. is expressd in the Kinge and Queene, whil'st
> They play the wantons with their woes.[43]

As Wells explains, here Scott took Richard's "Or shall we play the wantons with our woes?" as his starting point.[44] At other times, Scott borrowed words from plays to ameliorate his own sentences. For instance, the Duchess of York's "Where are the violets now / That strew the green lap of the newcome spring" informs Scott's "besides there is much sweetenes in the wyttie conceipts, apt sentences, proper allusions and applications to be dispearced in your Poeme, like soe many goodly Plotts of Lyllies and violetts strowed all over the newe springinge Meadowes."[45] In this case, Scott practiced what he preached: his writing included those "wyttie conceipts, apt sentences, proper allusions and applications" that he advised poets to employ. As outlined in the introduction, the adaptation of a playwright's lines in one's own writing is not, strictly defined, dramatic extracting, but rather, allusion, or, in this case, imitation.

Scott's unusual manuscript blurs the line between extract, allusion, and quotation. Other dramatic extracts, by contrast, are easy to identify because they are found in commonplace books and verse miscellanies. In some cases, Scott simply mentioned authors or works, such as his allusion to *Gorboduc*: "especially you must avoyde repeticion of the same conceipt; as in that commended Tragedy of Gorboduck, you may in one leafe obserue, to the same purpose, the storye of Phaeton twyse to be alluded vnto, as if the worlde afforded noe other example, to shewe the vnhappy successe of rashe aspiringe" (f. 21v). While the case of name-dropping a literary work or author is obviously not a dramatic extract, other cases where Scott cites full lines of text (occasionally changing them to suit his needs) could indeed be considered dramatic extracts.

Scott's "The Modell of Poesye" is the earliest example of a manuscript that contains dramatic extracts with commentary. While later manuscripts include dramatic extracts with commentary, Scott's work is unlike even these. Mid- to late seventeenth century manuscript compilers who offer commentary, such as Abraham Wright, PD, and the Lansdowne compiler, treat their reflections as separate from, yet related to, extracts—these will be discussed at length in Chapters 3 and 4. Most other manuscripts with commentary are arranged with marginal notes surrounding the extracts, but for Scott, the commentary is not peripheral to the extracts.

Scott's dramatic extracts are dissimilar to others because he was writing a guidebook for poets on how to be a better writer. We can compare his mention of dramatic works and playwrights to later commentaries, such as John Dryden's *Of Dramatick Poesie, An Essay* (1668); this use of quotations as examples is closer to literary criticism than to the commentary associated with most dramatic extracts. Scott designed his work to be read by other people—if he did not mean to print it, he intended it for scribal publication, evidenced by his inclusion of a dedication and other paratexts associated with publication. While some verse miscellanies and commonplace books circulated, others were kept for personal use, and so likely would not have necessitated the kind of commentary Scott offers. BL MS Add. 81083 is, in the end, a rare example of dramatic extracts used as textual evidence, while also being one of the few known pre-1600 extracts.

BL MS Add. 64078, unlike the Longleat MS and BL MS Add. 81083, presents a more typical example of dramatic extracting that anticipates the appearance and use of later manuscript extracts. This manuscript, probably compiled around 1596–early 1600/01, contains sixty-three lines from *1 Henry IV*, one of Shakespeare's most popular plays, reprinted in at least six quartos before the 1623 First Folio.[46] Hilton Kelliher's in-depth analysis of this manuscript and its Shakespearean content suggests that these extracts could have been reconstructed from notes taken during a performance. According to Kelliher, the compiler's interests included "the commonwealth and its great ones, war, dishonour, fear, and cowardice" and particularly "how a subject might command personal popularity exceeding even that of the sovereign."[47] Strikingly, the compiler changed Shakespeare's "even in the presence of the crowned king" to "Queene," making these extracts relevant to his current political situation.[48] Kelliher suggests that the copyist was possibly linking Henry IV to the Earl of Essex, although the exact topicality of these extracts remains unknown.[49]

The excerpts in BL MS Add. 64078 were copied in the late 1590s from a highly popular and political play that was written, performed, printed, and reprinted at a time when English theatre was flourishing. BL MS Add. 64078 resembles many later dramatic extracts due to the page layout. The extracts are left-aligned, written as blank verse with occasional marginal comments, and at times the extracts are separated from each other with a horizontal line. The extracts feature little commentary, except for a few marginal explanations: for instance, next to the lines, "my bloud hath bin too cold & tem<perat>," the compiler has written "of a Tem|perat ma*n*."[50] Like most other dramatic extracts, the extracts from *1 Henry IV* are side-by-side with non-dramatic material—in this case, Thomas Harriot's metaphysical notes. Manuscripts were commonly put to multiple uses; the compiler turned this one upside down before entering the dramatic extracts from the end, another practice found in multiple commonplace books and verse miscellanies. The topicality of the extracts, albeit lost on present-day readers of the manuscript, is also not uncommon for the many dramatic extracts that followed during the seventeenth century.

The final 1590s manuscript known to contain dramatic extracts, the Houghton manuscript, also includes topical and political dramatic extracts.[51] Sometime between 1587 and 1605, William Briton of Kelston (1564–c. 1636) copied excerpts from Thomas Sackville and Thomas Norton's *Gorboduc*. This deeply political play was first presented at the Inner Temple during the 1561 Christmas festivities and then acted before Queen Elizabeth in January 1562. Unlike the Shakespearean extracts discussed above, *Gorboduc* is not a professional play, and as a performance for court, could also be considered in Chapter 2, which treats masques and entertainments, or even, perhaps, as a very late medieval play. As the first English Senecan-style tragedy in blank verse, however, Sackville and Norton's play is most often treated as a precursor to early modern professional plays. *Gorboduc* was first published in 1565 (Q1) and republished with slight changes in 1570 (Q2) and 1590 (Q3).[52] Even though *Gorboduc* had been in print for decades, Briton is the first (and, to date, only) known person to copy excerpts from Sackville and Norton's play.

Briton copied three pages of extracts from *Gorboduc* in the section of his manuscript titled "Pithie sentences and wise sayinges," effectively announcing his interest in reading the play for commonplaces.[53] Some of the extracts Briton selected are, indeed, commonplaces: for instance, the first selection taken from the play is Ferrex's "a causles wronge & so unjust dispight / maie have redresse or at least revenge."⁵⁴ Briton also copied other, longer speeches, which suggests that his interest was not only in "pithy" or short sentences but also in the wisdom to be gleaned from the play. The "Pithie sentences and wise sayinges" section of his manuscript contains extracts from guidebooks, including Thomas Elyot's *The Boke named the Governour* (1531), William Baldwin's *A Treatise of Morall Phylosophie* (1547), as well as more than fifty passages from Thomas Blenerhasset's *The Seconde Part of the Mirrour for Magistrates* (1578).⁵⁵ For Briton, *Gorboduc* is as much a piece of political advice as it is a play. Briton's marginal notations, including comments such as "usurped Reigne" (f. 90) and "the differenc betwene unyon & divysion" (f. 89v) indicate that he was reading *Gorboduc*, at least in part, for the political message.

One early audience member's notes on the play have influenced our understanding of the play's political message. Robert Beale (1541–1601), an administrator, wrote that the chorus explained the message of the play: "yt was better for the Quene to marye with the L[ord] R[obert Dudley] knowen then with the K[ing] of Sweden."⁵⁶ This interpretation of the play's political message has since been widely accepted. Understanding Briton's extract, however, requires maintaining two historical points of focus: the original circumstances of the play's composition and performance, as well as the later moment when the extract was recopied. Although in the early 1560s, Queen Elizabeth had time to make a match, by the time Briton was copying selections into this manuscript (likely the early 1590s),⁵⁷ Elizabeth was over fifty and would have been unable to bear children. Briton highlighted the dangers brought about by those who strive for the throne:

> when growing pryd dothe fill the swelling brest
> & gredie lust doth rayse the clymminge mynde
> oh hardlie may the perrill be represt
> ne feare of angry goods [Gods] ne lawes kynd
> ne contry care cann fiery harte restraine
> when force hath armed envie & disdaine.⁵⁸

> when cruel hart, wrath, Treason, & dysdaine
> within the ambitious brest are lodged then
> behold howe myschiefe wyde herself displaies⁵⁹

All of the extracts from *Gorboduc* in the Houghton manuscript were copied in the order they appear in the play, save the last. For the last words from this play, Briton chose the words of one of Gorboduc's faithful advisors, Eubulus, upon hearing that the royal line has ended, "& loe the entry to the wofull wrack, / & utter Ruyne."⁶⁰ In the 1590s, Sackville and Norton's advice to the queen could only be read as hindsight, or, more optimistically, as the potential for the queen and her advisors to choose the right successor.

Briton's extracts reveal his interest in the role of the advisors to the throne. He copied the play's caution to advisors to "be playne without all wrie respect/or poysonous craft to speake in pleasing wyse."[61] Briton noted in the margin, "a councellour" next to Gorboduc's explanation of his decision to give each of his sons an advisor:

> I meane to joyne to eithere of my Sonnes
> some one of those whose longe approved faithe
> & wysdome tryed maie well assure my harte
> that myninge frawd shall fynde no waie to creepe
> into their fenced he eares with grave advyse.[62]

Later, Briton copied, "Wo to the prynce that plyent eare enclynes / & yelds his mynde to poysonous tale that floweth / from flattering mouth,"[63] further warning about the perils of poor counsel. Among the first extracts from the play that interested Briton was the claim of Arostus (one of Gorboduc's advisors) that if Gorboduc gave the throne to his sons while he still lived, he could "guyd & traine in tempered staie / their yet grene witts."[64] Even though Queen Elizabeth would have been unable to bear children when Briton transcribed these selections, she would have been able to name an heir and offer guidance before she died.

In his manuscript arrangement, Briton aligned extracts from *Gorboduc* with selections from major Renaissance political writers and classical philosophers. Briton's manuscript also situates these dramatic extracts alongside a major vernacular poetic work: the final extracts from *Gorboduc* (f. 90v) face the opening of twenty pages of sonnets from Sidney's *Astrophil and Stella* (ff. 91–103; see Figure 1.1).[65] At the time Briton was writing his manuscript, Sidney was regarded as a national hero and Protestant martyr, as well as one of England's foremost writers. By placing the extracts from *Gorboduc* alongside the sonnets from *Astrophil and Stella*, Briton legitimized the play's standing and cast the play in a literary light, while also perhaps highlighting the English and Protestant elements of the play.[66] Both *Astrophil and Stella* and *Gorboduc* can be seen as catalysts for two genres that gained popularity while Briton was writing: sonnet sequences and history plays, respectively. The 1591 publication of *Astrophil and Stella* precipitated the 1590s vogue for sonnet sequences.[67] History plays flourished in the 1590s, including Shakespeare's tetralogies and *King John* as well as plays by Christopher Marlowe, Robert Greene, George Peele, and Anthony Munday. Briton's choice of *Gorboduc* reflects not only the politics of his era and the rising prestige of history plays but also contemporary literary tastes.

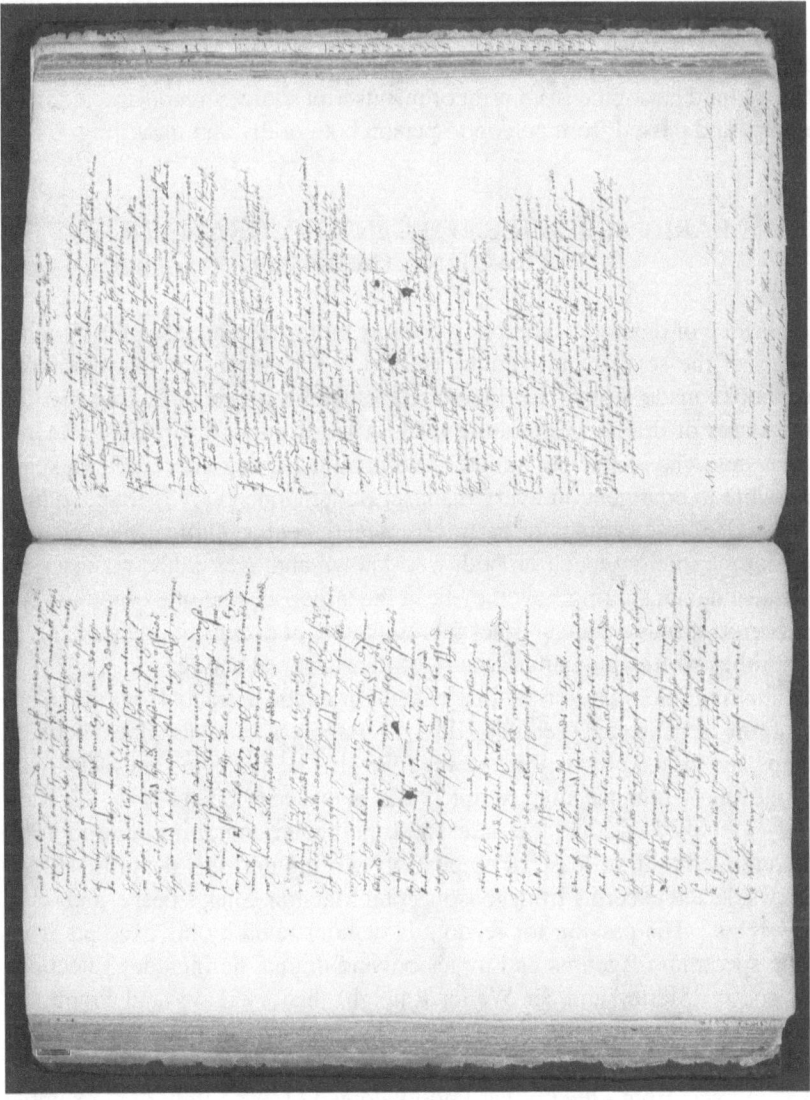

Figure 1.1 © The British Library Board, BL MS Add. 61822, f. 90v–91.

The famous drawing of *Titus Andronicus* and the recently discovered "Modell of Poesye" are anomalous in the context of dramatic extracting, with their illustration and literary criticism, respectively. The late fifteenth-century Reynes extracts, the selections from *1 Henry IV* in BL MS Add. 64078, and Briton's *Gorboduc* passages are typical of later extracts. We find an increasing number of dramatic extracts after 1600, particularly in commonplace books and miscellanies. As the next section demonstrates, these extracts could be copied from print or manuscript sources, reconstructed from memory, and passed from person to person both orally and in writing.

EARLY SEVENTEENTH-CENTURY DRAMATIC EXTRACTING (1600–1620)

The practice of dramatic excerpting became more widespread in the opening decades of the seventeenth century. David J. Knauer argues that commonplace books made drama into literature,[68] although it is equally true that the rising status of drama as literature made it worth mining for witty remarks and truisms. The increasing number of dramatic extracts after 1600 makes it impossible to comment on every manuscript, let alone every extract, so here I offer judicious examples of early seventeenth-century dramatic extracting. The examples below touch on both well-known and overlooked manuscripts while also demonstrating how they fit in the larger scheme of extracting. The manuscripts discussed are at times representative of dozens of other examples and at times worth analyzing because of their unusual nature.

Of the multiple manuscripts that contain dramatic extracts from the opening of the seventeenth century, Edward Pudsey's commonplace book is perhaps the best known. Pudsey (c. 1573–1612/13) copied extracts from multiple plays into his manuscript.[69] His manuscript opens with "Edward Pudsey's booke" and has the date 1600: he began compiling around 1600 and continued until at least 1609, possibly writing until his death in 1613.[70] Pudsey selected excerpts from Jonson, John Marston, Shakespeare, and other playwrights.[71] His passion for reading is demonstrated by his excerpts from a wide spectrum of genres and topics beyond drama: he includes selections from poetry (Sidney and Sir Walter Raleigh), history (Livy and Francesco Guicciardini), moral philosophy (Bacon), geography (Tomás de Torquemada), and religion (Thomas Lodge).

The extracts from *Othello* that Pudsey copied offer an important example of dramatic extracting. *Othello*, written around 1603, was not published until 1622, which means that Pudsey was not working from a print source—though, for the majority of his dramatic extracts Pudsey did rely on print sources. For his selections from *Othello*, however, Pudsey could have jotted notes during the performance in a table-book, a small book with waxed pages that could be written on (sometimes with pencils, pens, or styluses) and then erased.[72] Table-books would have been ideal for taking to the theatre because an audience member could take a few notes during the performance and then recopy the notes into a more permanent form, such as a personal miscellany. If he were taking notes during a performance, Pudsey would not have been the only one scribbling in the theatre. Thomas Heywood complained that his play *If you know not me, You know no bodie* was so popular that audiences "Did throng the Seates, the Boxes, and the Stage / So much; that some by Stenography drew / The plot: put it in print: (scarce one word trew:)."[73] Stenography, the art of writing things in code or shorthand, made it easier to transcribe rapid speech.

It is reasonable to conjecture that Pudsey was using a table-book to take at a performance, but it is also possible that Pudsey wrote down his recollections after attending a play without using any notes.[74] Or, Pudsey might have copied from another manuscript source—although full-text plays did not circulate as widely in manuscript as poetry, songs, or extracts from plays. Richard Savage, a nineteenth-century scholar, went so far as to suggest that Pudsey might have transcribed these extracts from Shakespeare's original manuscripts, although his speculation is far-fetched.[75] Pudsey's extracts from *Othello* demonstrate the wide variety of possible sources from which early modern manuscript compilers began taking dramatic extracts. One reason scholars continue to return to his manuscript is that there is no definitive account of his source.

Even though Pudsey likely did not copy his extracts from full-text plays in manuscripts, the circulation of full-text plays bears mentioning as context for dramatic extracts. T. H. Howard-Hill concludes that although manuscript poetry continued to flourish after the advent of printing, full-text plays in manuscript did not did not compete with their print counterparts.[76] Although we have numerous printed Elizabethan and Stuart play-texts, far fewer manuscript versions of these plays survive.[77] Despite modern scholarly concerns with categorizing these manuscripts as "fowle papers" or "fair copy" (or complicating these categories or repudiating them altogether), for the purpose of this discussion, it is more practical to consider the purpose of full-text play manuscripts: some were written for use in the theatre, others were written to be used by printers, and others were commissioned or presentation copies given to patrons.[78] The few existing complete manuscript plays reveal little about how widely each of these plays circulated. While a number of dramatic extracts can be traced back to particular playbooks and other print sources, a few dramatic extracts might have been copied from manuscript full-text plays. Although we have no proof that any manuscript dramatic extracts were copied from complete manuscript plays, there is evidence of print dramatic extracts being taken from full-text manuscript plays. John Cotgrave's *English Treasury of Wit and Language* (1655), discussed at length in Chapter 3, includes multiple passages from Thomas Middleton's *Hengist, King of Kent* (also known as *The Mayor of Queenborough*), predating the play's 1661 publication.

Predictably, dramatic extracting increased as the publication of playbooks increased: both can be attributed to the rising popularity and literary legitimation of theatre. Peter Blayney demonstrates that plays began being regularly (though still infrequently) published in 1590—the publication of plays was indubitably one contributing factor to the dramatic excerpting that began in the same period. While most years from 1585 to 1600 saw the publication of only two or three plays, there were two notable jumps in play publication: around 1594, which coincides with when we find the first dramatic extracts in manuscript, and around 1600, when dramatic extracting increased in popularity.[79] Blayney notes that before the end of Elizabeth's reign, there were very few printed playbooks and that the publication of playbooks increased during the first twenty years of James's reign and continued to rise during the Caroline period.[80] The relation between the publication of plays and the copying of dramatic extracts is chiastic: the publication of plays offers texts from which to extract, and compilers interested in drama increase the demand for play publication.

The first decade of the seventeenth century showed a rise in the numbers of plays published as well as a change in how these plays were published—plays began to be published with commonplace markers. G. K. Hunter's influential study lists a variety of typographical elements used in the sixteenth and seventeenth centuries to point out commonplaces: inverted commas (single or double), asterisks, manicules (pointing hands), and varying the typeface (italicization, for example).[81] The typographical marker we recognize as quotation marks (more properly called "commonplace markers" when found in early modern plays) functioned differently than they do today: rather than demarcating the start and end of someone's speech, in Margreta De Grazia's words, "they signalled what was memorable or worth commemorating, what deserved to be inscribed, or reinscribed, on those two writing surfaces or tables: the memory or the commonplace book."[82] Zachary Lesser and Peter Stallybrass's extensive research shows that 1570 marked the first play published with commonplace markers (the second edition of *Gorboduc*, which Briton may or may not have seen), but the practice was relatively rare up to 1599.[83] From 1600 on, however, the rate of using commonplace markers in plays skyrocketed. From 1600–1603, there were thirteen plays printed with commonplace markers.[84] By printing playbooks with commonplace markers, printers (and, at times, authors) were literally marking plays as significant and authoritative texts;[85] that is to say, drama was gaining the gravitas and cultural influence to be considered a literary genre worthy of mining for wisdom in the form of extracts.

Increases in printed plays and the inclusion of commonplace markers both contributed to (and perhaps reflected) increased dramatic extracting, but one particular early seventeenth-century example illustrates how inseparable print and manuscript culture are in the discussion of manuscript dramatic extracts. A slip of paper once used as a bookmark in a German book (c. 1620) is now included in BL MS Add. 41063, a large composite volume of miscellaneous letters and papers ranging from a fourteenth-century petition to nineteenth-century letters. This bookmark contains extracts from *Pericles* and *Richard III*.[86] Copied from one print source and presumably forgotten in another, these extracts remind us of the close relationship (and in this case, physical proximity) of print and manuscript culture throughout the seventeenth century.

William Drummond of Hawthornden's (1585–1649) dramatic extracts are similarly found in a volume that remind readers of the material conditions of reading, writing, and extracting at the beginning of the seventeenth century. Noted for his wide-ranging correspondences with literary figures including Michael Drayton, Sir Robert Kerr, Sir Robert Aytoun, Sir David Murray, and Ben Jonson, Drummond was himself one of the premier Scottish poets of the seventeenth century.[87] Drummond and Jonson's friendship is now mostly remembered through Drummond's notes on a conversation he shared with Jonson, where Jonson bluntly shared his opinions about other writers and their works. Jonson's acerbic remarks include "Samuel Daniel was good honest man . . . bot no poet" and "[John] Don[n]e, for not keeping of accent, deserved hanging."[88] Drummond never intended these notes to be published, but they were nevertheless posthumously printed in an abridged form in his 1711 *Works*. Drummond's dramatic extracts, like his now-famous conversation with Jonson, reflect his copious note-taking and his interest in his literary contemporaries and their works. As Robert MacDonald puts it, Drummond was "a collector, a hoarder, a kind of literary squirrel who saved anything that came his way."[89]

Drummond's dramatic extracts show that he read a variety of plays. Many of Drummond's papers are now in the National Library of Scotland (MSS 2053–2067, as well as others in the Advocates Manuscript collection). Volumes 7 and 8 of Drummond's papers (MSS 2059 and 2060) are his "commonplace-books," titled in his hand, "Ep^h^emeris."[90] The first dramatic extracts in Drummond's manuscript are from *The Honest Whore* (part one), which he titled "The [Conver]ted Curtizan," and topped with Thomas Dekker's name.[91] Drummond copied selections from a wide number of plays, making it particularly notable that he did not copy extracts from three of the most important playwrights of the time: Shakespeare, Jonson, and John Fletcher.[92] From Drummond's list of "bookes red be me [sic], anno 1606," we know that he read plays by Shakespeare, including *Love's Labour's Lost* and *A Midsummer Night's Dream*.[93] This, of course, does not suggest that Drummond chose not to extract from Shakespeare: perhaps Drummond's dramatic extracts from plays by his friend Jonson and by Shakespeare are in another manuscript that has been lost. We also have Drummond's "Catalogue of Comedies" that lists fifty-seven plays, including now-canonical works such as Christopher Marlowe's *Edward II* and *Doctor Faustus* alongside lesser-studied plays such as Edward Sharpham's *The Fleire* and Nathan Field's *A Woman is a Weathercock*.[94] Drummond's list of plays includes both sources he excerpted from (for instance, George Chapman's *All Fools*) as well as those not documented in his extant miscellanies.

Drummond's dramatic extracts, lists of book read, and list of plays reflect his interest in early modern English drama, as does his library. More than ten percent of the English books that Drummond had were playbooks.[95] MacDonald's claim that Drummond "had a normal attitude to plays: like his contemporaries, he regarded them as not quite respectable, but he read them in quantity"[96] is refuted by the dramatic extracts Drummond copied in NLS MS 2059: Drummond read at least some plays for wit and wisdom worth noting and remembering. Drummond's commonplace books offer a snapshot of his play reading habits: some of the playbooks he owned remain in the Drummond Collection at the University of Edinburgh. The marks Drummond left in particular extant physical playbooks show that his engagement with drama extends beyond those dramatic extracts. His copy of William Alexander's *The Monarchicke Tragedies: Crœsus, Darius, The Alexandrean, Julius Cæsar* (1607) is heavily annotated (NLS MS 1692). Drummond's *Romeo and Juliet* (1599) includes extensive underlining of interesting words and phrases, like "as the alcheering Sunne, / should in the farthest East begin to draw."[97] Studying Drummond's dramatic extracting adds to our understanding of how one reader (and writer) interacted with early modern playbooks: he was not a passive consumer, but an active copyist seeking apt phrases and interesting ideas.

In NLS MS 2059, Drummond's extracts from *Parasitaster* appear on a sheet of paper that has two blots of sealing wax, one on the recto and one on the verso (f. 345). The page was not folded as if to be sent, the wax is simply two small drops with no sign of a seal, there is no name or address noted. The sealing wax likely dripped onto the page while Drummond sealed something else (perhaps a letter to one of his literary contacts). The sealing wax is at the bottom of the page, so we cannot tell if the wax fell on the paper before or after Drummond copied his dramatic extracts. Either way, it offers a provocative mental image: Drummond, at a desk with his papers, taking a page or notebook out from under a letter to copy a dramatic extract, or Drummond sealing a letter near a page on which he has already copied selections from Marston's play. This physical mark of history, these two dots of sealing wax, demonstrates the quotidian nature of dramatic excerpting for literate people in the British Isles in the seventeenth century.

The sealing wax in NLS MS 2059 indicates that Drummond's extracts were physically near manuscripts in active circulation; another early seventeenth-century manuscript shows how dramatic extracts themselves could be disseminated from person to person (orally or in writing) and so were not always taken from the contexts of the full play. Stephen Powle (c. 1553–1630) was a government administrator who, like Drummond, kept copious records and personal letters.[98] Bodleian MS Tanner 169 is the second part of what is known as his commonplace book, compiled around 1596–1622.[99] On 29 November, 1606, Powle copied a couplet, which was then in wide circulation: "Treason is like unto a Cocatrices eies / First sees & ^then^ kills: but firste seene dies" (f. 43). Powle wrote that it was given to him by "Mr Clapham from Mr Foucke Grevill"; John Clapham was a writer in correspondence with Powle, and a version of the couplet later appeared in Sir Fulke Greville's play *Mustapha* (1609).[100] Greville, however, was likely quoting from Robert Pricket's *Times Anotomie* [sic] (1606), which includes "A Song of rejoicing for our late deliverance" that has a stanza that concludes with, "Treason is like,the *Baziliske* his eyes / First seeing, kills, first being seene, it dies."[101] Greville adapted the couplet slightly before including it in his play: in the 1609 quarto of *Mustapha*, the couplet runs "Mishchiefe is like the Cockatrices eyes; / Sees first and kils, or is seene first and dies";[102] the version of the play in Greville's 1633 *Workes* has the same wording, although notably the second sentence is italicized.[103] In the copy of the play that also includes commonplace markers to highlight some passages (1633), italics signal this sentence as important. One mid-century reader copied only selections from the play highlighted by italics, including the "Mischeife is like the Cocatrices Eyes" couplet.[104]

Most of the versions of this couplet found in manuscript follow Pricket's original formulation.[105] In early modern miscellanies, there are few extracts from *Mustapha* other than this particular couplet, although one other manuscript, an early seventeenth-century miscellany, includes a different passage from the play headed "Sir Fulke Greville of ambition."[106] Greville's couplet circulated alongside Pricket's formulation and was changed and adapted as it was conveyed from person to person. For instance, in *The Rich Cabinet furnished with varietie of Excellent discriptions, exquisite Charracters, witty discourses, and delightfull Histories, Devine and Morrall* (1616), which has been *digested Alphabetically into common places*, the author, T. G., reworked the couplet into a prose commonplace found under the heading "Lawes": "Lawes make treason like the eyes of a Cockatrice, which kill, if they espy us first with their venom: but are killed, if we discover it in his poyson."[107] T. G.'s commonplace draws both on Pricket ("treason") and Greville ("Cockatrice"). The basilisk/cockatrice couplet that Greville incorporated into his play reminds us of the close relation of dramatic extracts to commonplaces, both of which could be rephrased as they were remembered, spoken, and copied.

These early manuscripts demonstrate that early modern dramatic extracts could be taken from performances (Pudsey), copied from print sources (Pudsey and Drummond), and could be passed from person to person orally or in manuscript (Powle). The bookmark serves as a pointed reminder of the close relation between manuscript and print, while also suggesting the prevalence of dramatic extracts: if selections from plays were copied on loose slips of paper, the majority of them would now be lost. These manuscripts remind us of the importance of the print history of early modern plays in relation to their reception as works to be divided, excerpted, and passed along.

PROLIFERATING MANUSCRIPTS, PROLIFERATING EXTRACTS (1620s–1640s)

Greville's couplet illustrates not only the circulation of dramatic extracts beyond the initial scope of the play but also the increasing number of dramatic extracts as the seventeenth century progressed. Although Powle copied Greville's lines in 1606, the majority of manuscripts that contain the couplet were compiled at Oxford around the 1630s (such as Bodleian MSS Eng. poet e. 14, Eng. poet. e. 97, Malone 19, and Harvard MS Eng. 686). From 1620 to around 1645, there was a boom in the compilation of poetic anthologies and miscellanies at the universities, particularly Oxford.[108] It is unsurprising that environments that fostered increased manuscript circulation also cultivated an increased number of dramatic extracts.

Many manuscripts written during the 1620s and 1630s at Christ Church contain extracts from plays by Shakespeare, Jonson, James Shirley, and others.[109] For instance, BL MS Add. 30982 contains extracts from Middleton's *The Witch* (f. 36v); BL MS Egerton 2421 contains the lyrics from all of the songs in Shakespeare's *The Tempest* (ff. 6v–7); Bodleian MS Eng. poet. e. 14 contains extracts from Fletcher's (perhaps Middleton's?) *The Nice Valour* (f. 84), and Jonson's *Poetaster* (f. 21) and *Epicoene* (f. 12). This manuscript culture included extracts from masques, as well as plays—many Christ Church manuscripts contain extracts from Jonson's *The Gypsies Metamorphosed*.[110] These Christ Church manuscripts are only a few examples of the many that were written in the 1620s and 1630s that contain dramatic extracts.[111]

Bodleian MS Eng. poet. e. 97, one such Christ Church manuscript (c. 1630s–1640s), includes both seventeenth-century elements and nineteenth-century components that interact with early plays. This quarto-sized manuscript, primarily a verse miscellany, contains over 150 poems and one extract from *Love's Labour's Lost*.[112] In the same manuscript, a nineteenth-century copyist reproduced an early spoof on almanacs in its entirety, *A Mery P[rog]nosticacion* (1544), even mimicking the typeface and drawing the images; a marginal comment compares one of the fool's speeches from *King Lear* (3.2.81–94) to *A Mery P[rog]nosticacion* because both mock prophecies: "The Fool in Lear closes his burlesqe prophecy, much in the strain of the bible."[113] The same ninenteenth-century copyist transcribed a complete sixteenth-century morality play, *The Nice Wanton* (1560).[114] Shakespeare appears in two forms in Bodleian MS Eng. poet. e. 97: a seventeenth-century compiler quoted from *Love's Labour's Lost* yet did not title or ascribe the piece. Later, a nineteenth-century contributor did not quote from Shakespeare, but instead used his name in a scholarly comparison.

The seventeenth-century Shakespearean extract from *Love's Labour's Lost* in Bodleian MS Eng. poet. e. 97 runs: "The Fox, the Ape, the Humble-bee / were still at odds, being but three / untill the goose came out of doore / Staying the odds by adding Foure."[115] While most of the other poems in the collection are titled, and several are ascribed, the extract from *Love's Labour's Lost* offers no mention of author or title. In Shakespeare's play, Moth and Armado speak these lines repeatedly during their banter about the definition of an "envoy." Armado explains, "it is an epilogue or discourse, to make plain / Some obscure precedence that hath tofore been sain" (3.1.81–82). Although Armado believes that the purpose of an envoy is to explain obscure meanings, the meaning of this particular envoy has puzzled scholars for decades.[116] The compiler has positioned the four lines (which are separated in the play) as one unit, unbroken by dialogue. Moth and Armado's bawdy, clever repartée surrounding the epigram did not interest the compiler the way it does modern scholars.

Bodleian MS Eng. poet. e. 97 contains two songs that circulated separately from their plays in manuscript and eventually in print: Jonson's "Though I am yong & Cannot tell," from *The Sad Shepherd* and Sir John Suckling's "Why so pale & wan; Fond Love?" from *Aglaura*.[117] The compiler did not ascribe either poem, and titled Jonson's piece simply "Songe."[118] Numerous manuscripts contain versions of these two songs, both with musical settings and without.[119] Suckling's song was first printed in *Aglaura* in 1638 and later printed in his posthumous complete works, *Fragmenta Aurea*.[120] This extract was itself extracted in the miscellany and guidebook *The Academy of Complements*.[121] Similarly, Jonson's song was also published posthumously in a collection of his poems, *The Execration Upon Vulcan* (titled "A Sonnet") and was later published in a printed verse miscellany, *The New Academy of Complements*.[122] The rhyming animal fable and songs found in Bodleian MS Eng. poet. e. 97 are easy to memorize and have an understandable meaning even when removed from the context of the play, which makes them ideal selections for extracting. Indeed, from 1600 onwards, extracts such as these (songs, epilogues, prologues, and couplets) were the most commonly copied selections from plays.

As dramatic extracting became more widespread after 1600, songs were especially popular: the majority of dramatic extracts in seventeenth-century manuscript are songs. Songs are not only easily removed from a play's context; often, they were not published with the play-texts, partly because songs were not always composed with the play itself (these could be old songs, adaptations of old songs, or collaborations with a composer).[123] Tiffany Stern notes that even when "songs circulated without their music, as their verbal content alone, they were likely not to be written into the playtext from the start, and to circulate in a bundle containing prologues and epilogues"; songs from plays are arguably as paratextual as the prologues and epilogues. Stern asks, "If a playwright was always conscious that a song would be extracted from his play, and if he even, himself, was part of the extraction process, what does that say about the way he conceived of the lyrics: was the song, at the moment of writing, part of the drama, or was it always aside from the text?"[124] If playwrights conceived of songs as something "aside from the text," and knew that songs "would be extracted," songs then function like phrases marked with commonplace markers in the print text, designed to be taken separately from the play.[125]

Many songs from plays circulated both with musical settings and without. For instance, "If I freely may discover," from Jonson's *Poetaster*, is found in Giles Earle's songbook (comp. c. 1615–26) with music and also in BL MS Stowe 961 (comp. c. 1623–33), a verse miscellany, without music.[126] "If I freely may discover," like "Though I am young and cannot tell" from *The Sad Shepherd*, is an example of a song from a play that likely became more popular than the play itself. "If I freely may discover" is found in dozens of manuscripts from throughout the seventeenth century, although BL MS Stowe 961 is one of the earliest. Jonson's song circulated widely during the 1620s and 1630s, both with and without music, and generally with no reference to the play (*CELM*, JnB 693–714.5). Some music books contain multiple songs from plays and masques. Elizabeth Davenant (sister to playwright William Davenant) owned a manuscript music book that included songs from, for instance, Jonson's *The Devil is an Ass* ("Have you seene the white lilly grow?"), Thomas Goffe's *The Courageous Turke* ("Dropp drop goulden showrs"), and Fletcher's *Valentinian* ("Care charming sleepe").[127] New York Public Library MS Drexel 4175 (c. 1620) and MS Drexel 4257 (c. 1630s–1650s) are similarly replete with songs from plays.[128] Circulating with or without music, in print, manuscript, and orally, songs from courtly entertainments or from professional plays were typically the most copied parts of plays because, as Stern explains, they were often meant to be taken separately from the whole.

Margaret Bellasys's verse miscellany, BL MS Add. 10309, illustrates the generic indeterminacy of dramatic extracts, poems, epilogues, and songs. The dramatic extracts in Bellasys's miscellany exemplify the heterogeneric nature of many dramatic extracts: they are dramatic, but they can be simultaneously a poem or a song. Bellasys's miscellany, a more-than-300-page duodecimo manuscript written in the late 1620s and early 1630s, begins with a seventy-five page moralizing tract based on works by the Puritan preacher Thomas Adams and Bishop Joseph Hall, "The Characterismes of Vices."[129] The rest of the miscellany is filled with poetry by Donne, Carew, Jonson, Herbert, and others. We do not know for certain who Margaret Bellasys was, or if she wrote this manuscript by hand, had it commissioned, or simply signed the last page.[130]

One item in BL MS Add. 10309, "Verses before a masque," begins "Gentlemen, y'are welcome, but not from me" and is possibly unique in manuscript poetry.[131] This piece might be a prologue to a lost masque, or perhaps a prologue not yet associated with a masque.[132] Although it is unclear which masque this prologue prefaced, its presence in the manuscript perhaps points to the compiler's interest in drama. As a woman, Bellasys is excluded from the anticipated male audience of the performance. This prologue is an example of a dramatic extract whose dramatic origins are now lost: now it can only function as a self-contained piece without referring to its larger work. As mentioned above, Stern positions both prologues and songs in the liminal, paratextual space bordering the plays, and notes that they often circulated together. Bellasys's manuscript shows how both prologues and songs could become stand-alone poems.

Bellasys's manuscript contains three songs from plays: Middleton's *The Widow* and Jonson's *Epicoene* and *Volpone*. *The Widow* revolves around numerous suitors seeking to marry Valeria, who, like all the most attractive widows in Renaissance plays, has a lot of money. The song found in BL MS Add. 10309 comes at the beginning of the third act, when Ansaldo, a handsome youth, meets Latrocinio, who is singing. In this context, Middleton could have chosen almost any song to entertain his audience.[133] Middleton's thief, however, sings, "I keep my horse, I keep my whore," a song about a purse-taker, as the title in Bellasys's manuscript reminds us. The speaker in the song (just like the singer in the play) is a thief. With the last line of the song, "Deliver your purse, Sir," Latrocinio draws his weapon and attempts to mug Ansaldo. Ansaldo pulls out his gun and orders the thief to sing a new song as punishment. In the end, though, Latrocinio is as triumphant as the thief in the song who has his choice of women and gets the money: Latrocinio's friends arrive and they steal everything from Ansaldo, including the shirt from his back. To celebrate, the thieves sing yet another song.

"I keep my horse" is not only appropriate for the play because of the parallels the song's speaker has with Latrocinio but also because it comments on the themes in the play. The opening line, "I keep my horse, I keep my whore" is about gender and ownership, just like the main plot of the play. The singer calls the whore "mine," highlighting his ownership of the woman in the song; this contrasts with Valeria, the rich widow, who is an owner in her own right. The song jokingly suggests the possibility of rape: "the cook maid has no mind to sin" but feels forced to please the thief. Likewise, the scene itself brings up the potential of rape, particularly for audience members and readers familiar with the play, who know that Ansaldo will later be revealed to be a woman. Latrocinio's theft, then, takes on sexual overtones when he and his companions rob and strip Ansaldo/Martia. While Middleton's song can be read as a microcosm of the different themes in the play, in Bellasys's manuscript "I keepe my horse" is entirely recontextualized. The compiler of BL MS Add. 10309 did not copy the song from a print edition of the play: although the play was probably written around 1616, it was not published until 1652, well after this manuscript was compiled.[134]

The dramatic extracts and poems in Bellasys's manuscript contain multiple and opposing views: the poems surrounding "I keepe my horse" can emphasize the themes of sexual dominance over women, yet a reader familiar with the play might find the song a reminder of Middleton's strong female protagonist, Valeria, the titular widow. In Bellasys's manuscript, "I keepe my horse" follows "Why should passion leade the [thee] blinde."[135] "Why should passion" is a poem about loving a girl who is "too young to tast delight," but when autumn comes, it will "mak[e] her tast & colour sweeter." Both of these poems focus on women's bodies as sexual objects to be enjoyed by a male at his leisure: when she "tastes" best or, in Middleton's song, even against her will. These two very sexual poems are followed by an elegy, "Come Fates, I feare thee not,"[136] that takes an abstract view of love where Fate, Love, and Chastity are among those ideas personified. Ian Moulton concludes that the poems in this manuscript express "arguments for and against women," spoken by a variety of speakers.[137] "I keep my horse" can gesture to the proto-feminist elements of *The Widow* while also conforming to the misogynistic poems that surround it. Sasha Roberts argues that the "multiple perspectives" presented by opposing poems often juxtaposed in miscellanies "add up to something more than the proliferation of points of view as *neither* poem emerges with an authentic, authoritative, or dominant voice on the position of women."[138] As Roberts explains, all miscellanies foster "intertextual scepticism" in readers by juxtaposing different voices and points of views, while also creating an awareness of different forms, genres, and generic conventions.[139]

In the Restoration, "I keep my horse" was printed separately from *The Widow* decades after the play was written;[140] Jonson's "Come, my Celia,"

("Come sweet Celia" in Bellasys's manuscript) was reprinted by the author in a collection of poems during his lifetime.[141] "Come, my Celia" was initially written for *Volpone*, but was also included in Jonson's collections of poems, *The Forrest*.[142] In the 1616 folio of Jonson's *Workes* that contains both *Volpone* and *The Forrest*, this song appears twice.[143] Generically, this piece is both a dramatic extract, that is, a section taken from the play (in this case, by Jonson himself), and also a self-contained piece, that exists outside the play and circulates alone. In Bellasys's manuscript, the poem is followed by "Kisse me sweet, the wary lover," the companion piece to "Come, my Celia" in *The Forrest*.[144] We cannot know if the compiler of BL MS. Add. 10309 recognized this song as a selection from a play or appreciated it as a poem with no dramatic connections.

The generic boundaries of "Come, my Celia" are further blurred when we consider the musical factor. When the lyrics are written out, this song appears to be simply a poem, even if (as in *The Forrest* and *Volpone*), it is titled "Song." Even when printed with music (as in Alfonso Ferrabosco's 1609 songbook *Ayres*), the song on the page is not the same as a performed song. Both versions of the song on the page (with and without music) can conjure mental performances of the song and the title reminds us of the insistent orality of theatre, music, and poetry. "Come, my Celia" is simultaneously a song and a poem, simultaneously part of *Volpone* and separate from *Volpone*.[145] When recontextualized in Bellasys's miscellany, "Come sweet Celia" can be read in relation to the play, in relation to the poems in *The Forrest*, and without either context.

The second dramatic extract in BL MS Add. 10309 is the anti-cosmetic diatribe "Still to be neat" from Jonson's *Epicoene*. *Epicoene* shares a major plot point with *The Widow*: cross-dressed marriages. In the secondary plot of *The Widow*, the character of Martia/Ansaldo assumes multiple gender roles: a male actor performs a female character (Martia), who spends most of the play disguised as Ansaldo, the handsome male youth. In the last act, Ansaldo dresses as a woman, and Francisco falls in love with her, much to the amusement of the other women who believe that Ansaldo is a man. At the end of the play Ansaldo is revealed to be Martia and her marriage to Francisco is saved.

The cross-dressing in *Epicoene*, however, functions in the opposite way than in *The Widow*: it dissolves a marriage. Dauphine, intent on earning his inheritance early, convinces his rich uncle Morose to marry Epicoene, who is a boy dressed as a woman. At first, Epicoene seems like the perfect and quiet wife, but after they are married, she becomes a loud shrew. Finally, Morose offers Dauphine 500 pounds a year to end the marriage, whereupon Dauphine reveals that Epicoene was never a woman so his uncle can have a divorce. In a play about performing (false) gender, "Still to be neat" comments on the inherent falseness of cosmetics and fashion, the external markers typically associated with femininity. Clerimont, a friend of Dauphine who sings the song, rejects "powder'd" and "perfum'd" exteriors, claiming that they do not reflect interior beauty.[146] As a dramatic extract, "Still to be neat" encapsulates the idea of gender as performance on which Jonson bases his cross-dressing plot.

Like "I keep my horse" and the other extracts in this manuscript, this song can be read without the context of the play, however thematically linked to the rest of the play it may be. "Still to be neat" appears in at least six other manuscripts from the 1620s and 1630s.[147] These other manuscript versions suggest that this song may not have been copied from a print version of the play; it could have been copied from another manuscript, or it could have been written from memory. After its initial 1609 performance, *Epicoene* was revived twice before the Restoration: the first time, in 1619/20, and the second time, at court, in 1636.[148] When BL MS Add. 10309 was being compiled, "Still to be neat" and other songs from *Epicoene* were not dated poems fading from memory, but rather, songs that were performed and sung.[149] When a reader comes across the lyrics to a familiar song, it changes the interaction with the words: the tune of the song springs to mind and influences the rhythm and prosody with which a poem is read, even if the poem is being read silently or read aloud and not sung. Today, readers can approach "Still to be neat" (or, for that matter, other songs from plays) as a poem bereft of performed elements; many early modern readers, however, would have had read and heard a song.

Jonson's "Still to be neat" praises "sweet neglect" and natural beauty above "all the adulteries of art." In this case, adultery means, according to the *Oxford English Dictionary*, "adulteration, debasement, corruption."[150] Adulteration is "corruption by spurious admixture."[151] I believe the notion of adulterous art plays out in two different levels (beyond Jonson's original meaning) with regards to Bellasys's miscellany. As a miscellany, this manuscript can perhaps be considered to be filled with "spurious admixture": it contains poems, songs, and selections from plays regardless of their literary or performed lineage. The dramatic extracts in this manuscript, furthermore, are also adulterated because each one embodies a mixture of drama, song, and poetry. Drama is, by its nature, already a site of generic indeterminacy (or perhaps, interdependency): it is often filled with both prose and verse, songs and spoken words. A dramatic extract, then, while being in the most basic sense a selection from a play, can also be a copy of a selection from a play, a song, a poem, or a combination of these genres.

The manuscripts surveyed in this chapter represent only a fraction of the archival evidence about English dramatic extracts from 1590–1642, yet can also be taken as representative of the larger cultural attitudes toward dramatic extracting. As this chapter has traced, the practice of printing plays and miscellanies were some of the changes that influenced and were perhaps influenced by dramatic extracting. While some of the manuscripts from this early period of dramatic extracting are unusual (such as Peacham's illustration or Scott's literary commentary), others (like Bellasys's songs, Briton's "pithy sentences," and Powle's letter) exemplify prevalent patterns in dramatic extracting, such as the popularity of songs, the interest in commonplaces, and the social circulation of extracts. These manuscripts reveal that both play-readers and playgoers copied selections from plays; furthermore, these selections from plays often continued to circulate without the context of the full play.

Dramatic extracts remind us that the smallest part of a play can contain the meaning of that play, can stand alone with its own significance, and can gain new implications in different print and manuscript contexts. Early modern plays were not created as monolithic texts, nor were they received as complete units; rather, these plays circulated orally, in print, and in manuscript as snippets of wit and wisdom, song, and poem. The next chapter in this book turns to extracts from masques and entertainments that were written from 1590–1642; the evolution of copying selections from professional plays continues in Chapter 3.

NOTES

1. Boston Public Library G. 3973.6, sig. E. This book is signed "Margarett Ettrick" (sig. Nv). This saying, while likely proverbial, is found verbatim in Alexander Niccholes, *A Discourse, of Marriage and Wiving* (1615).

2. Classical texts on commonplacing include Aristotle's *Topics*, Cicero's *Topica* and *De Inventione*, the anonymous *Rhetorica Ad Herennium*, and Quintilian's *Institutio Oratoria*. For an overview of the ancient views of commonplacing as it relates to rhetoric, see Ann Moss, "Ancient and Medieval Places," in *Printed Commonplace-Books and the Structuring of Renaissance Thought* (Oxford: Clarendon, 1996), 1–23.

3. Trans. Moss, *Printed Commonplace-Books*, 12.

4. Moss explains that Seneca is "imitating many who said it before" (*Printed Commonplace-Books* 12). Seneca, for instance, quotes Virgil, who said, "pack close the flowing honey / and swell their cells with nectar sweet," trans. Peter Schubert, "Musical Commonplaces in the Renaissance" in *Music Education in the Middle Ages and the Renaissance: Reading and Writing the Pedagogy of the Past*, ed. Russell E. Murray, Jr., Susan Forscher Weiss, and Cynthia J. Cyrus (Bloomington, IN: Indiana University Press, 2010), 162.

5. Peter Stallybrass and Roger Chartier, "Reading and Authorship: The Circulation of Shakespeare 1590–1619," in *A Concise Companion to Shakespeare and the Text*, ed. Andrew Murphy (Oxford: Blackwell, 2007), 45.

6. Earle Havens, ed., *"Of Common Places, or Memorial Books": A Seventeenth-Century Manuscript from the James Marshall and Marie-Louise Osborn Collection* (New Haven, CT: Beinecke Rare Book and Manuscript Library, 2001), 5.

7. Stallybrass and Chartier, "Reading and Authorship," 45.

8. Mary Thomas Crane, "Seed or Goad: Educating the Humanist Subject" and "Educational Practice in Sixteenth-Century England," in *Framing Authority: Sayings, Self, and Society in Sixteenth-Century England* (Princeton: Princeton University Press, 1997), 53–76 and 77–92. See also Marjorie Donker, "Tudor Schools," in *Shakespeare's Proverbial Themes: A Rhetorical Context for the "Sententia" as "Res"* (Westport, CT: Greenwood Press, 1992), 77–112.

9. William Kempe, *The Education of Children in Learning* (1588), ed. Robert D. Pepper, *Four Tudor Books on Education* (Gainesville, FL: Scholars' Facsimiles and Reprints, 1966), 220. See also Crane, *Framing Authority*, 63.

10. English booksellers were not the first to see the potential gains in printing commonplace books. For more on the continental forebears of English printed commonplace books, see Moss, "Commonplace-Books in Print," in *Printed Commonplace-Books,* 186–215.

11. Adam Smyth, *"Profit and Delight": Printed Miscellanies in England, 1640–1682* (Detroit: Wayne State University Press, 2004), 20.

12. Foxe, *Pandectae Locorum Communium* (1585), f. 43 [no signature numbers].

13. Foxe, *Pandectae Locorum Communium* (1585), f. 30. Translation mine. (Original: "Afflictio. Afflictiones. Tribulatio. Vexatio, Crux. Angustia. vide titulum de Martyribus"). The 1572 edition does not include the specification that these words apply to martyrs.

14. Foxe, *Pandectae Locorum Communium* (1572), f. 272 [no signature numbers]. Translation mine. (Original: "Jejunium. Abstentia. Abstemii. Ciborum delectus. Temperantia.")

15. Hilton Kelliher, "Contemporary Manuscript Extracts from Shakespeare's *Henry IV, Part 1*," *English Manuscript Studies 1100–1700* 1 (1989): 160.

16. One volume that was often reprinted was *Floures for Latine spekynge selected and gathered oute of Terence*, with versions published in 1534, 1538, 1544, 1560, 1570, 1575 and 1581.

17. Kelliher, "Contemporary Manuscript Extracts," 160. For a discussion of the other people involved with creating these miscellanies, see Celeste Turner Wright, "Anthony Mundy and the Bodenham Miscellanies," *Philological Quarterly* 40 (1961): 449–61.

18. For a discussion of the Shakespearean extracts in *Englands Parnassus* and *Bel-védere*, see Sasha Roberts, "Reading Shakespeare's Tragedies of Love: *Romeo and Juliet*, *Othello*, and *Antony and Cleopatra* in Early Modern England," in *A Companion to Shakespeare's Works: The Tragedies*, ed. Richard Dutton and Jean Elizabeth Howard (Malden, MA: Blackwell, 2003), 125–29.

19. Neil Rhodes, "Commonplace Shakespeare," in *Shakespeare and the Origins of English* (Oxford: Oxford University Press, 2004), 170.

20. For instance, Smyth lists more than two dozen examples of extracts taken from John Fletcher plays in miscellanies from the period 1640–1682 in his index. Smyth introduced his online index in 2002 with his article "An Online Index of Poetry in Printed Miscellanies, 1640–1682," *Early Modern Literary Studies* 8 (2002): 1–9, http://purl.oclc.org/emls/08–1/smyth.htm. Smyth's online index can now be accessed here: http://tinyurl.com/3xadpbd.

21. This argument builds on arguments by Moss (*Printed Commonplace-Books*, 209–10), Rhodes ("Commonplace Shakespeare," 170) and Stallybrass and Chartier ("Reading and Authorship," esp. 48–55). Moss explains that initially, English writers appeared alongside classical authorities, but in the late 1590s, selections from English writers were copied for their own merits. Rhodes agrees that the printed commonplace books from the 1590s printed by Nicholas Ling, Frances Meres, and Robert Allott "celebrate the birth of a national literary canon" with the authority and cultural value of Latin works (170). Stallybrass and Chartier suggest that Shakespeare gained fame and respect as a poet first and dramatist second.

22. Peter Beal, "Notions in Garrison: The Seventeenth-Century Commonplace Book," in *New Ways of Looking at Old Texts: Papers of the Renaissance English Text Society, 1985–1991*, ed. W. Speed Hill (Binghamton: Renaissance English Text Society, 1993), 138–39.

23. R. Hathway, "Of the Booke," in *Bel-vedére, or The Garden of the Muses* (1600), sig. A7v.

24. Robert Allott, *Englands Parnassus: Or the choysest Flowers of our Moderne Poets...* (1600), sig. A5v.

25. Francis Bacon, *De augmentis Scientarum*, in *The works of Francis Bacon*, ed. and trans. James Spedding, Robert Leslie Ellis, and Douglas Denon Heath (London, 1858), 4.435. For a discussion of the relation between commonplace books and memory, see Richard Yeo, "Notebooks as Memory Aids: Precepts and practices in Early Modern England," *Memory Studies* (2008): 115–36.

26. *Dux Moraud*, Bodleian MS Eng. poet. f. 2 (back of roll); Shrewsbury fragment, Shrewsbury School MS VI. See Norman Davis, *Non-Cycle Plays and Fragments* (Oxford: Oxford University Press, 1970), xiv–xxi, c-cx, 1–7, and 106–13. For a further discussion of later acting parts, see Simon Palfrey and Tiffany Stern, *Shakespeare in Parts* (Oxford: Oxford University Press, 2007). The Ashmole fragment (Bodleian MS Ashmole 750, f. 168) and the Rickinghall fragment (also called the Bury St Edmunds fragment, BL Add Roll 63481B) each only contain one part as well (Davis cxviii–cxx). For a discussion of many of these manuscripts, see also Richard Rastall, *Music in Early English Religious Drama*, 2 vols. (Cambridge: D. S. Brewer, 1996 & 2001).

27. Durham Prologue, Durham Dean and Chapter MS 1.2 Archidiac, Dunelm 60 dorse; Cambridge Prologue, Cambridge University Library Mm I.18, f. 62. See Davis, *Non-Cycle Plays*, cxi–cxiii; cxv–cxvii; 114–15; and 188–119.

28. Some potential dramatic extracts that are excluded from this discussion but might be of interest include the Charter Fragment (in Cornish, BL MS Add. Charter 19491) and the Winchester Dialogues (Winchester College MS 33), which might never have been meant to be performed. For the Winchester Dialogues, see Rastall, *Music*, 2.485–89; for the Charter Fragment see Whitley Stokes, "Cornica IV: The Fragments of a Drama in Add. Ch. 19.491, Mus. Brit.," *Revue Celtique* 4 (1879–80): 258–62.

29. See Cameron Louis, ed., *The Commonplace Book of Robert Reynes of Acle: An Edition of Tanner MS 407* (New York: Garland, 1980). See also Iris G. Calderhead, "Morality Fragments from Norfolk," *Modern Philology* 14 (1916): 1–9; Davis, *Non-Cycle Plays*, cxx–cxxiv, 121–23; and Rastall, *Music*, 2.484–85.

30. Louis, *Commonplace Book*, 432–35.

31. Bodleian MS Rawl. poet. 26, ff. 16v–17. Chapter 2 discusses some of the attention given to early masques; see *CELM* for more examples, including, for instance, selections from Gascoigne's entertainment *The Tale of Hemetes the Heremyte* (GaG 4 and 4.5).

32. Seymour de Ricci's *Census of Medieval and Renaissance Manuscripts in the United States and Canada* (New York: H. W. Wilson, 1935–1940) lists Folger MS X.d.177 as containing a misquotation from Peele's *The Old Wives Tale*, but I examined the manuscript and was unable to find the misquotation. Victoria Burke catalogued the contents of this short manuscript for the online edition in the *Perdita Manuscripts* collection and does not mention the misquotation from Peele listed by De Ricci. *Perdita Manuscripts*, Adam Matthew Digital; catalogue available from *Perdita Archives*, University of Warwick, http://web.warwick.ac.uk/english/perdita/html/.

33. The Marquess of Bath, Longleat House, Harley Papers, Vol. I, f. 159v.

34. See June Schlueter, "Rereading the Peacham Drawing," *Shakespeare Quarterly* 50 (1999): 171–84 and Richard Levin, "The Longleat Manuscript and *Titus Andronicus*," *Shakespeare Quarterly* 53 (2002): 323–40. Schlueter asserts that the drawing is of a German play and not Shakespeare's *Titus Andronicus*. Levin counters Schlueter's argument and summarizes a continuum of interpretations of the drawing: it is seen as representing more than one scene from the play, as symbolically reflecting the action in the play, or as portraying the staging and theatricality of the play.

35. Herbert Berry, "The Date on the 'Peacham' Manuscript," *Shakespeare Bulletin* 17 (1999): 5–6.

36. Berry ("Date," 5–6) asserts that the signature is in a different hand than the text. If the date was added after, it might make sense that the person adding the date chose 1594 if they recognized the material as *Titus Andronicus*. Another hand has added "Henrye Peachams Hand 1595" in the right-hand margin. Although this other hand looks early modern, it may have been added by the notorious scholar and forger John Payne Collier. See Jonathan Bate, ed., *Titus Andronicus* (1995; repr. London: Arden Shakespeare, 2002), 40.

37. Alan Hughes, ed., *Titus Andronicus* (Cambridge: Cambridge University Press, 2006), 20; Levin, "Longleat Manuscript," 328; Bate, *Titus*, 41. Bate notes that the unified composition and uniformity of ink used suggest the image and text were written at the same time.

38. Bate, *Titus*, 40.

39. Other scholars, however, suggest that Peacham wrote the manuscript after 1623. Beal notes that the text was "possibly copied later from the First Folio" (*CELM* ShW 104). J. Q. Adams argues that the text was copied from the 1623 First Folio. Adams points out that the added stage direction, referring to Tamora's "sonnes," does not coincide with any of the early quartos, but only the folio. If Peacham copied these extracts after 1623, this not an example of the early stages of dramatic excerpting, but rather, of the popularity of dramatic extracting in the 1620s and 1630s. Further complicating the date of this manuscript, it might not have been copied from a print source at all. Peacham may have been working from memory; he could have been copying from another manuscript source; or he could have expanded notes that he had jotted

down during an earlier performance. See J. Q. Adams, introduction to *Shakespeare's "Titus Andronicus": The First Quarto* (New York: C. Scribner's sons, 1936), 31–40; Hughes, *Titus*, 21; and Katherine Duncan-Jones, *Shakespeare: Upstart Crow to Sweet Swan, 1592–1623* (London: Methuen, 2011), 55–72.

40. Duncan-Jones, *Shakespeare*, 56. Duncan-Jones discusses Peacham's extracts in relation to his other published works and is an example of the productive research that can be gained by the study of dramatic extracts.

41. Hannah Leah Crummé, "William Scott's Copy of Sidney," *Notes and Queries* 56 (2009): 553–54.

42. Gavin Alexander, ed., *The Model of Poesy*, by William Scott (Cambridge: Cambridge University Press, 2013), xxxvi–xxxvii.

43. BL MS Add. 81083, f. 26; *Richard II*, 3.3.163 (1597), sig. G1v. I was unable to see this physical manuscript, but was able to consult the color digital facsimile at the British Library. I take my transcriptions from Gavin Alexander, *The Modell of Poesye: An Original Spelling Edition*, by William Scott (Cambridge: Cambridge University Press, 2013), available as a pdf download from Cambridge University Press's website as a supplement to Alexander's edition (see previous note).

44. Stanley Wells, "By the Placing of his Words: Scott never refers to Shakespeare by name, but is his first close critic," *Times Literary Supplement*, September 26 2003, 15.

45. BL MS Add. 81083, f. 22v; *Richard II*, 5.2.46–47 (1597), sig. H4.

46. Kelliher, "Contemporary Manuscript Extracts," 144, 175.

47. Ibid., 162.

48. Ibid., 173.

49. Ibid., 174.

50. For a transcription of all the extracts from this manuscript, see Kelliher, "Contemporary Manuscript Extracts," 155–58. Transcriptions from this manuscript are taken from Kelliher and follow his conventions.

51. BL MS Add. 61822. For a description of this manuscript, see Henry Woudhuysen, *Sir Philip Sidney and the Circulation of Manuscripts 1558–1640* (Oxford: Clarendon, 1996), 409–10 and William Ringler's typed notes held with the manuscript at the British Library (also available with the facsimile on *British Literary Manuscripts Online*, Gale Cengage Learning, Gale Document Number MC4400000190). An expanded version of this argument appears in Estill, "New Contexts for Early Tudor Plays: William Briton, an Early Reader of *Gorboduc*" *Early Theatre* 16 (2013): 197–210, where I focus on how Briton's extracts are both commonplace and applicable to the succession crisis; I also provide a list of the extracts by line number.

52. Russell A. Fraser and Norman Rabkin, eds, *Drama of the English Renaissance* (New York: MacMillan, 1976), 81. All line numbers from *Gorboduc* are taken from this edition.

53. BL MS Add. 61822, f. 77. The 1570 edition of *Gorboduc* was printed with commonplace markers (unlike Q1, 1565). Briton does not copy the passages highlighted for extracting by commonplace markers—though we cannot be sure of the edition Briton used (and whether or not there were commonplace markers in his edition) because of the similarity between the so-called "pirated" first quarto and the second.

54. BL MS Add. 61822, f. 89v; Thomas Sackville and Thomas Norton, *Gorboduc* 1.1.12–13.

55. Both Elyot's and Baldwin's works were frequently reprinted in the sixteenth century; we do not know which edition Briton used.

56. BL MS Add. 48023 (Yelverton MS 26), f. 359v. For a discussion of the politics as it relates to the eyewitness account of the performance, see Henry James and Greg Walker, "The Politics of *Gorboduc*," *English Historical Review* 110 (1995): 109–21; Greg Walker, "Strategies of Courtship: The Marital Politics of *Gorboduc*," *The Politics of Performance in Early Renaissance Drama* (Cambridge: Cambridge University Press 1998), 196–221; Norman Jones and Paul Whitfield White, *"Gorboduc* and Royal Marriage Politics: An Elizabethan Playgoer's Report of the Premiere Performance," *English Literary Renaissance* 26 (1996): 3–26; and Mike Pincomb, "Robert Dudley, *Gorboduc*, and 'The Masque of Beauty and Desire': A Reconsideration of the Evidence for Political Evidence," *Parergon* 20 (2003): 19–44.

57. Although many items in this manuscript are dated (and the latest date in the manuscript is 1605), Ringler points out in his notes that the "Rules of Husbandry" (ff. 55–62v) preceding the "Pithie sentences" were written in the late 1580s or early 1590s with later marginal notations added from 1594–1602. Following the "Pithie sentences" and sonnets from *Astrophil and Stella* is another section on "Rules of husbandry. . .taken owt of other authors in Anno 1596" (f. 104v). Ringler acknowledges that we cannot assume that the manuscript was written seriatim, but suggests that the sonnets were written in the period before 1596; by this token, the extracts from Gorboduc were likely copied in the early 1590s as well. If the extracts were copied closer to the *terminus ad quem* of 1605, Briton would have seen firsthand the effects of Elizabeth's refusal to marry: the end of the Tudor line and the accession of James I.

58. BL MS Add. 61822, f. 90; Sackville and Norton, *Gorboduc*, 2.2.89–94.

59. BL MS Add. 61822, f. 90v; Sackville and Norton, *Gorboduc*, 4.2.269–72.

60. BL MS Add. 61822, f. 90v; Sackville and Norton, *Gorboduc*, 5.2.181–82.

61. BL MS Add. 61822, f. 89v; Sackville and Norton, *Gorboduc*, 1.2.29–30.

62. BL MS Add. 61822, f. 89v; Sackville and Norton, *Gorboduc*, 1.2.360–64.

63. BL MS Add. 61822, f. 90; Sackville and Norton, *Gorboduc*, 2.2.103–5.

64. BL MS Add. 61822, f. 89v; Sackville and Norton, *Gorboduc*, 1.2.117–21.

65. Briton copied 100 of the 108 sonnets included in the 1591 edition of *Astrophil and Stella*. Although many of Sir Philip Sidney's other works circulated widely in manuscript, this manuscript is the only one to contain extensive selections from *Astrophil and Stella* (Martin Garrett, *Sidney: The Critical Heritage* [New York: Routledge, 1996.]) See also Ringler, *The Poems of Sir Philip Sidney* (Oxford: Clarendon, 1962), 541–42 and Woudhuysen, *Sir Philip Sidney*, 347–48, 409–10.

66. Briton was probably writing this after the execution of Mary, Queen of Scots (1587), who was a Catholic who had a genuine claim to the English crown after Elizabeth's death.

67. Arthur F. Marotti, "'Love is Not Love': Elizabethan Sonnet Sequences and the Social Order," *English Literary History* 49 (1982): 396.

68. David J. Knauer, "Playing Alone: Dramatic Literature in the English Renaissance" (PhD diss., Northern Illinois U, 1998), 147–48.

69. Pudsey's manuscript is Bodleian MS Eng. poet. d. 3, with some leaves now housed at the Shakespeare Birthplace Trust Record Office, ER 81/1/21.

70. Bodleian MS Eng. poet. d. 3, f. 1. See also Juliet Gowan, "An Edition of Edward Pudsey's Commonplace Book (c. 1600–1615) from the Manuscript in the Bodleian Library," (MPhil thesis, University of London, 1967), 13–14. Gowan's thorough yet unpublished edition of Pudsey's manuscript addresses the main scholarly concerns surrounding this manuscript. For a transcription of the Shakespearean extracts, see Richard Savage, *Shakespearean Extracts from "Edward Pudsey's Booke"* (London: Simpkin and Marshall, [1888]). For a discussion of Pudsey's Shakespearean extracts, see Duncan-Jones, *Shakespeare*, 72–83; for a discussion of his recreational and educational reading intentions, see Fred Schurink, "Manuscript Commonplace Books, Literature, and Reading in Early Modern England" *Huntington Library Quarterly* 73 (2010): 453–69.

71. Pudsey excerpted from Thomas Nashe's *Summer's Last Will and Testament* (f. 21v); Ben Jonson's *Every Man Out of His Humour* (f. 39v), *Cynthia's Revels* (f. 40v), *Every Man In his Humour* (f. 41), *Poetaster* (f. 41v), and *The Case is Altered* (f. 80); John Marston's *Jack Drum's Entertainment* (f. 40v), *Antonio and Mellida* (f. 41v), *Antonio's Revenge* (f. 41v), and *What You Will* (f. 81); Thomas Dekker's *Satiromastix* (f. 42v), and *The Honest Whore* (part 1; f. 80); Cyril Tourneur's *The Atheists Tragedy* (f. 80v); John Webster's *The White Devil* (f. 81); Thomas Heywood's *How to Choose a Good Wife* (f. 86); John Lyly's *Love's Metamorphoses* (f. 86v) and *Alexander and Campaspe* (f. 86v); and the difficult-to-attribute *Blurt Master Constable* (f. 86). In the leaves at the Shakespeare Record office are Pudsey's extracts from Shakespeare's *Merchant of Venice*, *Titus Andronicus*, *Romeo and Juliet*, *Richard II*, *Richard III*, *Much Ado About Nothing*, and *Hamlet*, as well as selections from George Chapman's *Blind Beggar of Alexandria*.

72. For more information on how Pudsey could have copied his notes while at the theatre (using a table-book), see Peter Stallybrass, Roger Chartier, J. Franklin Mowery, and Heather Wolfe, "Hamlet's Tables and the Technologies of Writing in Renaissance England," *Shakespeare Quarterly* 55 (2004): 379–419. A late nineteenth-century owner or archivist suggests (in a note written in the manuscript front pages), that the extracts are "in all probability, copies of brief short-hand or other notes taken by Pudseye at the theatres." See also Andrew Gurr, *Playgoing in Shakespeare's London*, 3rd ed. (Cambridge: Cambridge University Press, 2004), 240.

73. Thomas Heywood, *Pleasant Dialogues and Dramma's* (1637), 248–49. Kelliher offers a series of early modern references to table-books and taking notes while at the theatre ("Contemporary Manuscript Extracts," 168–71). I have used a few of his examples here, although there are many others.

74. David Kathman, "Pudsey, Edward. (*bap.* 1573, *d.* 1612/13)," *ODNB*.

75. Savage, *Shakespearean Extracts*, vii–viii.

76. T. H. Howard-Hill, "'Nor Stage, Nor Stationers Stall Can Showe': The Circulation of Plays in Manuscript in the Early Seventeenth Century," *Book History* 2 (1999): 28–41.

77. For an idea of the relative paucity of full-text manuscript plays compared to print plays, consider that there are 160 printed plays that can be linked back

to the Lord Chamberlain's Men/The King's Men, but only nineteen full-text play manuscripts that can be linked to this company. See Gurr, *The Shakespeare Company: 1594–1642* (Cambridge: Cambridge University Press, 2004), 121.

78. For a close analysis of manuscripts used in the theatre, see Paul Werstine, *Early Modern Playhouse Manuscripts and the Editing of Shakespeare* (Cambridge: Cambridge University Press, 2012). For a discussion of presentation or commissioned copies, see Grace Ioppolo, *Dramatists and Their Manuscripts in the Age of Shakespeare, Jonson, and Middleton* (New York: Routledge, 2002), 145–47.

79. Peter Blayney, "The Publication of Playbooks," in John D. Cox and David Scott Kastan, *A New History of Early English Drama*, (New York: Columbia University Press, 1997), 385.

80. Blayney, "Publication of Playbooks," 384–85. Although Blayney shows the increase of playbook sales and printing, he cautions modern scholars against assuming that early modern printers, publishers, and booksellers could easily make money selling plays to meet "the insatiable demands of hordes of eager play collectors" (415). Blayney reminds modern scholars that play sales accounted for only a small percentage of London book sales (385). Alan B. Farmer and Zachary Lesser assert that Blayney underestimated the popularity of playbooks, but their figures on play publications and republications are similar to Blayney's. Their debate exists in multiple articles: Blayney's "The Publication of Playbooks"; Lesser and Farmer's "The Popularity of Playbooks Revisited," *Shakespeare Quarterly* 56 (2005): 1–32; Blayney's "The Alleged Popularity of Playbooks," *Shakespeare Quarterly* 56 (2005): 33–50, and Lesser and Famer's "Structures of Popularity in the Early Modern Book Trade," *Shakespeare Quarterly* 56 (2005): 206–13.

81. G. K. Hunter, "The Marking of *Sententiae* in Elizabethan Printed Plays, Poems, and Romances," *The Library*, 5th ser., 6 (1951): 180. For more on commonplace markers, see Moss, *Printed Commonplace-Books*, 210–11 and Stallybrass and Chartier, "Reading and Authorship," 46–47.

82. Margreta de Grazia, "Shakespeare in Quotation Marks," in *The Appropriation of Shakespeare: Post-Renaissance Reconstructions of the Works and the Myth*, ed. Jean I. Marsden (Hemel Hempstead: Harvester Wheatsheaf, 1991), 59. See also Estill, "Commonplace Markers and Quotation Marks," in *ArchBook: Architectures of the Book* ed. Alan Galey et al., University of Saskatchewan, www.archbook.ca.

83. Zachary Lesser and Peter Stallybrass, "The First Literary *Hamlet* and the Commonplacing of Professional Plays," *Shakespeare Quarterly* 59 (2008), 405.

84. Comparing Blayney's figures on the publications of playbooks ("Publication" 384–85) with Lesser and Stallybrass's figures on the use of commonplace markers ("The First Literary *Hamlet*," 398–400) suggests that this increase in the number of plays printed with commonplace markers is also an increase in the percentage of plays printed with commonplace markers. Blayney counts 52 plays published between 1585 and 1599 and claims that there were no more than 30 plays published the decade before, which suggests that around 72 plays were published over the twenty-six years before 1600, of which only nine (roughly 12.5%) were published with commonplace markers. In the three years from 1600–1603, however, 13 of 42 plays were published with commonplace markers, that is, roughly 31% in total, or an increase of almost 20%.

85. Lesser and Stallybrass, "The First Literary *Hamlet*," 417

86. BL MS Add. 41063, f. 87. Stanley Wells and Gary Taylor suggest that the *Pericles* extracts were copied from the 1619 fourth quarto in *William Shakespeare: A Textual Companion* (Oxford: Oxford University Press, 1987), 567.

87. Michael R. G. Spiller, "Drummond, William, of Hawthornden (1585–1649)," *ODNB*, 4. For a transcription of some of Drummond's correspondence, see David Laing, "A Brief Account of the Hawthornden Manuscripts. . ." *Archaeologia Scotia* 4 (1857), 83–98.

88. R. F. Patterson, ed., *Ben Jonson's Conversations with William Drummond of Hawthornden* (London: Blackie and Sons, 1923), 3, 5.

89. Robert MacDonald, ed., *William Drummond of Hawthornden: Poems and Prose* (Edinburgh: Scottish Academic Press, 1976), xiii.

90. NLS MS 2059, f. 1. Drummond's volumes were bound around 1827, "somewhat confusedly" according to the National Library of Scotland catalogue.

91. NLS MS 2059, f. 208. *The Honest Whore* was published as *The Converted Curtezan* in late 1604 or early 1605: this is the edition Drummond read.

92. Following *The Honest Whore*, Drummond copied from Chapman's *All Fools* (f. 209r-v), Thomas Middleton's *Your Five Gallants* (ff. 209v–10), John Day's *Law-tricks or Who Would Have Thought It* (ff. 210v–11), Heywood's *How a Man may Chuse a Good Wife from a Bad* (f. 212), and Dekker and Webster's *Westward Hoe* (f. 214). After a few blank pages are extracts from the anonymous *No-body and Some-body* (f. 218), Chapman's *Sir Giles Goose-cappe* (ff. 218v–20v), Middleton's *A Mad World My Masters* (ff. 221–22v), and Day's *The Ile of Guls* (f. 222v). Later on in the manuscript, Drummond selected extracts from three other plays, including the anonymous *Liberality and Prodigality* (f. 236), from which Drummond took two verses of songs and some dialogue, and Marston's *The Fawn, or Parasitaster* (ff. 344–48v). Drummond's commonplacing also preserves a fragment of a work by George Peele, *The Hunting of Cupid* (ff. 352–53): this extract led scholars to believe that *The Hunting of Cupid* was a lost play by Peele, although Cutts later argued that *The Hunting of Cupid* is a pastoral poem, part of which was set to music. John P. Cutts, "Peele's *Hunting of Cupid*," *Studies in the Renaissance* 5 (1958): 121–132. For W. W. Greg's complete transcription of *The Hunting of Cupid* extracts from Drummond's manuscript, including a facsimile, see *"The Hunting of Cupid*, a lost play by George Peele," *The Malone Society Collections* 1, parts 4 and 5 (1911): 307–14.

93. NLS MS 2015, f. 359. For a transcription of the Drummond's reading list, see Robert H. MacDonald, ed., *The Library of Drummond of Hawthornden* (Edinburgh: Edinburgh University Press, 1971), 228–31.

94. NLS MS 2060, f. 122–23. MacDonald conjectures this "is presumably a list of plays Drummond had read or plays that he had bought," compiled after 1621 (231). For a complete transcription of Drummond's list of plays, see MacDonald, *The Library of Drummond*, 231–32.

95. This figure was achieved by comparing MacDonald's reconstruction of Drummond's library (*The Library of Drummond*, 187–203) to the *Database of Early English Playbooks*, ed. Alan B. Farmer and Zachary Lesser, University of Pennsylvania, deep.sas.upenn.edu.

96. MacDonald, *Library of Drummond*, 139.

97. Edinburgh University Library, De.3.7.3; a facsimile is available at "Shakespeare Collected," National Library of Scotland and University of Edinburgh, shakespeare.nls.uk.

98. For a biography of Powle, see Virginia Sterne, *Sir Stephen Powle of Court and Country: Memorabilia of a Government Agent for Queen Elizabeth I, Chancery Official and English Country Gentleman* (Toronto: Associated University Presses, 1992).

99. Jason Scott-Warren, "Reconstructing Manuscript Networks: The Textual Transactions of Sir Stephen Powle," in *Communities in Early Modern England*, ed. Alexandra Shepard and Phil Withington (Manchester: Manchester University Press, 2000), 18–37. As Scott-Warren points out, Tanner MSS 168 and 169 should more appropriately be called miscellanies because they are not organized, least of all by commonplace headings (20). The same can be said for Drummond's "common-place books" (NLS catalogue).

100. For a discussion of the relationship of and correspondence between Powle and Clapham, see Scott-Warren, "Reconstructing Manuscript Networks," 23–27.

101. Robert Pricket, *Times Anotomie* (1606), sig. H1v.

102. Fulke Greville, *Mustapha* (1609), sig. E3v.

103. The 1633 version reads, "Mischiəfe is like the Cockatrices eyes; / Sees first, and kills ; or is seene first ; and dies" (sig. X). The inverted e is an example of flipped type. Greville, *Certaine Learned and Elegant Workes. . .* (1633).

104. Folger MS V.a.219 (c. 1650), f. 52.

105. See *CELM* GrF 35–46 for a list of the manuscripts from the 1630s and beyond that include this couplet with "Treason" instead of "Mischief" and "Basilisk" instead of "Cockatrice."

106. University of Leeds Brotherton MS Lt. 25, f. 6v. Facsimile available from *Literary Manuscripts: 17th and 18th Century Poetry from the Brotherton Library, University of Leeds*, Adam Matthew Digital.

107. T. G., *The Rich Cabinet...* (1616), sig. M.

108. Arthur F. Marotti, *Manuscript, Print, and the English Renaissance Lyric* (Ithaca: Cornell University Press, 1993), 32.

109. I rely on Marotti (*Manuscript, Print, and the English Renaissance Lyric*, 32) for identification of Christ Church manuscripts.

110. For example, Westminster Abbey MS 41 (ff. 28v–29v), Bodleian MS Eng. poet. e. 14 (f. 16r-v), BL MSS Add. 30982 (f. 155) and Sloane 1792 (f. 123), and Folger MS V.a.345 (p. 160), among others.

111. See *CELM* for a list of further manuscript copied around this time. Just a few examples of manuscripts containing dramatic extracts from this period include BL MS Harley 6057, BL MS Sloane 542, and Bodleian MS Ashmole 38.

112. This manuscript contains many poems featured in *Early Stuart Libels*, ed. Alastair Bellany and Andrew McRae, Early Modern Literary Studies Texts Series I, http://purl.oclc.org/emls/texts/libels/. *CELM*'s explanation that the manuscript is related to Christ Church, Oxford is borne out by the high number of poems by Christ Church authors, including William Strode, William Corbett, William Cartwright, and

the lesser known Jerameel Terrent. Bodleian MS Eng. poet. e. 97 also includes a poem about Christ Church, "On the death of Jo: Dawson, Butler of Ch[rist] ch[urch]" (p. 170), and "On Bishopp Laud Chan[cellor] of Oxon" (p. 31), about Oxford more generally.

113. Bodleian MS Eng. poet. e. 97, pp. 197–213. I follow the Bodleian Summary Catalogue (entry 46487) dating of this hand. At the bottom of the first page of *A Mery P[rog]nosticacion* is a note reading, "This probably is one of the earliest attempts to satyrize sham predictions, prognostications" (p. 197). The phrase "burlesque prophecy" in relation to the Fool's speech in 3.2 is used in a few nineteenth-century sources, including James Rees, *Shakespeare and the Bible* (1876) and *Three Essays on Shakespeare's Tragedy of King Lear* (1851).

114. Bodleian MS Eng. poet. e. 97, pp. 196. *The Nice Wanton* runs from pp. 225–77. *The Nice Wanton* copyist noted the challenges of copying the original text: "not plain to read in the M.S." and offered conjectured readings, "I suppose nursed" (p. 226). At other times, on the page facing the play-text, the scribe explained challenging words, acting as a modern-day editor: "M.S. hodypeke, (very likely,) a word of ridicule in those times" (p. 230).

115. Bodleian MS Eng. poet. e. 97, p. 180; Shakespeare, *Love's Labour's Lost* 3.1.89–92, 95–99.

116. For allegorical readings, see, for instance, M. C. Bradbrook, *The School of Night: A Study in the Literary Relationships of Sir Walter Ralegh* (Cambridge: Cambridge University Press, 1965), 165; Anthony Petti, "The Fox, the Ape, the Humble-Bee and the Goose," *Neophilologus* 44 (1960): 208–15; Horst Breuer, "Shakespeare's 'Humble-Bee': A Note on *Troilus and Cressida*, 5.10.41–44," *Revue des langues vivantes* 43 (1977): 380–83; and Stanley B. Greenfield, "Moth's L'envoy and the Courtiers in *Love's Labour's Lost*," *The Review of English Studies* 5 (1954): 167–68. Recent scholarship has been less interested in finding one-to-one allegories for the fox, the ape, and the humble bee, but instead has turned to the wordplay for meaning, including Philippa Berry, "'Salving the Mail': Perjury, Grace, and the Disorder of the Things in *Love's Labour's Lost*, in *Spiritual Shaekspeares*, ed. Ewan Fernie (New York: Routledge, 2005), 94–108; and Patricia Parker, "Preposterous Reversals: *Love's Labour's Lost*," *Modern Language Quarterly* 54 (1993): 435–82.

117. For Jonson: Bodleian MS Eng. poet. e. 97, p. 215, 1.6.65–80; for Sir John Suckling, p. 218, 4.2.24–28. For a thorough explication of the latter, particularly a discussion of the dual audience, see L. A. Beaurline, "'Why So Pale and Wan': An Essay in Critical Method," *Texas Studies in Literature and Language* 4 (1963): 553–63. All line numbers for Suckling's work are taken from L.A. Beaurline and Thomas Clayton, eds., *The Works of Sir John Suckling* 2 vols. (Oxford: Oxford University Press, 1971).

118. The compiler initially skipped two lines of the first verse, and then added them below, "And then ag:[ain] I have bin told, / Love wounds with heat & d[ea]th with Cold; So that &c ut Supra [as above]" (p. 215).

119. For instance, NYPL MS Drexel 4041 (ff. 7v–8v) includes a musical setting for Suckling's song. In BL MS Egerton 923, Suckling's poem is titled "A Song by Sir Jo: Suckling" (f. 85v) but is offered without an accompanying score. Jonson's poem

is found in a slightly later manuscript, Bodleian MS Mus. b. 1 (ff. 137v–138, comp. c. 1656) with music, and without in verse miscellanies such as Folger MS V.a.96.

120. Suckling, *Fragmenta Aurea* (1646), sig. A8v. Some critics have suggested that Suckling might have written the song before the play because of Orsames's claim it is "A little foolish counsell (Madam) / I gave a friend of mine four or five yeares agoe" (4.2.31–32). See Clayton, *Works of Sir John Suckling*, 260–62.

121. *The Academy of Complements* (1646), sig. I12v.

122. Jonson, *The Execration Upon Vulcan* (1640), sig. G3; *The New Academy of Complements* (1669), 242.

123. Tiffany Stern, *Documents of Performance in Early Modern England* (Cambridge: Cambridge University Press, 2009), 171.

124. Ibid., 171, 173.

125. Some songs, such as those from *The Gypsies Metamorphosed*, circulated as independent works of art. Others, like the greensickness song from *The Miser* in Muddyclift's BL MS Sloane 161, were copied directly from the play itself. See Chapters 2 and 4.

126. Giles Earle's songbook, BL MS Add. 24655, ff. 59v–60; BL MS Stowe 961, f. 79v. BL MS Stowe 961 contains primarily poetry by John Donne. Jonson's song is found in other similar "Donne" manuscripts such as Yale Osborn MSS b 114 and b 148, BL MS Stowe 962, and the Crewe manuscript at Meisei University. For more information on these manuscripts, see *DigitalDonne: The Online Variorum*, ed. Gary A. Stringer, Texas A&M University, donnevariorum.tamu.edu.

127. Christ Church, Oxford, MS Mus. 87 (compiled in the mid 1620s): Jonson, ff. 4v–5; Goffe, f. 3v; Fletcher ff. 5v–6. Complete facsimile available in Elise Bickford Jorgens, ed., *English Song 1600–1675: Facsimiles of Twenty-six Manuscripts and an Edition of the Texts* (New York: Garland, 1987), vol. 6.

128. Facsimiles of these manuscripts are available in Jorgens, *English Song*, vols. 10 and 11. NYPL MS Drexel 4257 contains songs from Abraham Cowley's *Love's Riddle*, multiple plays by James Shirley, William Cartwright's *The Royal Slave*, and John Ford's *The Lady's Trial*. NYPL MS Drexel 4175 includes songs from Middleton's *A Chaste Maid in Cheapside* and *The Witch*, Francis Beaumont and John Fletcher's *The Captain*, Jonson's *The Devil is an Ass*, Webster's *The Duchess of Malfi*, and Shakespeare's *The Winter's Tale*.

129. Lambert Ennis, "Margaret Bellasys' 'Characterismes of Vices,'" *PMLA* 56 (1941): 141–50. Ennis argues that Bellasys wrote the opening tract and altered the source texts enough to make it an original work.

130. Most scholarship accepts the British Library Catalogue's identification of Margaret as the daughter of Thomas Belasyse (1577–1652), first Viscount Fauconberg of Henknowle, a royalist who eventually embraced Cromwell and who converted to Catholicism later in his life. See Ian Frederick Moulton, *Before Pornography: Erotic Writing in Early Modern England* (Oxford: Oxford University Press, 2000), 57–58, 230 and Gary Taylor, "Some Manuscripts of Shakespeare's Sonnets," *Bulletin of the John Rylands Library* 68 (1985–86): 210–46. As Moulton points out, however, this Margaret died in 1624. Gary Taylor suggests that another Margaret (d. 1671, daughter of Sir George Selby and wife of William Bellasys) might have written the

manuscript. Moulton (*Before Pornography*, 58) suggests that this collection was written by a professional scribe, because of the neat hand and use of catchphrases, although Ilona Bell and Margaret Hannay point out that neither of these elements rule out a woman compiler (discussion, Renaissance English Texts Society panel, "Early Modern Women's Manuscripts," at the International Congress on Medieval Studies in Kalamazoo, Michigan, 2010). Without assuming that Bellasys had the agency of a compiler, I follow Sasha Roberts and Bruce R. Smith in considering Bellasys the primary reader of these texts even if an amanuensis created the compilation. Roberts, *Reading Shakespeare's Poems in Early Modern England* (Basingstoke: Palgrave, 2003), 179–83; Bruce R. Smith, *Homosexual desire in Shakespeare's England: A Cultural Poetics* (Chicago: University of Chicago Press, 1994), 239.

131. BL MS Add. 10309, f. 140v. This piece is not listed in any other manuscript in the Folger Shakespeare Library's *Union First Line Index of English Verse: 13th-19th Century (bulk 1500–1800)*, firstlines.folger.edu or *Literature Online*, ProQuest.

132. Stern considers "'found' songs in music manuscripts, the plays of which are lost"; rather than a "playless song" (*Documents of Performance*, 168), "Gentlemen, y'are welcome" is a masque-less prologue.

133. Stern gives some examples of plays that contain "random song," with stage directions such as "He plays and sings any odde toy, and Orlando wakes" in Greene's *Orlando Furioso* (*Documents of Performance*, 125). For updates or to contribute information about this prologue, visit the *Lost Plays Database*, ed. Roslyn L. Knutson and David McInnis, University of Melbourne, www.lostplays.org.

134. See Gary Taylor, "*The Widow*," and Gary Taylor and Andrew J. Sabol, "Middleton, Music, and Dance" in Gary Taylor and John Lavagnino, eds., *Thomas Middleton and Early Modern Textual Culture* (Oxford: Clarendon, 2007), 1084–93 and 119–81, esp. 152. In Taylor's textual notes to *The Widow*, he notes that Bellasys's manuscript is the furthest from the printed 1652 quarto of all extant versions of the songs ("*The Widow*," 1087). Taylor claims the variants "either represent an authorially variant version of the song or a very corrupt transcription" ("*The Widow*," 1087, n. 3.1.22–37). This song is also found in Bodleian MS Ashmole 38 (where the play is acknowledged), which suggests that the play was revived around 1636–1638. The generally accepted dates of manuscript compilation for BL MS Add. 10309 run from the 1620s to the early 1630s, although this manuscript might have been written during the mid-1630s revival (Taylor and Sabol, "Middleton, Music, and Dance," 152).

135. BL MS Add. 10309, f. 95v-96. "Why should passion" was first published in *The Academy of Complements* (1646), sig. K1v, and later published in *The Poems of Pembroke and Rudyard* (1660), sig. F6v; however, the poem could be by Walton Poole. This poem was popular in manuscript circulation: *CELM* lists more than a dozen extant manuscripts that contain it. "Why should passion," like "I keep my horse," is also sometimes titled "a ditty" or "song."

136. BL MS Add. 10309, f. 96v. Although this elegy was at one time considered part of the Donne canon, it is now accepted as the work of John Roe. See Gary Stringer, *The Variorum Edition of the Poetry of John Donne*, vol. 2, The Elegies. (Indiana: Indiana University Press, 2000), esp. lxxxvii–lxxix, 429, and lxxxv note 7.

137. Moulton, *Before Pornography*, 62.

138. Sasha Roberts, "Women's Literary Capital in Early Modern England: Formal Composition and Rhetorical Display in Manuscript and Print," *Women's Writing* 14 (2007): 259.

139. Ibid.

140. *The Widow* was revived in the Restoration and William Lawes composed new music for "I keep my horse." In 1686, John Playford printed a version of Lawes's music and claimed the song was taken from Shakespeare's *1 Henry IV*. The song was printed, without music, in the 1684 *Academy of Complements* (354–55).

141. This song is more commonly written as "Come my Celia, let us prove," but Bellasys's manuscript says "sweet" (BL MS Add. 10309, f. 117).

142. Jonson, *Volpone* 3.7.165–82 (1607), sig. H2; Jonson, *The Forrest* (1616 folio), sig. Zzz5v.

143. Jonson, *Volpone* 3.7.165–82 (1616 folio), sig. Ss5; Jonson, *The Forrest* (1616 folio), sig. Zzz5v.

144. "Kiss me Sweet," BL MS Add. 10309, f. 117v. These pieces also appear together in Bodleian MS Rawl. poet. 31 and Edinburgh University MS Halliwell-Phillips 401. "Come, my Celia" and "Kiss me, sweet," however, are more frequently found separately in manuscript (see *CELM* JnB 443–50.5 and JnB 542–48). For instance, Bodleian MS Rawl. poet. 172, Folger MSS V.a.262 and V.a.339, and Yale Osborn b 356 contain only "Come, my Celia," whereas Bodleian MSS Eng. poet. e. 14, Firth e. 4, and Folger MS V.a.345 contain only "Kiss me, sweet."

145. For a reading of the significance of "Come my Celia" in relation to the events of the play and Ferrabosco's music, see Mary Chan, *Music in the Theatre of Ben Jonson* (Oxford: Oxford University Press, 2002), 89–98.

146. For a further analysis of the significance of "Still to be neat" in relation to the events in *Epicoene* see Chan, *Music*, 70–72. Chan argues that the song "stands on its own, as an ideal never achieved" in the play (72); this examination further shows how the song stands on its own in manuscript circulation.

147. *CELM* dates Bodleian MSS Malone 19, Rawl. poet. 31, and Rawl. poet. 199 to 1620s–1630s. Bodleian MSS Ashmole 38, Eng. poet. e. 14, and BL MS Egerton 2230 were probably compiled in the 1630s. Folger MS V.a.162 and Bodleian MS Don. d. 58 were written in the mid-seventeenth century and also contain this poem.

148. Richard Dutton, ed., *Epicene, or, the Silent Woman*, by Ben Jonson (Manchester: Manchester University Press, 2003), 76.

149. Like "I keep my horse," "Still to be neat" continued to circulate in the mid-to-late seventeenth century. New York Public Library MSS Drexel 4041 (c. 1630–1650) and 4257 (c. 1630–1659) both contain "Still to be neat" with musical notation. *Epicoene* was one of the first plays revived after the Restoration. The song was printed with music in Playford's *Select Ayres and Dialogues* (1669), and without music in the print verse miscellany, *Westminster Drollery* (1671).

150. "adultery, n.2." *OED*, 2nd ed.

151. "adulteration, n.1" *OED*, 2nd ed.

Chapter 2

Dramatic Extracts from Elizabethan and Stuart Masques and Entertainments

John Milton's *Comus* is an entertainment about how great a writer Milton thinks he is. Ben Jonson's *The Gypsies Metamorphosed* is a masque about abusive husbands, adultery, and cross-dressing escapes. Sir Philip Sidney's *The Lady of May* is a masque about a bumbling schoolmaster and has nothing to do with Queen Elizabeth. While none of these statements is categorically true, they are all reflected in early modern manuscripts that contain extracts from these masques.[1] As parts of a whole, extracts do not necessarily capture the same meaning as the complete text. Furthermore, as this chapter shows, the meaning of dramatic extracts change in new textual and historical contexts.

Although extracts from masques and extracts from professional plays at times function similarly, this is not always the case; selections from masques and entertainments follow a separate yet parallel trajectory to those from plays.[2] For instance, to date, we have no examples of selections from professional plays in volumes of state papers. This chapter begins by looking at masque extracts that function similarly to those from plays (such as songs and commonplaces), turns to the particular and courtly nature of masque extracts, and concludes by reinforcing one of this book's major arguments, that there is no one-size-fits-all approach to dramatic extracts: each writer, each dramatic work, each manuscript, each compiler, and each extract needs to be considered on its own terms.

Until the latter half of the twentieth century, literary critics largely ignored masques or only discussed them as minor dramatic works by familiar authors.[3] Stephen Orgel, Roy Strong, and others renewed scholarly interest in the study of occasional pieces by demonstrating that masques were inherently political and connected to particular cultural moments.[4] The trend of reading masques politically continues today; recent scholarly discussions of masques have titles that include such terms as "Political Intervention," "Performance,

Politics, and Religion," and "Political Possibilities," or "Jacobean Politics," "Stuart Court Culture," "Gender and Politics," and "Court Culture and Ideology," among others.[5] A handful of scholars such as C. E. McGee, James Knowles, and Gabriel Heaton have worked on the circulation and afterlives of masques, and, in a few cases, extracts from masques; my work builds on and continues this type of research.[6] In this chapter, I show how dramatic extracts can lead to productive ways of reading masques and entertainments that goes beyond the politics of the original moment of performance.

In this chapter, I posit that the act of excerpting from a masque or entertainment not only creates a different meaning from that implicit in the moment of performance but also offers new readings that differ from the significance of a complete print or manuscript version.[7] To prove this point, I show how extracts can be decontextualized from their full-text sources and how they can be recontextualized, for instance, in state papers or alongside classical authors. While acknowledging that masques were often political texts tied to their initial performance, this study offers an examination of excerpts from these works as they are embedded in new manuscript and print contexts. To put it another way, this chapter looks at the occasions of excerpting and the circulation of those excerpts rather than the occasions of performance.[8]

The first section of this chapter focuses on songs and other self-contained extracts from masques in order to demonstrate how these extracts circulated separately from their masques and were taken as complete units unto themselves, decontextualized from the full masque and its performance. The second section shows how early readers could be interested in the author of a masque for courtly or political reasons. This discussion of authorship and interest in masques includes Milton's unusual self-extracting from *Comus*. The chapter concludes by offering a vivid example of how changing historic circumstances can alter the meaning of a dramatic extract. By considering a range of texts (including those by Jonson, Nicholas Breton, John Lyly, Sir Francis Bacon, and anonymous writers) in a variety of manuscripts (such as commonplace books, miscellanies, songbooks, and composite volumes) and, when known, a gamut of readers from William Cavendish, Duke of Newcastle to unidentified university students, this chapter provides an overview of many ways masque extracts functioned and were part of early modern manuscript culture.

We can learn about early modern culture, courtly entertainments, and social history by examining dramatic extracts from masques and entertainments. Most important, examining dramatic extracts from masques shows that early readers did not consider masques as unified works tied solely to one occasion: rather, like professional plays, masques were sources that could be dismantled, and, in some cases, never existed as complete authorial texts. By considering extracts taken from complete masques as well as those copied from incomplete sources and those that add new material, this work destabilizes our idea of the source text.

SONGS AND SELF-CONTAINED EXTRACTS FROM MASQUES

While it might surprise scholars to learn that songs are the most common parts of plays in manuscript circulation, the popularity of songs from masques is perhaps more intuitive. Masques and entertainments are known for their dancing, music, and, of course, songs. In many cases, we have composers' manuscripts with the original score of the masque; as these are not examples of dramatic extracts, they will only be touched on in passing.[9]

As with professional plays, some masques incorporated preexisting songs, and others included songs that were composed separately from the rest of the performance. Both of these possibilities could be true for "The Plowman's Song" from *The Honorable Entertainment at Elvetham*, which begins "In the merrie moneth of May."[10] "The Plowman's Song" was written by Nicholas Breton and included in a larger entertainment that was likely written collaboratively.[11] *The Honorable Entertainment at Elvetham* was a four-day celebration for Queen Elizabeth in 1591, published later that year.[12] Breton's pastoral song was sung before the queen on the third morning of the entertainment (23 September 1591), and, the printed text tells us, "The song . . . pleased her Highnesse, after it had beene once sung, to command it againe, and highly to grace it with her chearefull acceptance and commendation."[13]

Breton's song was a hit, appearing in multiple print and manuscript sources. One reason "In the Merry Month of May" circulated so widely is that it was published separately from the entertainment as both a poem and a song in the early seventeenth century. Similarly, modern editors regularly treat Breton's song as a stand-alone piece, with perhaps just a footnote to indicate that at one time, it was part of a larger entertainment.[14] In 1600, this selection was published amid other pastoral poetry in *Englands Helicon*, titled "Phillida and Coridon" and attributed to Breton.[15] In 1604, Michael East (Este) printed the song with a musical setting in *Madrigales to 3. 4,.and 5. Parts*. The early availability of this extract in print—in the complete published masque and the song alone both a verse miscellany and songbook—undoubtedly contributed to its appearance in manuscript.

Multiple composers throughout the seventeenth century set Breton's lyric to music, undoubtedly furthering its stand-alone popularity outside the context of the masque. John Baldwin's original music for the entertainment exists in only one known manuscript.[16] "In the Merry Month of May" was later set to music by Richard Nicholson (after 1600), Michael East (c. 1604), Giovanni Giaocomo Gastoldi (before 1609), John Wilson (c. 1659), Benjamin

Rogers (c. 1660) and at least one other unknown composer (c. 1666).[17] Both Gastoldi's and Rogers's arrangements were printed in music textbooks after the Restoration: the song was used for teaching, which would only expand its dissemination.[18] Wilson's arrangement appears in multiple manuscripts, many of which include other songs from plays and masques.[19] For many who copied Wilson's song, it was his name and involvement that is important: it is attributed to "John Wilson" or "J. W." but its relation to Breton or to the Elvetham entertainment is not noted.[20] This masque extract was likely not ever copied from the entire print text of the masque; rather, the song itself was copied and recopied into multiple manuscripts.

Not only did "In the Merry Month of May" surface in both manuscript and printed music books, it was copied into multiple verse miscellanies over the course of the seventeenth century. The poem appears in one early miscellany that also includes extracts from Shakespeare's *Rape of Lucrece* and a dramatic exercise from Cambridge University.[21] In this particular manuscript, Breton's song appears on a page where religious passages attributed to Dr. Hall have been added. In a mid-century manuscript, Breton's poem can be found, titled "Phillida & Corydon," alongside other pastoral poems.[22] At the end of the century, or perhaps in the early eighteenth century, this poem was copied into a verse miscellany, in a series of poems titled "Sonnets." This section of the manuscript includes more than one song from early seventeenth-century plays and masques, such as "Oh! that Joy so soon should waste" from Jonson's *Cynthia's Revels* and "Why so pale and fond wan lover" from Sir John Suckling's *Aglaura*.[23] These three miscellanies represent "In the Merry Month of May" as a poem without reference to Breton or to *The Entertainment at Elvetham*. "In the Merry Month of May" typifies many lyrics, which circulated as both songs and poems and could be found literally alongside a variety of intertexts.

Of the verse miscellanies that include Breton's song, two add an extra couplet not found in other sources. BL MS Add. 34064, compiled c. 1596, includes two extra lines:

> In the merrie moneth of may
>   in a morne by breake of daie
> *with a troope of damsells playinge*
>   *forthe the wood forsooth a maying*
> when anon by the wood side
>   where that may was in his pride
> I espied all alone
>   Phillida and Choridon. (addition italicized)[24]

Scholars have known of this manuscript ever since Bishop Thomas Percy used it as a source for his *Reliques of Ancient English Poetry* (1765).[25] Similar extra lines are found in Bodleian MS Rawl. poet. 85:

> In the merye monthe of May
> by in a morne by breake of daye
> *I sawe a troupe of damsels playenge.*
> *Forthe they wente than one a mayenge*
> And anon by the wood syde
> Where that may was in his pride
> There I spyed all alone. ~~Ph~~
> Phillida and Corridon. (addition italicized)[26]

These added lines are clearly related, but likely not directly copied from one another. These variant lines reveal that "In the Merry Month of May" circulated orally well beyond the initial performance.

The widespread circulation of "In the Merry Month of May" separately from the source entertainment is not unusual for songs, both from masques and professional plays. One of the most popular songs in early modern manuscript circulation is James Shirley's dirge from *The Contention of Ajax and Ulysses*, "The Glories of our Blood and State," which is found in over three dozen manuscripts.[27] Jonson's scatological "Cock Lorell would needs have the devil his guest" also circulated widely and was often adapted and changed.[28] The transmission and circulation of "In the Merry Month of May" separately from *The Entertainment at Elvetham* is not an unusual case: in actuality, for many songs attached to larger performances, it was the norm.

The popularity of "In the Merry Month of May" continued well into the Restoration; the song was published in multiple printed verse miscellanies and songbooks in the latter half of the century.[29] Breton's song was not popular because it was associated with *The Honorable Entertainment at Elvetham*, or even because it had gained Queen Elizabeth's approval when presented before her. Rather, the song's popularity far eclipsed that of its original source text.

Although some songs circulated broadly, other songs were only copied once or twice. For instance, Peter Daniell's verse miscellany is the only known manuscript to contain a song from *The Masque of the Inner Temple and Grayes Inne*.[30] The song, "peace and silence be the guyde" appears untitled on a page below a poem about wooing a woman, "Bee not soe foolish nice," that concludes "Come bill & kisse & Ile shew you," and above some pieces "writt in a window at Litchfeild" about whether or not love is a sin.[31] Although Francis Beaumont originally wrote the masque to celebrate the marriage of Elizabeth of Bohemia and Frederick V, the Elector Palatine in 1613, Daniell's miscellany offers the piece as a generalized poem about marriage. The decontextualization of this piece in Daniell's miscellany foreshadows the song's later printing in verse miscellanies such as *The New Academy of Complements* (1669). This could also be an instance where a preexisting song was brought into a performance rather than a new song being written specifically for performance. While some songs, like "Cock Lorell" and "In the Merry Month of May," circulated widely, others, such as "peace and silence be the guyde," were less popular and turned up in one or two manuscript sources. As this section has shown, throughout the seventeenth century, it was not uncommon to find songs from masques (and plays) in manuscript, most commonly in verse miscellanies and songbooks. These songs generally appear without reference to their dramatic source or author, and as such, can be taken independently from the full masque.

In some extreme cases, decontextualized songs found in manuscript are the only record of a masque's performance. Peter Beal has identified the songs in National Library of Wales MS 5308E as part of a now-lost masque by the Merchant Adventurers that was likely performed around the 1630s.[32] It seems likely that there are more songs and extracts from both masques and plays scattered about verse miscellanies, commonplace books, and music books that are not identified as dramatic extracts because their source text is now lost. Although some early readers would associate certain songs with longer performances, others would have read the songs without knowledge of their origin. Scholars could also approach the meaning of songs from masques without the masque's original context, as that is how the songs would have been taken (that is, both copied and understood) by some readers.

In some ways, the appeal of copying a speech is comparable to that of a song: some speeches can be read as self-contained units: pieces that make sense without having to know the circumstances of the original dramatic performance or the complete work. Like songs, certain speeches were composed separately as individual parts of an entertainment, as was often the case for tilts.[33] Stand-alone dramatic extracts could fulfill two different purposes: they could be entirely decontextualized from the original performance, or they could, synecdochically, stand as representatives of the whole. While some speeches make sense independent of their ties to a complete text, there are also those compilers who copied a speech from a complete entertainment in order to refer to the original performance. Conversely, other small self-contained segments, such as couplets, can be easily removed from the context of the entire masque. Some couplets, epigrams, and short extracts are commonplaces that are meant to be taken from the source text and abstracted.

Gilbert Frevile's miscellany, BL MS Egerton 2877, which includes the opening speech from Jonson's *The entertainment of the two Kings of Great Britaine and Denmarke at Theobalds, July 24. 1606*, offers one example of a dramatic extract that attempts to capture the original moment of performance, Jonson published the entertainment in his 1616 *Workes*, along with a brief description of the events; Frevile's copy includes information not in the printed version. Jonson's explanatory introduction runs thus: "The Kings being entred the inner Court; above, over the porch, sate the three Howers, upon clouds, as at the ports of Heaven; crown'd with severall flowers: of which, one bore a Sunne-diall; the other, a Clock; the third, an Hower-glasse; signifying as by their names, Law, Justice, and Peace. And for those faculties chosen to gratulate their comming with this speech."[34] Frevile's manuscript does not offer this description from the printed play; instead, the extract is titled, "The speeche by Ewmone, by Dice, & Irene the .3. houres which do represent Time" and the margin reads, "made in a showe at the entertaignment of our king James, & the K[ing] of Den[mark] at Thebaulds, by the Earle of Salisburie" (f. 162v rev.). Frevile provided only the opening speech and not the Latin translation for King Christian IV of Denmark nor the Latin inscriptions on the walls. Following the speech, he included a description of the action: "Then fell downe presently, a showre of leaves, & the word (welcome) written on each of them in lettres of gold" (f. 162v rev.). The extract preserved in BL Egerton 2877 offers information on the original staging—including specific names—that would have otherwise been lost.

Beyond offering insight into original staging, Frevile's extract shows how an entertainment can be described differently, which destabilizes the notion of source text. If Jonson had not chosen to print this entertainment in his collected works, scholars could assume that the 1606 Theobald's entertainment as described in the manuscript is complete.[35] Frevile copied another speech for Queen Elizabeth upon her entry to Greenwich, and as there are no other extant sources for this pageant, this text is taken as complete and authoritative.[36] Jonson's printed text and Frevile's extract remind us that our source texts, particularly for entertainments, are rarely definitive accounts of the events that occurred. Furthermore, Frevile's manuscript affirms the importance of studying dramatic extracts specifically. While prose and poetry can be malleable and changing, there is an inherent instability in dramatic source texts as they chronicle performed events that can change to adapt to unforeseen circumstances and can be remembered differently by each audience member and participant.[37]

In contrast to Frevile's extract, which points readers to the original moment of performance, other self-contained dramatic extracts are fully removed from their original sources. For instance, some compilers chose to excerpt from the "Lotterie" in *The Queen's Entertainment at Harefield*.[38] The lottery is a series of discrete couplets on various topics, such as this lot on "A Fanne": "You love to see, and yet to be unseene, / Take you this fan to be your beauties skreene."[39] In one case, a selection from *The Entertainment of Harefield* was republished in *A Poetical Rapsodie* (1608) with an erroneous date and place of initial performance.[40] Similarly, the compiler of BL MS Add. 22601 included extra lots that may not have been in the original performance.[41] In these cases, the lots from *The Queen's Entertainment at Harefield* circulated because they were apt and memorable—both in form and content—and not as a gesture of patronage of or celebration of Elizabeth.

In contrast to the decontextualized lots in BL MS Add. 22601 and *A Poetical Rapsodie*, the lots in John Manningham's miscellany (BL MS Harley 5353) include information specific to the original performance. Manningham, although not in the inner courtly circle of initial recipients of the masque, included the names of which noble drew each lot: for instance, "A Bodkin. La[dy] Dorothy [Hastings] / Even with this bodkin you may live unharmd/ Your beauty is with virtue soe well arm'd."[42] Manningham did not copy the entire lottery, either by choice or because his source text was incomplete.[43] Even though Manningham's extracts refer to the original performance, each of these small tidbits can also stand on its own, similar to a fortune from a fortune cookie. Entertainments that are not plot- and character-driven provide fodder for easily extractable material because much of it can be understood without context.

Like the lots from *The Entertainment at Harefield*, the paradoxes from *The Masque of Mountebanks* are small snippets that were taken from the original masque and recopied in print and manuscript.[44] In *The Masque of Mountebanks*, Paradox personified enters and offers a series of disconnected pithy remarks on a variety of topics, such as, "It is Better to be a Coward then a Captaine for a goose lives longer then a Cock of the game" or "Tis Dangerous to mary a widdow for she haith cast her rider" (Gray's Inn MS 29, pp. 9, 10). These epigrammatic jests were republished and recopied, not because of their original performance at Gray's Inn, but rather, because of their wit and brevity. Some manuscripts include unique paradoxes, which shows how people not only memorized, copied, and wrote these one-liners, they also emulated and expanded them.[45] The variation in the extant witnesses of *The Masque of Mountebanks* shows the modularity of the paradoxes: they could be added, removed, or changed at will. *The Masque of Mountebanks* is a series of only vaguely connected plots and events; so, for these paradoxes to be copied alone or in a series makes almost more sense than their original performed context, alongside knights, mountebanks, and songs. Indeed, many of the paradoxes from *The Masque of Mountebanks* appear in early modern proverb books and conversational guides.[46] Compilers who copied the lots from *The Entertainment at Harefield* and the paradoxes from *The Masque of Mountebanks* certainly follow the commonplacing tradition outlined in Chapter 1. These small segments, while incorporated into larger entertainment, were also meant to stand alone. Writers often included existing epigrams in their plays—and readers and playgoers could take these and other epigrams from the complete text.

As this analysis of songs and self-contained extracts demonstrates, excerpting from masques could function similarly to extracting from professional plays. It is particularly important to point out decontextualized extracts from masques and entertainments because scholars often consider masques as complete texts and performed works. Although some early readers (such as Frevile) looked to extracts as a way to illuminate a masque's initial purpose and performance, other early readers, such as those who copied songs or epigrams, were not always concerned with the source text as a whole and meaningful entity. Masques and entertainments could be a series of loosely connected moments that cumulatively create one event or spectacle, which explains why some extracts could be self-contained and others refer to the event. Other manuscripts, like John Abbott's discussed in Chapter 4, show how some extracts can simultaneously stand alone while also referring back to a complete text.

MILTON'S SELF-EXTRACTING AND SELF-AUTHORIZING

If it were not for the songs from Milton's *Comus*, we would have only a single example of a dramatic extract from this work, and a particularly unusual example at that: one by Milton himself. The extracts from Milton's *Comus* underscore both the power of songs to circulate beyond the original masque and the self-contained nature of some dramatic extracts, particularly couplets. Most important, however, Milton's self-extracting is a form of self-authorizing: he presents his work as worthy of commonplacing, which in turn, situates himself as not only an author worth quoting but as a source of wisdom.[47] Milton's self-extracting from *Comus* is unusual because it is our only known example of an early modern playwright extracting from his or her own work in a commonplace book, verse miscellany, or, in this case, an *album amicorum*.[48]

Milton wrote *Comus* for John Egerton, Earl of Bridgewater's appointment as Lord President of Wales. The masque was first performed in 1634 at Ludlow Castle, the Egerton/Bridgewater family estate; the roles of the brothers and the sister were played by Bridgewater's children, who were all around 11–13. *Comus* is a masque about two brothers and a sister who go walking in the forest. The sister gets tired and the brothers head off to fetch help. Comus arrives, tricks her into following him, takes her to his evil pleasure palace and traps her on a chair, where she's stuck by "gummes of glutenous heate."[49] Comus keeps trying to persuade the girl to drink and to perform sexual acts, but she refuses, clinging to virtue. Meanwhile, her brothers run into a good spirit disguised as a shepherd who tells them how to save her; they find her, chase off Comus, and a water nymph comes to unstick Lady from her chair. They dance, happily, and the Attendant Spirit "epilogizes" about virtue.[50] Milton's self-quotation is the final couplet of the Attendant

Spirit's epilogue. *Comus* has been considered for its moralizing nature for the child actors, for the politics surrounding Bridgewater's promotion, or in relation to the Castlehaven sex scandal, when Bridgewater's brother-in-law was arrested, tried, and executed for arranging servants to rape his wife and committing sodomy with other servants.[51] Here, however, I focus on how Milton's self-extracting positions *Comus* as an important early step in his literary career.

Milton signed his name and quoted from *Comus* in an *album amicorum* ("book of friends"), an early modern autograph book (see Figure 2.1).[52] The autograph book, Harvard MS Fr 487, belonged to an Italian named Camillo Cerdagni (often referred to as "Monsieur Cardouin" in his book) and includes signatures from people of many nationalities, including English, French, Italian, and Dutch. When people signed their name in the volume, they sometimes drew a coat of arms or wrote a declaration of friendship. Often, those who signed included a short quotation, the majority in Latin, with some in other languages, including Greek and Hebrew. As in other *alba amicorum*, the classical writers are well-represented in Cerdagni's autograph book, which includes many quotations from Cicero and Horace, and even some from drama, namely, Seneca. In Cerdagni's autograph book, Milton positioned his writing alongside Horace's by copying first his own couplet and then a line from Horace's *Epistles*.[53]

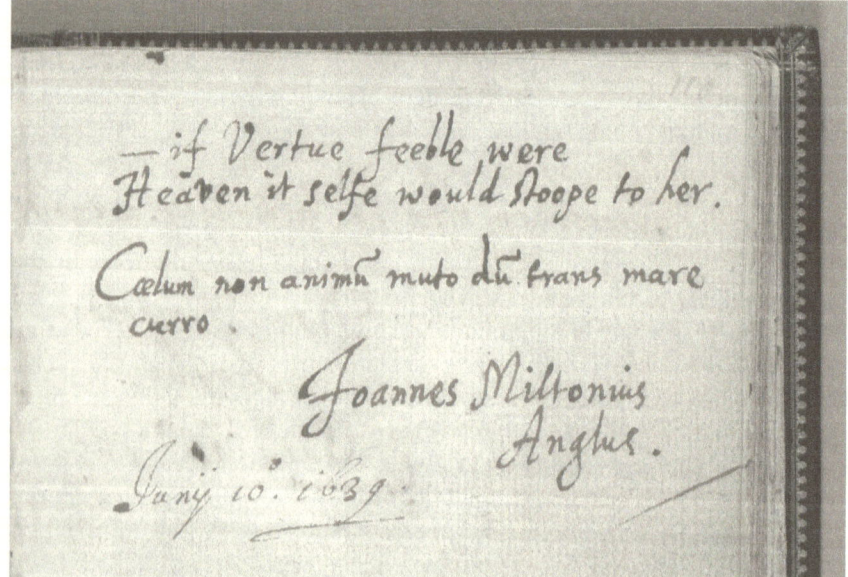

Figure 2.1 Milton's autograph. Harvard MS Fr. 487, p. 110, Houghton Library, Harvard University.

In Cerdagni's book, very few of those who signed wrote quotations in English like Milton did. He quoted the last couplet of *Comus*, "—if Vertue feeble were/Heaven it selfe would stoope to her," followed by a line from Horace (see Figure 2.1).[54] Milton could likely not have expected the (mainly continental) users of Cerdagni's autograph book to recognize his masque, let alone identify the source of these two scant lines. Milton, however, began his couplet with a dash and a miniscule letter, suggesting to any reader that the line is metrically incomplete and taken from a larger work.[55] Choosing to omit the first syllable of the line, "Or," makes Milton's extract stand alone in meaning without relying on the opening part of the sentence. Eliding the first word shapes Milton's self-quotation into a commonplace; simultaneously, by marking the elision, Milton gestured toward the fact that this commonplace is taken from a larger work.

Milton did not attribute the quotation to either *Comus* or himself; similarly, when the entertainment was printed two years earlier (1637), it did not include Milton's name, as he had not authorized its publication. *Comus* was published by its other creator, Henry Lawes, who wrote all of the music for performance. Lawes explained in his dedication to Bridgewater's son (one of the former child actors), "Although not openly acknowledg'd by the Author, yet it is a legitimate off-spring, so lovely, and so much desired, that the often copying of it hath tir'd my pen to give my severall friends satisfaction."[56] Despite not claiming authorship of his extract from *Comus*, Milton's inclusion of it in Cerdagni's album amicorum shows that he recognized its literary value. Later, Milton published and acknowledged *Comus* in his 1645 *Poems*; moreover, he mentioned its inclusion by highlighting that Lawes set the songs to music on the title page. *Comus* became part of the Miltonian canon relatively early on, well before *Paradise Lost* was published (1668).

Even though when he signed Cerdagni's book (likely 1639), Milton was a young writer at the beginning of his career, he already saw his work as comparable to the classics. Not only does Milton's dramatic extract present his esteem for his own writing, it also shows that he valued entertainments and masques as a source of commonplace wisdom. With most dramatic extracts, we consider a reader's perspective on a written text: in Milton's case, we have the author's reading of his own work. Milton saw his work as having wisdom that merited imparting beyond the original circumstances of the entertainment's modest initial audience.

Milton was one of only four people to write a note in English in Cerdagni's book, yet he was not the only one who signed with an English dramatic extract. Edmund Batty signed Cerdagni's book in 1637 and included the final lines from act one of James Shirley's *The Traytor* (1635): "When wee expect= / Our Blisse time creeps, but when the hapier things / call to enjoy, each sawcie howre hath wings" (p. 67). Batty, like many of the others who signed Cerdagni's book, included a commonplace; he was, however, the only one to choose a selection from an English professional play. Before now, this Shirley extract had been hitherto uncatalogued and unnoticed; its discovery suggests that there are more dramatic extracts to be found in *alba amicorum*.[57]

With most dramatic extracts, we consider a reader's perspective on a written text: in Milton's case, we have the author's reading of his own work. Milton saw his work as having wisdom that merited imparting beyond the original circumstances of the entertainment's modest initial audience. Milton himself knew how powerful drama could be for building reputation. As he wrote in his praise of Shakespeare: "Dear Sonne of Memory, great Heire of *Fame*, / What needst thou such dull witnesse of thy Name? / Thou in our wonder and astonishment / Hast build thy selfe a lasting Monument."[58] Shakespeare, Milton suggests, does not need paeans in his honor or paratexts to shore up his status as an author. Milton titled his commendatory poem "An epitaph on the admirable Dramaticke Poet W.Shakespeare," emphasizing that Shakespeare's plays are their own monument: just as *Comus* had the potential to highlight Milton's strength as a "Dramaticke Poet." Milton was interested in enduring literary monuments even before he began composing the epic that would come to define his career, *Paradise Lost*.

With his extract from *Comus*, Milton positioned himself as a writer worth commonplacing like classical authors. Milton's self-extracting provides a particular new occasion in which to consider his work: a moment of self-authorizing, and perhaps even self-promotion. Like Milton, who commonplaced his own words to increase his status as a writer and to associate himself with canonical authors, other readers copied extracts from masques in order to align themselves with particular courtly events and authors.

COURTLY MOTIVATIONS FOR EXTRACTING FROM COURTLY ENTERTAINMENTS

Although some compilers copied extracts from both masques and professional plays, others were attracted to courtly entertainments but not the London stage. By gathering masque extracts into a composite volume or by copying selections into a miscellany, these compilers revealed their interest in court culture. This section first touches on Sir Julius Caesar's preservation of documents related to the queen's visit to his house, then shows how extracts from Sir Francis Bacon's dramatic work were valued for his authorship and political cachet, and concludes by examining the importance of Jonson's masques to William Cavendish in the 1630s.

Sir Julius Caesar, Judge of the Admiralty and Master of Requests, hosted Queen Elizabeth at his manor at Mitcham on September 12th, 1598.[59]

The only documentary evidence we have about *The Queen's Entertainment at Mitcham* is from Caesar's papers: some dialogue, accounts (including the provisions for the kitchen), and the songs.[60] The dialogue and the songs were gathered from separate pages in different hands, suggesting that this entertainment was never collected as a whole.[61] The sections of this masque are found in a composite volume with his other business papers, including notes on the Star Chamber, petitions, letters, and notes about money, land ownership, foreign affairs, and courtly matters. *The Queen's Entertainment at Mitcham* did not circulate widely in manuscript, but where it is preserved, in Caesar's papers, it is equated with business. Caesar may have saved these documents for posterity, but not a theatrical or literary posterity; rather, for Caesar, the entertainment was a political and financial undertaking. Caesar's documents remind us that masques, although not commercial undertakings like professional plays, were costly ventures embarked on with the hope of gain, often of reputation.

The dialogue and songs from *The Queen's Entertainment at Mitcham* survive unattributed in Caesar's manuscripts, although modern scholars accept John Lyly's authorship.[62] Conversely, many extant copies of and extracts from Bacon's masques exist likely because they were attributed and explicitly associated with his name. In both cases, however, the importance of the texts lies in their inherent courtliness. Two manuscripts, BL MS Harley 6797 and Alnwick Castle MS 525, include extracts from Bacon's dramatic work along with his non-dramatic work. BL MS Harley 6797 is an early composite volume of Bacon's own papers that includes two speeches from *Of Tribute, or Giving That Which is Due* (also called *A Conference of Pleasures*).[63] These two speeches from *Of Tribute* are found amid other primarily non-literary papers, including Bacon's essays, speeches, and notes on English law. These two speeches were gathered and bound with the others in the composite volume not because of their inherent literary value, but because they are part of Bacon's oeuvre, as their title in the manuscript demonstrates: "Mr Bacon in prayse of knowledge" and "Mr Bacons Discourse in the praise of his Soveraigne" (BL MS Harley 6797, ff. 47 and 48v). Alnwick Castle MS 525 includes *Of Tribute* in its entirety as well as other Baconian dramatic extracts.[64] Both these manuscripts preserve Bacon's dramatic output as a testament to his authorship, and presumably, Bacon's status as author relies on his standing at court.

When not preserved amid other Baconian documents, extracts from Bacon's masques are often found in volumes of state papers, which demonstrates their status as political or courtly documents. *A Device to Entertain the Queen at Essex House* (1595, also called *Of Love and Self-Love*) was regularly gathered with state papers.[65] Some of the volumes of state papers that include selections from this Baconian entertainment are large books meant to serve as reference volumes for political affairs, such as Queen's College Oxford MS 121, which has 614 folio-sized pages. Conversely, Folger MS V.b.213 is a short manuscript with only two parts: the first, speeches from *A Device to Entertain the Queen at Essex House*, the second, parliamentary speeches by Nicholas Bacon (1510–1579).[66] All of the manuscripts that include even parts from this entertainment are non-dramatic, and in most cases, non-literary.[67] Most manuscripts include a fairly long portion of the entertainment, that is, speeches between a squire, a hermit, a statesman, and a soldier. This segment may have been presented without the outer plot;[68] as such, some of these might not be dramatic extracts in the strictest sense, although they are still valuable to consider here as they show how Bacon's name and reputation influenced the reception of his dramatic work. These state paper volumes do not include extracts from other masques or entertainments, which also highlights that these selections were copied and kept because of Bacon's involvement rather than their dramatic or literary value.

Folger MS V.b.214 includes a late sixteenth-century copy of a single speech from *A Device to Entertain the Queen at Essex House*. Richard Green, likely one of the manuscript's primarily compilers, was interested in the speech as a document related to Essex—and not, as in the case of the Alnwick MS, as a document relating to Bacon.[69] Here, the extract is titled, "A speech at the tilte by the E[arl] of Essex" (f. 200). In Green's manuscript, the Statesman/Secretary's speech is given without the scathing retort of the squire. Part of the speech is meant to be taken ironically, as when the Statesman advises, "Lett him not trouble him self too Laboriouslie to sounde into any matter deeplie, or to execut any thinge exactlye" (f. 200v).[70] Couched with good advice including "in his demonstration of Love, let him not goe too farr" and "Let pollicye and matter of state be the chiefe and allmost onlye matter he intends" (f. 200), the ironic parts of the speech can almost pass a reader of this volume by without notice. The Squire's retort to the "hollow Statesman" helps condition a reader or audience member to not take the Statesman's words at face value; this caveat is lost in Green's manuscript. In Folger MS V.b.214, this dramatic extract is surrounded by writing by and about Essex, including two copies of his *Apology*, Queen Elizabeth and others writing about his Cadiz exploration, and copies of letters to and from the Earl.[71] The extract from the Essex House entertainment in Green's manuscript does not reflect the initial performance or even carry the original meaning. Taken with the surrounding documents, it further shows Green's interest in one particular courtly figure, in this case, Essex.

Unlike the masque extracts found in legal or state papers, or in single-author collections of Bacon's work, the Newcastle manuscript (BL MS Harley 4955) offers an example of the importance of Jonson's masques as both courtly *and* literary texts. While extracts from masques are sometimes found alongside extracts from plays, the Newcastle manuscript features both complete masques and masque excerpts prominently, without any reference to the professional stage. Although today Jonson is best known for his professional plays, the Newcastle manuscript positions him as, above all, a courtly writer: an author of masques and poetry.

The Newcastle manuscript was written for William Cavendish, Earl (later Duke) of Newcastle, by his secretary, John Rolleston.[72] The Newcastle manuscript is perhaps best known for its collection of poems by John Donne, Richard Andrews, and Jonson, although the full-text masques and entertainments in the manuscript, particularly *The Gypsies Metamorphosed*, have also garnered scholarly attention. The appearance of the complete texts of *The King's Entertainment at Welbeck, The King and Queen's Entertainment at Bolsover* (*Love's Welcome*), and the *Cavendish Christening Entertainment* (sometimes called *The Entertainment at Blackfriars*) in this manuscript is not surprising, as all of these were written by Jonson for the Cavendish family.[73] The three masque extracts in the text, taken from *The Vision of Delight, Christmas His Masque,* and *The Fortunate Isles and Their Union*, show Cavendish's enduring interest in Jonson's writing. In his later years, Jonson recognized Cavendish as his "best patron."[74] Cavendish and Jonson's mutually constitutive relationship of patron-playwright appears not only in the entertainments that Jonson wrote specifically for Cavendish but also in the earlier masques and entertainments excerpted in the Newdigate manuscript. This handsome folio volume features Jonson's work in three series, with large running heads proclaiming his name.[75] The professional, neat, presentation-style folio format of the Newcastle manuscript further authorizes Jonson's poetry and masques.

I propose considering new occasions for these masques: that is, their meaning to Cavendish in the early 1630s. The Newcastle manuscript reflects Cavendish's social aspirations during the 1630s and shows the value he placed on courtly entertainments as a reflection of coterie belonging. Responding to the scholars who consider the universal themes or artistic merits of Jonson's masques, Leah Marcus effectively reads *Christmas His Masque* and *The Vision of Delight* as topical works that relate to the events of 1616–1617.[76] Marcus argues that "the court masque was perhaps the most inherently topical of all seventeenth-century art forms."[77] Examining the value and meaning of these masques for Cavendish in the 1630s builds on Marcus's research while also showing that Jonson's masques can be read beyond their original performances. Using the extracts in the Newcastle manuscript as a vector, I show how these masque extracts are both separate from and linked to their sources.

Rolleston, the scribe of the Newcastle manuscript, had access to multiple holograph manuscripts to copy Jonson's poems, which underscores the close ties between Jonson and Cavendish.[78] *The Vision of Delight* and *Christmas His Masque* were performed for the Christmas 1616 season after the first folio of Jonson's works was published earlier that year. The Newcastle manuscript was likely completed between 1630–1634, before *The Vision of Delight* was published in the 1641 folio.[79] The Newcastle manuscript contains one long excerpt from the *Vision*, Fantsy's speech on gluttony, fashion, and the court. Rolleston could not have copied the selection from *The Vision of Delight* from a print source and therefore likely used an authorial copy.

While the manuscript generally coincides with the printed version of *The Vision of Delight*, the main substantive departure shows how Rolleston and the printers of the 1641 folio treated their (possibly shared but certainly related) source: the stage directions in the Newcastle manuscript are in the present tense.[80] The printed text preserves *The Vision of Delight* as part of Jonson's posthumous oeuvre, whereas for readers of the Newcastle manuscript, this dramatic extract offers a present-tense imaginative space. Although it is not unusual for dramatic extracts to retain the present tense in their source texts, when contrasted with the past-tense print sources, the present tense reinforces the continued relevance rather than the past political import of these masques.

Both other dramatic excerpts in the Newcastle manuscript are songs, from *Christmas His Masque* and *The Fortunate Isles*. The printed version of *Christmas His Masque* (which, like *The Vision of Delight*, first appeared the 1641 second folio) includes particularly detailed descriptions of costume and character, particularly for Christmas and his ten children. The Newcastle manuscript omits these descriptions and includes the majority of the sung portions of the masque (all save the epilogue), with all the dialogue and interruptions omitted. In the full masque, the song "Our dances' freight is a matter of eight" is interrupted by Venus's arrival. This excerpt fuses the interrupted verses. While Rolleston may have excised the dialogue, perhaps at Cavendish's behest, it is also possible that Rolleston was working from a complete version of the song that Jonson wrote before including it in the masque. If this is the case, Jonson's manuscript offers an example of his creative process: he wrote the song, probably for the Christmas celebration at court, and then created the dialogue surrounding it.

Of all the masque extracts in the Newcastle manuscript, the song from *The Fortunate Isles* is closest to the printed version. Where the other extracts include substantive changes in nouns and verb tenses, "Come noble Nymphs and doe not hide" varies only in spelling from the other known version. The song, however, as with the songs from *Christmas His Masque*, differs from the printed masque in that it does not mention the singers. Whereas the printed masque shows that the song is sung by Proteus, Saron, and Portunus, in turns, the Newcastle manuscript presents a unified version that could be sung by one voice. Jonson originally wrote "Come Noble Nymphs" for his masque *Neptune's Triumph for the Return to Albion* (to be sung by the same three characters), but the performance scheduled for January 6th, 1624 was cancelled, so he repurposed quite a bit of the material for the following year's Christmas celebration, *The Fortunate Isles*.[81] While the title of the song in the Newcastle manuscript, "A song at Court to invite the Ladies to Daunce" (emphasis in the original), suggests that it is taken from *The Fortunate Isles* and not *Neptune's Triumph*, the title is also vague enough that the song is not tied to one particular Jonsonian source text (f. 192). Rather, this piece is one of the many poems under the running head "Ben: Jonson," "Benjamin Johnson," or similar. In the Newcastle manuscript, "Come Noble Nymphs" is both separate from and connected to its performed and courtly origins.[82]

As Joshua Eckhardt notes, we cannot know the exact involvement of Cavendish or his scribe, Rolleston, but we can show that Cavendish collected the texts to be transcribed from his literary network, and we can assume that Rolleston copied these texts in order to please Cavendish.[83] At the time the Newcastle manuscript was being written (1630–1634),[84] Cavendish staged two royal masques by Jonson, both of which are also preserved in this manuscript, *The King's Entertainment at Welbeck* (1633) and *The King and Queen's Entertainment at Bolsover* (1634). Cavendish, who was at his financial apex, hosted the lavish performances at Welbeck and Bolsover as part of his striving for a court appointment from King Charles.[85] The dramatic extracts in the Newcastle manuscript reflect Cavendish's desire to be part of Charles's court. Decades earlier, when *Christmas His Masque* and *The Vision of Delight* were performed (both December 1616–January 1617), Cavendish was not nobility, although he was Viscount Mansfield by the time *The Fortunate Isles* (Jan. 1625) was performed. In 1628, Cavendish became the Earl of Newcastle; and it was not until after this manuscript was completed that he was appointed to court (1638), later created Marquess (1643) and, finally, Duke (1665). The Newcastle manuscript shows how access to earlier, unprinted masques could be a sign of social status: they can provide a retrospective belonging to coterie audiences.

The Newcastle manuscript shows that masques and masque excerpts can and should be read beyond their original performances as they gain new meanings to new readers. William Cavendish offers an example of one such reader, and these masque extracts show his continued interest in royal entertainments, his patronage and respect for Jonson, as well as his ambition.

NEW OCCASIONS FOR OCCASIONAL DRAMA: *THE GYPSIES METAMORPHOSED*

If the chapter so far has demonstrated the value of reading occasional drama beyond its original performances, our final example shows that this kind of reading is not only possible but necessary to understanding why masque extracts circulated. This last section of the chapter looks at new occasions for examining occasional drama by tracing the circulation of an extract from Jonson's *The Gypsies Metamorphosed* after the initial performance. I demonstrate that one particular extract, Lady Purbeck's fortune, was recontextualized by being copied into multiple manuscripts because of changing historical circumstances, and then decontextualized from both her and Jonson's masque when recopied into further manuscript sources. Early modern readers would not have been able to consider Jonson's words about her without thinking of the scandal that postdated Jonson's masque.

The extracts from *The Gypsies Metamorphosed* indicate that many readers were interested in the masque not because of its original performance, but because of later events involving those who participated in the masque. *The Gypsies Metamorphosed* (1621) was both commissioned by and performed by George Villiers, then Earl of Buckingham, who later became the Duke of Buckingham. The original occasion of this masque was a celebration of Buckingham's role at court. The masque is not plot-driven, but instead, thematically tied together. The gypsies arrive, played by Buckingham and his family members; they sing and dance and tell fortunes for notable audience members, including the king. After the fortunes, the townspeople, dressed as clowns, entertain the audience with bawdy libels, dances, and jest. *The Gypsies Metamorphosed* provided fodder for many dramatic extracts, primarily songs: "Cock Lorell" circulated widely, as did "From a gypsy in the morning."[86] The metamorphosis occurs when the "gypsies" return, now white-skinned and in their aristocratic clothing. As the epilogue explains, "You have beheld (and with delight) their change / . . . / Know, that what dy'd our faces, was an ointment."[87]

The manuscripts that contain Lady Purbeck's fortune suggest that the compilers were not interested in the occasion for and events of Jonson's masque, but in the sensational scandal involving her and her husband John Villiers, who was Buckingham's brother. *The Gypsies Metamorphosed* presented a memorable fortune-telling scene where the noble actors told the fortunes of other nobles in the audience. Buckingham himself, dressed as gypsy, brazenly asked for the king's hand and delivered his fortune, but it is not this moment that later manuscript compilers chose to set down. Of all the fortunes told that day, including the king's fortune and the prince's, the most popular fortune that circulated in manuscript was Lady Purbeck's.

The Gypsies Metamorphosed is unusual in that it was an occasional performance that was repeated. It was performed three times: first, on August 3rd, 1621 at Burley-on-the-Hill in Rutland at Buckingham's large and costly new estate; second, on August 5th, 1621 at Belvoir Castle, owned by the Earl of Rutland, Buckingham's father-in-law; and third, at Windsor, during September 1621.[88] The fortunes extracted from *The Gypsies Metamorphosed* do not have a clear print source. This masque was not published until 1640, when it was included in John Benson's duodecimo collection of Jonson's poems; it reappeared in the second volume of Jonson's *Workes* (1641).[89] Manuscripts as early as the 1620s include excerpts and songs from *The Gypsies Metamorphosed*.[90] Two manuscripts contain the entire masque in composite forms of both the Burley and Belvoir versions: the Newcastle Manuscript, discussed above (BL MS Harley 4955, c. 1630–1634) and Huntington HM 741 (c. 1620s). There are only a few other early manuscripts that contain fortunes other than Lady Purbeck's.[91]

Orgel claims that *The Gypsies Metamorphosed* "was the King's favorite masque, and the court's" and goes on to posit that "it is difficult to believe that it was not Jonson's favorite masque as well."[92] Although modern critics concur that this masque is a political statement of some sort, scholars cannot agree on Jonson's intentions.[93] In the case of *The Gypsies Metamorphosed*, then, the indeterminacy of Jonson's intentions complicates any reading of the occasions of performance. Rather than speculating on Jonson's motivations, this examination focuses on the later contexts in which readers encountered the masque and its extracts. Regardless of Jonson's intentions, the extracts from *The Gypsies Metamorphosed* took on unanticipated meanings in manuscript circulation. To understand these unanticipated meanings requires considering the Lady Purbeck's tumultuous marriage both before Jonson wrote the masque and after.

When he wrote *The Gypsies Metamorphosed*, Jonson would certainly have been familiar with the strained relationship between John Villiers (Viscount Purbeck) and his wife, Frances Coke (Viscountess Purbeck). Lady Purbeck (1599–1645) was the daughter of Lady Elizabeth Hatton, née Cecil (1578–1646), and Sir Edward Coke (1552–1634).[94] Lady Purbeck's father, Coke, forced her to marry John Villiers in an attempt to regain political power by aligning himself with Buckingham's rising star. Lady Purbeck and her mother, Lady Hatton, rejected the match, fled to a country house, and were later captured by Coke.[95] One seventeenth-century source claimed that Lady Purbeck had to be tied to a bedpost and beaten into submission.[96] Lady Hatton petitioned Francis Bacon, then Lord Keeper, to have power over her daughter's marriage because it was her fortune that would be used as dowry. Bacon agreed that both parents should have a say, and Lady Hatton ultimately accepted the match with Villiers when she secured an income for her daughter.[97]

In 1621, the year *The Gypsies Metamorphosed* was written and performed, people abreast of current gossip knew that Lady Purbeck was unhappily married. By the late 1620s, the unhappiness of her marriage was public knowledge as she was arraigned for adultery.[98] As early as 1620, John Villiers's mental state was deteriorating; later, he "suffered from periodic fits of insanity of a manic nature which might lead him to smash glass and 'bloody' himself."[99] Viscount Purbeck was kept under doctor's supervision away from his wife. While separated from her husband, Lady Purbeck had a son in 1624. Rumors abounded that Sir Robert Howard was the father, and in 1625, protesting their innocence, Lady Purbeck and Howard were summoned to the court of high commission.[100] Buckingham had been trying to secure Lady Purbeck's marriage portion for himself: James, in a rare act against his favorite, intervened to guarantee Lady Purbeck an annual income, as long as she left her estates to her husband. The Villiers were especially upset by Lady Purbeck's pregnancy because at this point Buckingham did not have an heir so his fortune, too, might pass to Howard's bastard son.[101]

Six years after the initial performance of *The Gypsies Metamorphosed*, Lady Purbeck was found guilty of adultery and ordered to do public penance, but she escaped by going to her father at the Savoy.[102] In 1635, when her father died, she returned to London, but King Charles had not forgotten her crime and was determined for her to do public penance.[103] This time, Lady Purbeck escaped by donning male clothing and fleeing to France, creating sensational news for the court. As James Howell wrote to Thomas Wentworth, the Earl of Strafford, in May 1635: "My Lady *Purbeck* cannot be heard of, having lately broken out of the *Gate-house* in Man's Apparel to prevent doing of Penance barefooted hence to *Paul's*. Sir *Robert Howard* is still close Prisoner in the *Fleet*; in the interim, 'tis said, she is gone to *France*."[104] Howard joined Lady Purbeck in France. Rather than letting matters lie, Charles "attempted to have the writ served on her in Paris, which aroused French Nationalist fury" and kept the scandal in the public eye.[105] Lady Purbeck returned to England by 1640 to petition unsuccessfully for the return of her estates, where she died in 1645.

In *The Gypsies Metamorphosed*, Jonson praised Lady Hatton's (Lady Purbeck's mother) mettle: "Others fortunes may be showne, / You are builder of your owne."[106] Jonson could have even been alluding to Hatton's intervention in her daughter's marriage to protect her inheritance when he wrote, "And what ever Heave'n hath gi'n you, / You preserve the state still in you."[107] Although ostensibly discussing Lady Hatton's unfading beauty, this fortune is clearly about her indomitable spirit and could include a veiled reference to the fact that she chose to keep her first husband's name instead of taking Coke's.[108] Lady Hatton's own marital troubles were well known:

she had initiated more than one legal action against Coke before *The Gypsies Metamorphosed* was written and performed. She had also fought strongly for her daughter not to marry Villiers by hiding her daughter, by trying to engineer a different marriage, and by turning to Bacon.

Jonson encouraged the kind of biographical reading that uses Lady Hatton's life to understand the full meaning of her fortune. Jonson told his audience to seek layers of meaning in his text: "If we here be a little obscure, it is our pleasure, for rather than we will offer to be our own interpreters, we are resolved not to be understood."[109] The Jackman, who speaks these lines, cautions the audience that these are not simply meaningless words and refers "any man [who doubts] of the significancy of the language"[110] to read up on gypsy's canting, a means of communication designed to hide meaning from some and share it with a select group, just as Jonson's words held specific implications for particular audience members. Reading the fortunes as layered with multiple meanings, as Jonson encouraged, explains why Lady Purbeck's fortune circulated in manuscript more than the other fortunes.

It was not Jonson's talent or the popularity of *The Gypsies Metamorphosed* that led to the interest in this dramatic extract—rather, Lady Purbeck's fortune was copied into multiple manuscripts because of the later scandal associated with her name. Marginalia in a 1622 copy of Ralph Brooke's *A Catalogue and succession of the Kings, Princes, Dukes, Marquesses, Earles, and Viscounts of this Realme of England* shows the vitriolic reaction her name could induce in readers: a reader has changed "Frances, daughter of that great and worthy Lawyer, Sir *Edward Coke*" to "Frances, ^reputed daughter^" and added, "but was indeed a Bastard, begotten before marriag, by Sir Robert Howard knight and prooved an Errant Whoore."[111] This unknown reader is hazy on the facts of the case (Howard, being Lady Purbeck's lover and not her secret father), but casts both Lady Purbeck and her mother, Lady Hatton, as immoral women to scorn. Although this book was published in 1622, a later owner signed and dated the book 1679:[112] this harsh censure could have been added or read decades after the scandal. The only other editorializing comment in the marginalia in this volume is a comment on Bacon: "Hee was as wise a man, as ever England produced."[113] This chapter demonstrates that masques and extracts from masques are courtly texts linked to their creators and subjects well after the initial moment of their performance.

Arthur F. Marotti has documented the trend of verse miscellanies to contain poems that refer to political scandals;[114] this masque extract similarly gained popularity when scandal struck. Unlike verse libels or other political satires, however, this dramatic extract was not created because of a scandal; instead, it gained meaning from a scandal. The later manuscripts that contain Lady Purbeck's fortune include Folger MS V.b.43 (c. 1630), Rosenbach MS

239/23 (c. 1630s), Harvard fMS Eng. 626 (c. 1630s), as well as Folger MS V.a.96 (c. 1640) and Huntington HM 172 (c. 1640).[115] It was not the masque's publication that spurred manuscript writers to include this fortune in their verse miscellanies: it was an interest in the subject matter of the fortune, or, in later cases, perhaps in the fortune as a poem unconnected to the masque.

With her scandalous behavior throughout the 1620s and 1630s, it seems no wonder that Lady Purbeck's fortune remained of public interest. Jonson's words take on a new meaning when applied not just to an unhappy young wife but to an adulterous, cross-dressing criminal. Jonson's playful lines portray Lady Purbeck as the Queen of Love:

> Venus here doth Saturn move
> That you should be the queen of love
> And the other stars consent,
> Only Cupid's not content;
> For though you the theft disguise,
> You have robbed him of his eyes:
> And to show his envy further,
> Here he chargeth you with murther.[116]

For the masque audience, members of a courtly circle surrounding Buckingham and the king, this speech could have conjured images of Lady Purbeck's marriage, a match where "consent" was the contentious issue. This nuptial match did not just involve a battle between Lady Hatton and Sir Coke: the Villiers family also pushed for this match, particularly Lady Compton, Buckingham and Villiers' mother. *The Gypsies Metamorphosed* was presented just four years after King James presided over the marriage of Frances and John; the king himself gave Lady Purbeck away.[117] The "consent" that Jonson's fortune raises brings up the layers of meaning that he asked his audience to consider: the bride's parents' different opinions, the groom's family's and the king's approval, and lastly, the will of the unhappy couple. For later readers, the "disguise" could bring to mind Lady Purbeck's transvestite escape from the London; the "charges" that resonate are not fictitious murder charges but real charges of adultery.

Although it is likely that Lady Purbeck's fortune began circulating in manuscript because of her notoriety, it could have remained in circulation as a piece with its own artistic merits. The compiler of Folger MS V.b.43 titled the fortune "Looking on A Gentlewoman's Hand to tell her fortune."[118] This does not rule out the possibility that the compiler knew of the scandal or the original context of the excerpt, but it is also possible that the compiler might not have known about Lady Purbeck. This fortune that makes no mention of Lady Purbeck suggests two possible interpretations of its title: she could have been so notorious that her name was not needed, or, even though the extract began circulating because of her infamy, it continued to circulate without the context of the original performance or subsequent scandal.

Proposing that Lady Purbeck's fortune initially circulated because of her later notoriety is more than a simple historical scavenger hunt. This reading demonstrates how the multiple iterations of this fortune in manuscript gained new meanings due to changing historical contexts. It refutes the notion that occasional drama cannot be read outside the context of the original occasion of performance. Furthermore, this analysis of the circulation of Lady Purbeck's fortune begins to address the way manuscript circulation can remove a dramatic excerpt from the intended original audience and original context of the play, opening the extract up to new interpretations. Jonson compared reading a fortune in Lady Purbeck's hand to reading a book: "Help me wonder, here's a book."[119] To return to Jonson's words, Lady Purbeck is indeed "a book": her life is a text that affects the circulation of other texts. Examining the manuscript circulation of this particular dramatic extract leads to a better understanding of the politics and reception history of Jonson's masque because it shows how early readers associated Jonson's fictional characterization with later real-life events. Furthermore, Lady Purbeck's fortune exemplifies how the meaning of masque extracts can change in light of new circumstances, which underscores the need for scholars to consider not only the original moments of performance and publication but also later moments of reception for masques and entertainments.

While this chapter has provided an overview of many of the ways masque extracts circulated as songs, poems, and commonplaces in a variety of manuscript contexts including music books, miscellanies, and *alba amicorum*, there is further work to be done in this area. Undoubtedly, more extracts will be discovered: particularly from collaborative or anonymous masques and entertainments that are not yet indexed in the *Catalogue of English Literary Manuscripts*. Although this chapter has offered, in places, a century-long overview of masque extracts, particularly as it relates to the circulation of songs, other masque extracts will be briefly discussed in later chapters. Chapter 3 argues that many dramatic extracts taken from professional plays while the theatres were closed reveal a nostalgia for theatre, while other extracts, particularly the decontextualized songs discussed in this chapter, were often not taken from plays or masques, but rather, from intermediary sources.

From songs and speeches, to lots and epigrams, to commonplaces and fortunes, masque extracts function in myriad ways: they can enhance our knowledge of the original performance, destabilize the idea of a source text, and show how the meaning of one part of a text can change. Extracts from masques can be both decontextualized and recontextualized; they can circulate as abstract or commonplace texts with no reference to their source, or they can reveal later reinterpretations of their original text. Ultimately, extracts from masques provide new occasions for reading occasional drama.

NOTES

1. The extracts from *The Lady of May* and their significance in BL MS Sloane 161 are discussed in Chapter 4.

2. I use the term "masque" to refer to both masques and entertainments that were staged without elaborate sets. For a discussion of the complicated generic questions surrounding masques, see Lauren Shohet, *Reading Masques: The English Masque and Public Culture in the Seventeenth Century* (Oxford: Oxford University Press, 2010), esp. 37–80 and Jerzy Limon, *The Masque of Stuart Culture* (Newark: University of Delaware Press, 1990), esp. 17–28.

3. For a discussion of currently scholarly attitudes toward masques, see Shohet, *Reading Masques*, esp. 25–31 and Limon, *The Masque of Stuart Culture*, esp. 7–8.

4. For example, consider Stephen Orgel, *The Jonsonian Masque* (Cambridge, MA: Harvard University Press, 1965) and Stephen Orgel and Roy Strong, *Inigo Jones: The Theatre of the Stuart Court* (Berkeley: University of California Press, 1973).

5. Mike Pincombe, "Robert Dudley, *Gorboduc*, and 'The Masque of Beauty and Desire': A Reconsideration of the Evidence for Political Intervention" *Parergon* 20 (2003): 19–44; Eliza Fisher Laskowski, "Performance, Politics, and Religion: Reconstructing Seventeenth-Century Masque," PhD diss., University of North Carolina at Chapel Hill, 2006; "'All Emulation Cease, and Jars': Political Possibilities in *Chloridia*, Queen Henrietta Maria's Masque of 1631" *Ben Jonson Journal* 9 (2002): 87–108; Glenn A. Odom, "Jacobean Politics of Interpretation in Jonson's *Masque of Blackness*" *Studies in English Literature 1500–1900* 51 (2011): 367–83; Martin Butler, "*The Masque of Blackness* and Stuart Court Culture" in *Early Modern English Drama: A Critical Companion*, ed. Garrett A. Sullivan and Patrick Cheney (Oxford: Oxford University Press, 2006), 152–63; Elizabeth Zeman Kolkovich, "Work in Progress: Gender and Politics in Late Elizabeth Progress Entertainments," PhD diss., University of Illinois Urbana, 2009; and Guillaume Forain, "Culture de cour et idéology: De l'usage de la pastoral dans le masque *Pans Anniversarie* de Ben Jonson (1621)" *Etudes Epistémè* 3 (2003): 124–55.

6. Although Gabriel Heaton focuses on full-text masques and entertainments, he often touches on dramatic extracts. C. E. McGee's and James Knowles's research shows how the interpretation of a complete occasional piece can change. C. E. McGee and John C. Meagher included extracts in their influential series of four "Preliminary Checklist of Tudor and Stuart Entertainments" articles (*Research Opportunities in Renaissance Drama*, 1981, 1982, 1984, 1988), as do the *Records of Early English Drama* volumes (23 vols. Toronto: University of Toronto Press, 1979–2010, with more forthcoming). See Heaton, "Elizabethan Entertainments in Manuscript: The Harefield Festivities (1602) and the Dynamics of Exchange," in *The Progresses, Pageants, and*

Entertainments of Queen Elizabeth I, ed. Jayne Elizabeth Archer, Elizabeth Goldring, and Sarah Knight (Oxford: Oxford University Press, 2007), 227–44, as well as Heaton, *Writing and Reading Royal Entertainments: From George Gascoigne to Ben Jonson* (Oxford: Oxford University Press, 2010). See also McGee, "More than One Way to Skin a Cat(holic): Editing the Afterlife of an Occasional Entertainment," *Research Opportunities in Renaissance Drama* 34 (1995): 1–14; Knowles, "'In the purest times of peerless Queen Elizabeth': Nostalgia, Politics, and Jonson's use of the 1575 Kenilworth Entertainments," in Archer, Goldring, and Knight, *The Progresses, Pageants, and Entertainments of Queen Elizabeth*, 246–67; and Knowles, "'Songs of baser alloy': Jonson's *Gypsies Metamorphosed* and the Circulation of Manuscript Libels," *Huntington Library Quarterly* 69 (2006): 153–76.

7. This argument builds on Limon's differentiation of the theatrical and literary texts of masques. Limon asserts that the literary masque and the performed masque "create meanings in a different way, but also that these meanings are essentially different" (9); to this, I add the new meanings created by extracts from masques.

8. See R. Malcolm Smuts on the relation between occasional events and literature. Smuts calls for an understanding of literary texts as both "timeless cultural artefacts" and historical and social events. Smuts, "Occasional Events, Literary Texts and Historical Interpretations," in *Neo-Historicism*, ed. Robin Headlam Wells, Glenn Burgess, and Rowland Wymer (Cambridge: D.S. Brewer, 2000), 179–98.

9. For instance, we have William Lawes's autograph score for James Shirley's *The Triumph of Peace* (Bodleian MS Mus. Sch. B. 2) and other settings by Lawes for both masques and professional plays in BL MS Add. 31432. For further details, see John P. Cutts, "British Museum Additional MS. 31432: William Lawes' writing for the Theatre and the Court," *The Library*, 5th ser., 7 (1951): 225–34.

10. The full title as published runs, *The Honorable Entertainement gieuen to the Queenes Maiestie in Progresse, at Elue-tham in Hampshire, by the right Honorable the Early of Hertford* (1591).

11. Ernest Brennecke,"The Entertainment at Elvetham, 1591," in *Music in English Renaissance Drama* ed. John H. Long (Lexington, KY: University of Kentucky Press, 1968), 32–56.

Michael G. Brennan ("Nicholas Breton (1554/5-c.1626)," *ODNB*), James Nielson ("Nicholas Breton," *DLB*) and Alexander B. Grosart (*The Works in Verse and Prose of Nicholas Breton*, Private Circulation, 1879), also believe that Breton's song was included in a larger entertainment and that he did not write the entirety.

12. Harry H. Boyle, "Elizabeth's Entertainment at Elvetham: War Policy in Pageantry," *Studies in Philology* 68 (1971): 146–66.

13. *The Honorable Entertainement . . . at Elvetham* (1591), sig. D2v.

14. The most pointed example of the editorial practice of ignoring the song's relation to the entertainment is the inclusion of the song in George Reuben Potter's *Elizabethan Verse and Prose (Non-Dramatic)* (New York: H. Holt, 1928, republished through 1948).

15. *Englands Helicon* (1610), sig. D3r-v.

16. BL Music books and manuscripts, R.M. 24. d. 2, ff. 171v–73. See Brennecke, "Entertainment at Elvetham," 46–51.

17. Nicholson, BL MS Add. 17797; East, *Madrigales to 3. 4. and 5. Parts* (1604), song II; Wilson, *Cheerefull Ayres* (1659), sig Iv and *Select Ayres and Dialogues* (1659), sig. Cc; Rogers, University of Glasgow MS Euing R.d.58-61 (see *CELM*, BrN 74). An unattributed cittern score appears in John Playford's *Musick's Delight on the Cithren* (1666), sig. Gv.

18. Gastoldi in Philomus., *Synopsis of Vocal Musick* (1680), sigs. L5v-L6; Rogers in John Playford, *An Introduction to the Skill of Musick* (1674), sig. F.

19. Wilson's setting is found in Bodleian MS Don c. 57, which also contains "Hark, Hark, the Lark" from *Cymbeline* and in Edward Lowe's songbooks, Edinburgh University Library Dc. 1.69 and Bodleian MS Mus d. 238, which contain "Where the Bee Sucks" from *The Tempest.* See Elise Bickford Jorgens, ed., *English Song 1600–1675: Facsimiles of Twenty-six Manuscripts and an Edition of the Texts* (New York: Garland, 1987), vols. 6 and 8, for facsimiles and bibliographies for further reading.

20. Bodleian MS Mus. b. 1 includes Wilson's setting in a book of his songs (though, as Margaret Crum has argued, not in his hand). See Crum, "A Manuscript of John Wilson's Songs" *The Library*, 5th ser., 10 (1955) 55–57.

21. The Waferer Commonplace Book, BL MS Add. 52585, f. 57. Compiled in multiple hands.

22. NLS MS Adv. 19.3.4, f. 13v. This manuscript also includes "Charon, oh Charon" from Francis Beaumont and John Fletcher's *The Mad Lover* (f. 17) and "Come my Daphne" from Shirley's *The Cardinal*, where the speakers are clearly marked as Strephon and Daphne (f. 23).

23. Folger MS V.a.308, f. 8, compiled 1690–1730. For Sir John Suckling and Ben Jonson, see ff. 5v–6.

24. BL MS Add. 34064, f. 16. I consulted this manuscript using *British Literary Manuscripts Online*, Gale Cengage Learning, Gale Document Number MC4400003280.

25. For a critique of Percy's treatment of this poem and others, see William A. Ringler, Jr., "Bishop Percy's Quarto Manuscript (British Museum MS Additional 34064) and Nicholas Breton," *Philological Quarterly* 54 (1975): 26–39. Grosart noted the presence of these lines in *The Works of Nicholas Breton* (Privately Printed, 1879), n.p.

26. Bodleian MS Rawl. poet. 85, f. 3. This version was published in *The Gentleman's Magazine and Historical Chronicle* (1812): 647, as "From an old MS."

27. For more on the circulation of this song, please see *CELM*, ShJ 140-74.8, and the Folger Shakespeare Library's *Union First Line Index of English Verse: 13th–19th Century (bulk 1500–1800)*, firstlines.folger.edu

28. For a detailed discussion of the popularity of "Cock Lorell," see James Knowles, "'Songs of baser alloy.'"

29. *New Academy of Complements* (1669), sig. G4r-v; *Merry Drollery Complete* (1670), sigs. G2r-v; *Windsor Drollery* (1671 and later copies), sig. Mr-v; as lyrics below a simple vocal line in Henry Playford's expanded *Wit and Mirth* (1699), sig. D10v; and *The Academy of Complements with Many New Additions* (1684), sig. O2. The poem also appears in *Wits Academy* (1677) as "'Twas in the pleasant Month of May," sig. D2r-v (pp. 75–76; note that page signatures restart for the second part,

"A Collection of the Newest Songs and Merry Catches"). For eighteenth-century examples, see Abigail Williams, ed., Digital Miscellanies Index, Bodleian Library, University of Oxford, http://digitalmiscellaniesindex.org.

30. Bodleian MS Eng. poet. c. 50, f. 36v. Where the printed versions read, "Peace and silence be the guide / To the Man, and to the Bride," Daniell's copy substitutes "groome" for man. Printed versions: Beaumont, *The Masque of the Inner Temple and Grayes Inne* quarto (1612), sig. D3; Beaumont and Fletcher, *Comedies and Tragedies* (1647), sig. Dddddddd2v [8d2v] (p. 28, not paginated consecutively); Beaumont, *Poems* (1653), sig. Hv.

31. Bodleian MS Eng. poet. c. 50, f. 36v. Daniell also copied other dramatic extracts, including selections from *Valentinian* and *The Nice Valour*, among others. See *CELM* for more details.

32. Peter Beal, "Songs by Aurelian Townshend, in the hand of Sir Henry Herbert, for an Unrecorded Masque by the Merchant Adventurers," *Medieval and Renaissance Drama in England* 15 (2003): 243–60.

33. An in-depth discussion of the circulation of speeches from tilts as well as other documentary evidence, such as tilt-lists, is beyond the scope of this chapter. There are multiple known extant speeches from tilts: see Roy Strong, *The Cult of Elizabeth: Elizabethan Portraiture and Pageantry* (Hampshire, UK: Thames and Hudson, 1977), esp. Appendix A. See also McGee and Meagher, "Preliminary Checklist" articles.

34. Jonson, *The entertainment of the two Kings . . . at Theobalds* 5-10 (1616 folio), sig. Eeee5. For more on manuscripts with selections from this masque, see James Knowles, introduction to "An Entertainment at Theobalds" in *The Cambridge Edition of the Works of Ben Jonson*, ed. David Bevington, Martin Butler, and Ian Donaldson, et al., 7 vols. (Cambridge: Cambridge UP, 2012), 204.

35. Jonson did indeed choose to omit certain masques from his 1616 *Workes*, such as *The Entertainment at Britain's Burse*. For more on the recovery of this once-lost masque and on Jonson's selectivity, see James Knowles, "'To raise of a house of better frame': Jonson's Cecilian Entertainments," in *Patronage, Culture, and Power: The Early Cecils*, ed. Pauline Croft (New Haven, CT: Yale University Press, 2002), 180–95.

36. The manuscript also includes "Goodwill's Part," a speech for Queen Elizabeth: for an analysis and transcription, see C. E. McGee, "A Reception for Queen Elizabeth in Greenwich," *Records of Early English Drama Newsletter* 5 (1980): 1–8.

37. Limon, for instance, shows how a writer's text changes when staged: see *Masque of Stuart Culture*, esp. 28.

38. For a full text of the entertainment, see Gabriel Heaton, ed., "[The Queen's Entertainment at Harefield, 31 July–2 August 1602]" in *John Nichols's The Progresses and Public Processions of Queen Elizabeth I: A New Edition of the Early Modern Sources*, ed. Elizabeth Goldring, Faith Eales, Elizabeth Clarke, and Jayne Elisabeth Archer, eds., (Oxford: Oxford University Press, 2014), vol. 4, 174–95.

39. Francis Davison, *A Poetical Rapsodie* (1608), sig. B4.

40. Heaton, "Elizabethan Entertainments," 242. Heaton also argues that the extracts in *A Poetical Rapsodie* reflect a renewed interest in Sir John Davies's authorship.

41. BL MS Add. 22601, ff. 49–51. See also Heaton, "Elizabethan Entertainments," for a discussion of the various texts of this entertainment

42. BL MS Harley 5353, f. 95v. Heaton, "Elizabethan Entertainments," 241.

43. For more on Manningham's social status and access to the masque, see Heaton, "Elizabethan Entertainments," 241.

44. I will not rehearse the other manuscripts that include *The Masque of Mountebanks* and extracts as they have been discussed in Estill, "Politics, Poetry, and Performance: The Miscellaneous Contents of Arbury Hall MS 414," *Early Theatre* (2011), esp. 109–14, and Gabriel Heaton, "Textual Reproduction in a Scribal Community," an unpublished chapter from "Performing Gifts: The Manuscript Circulation of Elizabethan and Early Stuart Courtly Entertainments," PhD diss., Cambridge University, 2003. I would like to thank Heaton for sharing this chapter and Alan Nelson for sharing his research now published with *REED*: Nelson and John R. Elliott Jr, eds, *Records of Early English Drama: Inns of Court* (Cambridge: Boydell & Brewer, 2010), esp. 365, 488–99, 563–80, and 738–39.

45. Estill, "Politics, Poetry, and Performance," 109.

46. Edward Phillips's *The Mysteries of Love & Eloquence* (1658 and 1685) and his later *The Beau's Academy* (1699) both contain numerous paradoxes from *The Masque of Mountebanks*. For instance, multiple paradoxes "Q. Why is wealth better then wit? A. Because few Poets have had the fortune to be chosen Alderman" appears in *The Mysteries of Love & Eloquence* (1658), sig. N4. John Ray included "It's dangerous marrying a widow because she hath cast her rider" in *A Collection of English Proverbs* (expanded edition, 1678), sig. E5v. There are many further examples of the paradoxes appearing in print sources.

47. For a discussion of the scale of *Comus* and its status as a masque, see Stephen Orgel, "The Case for *Comus*," *Representations* 81 (2003): 31–45. Henry Lawes originally composed the music for *Comus*, but as with "In the Merry Month of May," later composers, notably Thomas Arne and George Frideric Handel, composed new music. BL MS Add. 11518 preserves Arne's elaborate eighteenth-century score bound with a small separate of Lawes's score at the opening of the volume. Other than the separate in BL MS Add. 11518, Lawes's autograph music book (BL MS Add. 53723) is the only other manuscript known to contain his setting. See Jorgens, *English Song 1600–1675*, vol. 3.

48. There are, of course, many examples of playwrights who repurpose their own material (or borrow from others' plays) in their plays, which can be more accurately considered as adaptation.

49. Milton, *Comus* (1637), sig. E4.

50. Ibid., sig. Fv.

51. For these readings of *Comus*, see, for instance, Stephen Orgel, "The Case for *Comus*" *Representations* 81 (2003): 31–45; John Creaser, "Milton's *Comus*: The Irrelevance of the Castlehaven Scandal" *Milton Quarterly* 4 (1987): 25–34; Barbara Brested, "*Comus* and the Castlehaven Scandal" *Milton Studies* 3 (1971): 201–224; Leah Marcus, "The Milieu of Milton's *Comus*: Judicial Reform at Ludlow and the Problem of Sexual Assault" *Criticism* 25 (1983): 293–327.

52. For a history of the *album amicorum*, see June Schlueter, *The Album Amicorum and the London of Shakespeare's Time* (Chicago: University of Chicago Press,

2011). Schlueter's book focuses on alba amicorum slightly earlier than Harvard MS Fr 487.

53. The signature is dated Junij 10 1639. The date is in a lighter ink than the signature.

54. "Cælum non animũ muto dũ trans mare curro," Harvard MS Fr. 487, p. 110; cf. *Epistles* 1.xi.27. Of the three other people who signed Cerdagni's book and included English phrases, none are monolingually English.

55. Milton began his Latin quotation from Horace with a majuscule. His use of a miniscule for "if" is purposeful.

56. Milton, *Comus* (1637), sig. A2r-v.

57. Wolfgang Klose's study of *alba amicorum* (1550–1600) does not list any further dramatic extracts, but, as this study has shown, dramatic extracting flourished in the seventeenth century and was not yet an established practice in the sixteenth century. Klose, *Corpus Alborum Amicorum* (Stuttgart: Anton Hiersemann, 1988).

58. Milton, "An Epitaph on the admirable Dramaticke Poet, W.Shakespeare," in Shakespeare (1632 folio), sig. A5.

59. Leslie Hotson, ed., *The Queen's Entertainment at Mitcham* (New Haven, CT: Yale University Press, 1953), 6. Caesar later became Master of the Rolls and Chancellor of the Exchequer under King James.

60. For more on Caesar's forms of textual engagement and his manuscripts, notably his commonplace book, BL MS Add. 6038 (Foxe's *Pandectae Locorum Communium*, discussed in Chapter 1), see William Sherman, *Used Books: Marking Readers in Renaissance England* (Philadelphia: University of Pennsylvania Press, 2008), esp. Chapter 7.

61. BL MS Add. 12497: the entertainment, ff. 253–62v; the accounts, ff. 237–44; the songs, f. 281. For more on this entertainment, including a transcription and a comparison to the entertainment at Chiswick, see Hotson, *Queen's Entertainment*. See also BL MS 4160, f. 21 ("a copy of Caesar's account in the hand of Thomas Birch"), published in Goldring, Eales, Archer, and Clarke, eds., *John Nichols's The Progresses*, vol. 4, 64.

62. Hotson argues that John Lyly wrote this entertainment, despite the fact that these documents are not in Lyly's hand (*Queen's Entertainment*, 4). When the entertainment was recopied remains a matter of conjecture.

63. This work was unpublished in the early modern period. Whether or not *Of Tribute* was actually performed is unknown. See Brian Vickers, ed., *Francis Bacon: The Major Works* (Oxford: Oxford University Press, 2002), esp. 514–15.

64. I was not able to consult this manuscript in person, so I rely on James Spedding, ed., *A Conference of Pleasure, Composed for Some Festive Occasion About the Year 1592 By Francis Bacon* (London: Whittingham and Wilkins, 1870) and Frank J. Burgoyne, ed., *Collotype Facsimile & Type Transcript of an Elizabethan Manuscript Preserved at Alnwick Castle*, 2 vols. (London: Longman, Green, & Co., 1904). *Of Tribute* runs from pp. 3–25, which Burgoyne calls folios instead of pages. The possible dramatic extracts include selections from *A Device to Entertain the Queen at Essex House* (1595) and a speech from a tournament.

65. This work was unpublished in the early modern period. Some of the volumes of state papers that include speeches from *A Device to Entertain the Queen at Essex*

House are BL MS Add. 40838, Lambeth Palace MS 933, Queen's College Oxford MSS 121 and 130, and Inner Temple Library Petyt MS 538, vol. 36. For a complete text of the entertainment, see Vickers, *Francis Bacon*, 61–68 and Paul E. J. Hammer, ed., "Device Exhibited by the Earl of Essex before Queen Elizabeth, on the Anniversary of her Accession to the Throne, 17 November 1595" in *John Nichols's The Progresses*, ed. Goldring, Eales, Clarke, and Archer, vol. 3, 862–76.

66. The two sections of Folger MS V.b.213 are paginated separately and written in different hands.

67. Heaton offers an overview of all the manuscripts that include most or all of this masque, as well as the related evidence such as descriptions of performance (*Writing and Reading Royal Entertainments*, esp. 76–89).

68. Vickers, *Francis Bacon*, 535.

69. Heaton, *Writing and Reading Royal Entertainments*, 86. James McManaway notes that this volume was "compiled by someone deeply interested in the affairs of the Earl of Essex," in "Elizabeth, Essex, and James," in *Elizabethan and Jacobean Studies Presented to Frank Percy Wilson in Honour of His Seventieth Birthday*, ed. Herbert Davis and Helen Gardner (Oxford: Clarendon, 1959), rpt. in *Studies in Shakespeare, Bibliography, and Theatre* (New York: Shakespeare Association of America, 1969), 165.

70. See Vickers's notes on the passage, *Francis Bacon*, 537–38.

71. To see the full contents of this manuscript, visit the Folger Shakspeare Library Digital Image Collections, luna.folger.edu.

72. Kelliher, "Donne, Jonson, Richard Andrews and The Newcastle Manuscript," *English Manuscript Studies 1100–1700* 4 (1993): 134–73. For a bibliographic description of the manuscript with particular attention to the Jonson pieces, see William Dinsmore Briggs, "Studies in Ben Jonson," *Anglia* 37 (1913): 463–93.

73. Gabriel Heaton, *Writing and Reading Royal Entertainments*, 244. See also Cedric C. Brown, "Courtesies of Place and Arts of Diplomacy in Ben Jonson's Last Two Entertainments for Royalty," *The Seventeenth Century* 9 (1994): 147–71.

74. For a discussion of the patronage relation between Jonson and Cavendish, see Brown, "Courtesies," and Nick Rowe, "'My Best Patron': William Cavendish and Jonson's Caroline Dramas," *The Seventeenth Century* (1994): 197–212.

75. BL MS Harley 4955, ff. 2–55, 173–82, 192–204.

76. Leah Sinanoglou Marcus, "'Present Occasions' and the Shaping of Ben Jonson's Masques" *English Literary History* 45 (1978): 201–25.

77. Marcus, "'Present Occasions,'" 201.

78. Kelliher, "Donne, Jonson, Richard Andrews," 151.

79. Kelliher, "Donne, Jonson, Richard Andrews," 144; *The Workes of Ben Jonson. The second Volume.* (London: Richard Meighen, 1640 [1641]). When I refer to Jonson's 1641 folio, I mean Meighen's publication, and not the reprint of the 1616 folio that also appeared in 1640–1641. See Peter Happé, "The 1640-1 Folio (F2(3))" in *The Cambridge Edition of the Works of Ben Jonson Online*, ed. Martin Butler, David Gants, et al., Cambridge University Press and King's College London, universitypublishingonline.org/cambridge/benjonson.

80. Where Jonson's 1641 folio reads "*Here the second* Anti-masque *of* Phantos'mes *came forth, which danced.* / PHANT'SIE *proceeded*" (l. 107-8, sig. Dv,

p. 18; note that signatures and pagination are not consecutive in this volume), the manuscript reads "Here the Anti=masque of **Phantomes** / comes forth, That danced **Phan'sy**, / proceeds" (BL MS Harley 4995, f. 41v). Another example of the folio's clarification can be seen in the description of Wassail in *Christmas His Masque*, who, in the printed text is "for Twelfe-night more meet too" (l. 194, sig. B3v; p. 6), but in the manuscript is "for this night most meet to" (f. 47). An audience member attending the performance would have known that it was part of the twelfth night revels: this emendation is for later readers.

81. Stephen Orgel, *Ben Jonson: The Complete Masques* (New Haven, CT: Yale University Press, 1969), 504.

82. "Come Noble Nymphs" is, like "The Glories of our Blood and State" or "In the Merry Month of May," a song that circulated widely beyond its original masque contexts. It was, for instance, published as a poem in Jonson's *Execration Against Vulcan* (1640) and circulated as a manuscript separate in Bodleian MS Ashmole 36/37. For more on the circulation of this song, see *CELM*, JnB 606-10.5 and the Folger *Union First Line Index*.

83. Joshua Eckhardt, *Manuscript Verse Collectors and the Politics of Anti-Courtly Love Poetry* (Oxford: Oxford University Press, 2009), 20.

84. Kelliher, "Donne, Jonson, Richard Andrews," 144.

85. Lynn Hulse, "Cavendish, William, first duke of Newcastle upon Tyne (*bap.* 1593, *d.* 1676)," *ODNB*.

86. Rather than citing an early modern print source that post-dates most of the manuscripts discussed here, the *Gypsies Metamorphosed* will be cited by line number from *The Cambridge Edition of the Works of Ben Jonson*, ed. David Bevington, Martin Butler, and Ian Donaldson, vol. 5 (Cambridge: Cambridge UP, 2012). "Cock Lorell," Burley 695–757; "From a gypsy," Windsor 978-1042. For an analysis of the circulation of "Cock Lorell" and other manuscript material in relation to anti-Buckingham sentiment of the 1620s, see Knowles, "Songs of baser alloy." See *CELM*, JnB 613-70.5, for a list of extracts from *The Gypsies Metamorphosed*. For a discussion of some of the other songs in *The Gypsies Metamorphosed*, see Mary Chan, *Music in the Theatre of Ben Jonson* (Oxford: Oxford University Press, 2002).

87. Jonson, *Gypsies*, Windsor, Epilogue 3, 9.

88. Mark Netzloff, "'Counterfeit Egyptians' and Imagined Borders: Jonson's *The Gypsies Metamorphosed*," *English Literary History* 68 (2001): 764.

89. Jonson, *Q. Horatius Flaccus: His Art of Poetry* (1639), sigs. C10-E12v. Jonson, *The Gypsies Metamorphosed*, (1641 folio), sigs. G4-L2v (pp. 47–80, signatures and pagination not consecutive).

90. National Archives SP 14/122/58, Bodleian MS Tanner 306, and Bodleian MS Rawl. poet. 172.

91. Bodleian MS Rawl. poet. 172, f. 78r-v, has the same four fortunes from the Windsor version of the masque as Bodleian MS Tanner 306, ff. 252–253 (the Lord Keeper's, the Lord Steward's, the Lord Treasurer's, and the Lord Chamberlain's) and shares a number of readings with this manuscript; they are, as Greg explains, closely related (75). The third and final early manuscript containing fortunes is the Conway Manuscript (National Archives SP 14/122/58, ff. 99–100v), composed by Henry Goodyer in the 1620s, and labeled "The Gypsies Maaske att Burley." The Conway

74   Chapter 2

manuscript names some of the gypsies who spoke the fortunes at the Burley performance. Buckingham himself read the king's fortune; Baron Feilding (later Earl of Denbigh) recounted the Prince's fortune and Lady Purbeck's fortune; and Endymion Porter (a courtier) told the Lady Marquess of Buckingham's fortune as well as the Countess of Rutland's. For a detailed description of these manuscripts, see W. W. Greg, *Jonson's Masque of the Gipsies in the Burley, Belvoir, and Windsor Editions* (London: Oxford University Press, 1952), esp. 9, 71–75. I consulted the Conway manuscript via *State Papers Online: The Government of Britain, 1509–1714*.

92. Orgel, *Ben Jonson*, 144.

93. For various readings of the original political meaning of the masque, see Martin Butler, "'We are one mans all': Jonson's *The Gipsies Metamorphosed*," *The Yearbook of English Studies* 21 (1991): 252–73; Richard Helgerson, *Self-Crowned Laureates: Spenser, Jonson, Milton, and the Literary System* (Berkeley: University of California Press, 1983), 178; and Dale B. J. Randall, *Jonson's Gypsies Unmasked: Background and Theme of* The Gypsies Metamorphos'd (Durham, NC: Duke University Press, 1975).

94. Both Lady Hatton and Sir Coke had been married previously, she to Sir William Hatton and he to Bridget Paston. Lady Hatton refused to take her second husband's name.

95. Thomas Longueville, *The Curious Case of Lady Purbeck: A Scandal of the XVIIth Century* (London, 1909), 36–39. Available through *The Making of Modern Law*, Gale/Cengage Learning, Gale Document Number: F3751096702.

96. Longueville, *Curious Case*, 54.

97. Kate Aughterson, "Hatton, Elizabeth, Lady Hatton [*other married name* Elizabeth Coke, Lady Coke] (1578–1646)," *ODNB*.

98. Aughterson, "Hatton, Elizabeth," *ODNB*.

99. Antonia Fraser, *The Weaker Vessel: Woman's Lot in Seventeenth-Century England* (London: Widenfeld and Nicolson, 1984), 13.

100. Stuart Handley, "Villiers, John, Viscount Purbeck (1591?–1658)," *ODNB*.

101. Fraser, *Weaker Vessel*, 17–18.

102. Handley, "Villiers, John," *ODNB*.

103. Longueville, *Curious Case*, 118.

104. William Knowler, ed. *The Earl of Strafforde's Letters and Dispatches . . .* (London: W. Bowyer, 1739), vol. I, 423.

105. Fraser, *Weaker Vessel*, 19.

106. Jonson, *Gypsies*, Burley 407–8.

107. Ibid., 409–10.

108. Randall, *Jonson's Gypsies*, 135.

109. Jonson, *Gypsies*, Burley 44–45.

110. Ibid., 46.

111. Ralph Brooke, *A Catalogue and succession of the Kings, Princes, Dukes, Marquesses, Earles, and Viscounts of this Realme of England, since the Norman Conquest, to this present yeere 1622* (1622), Cambridge University Library Syn.3.62.17 (available on *EEBO*), sig. Ll4v. Thanks to Katie Will for pointing out this marginalia.

112. Brooke, *Catalogue*, sig. [A]2v.

113. Ibid., sig. Ll4v.

114. Arthur F. Marotti, *Manuscript, Print, and the English Renaissance Lyric* (Ithaca: Cornell University Press, 1993), 94.

115. As Hobbs has shown, Huntington MS HM 172 and Folger MS V.a.96 were copied from the same manuscript source: *Early Seventeenth-Century Verse Miscellanies*, 124–25.

116. Jonson, *Gypsies*, Burley 386–93.

117. Fraser, *Weaker Vessel*, 12–13.

118. There are two groups of poems in Folger MS V.b.43 that highlight the indeterminacy of whether the compiler knew the subject of Lady Purbeck's fortune: the courtly poems perhaps suggest a familiarity with the court, whereas the poems about gentlewoman suggest the compiler's interest in the general topic. The manuscript contains multiple poems about political and courtly events, including a disparaging poem about the performance of *Technogamia* before King James at Woodstock (1621; f. 5) and an epitaph for John Felton, Buckingham's killer (1628; f. 34). This manuscript also, however, contains a number of poems about gentlewomen (often complimentary or rhapsodizing), with titles such as "On A Heart which a Gentlewoman wore in hir breast" (f. 23v), "On A Gentlewoman looking in a glass" (f. 23), "On A Gentlewoman like his mistris" (f. 27), and "on a Gentlewoman that Sung Excellently" (f. 16).

119. Jonson, *Gypsies*, Burley 382.

Chapter 3

Theatrical Nostalgia

Dramatic Miscellanies and the Closure of the Theatres, 1642–1660

In one of the most momentous events in early modern theatre history, on September 2, 1642, Parliament ordered the London theatres to be closed because, they reasoned, England was threatened by civil war, and "public sports do not well agree with public calamities, nor public stage-plays with the seasons of humiliation."[1] As we know today, the closure of the theatres did not end theatrical activity in London. Performances continued: some were illicit, some staged by amateurs, and others, termed operas, circumvented the ban. Beyond performances, theatrical activity persisted in the form of play publication, pamphlet plays, play translation, and drolls, to name just a few. In a prefatory poem for the 1653 publication of Richard Brome's plays, Aston Cockayne, the poet and playwright, exclaimed, "we shall still have Playes! and though we may / Not them in their full Glories yet display; / Yet we may please our selves by reading them."[2] Dramatic extracting reveals another way theatrical activity and play reading persisted after the public theatres were closed. The study of dramatic extracts can contribute to the growing body of scholarship on theatrical activities during 1642–1660.[3] The act of copying selections from a play is particularly important in relation to the closure of the theatres because it shows how some readers actively sought playbooks specifically, which, I contend, demonstrates a sense of nostalgia.

I argue that the closure of the theatres changed the way people read plays, while at the same time, dramatic extracting continued the way it had in the early seventeenth century; as the French say, *plus ça change, plus c'est la même chose*—the more things change, the more they stay the same. The greater part of this chapter examines the way dramatic extracting changed because of the closure of the theatres, although I gesture to the continuation of particular practices of dramatic extracting throughout, particularly in the conclusion. This examination also continues to explore the varied and perhaps paradoxical reading practices outlined in relation to masques in Chapter 2: on the one hand, people read plays politically and in relation to particular historic moments and events, and on the other hand, people read plays for the ahistorical and generalized wisdom of commonplaces.

This chapter introduces a key development in seventeenth-century dramatic extracting: the dramatic miscellany, a print or manuscript collection comprising primarily dramatic extracts. In addition to defining this new category of dramatic miscellany, I also discuss particular examples in depth. My chapter first treats Abraham Wright's BL MS Add. 22608 and John Cotgrave's print *English Treasury of Wit and Language* in relation to the complex political situation of mid-century England. Examining the politics of dramatic excerpting does not simply equate any theatrical activity during the 1640s and 1650s to royalism on the basis that Puritans and parliamentarians disliked theatre.[4] As Wright and Cotgrave show, dramatic extracting could be undertaken by royalists and parliamentarians alike, at times with political intentions and at times without. Like many of the extracts from masques discussed in Chapter 2, *The English Treasury of Wit and Language* demonstrates how the meaning of a dramatic extract can change when we consider it in later historical circumstances.

After comparing Wright's and Cotgrave's miscellanies at length, I turn to two less politicized miscellanies of the age, John Evans's *Hesperides* and Folger MS V.a.87. I show that Humphrey Moseley, the publisher of *The English Treasury* and anticipated publisher of *Hesperides*, both created and catered to a book-buying public who were interested in plays as well as works with dramatic extracts. While the first part of the chapter offers historically contingent and politically charged readings, I demonstrate how the compiler of Folger MS V.a.87 abstracted and generalized readings into commonplaces that are, in some senses, ahistorical or trans-historical—and separate from the plays they were taken from. I conclude the discussion of dramatic miscellanies by summarizing the importance of these overlooked texts: they offer tangible evidence of the plays and editions being read and reveal how early readers approached plays.

Two important contexts for considering dramatic extracts in the civil war and interregnum period are drolls and dramatic miscellanies, which, at first glance, might seem completely unrelated. The first, drolls, a theatrical innovation briefly discussed below, is beyond the focus of this book. The second, dramatic miscellanies, a new kind of book, emerged in both print and manuscript around this time. Much of this chapter is dedicated to exploring dramatic miscellanies, both as a genre of book and as particular texts that reveal one reader's views of theatre.

During the closure of the theatres, dramatic extracting flourished, as did the performed equivalent of extended dramatic extracts: drolls. The term "droll" is a post-Restoration term (short for "drollery") applied anachronistically to a range of civil war and interregnum entertainments, including sung dialogues, jigs, masques, interludes, and adapted and abridged plays.[5] Drolls relate to dramatic extracts because, like extracts, they often consist of selections from a larger dramatic work. Generically, I differentiate drolls from extracts—and, in doing so, align them with abridgments—because drolls were meant to be performed, unlike the majority of extracts. Drolls, like dramatic extracts, demonstrate a continued interest in drama and dramatic activities after the theatres closed.

The strategies of adapting drolls from long plays vary as much as the strategies for extracting from plays. Henry Marsh's *The Wits, or Sport upon Sport* (1662) exemplifies how drolls appropriate earlier plays, as it contains scenes and characters from Renaissance plays including James Shirley's *The Scornful Lady*, John Fletcher's *A King and No King*, and Ben Jonson's *The Alchemist*.[6] John James Elson's modern edition of *The Wits* shows the range of approaches taken in lifting drolls from five act plays: *Hamlet*'s gravediggers scene is copied with only a few alterations, whereas the droll "Bottom the Weaver," from *A Midsummer Night's Dream*, involves stitching together different scenes, abridging speeches, and reassigning roles to accommodate a smaller cast.[7] Similarly, we have dramatic extracts that were copied faithfully from the source and others that were altered almost beyond recognition. One of the main differences between drolls/abridgments and extracts is the intended use: drolls and abridgments were often intended as performance pieces, whereas extracts were written. Extracts were often meant for reuse in conversation, or were gathered in a literary or scholarly vein.

The civil wars and closure of the theatres generated both theatrical and literary innovation—the dramatic miscellany is one such innovation that has not been studied.[8] A new kind of manuscript emerged: the dramatic miscellany, that is, books filled entirely or mainly with dramatic extracts. In his *Dictionary of English Manuscript Terminology*, Peter Beal defines a miscellany as "any kind of volume in which a mixture of literary compositions, of different genres or by different authors, are collected together."[9] Beal then offers two subcategories of miscellanies, verse miscellanies and commonplace books.[10] I propose a related subcategory, the dramatic miscellany, which overlaps with both verse miscellany and commonplace book, but also has distinct characteristics.[11] For instance, a dramatic miscellany can be a commonplace book when it is organized by subject headings, as with Cotgrave's *English Treasury of Wit and Language, Collected Out of the most, and best of our English Drammatick Poems; Methodically digested into Common Places for Generall Use* (1655). Cotgrave's miscellany is also a poetical miscellany; he printed the extracts as verse, even changing prose to poetry. Other dramatic miscellanies, such as Folger MS V.a.87 are neither arranged by commonplace headings nor written as poems. In their focus on extracts from plays, dramatic miscellanies are equivalent to *flores poetarum*, collections of extracts from poems.[12] Like *flores poetarum*, dramatic miscellanies have classical roots: one Latin dramatic miscellany, comprising extracts from Terence's plays, was republished multiple times in England over the sixteenth century.[13] Dramatic miscellanies reflect a shift in dramatic extracting where manuscript compilers (or, in the case of Cotgrave, print miscellany compilers) turned specifically to drama for fodder, rather than including drama with other poetical or prose works.

Dramatic miscellanies comprise extracts from plays and not copies of complete plays themselves; collections of complete plays are better described as anthologies (collections printed as a whole) or composite anthologies/ sammelbände (collections bound together after each piece was created). For instance, BL MS Egerton 1994 is a well-known composite anthology of full-text manuscript plays that includes John Fletcher and Philip Massinger's *The Elder Brother* and the anonymous *Thomas of Woodstock*, among other plays.[14] As there are very few full-text manuscript plays, the majority of composite dramatic anthologies are made by binding printed play quartos: some of these were bound by early readers and others, by later archivists.[15] Unlike dramatic miscellanies, we have many examples of printed dramatic anthologies (collections of plays printed and sold as a unit, such as Shakespeare's first folio, 1623) and composite dramatic anthologies (often printed play quartos bound together).[16]

Although there are only a handful of print and manuscript dramatic miscellanies, the study of these texts is valuable because it reveals how early modern readers approached plays. As early as 1598, the playwright John Marston mentioned those who have a "common-place booke [made] out of plaies,"[17] but the earliest extant dramatic miscellanies date to after the closure of the theatres in 1642. Perhaps there are earlier dramatic miscellanies to be uncovered, but at the moment, existing archival evidence suggests that this type of manuscript began, or at the least, was popularized in the mid-seventeenth century. The dramatic miscellanies discussed in this chapter show a theatrical nostalgia: a longing for theatre that is no longer being performed.

Cotgrave's *English Treasury* (1655) is the only known seventeenth-century print dramatic miscellany, but there are multiple manuscript examples, including Abraham Wright's BL MS Add. 22608 (1630s and 1640s), Folger MS V.a.87 (1650s), William Deedes's Folger MS V.a.226 (1690s), Archbishop Sancroft's Bodleian MS Sancroft 29 (before 1693), and BL MS Lansdowne 1185 (c. 1700). The three chronologically later manuscripts will be discussed in Chapters 4 and 5; this section focuses on dramatic miscellanies that were compiled during the civil wars and interregnum (1642–1660). The practice of compiling dramatic miscellanies developed from commonplacing traditions where extracts from plays appeared alongside other literary works. Unlike other dramatic extracting, however, the compilation of dramatic miscellanies indicates that readers and booksellers differentiated drama from other literary genres.

ABRAHAM WRIGHT'S DRAMATIC MISCELLANY, BL MS ADD. 22608

Abraham Wright (1611–1690), a devout Church of England clergyman and royalist, compiled BL MS Add. 22608, a dramatic miscellany that I contend was written with a sense of royalist nostalgia.[18] In order to prove this point, I first demonstrate that one section of BL MS Add. 22608 is indeed a dramatic miscellany, while also redating at least parts of the manuscript to after the closure of the theatres. Closely attending to this manuscript corrects some long-standing scholarly oversights by bringing to light previously overlooked dramatic extracts from plays by William Peaps and Jasper Mayne. Although many of the dramatic extracts themselves are politically innocuous, the manuscript as a whole carries royalist implications. Wright later bequeathed BL MS Add. 22608 to his son with specific marginal notations, demonstrating how dramatic miscellanies and extracts could be used as a tool for both propagating particular political views as well as achieving the social polish needed to succeed in society.

The British Library catalogue explains that BL MS Add. 22608 is made of three parts: first, extracts from prose histories (ff. 3–68); second, dramatic extracts and extracts from Fuller's *Holy Wars* (ff. 69–116); and third, extracts from Anthony Stafford's *Niobe* (ff. 117–19v). The second section at one point stood as a complete unit—it was a dramatic miscellany—and was only bound with other sections some time after its initial composition.[19] The opening page of dramatic extracts is much more worn than the page preceding it in the bound volume. Further evidence that part of BL MS Add. 22608 once stood as a separate dramatic miscellany comes from the foliation. Wright numbered the folios in this section, beginning with the number 1 on folio 69. He also included a table of contents for just this section of the manuscript (see Figure 3.1 and Table 3.1). The table of contents lists each play twice, once in Wright's hand at the top, and then in a list with columns below, written in a shakier hand. The next section of the manuscript (Stafford's *Niobe*) begins with new pagination on folio 117. The dramatic extracts in this manuscript were conceptualized as a single unit; Wright compiled a dramatic miscellany, which was only later included in a composite volume.

Wright not only excerpted from multiple plays but also commented on the plays; he is now perhaps most famous for his commentary on two of

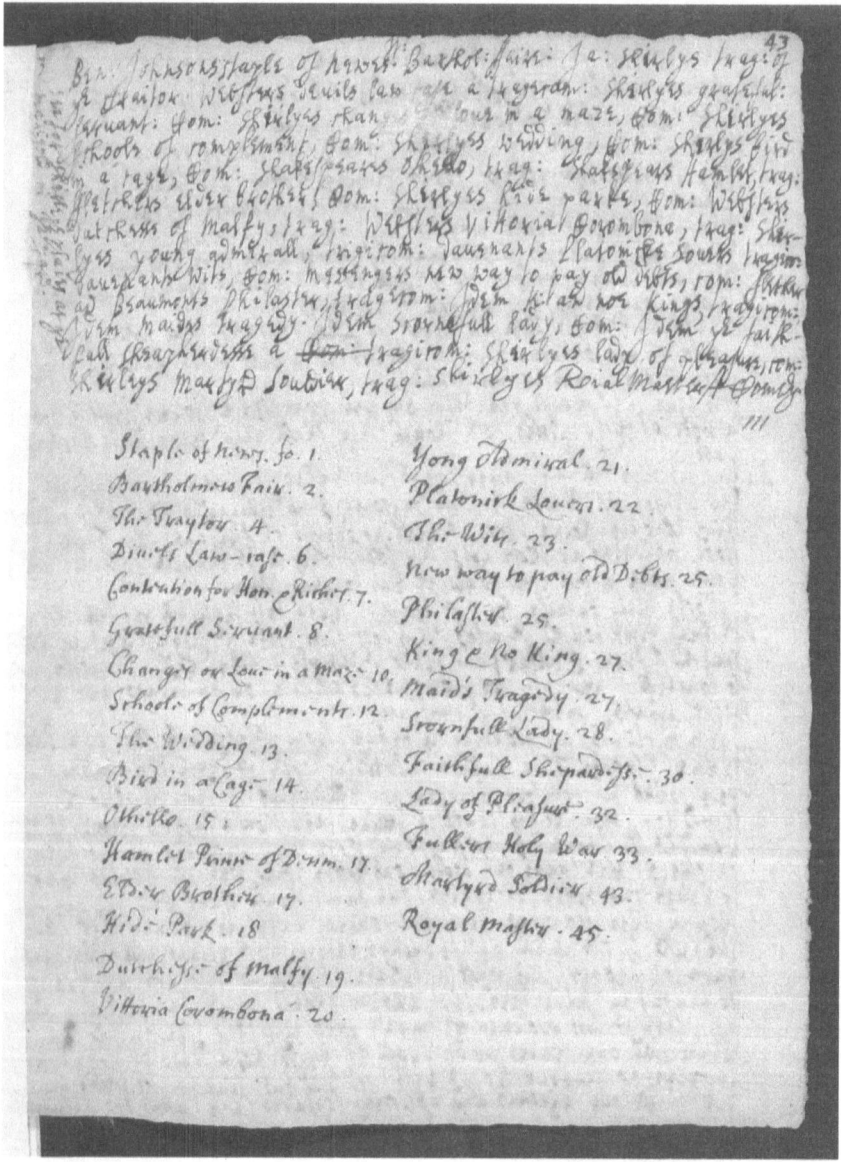

Figure 3.1 © The British Library Board, BL MS Add. 22608, f. 111, Wright's table of contents.

Shakespeare's tragedies.[20] Wright deemed *Othello* "A very good play both for lines and plot, but especially the plot. Iago for a rogue and Othello for a jealous husband 2 parts well pen[ne]d" (f. 84v) but he criticized *Hamlet* more harshly, noting that it was "But an indifferent play, the lines but meane, and

Table 3.1 Transcription, BL MS Add. 22608, f. 111, Wright's table of contents.

See for Shirley's plaies at the marigold in the yard.

Ben: Johnsons staple of Newes. ^Ib^: Barthol: ffaire: Ja: Shirlys trag: of the Traitor. Websters devils law case a tragecom: Shirlyes grateful: servant: Com: Shirlyes changes or love in a maze, Com: Shirlyes Schoole of complement, Com: Shirlyes Wedding, Com: Shirlys bird in a cage, Com: Shakespeares Othello, trag: Shakepears Hamlet, trag: ffletchers Elder brother, Com: Shirlyes hide parke, Com: Websters dutchess of Malfys trag: Websters Vittoria Corombona, trag: Shir- lyes young admirall, trigicom: davenants Platonicke Lovers tragic: davenants Wits, Com: Messengers new way to pay old debts, com: flether and Beaumonts Philaster, tragecom: Idem K: and noe Kings, tragicom: Idem Maides Tragedy. Idem Scornefull lady, Com: Idem the faithfull Sheapherdesse a ~~Com:~~ tragicom: Shirlyes lady of pleasure, com: Shirleys martyrd souldier, trag: Shirlyes Roial Master A Comedy.

Staple of news fo. 1.	Yong Admiral. 21.
Bartholomew Fair. 2.	Platonick Lovers. 22.
The Traytor. 4.	The Wits. 23.
Divels Law-case. 6.	New way to pay old Debts. 25.
Contention for Hon. & Riches. 7.	Philaster. 25.
Gratefull Servant. 8.	King & No King. 27.
Changes or Love in a Maze. 10.	Maid's Tragedy. 27.
Schoole of Complements. 12.	Scornfull Lady. 28.
The Wedding. 13.	Faithfull Shepardesse. 30.
Bird in a Cage. 14.	Lady of Pleasure. 32.
Othello. 15.	Fullers Holy War. 33.
Hamlet Prince of Denm. 17.	Martyrd Soldier. 43.
Elder Brothers. 17.	Royal Masters. 45.
Hide Park. 18	
Dutchesse of Malfy. 19.	
Vittoria Corombona. 20.	

Note: On this page, for frequent repetition of Shirley's name, it looks like Sherly or Sherlye has been overwritten to Shirly or Shirlye.

in nothing like Othello. Hamlet is an indifferent good part for a madman" (f. 85v).[21] Wright's commentaries show his recurring interest in "plot" and "lines": for Wright, Henry Shirley's *The Martyred Soldier* was "An indifferent good play. The plot easy and plaine; the lines indifferent" (f. 113v); James Shirley's *The Lady of Pleasure* was "The best play of Shirley's for the lines, but the plot is as much as none" (f. 101v); Massinger's *A New Way to Pay Old Debts* was "A silly play. the plot but ordinary ... without any new dress either of langu^a^ge or fancy" (f. 93v); and John Webster's *The Devil's Law Case* was "but an indifferent play, the plot is intricate enough, but if rightly scanned will bee found faulty, by reason many passages doe either not hang together, or if they doe it is so sillily as noe man can perceive them likely to bee ever done" (f. 75v). These examples of Wright's interpretation indicate his attention to both the language and the action of a play and partly explain his interest in dramatic extracting. Wright copied dramatic extracts as commonplaces; he chose the "lines" he found beautiful. Wright had a clear aesthetic motivation for copying extracts from plays, but he also had a political and educational agenda as well.

In the case of Wright's dramatic miscellany in BL MS Add. 22608, Wright's scribal publication of dramatic extracts is intentionally royalist, as demonstrated by his previous print publication, his selection of plays, the didactic marginal instructions, and the effect his opinions ultimately had on his son.[22] Wright's royalism is also evident in some of his own poetry, which he published anonymously in *Parnassus Biceps*.[23] One of these poems, "Upon the Kings-Book bound up in a Cover coloured with His blood" positions *Eikon Basilike* as second only to the Gospel and Christ's blood.[24] Another of Wright's verses, beginning "Were they not Angells sang, did not mine eares," was spoken to entertain Charles I at his visit to St. John's College in 1636.[25]

In *Parnassus Biceps* (1656), Wright exhibited royalist nostalgia by collecting verse that had circulated in the universities twenty years previously. He glowingly extolled the pre-civil war days in his epistle to the reader: "Then were these Poems writ, when peace and plenty were the best Patriots and Maecenasses to great Wits."[26] The same royalist nostalgia pervades Wright's dramatic miscellany; while he assembled many selections from Caroline plays, notably James Shirley's and William Davenant's, he also gathered extracts from a number of even earlier plays, including Francis Beaumont and John Fletcher's and Ben Jonson's. During the civil wars, Beaumont's and Jonson's poetry was often associated with royalism, for instance, in the royalist printed verse miscellany, *Harmony of the Muses* (1654).[27] *The Famous Tragedie of King Charles I* (1649), a pamphlet play, positions pre-war playwrights—"Johnson, Shakespeare, [Thomas] Goffe, and Devenant / Brave [John] Sucklin, Beaumont, Fletcher, [James] Shurley"—as antithetical to Puritan parliamentarians.[28] Wright's attention to Beaumont and Fletcher and Jonson in *Parnassus Biceps* can be seen as royalist; as can his dramatic extracts from Jonson, Shakespeare, Shirley, and Beaumont and Fletcher in his manuscript dramatic miscellany.

Understanding the politics of Wright's dramatic miscellany requires a clear understanding of the date of the manuscript. Although previous scholars have suggested that this manuscript was written in 1639 or 1640, the as-yet unnoticed extracts from William Peaps's *Love In it's Extasie* (sic, pr. 1649) and Jasper Mayne's *The Amorous Warre* (pr. 1648) reveal that Wright continued copying commonplaces from plays well after the closure of the theatres in 1642.[29] Henry Shirley's *The Martyr'd Soldier* (pr. 1638) and James Shirley's *The Royall Master* (pr. 1638) are the last plays that Wright cites in his table of contents, but Wright copied further dramatic extracts from Peaps and Mayne that he did not list in his table of contents. Based on the hitherto ignored plays from which Wright excerpted, we can safely date the compilation of his manuscript from c.1640–1650, rather than assuming that he completed it in a few years around 1640.[30] Redating the compilation of this manuscript alters its political importance, just as the turbulent years of the civil wars altered England's political landscape.

Knowing that Wright copied at least some of these extracts after the closure of the theatres and around Charles I's execution partly accounts for his tastes: he exhibits clear royalist nostalgia. Wright's interest in plays by James Shirley, Davenant, Beaumont and Fletcher, and Jonson can be understood for their aesthetic value, but some of his other choices, notably Peaps's *Love In it's Extasie*, leave much to be desired in terms of lines and plot, Wright's preferred standards for evaluation. Wright may have been drawn to this play by the royalist nostalgia expressed in its paratextual matter. The epistle to the reader of *Love In it's Extasie* admits the play's shortcomings compared to previous dramatic achievements: "Did the Stage enjoy its former lustre, this would have lien still neglected and forgotten: but since those pastimes are denied us wherein we saw the soule and genius of all the world lye contracted in the litle compasse of an English Theatre, I have thought fit . . . to venture this in publike."[31] On the title page, *Love In it's Extasie* declares its connection with times past by announcing itself as "A kind of Royall Pastorall written long since, by a Gentleman, Student at *Æton*, and now published." Annabel Patterson argues that pastoral was especially prominent during Charles I's reign.[32] While Dale B. J. Randall is more cautious, initially claiming, "clearly no political, religious, or social group had a patent on pastoral," he goes on to say, "Nevertheless, pastoral was characteristically an instrument of the royalists, especially in dramatic and quasi-dramatic writings."[33] Peaps's pastoral, while patently absurd, hearkens back to the Caroline pastorals and features multiple kings disguised as shepherds and a tyrannical regent. Had he been brave enough, his title page could have read "A kind of Royal*ist* Pastorall" (addition italicized). The epistle to the reader raises the very political reading it tries to deny: "You may be confident there lyes no Treason in it nor State invective, (The common issues of this pregnant age) It is inoffensive all, soft as the milkie dayes it was written in."[34] The subtitle to the play, *The large Prerogative*, is perhaps most telling: one concern of the civil war was the king's prerogative and whether it was or should be circumscribed by law. *The large Prerogative* summons to mind an image of a king with, if not absolute prerogative, a clear dominion. Wright shared the high regard for pre-civil war theatre and culture that Peaps exhibited in *Love In it's Extasie*.

Both Peaps's *Love In it's Extasie* and Mayne's *The Amorous Warre* were published after the closure of the theatres, which was, as Lois Potter explains, "a political act in its own right."[35] Alfred Harbage suggests that the publication of *Love In it's Extasie* was motivated by "royalist discontent at the prohibition of drama."[36] Mayne himself was a royalist sympathizer, which cost him his position at Oxford.[37] His previous play, *The Citye Match*, had been performed for the King and Queen in 1639. In *ΟΧΛΟ-MAXIA [Ochlo-machia], or, The Peoples War* (1647), Mayne argued against rising up against the king. The title page of *Ochlo-machia* includes an epigraph from Romans on the title page, "Let every soul be subject unto the higher powers" (13.1).[38] Mayne attributed this to Romans 13:2, a verse that has even stronger royalist connotations, "Whosoever therefore resisteth the power, resisteth the ordinance of God: and they that resist shall receive to themselves damnation." According to Dennis Flynn, Mayne "certainly engaged in the propaganda war";[39] it would be foolhardy to think that his plays were not a part of this effort. In *The Amorous Warre*, Mayne alludes to a civil war where part of society declared it lawful to fight against the king. In Mayne's story, the people's uprising results in rape and slaughter.[40] Not only did Mayne's royalism align with Wright's, both also revered earlier playwrights: Mayne is perhaps now best known for his commendatory poems that praised Shakespeare and Jonson.[41] While Wright may not have selected overtly political material from Peaps's and Mayne's plays, his choice of these plays reveals his royalism nevertheless.

Wright bequeathed his dramatic miscellany to his son, James (c. 1644–1713), and in passing along this manuscript, passed along his taste in plays and political views.[42] James adopted his father's nostalgic preferences. In *Country Conversations* (1694), James expressed a predilection for pre-civil war plays: "the New Plays, the Comedies especially . . . in my Esteem are nothing comparable to those Writ before the civil war, and some in the Reign of King *Charles* the Second."[43] New plays, he continues, "have neither the Wit, Conduct, Honour, nor Design of those Writ by *Johnson, Shakspear*, and *Fletcher*."[44] After hearing the counter-argument for new theatre, one speaker "produced out of *Ben. Johnson, Shakspear, Beaumont* and *Fletcher, Messenger, Shirley*, and Sir *William Davenant*, before the Wars, and some Comedies of Mr. *Drydens*, since the Restauration, many Characters of Gentlemen, of a quite different Strain from those in the Modern Plays."[45] James Wright's theatrical tastes were no doubt heavily influenced by his father: all save one of the authors that James mentions (John Dryden) are found in BL MS Add. 22608. James is now better-known for *Historia Histrionica: An Historical Account of the English Stage* (1699), a dialogue between two characters, Lovewit and Truman, that similarly glorifies pre-civil war theatre, although it focuses more on players than playwrights. Wright's comments to his son would have been added after James's birth (c. 1644); Wright either copied these extracts after the theatres were closed, or turned to them again in order to introduce his son to the plays that were written and performed before he was born.

Wright purposefully influenced his son's reading habits with his marginal comments and notes. Wright told his son where to shop for plays, "See for

Shirley's plaies at the marigold in the yard," a bookshop in St. Paul's Churchyard.[46] Francis Eglesfield, one of the booksellers and sometimes publisher at the Marigold from 1635 until the Restoration, was himself a royalist. Eglesfield was one of four publishers heavily involved in the printing of Charles I's absolutist *Eikon Basilike*, a work whose royalist implications were magnified after his beheading.[47] Shortly after the Restoration, Eglesfield is credited with writing the anonymously published *Monarchy Revived in the most illustrious* (1661 [actually 1660]), also published as *The Life and Reigne of Our Sovereign Lord King Charles the II* (1660), and written by "a Lover of his Prince and Countrey."[48] Particularly after the Restoration, Eglesfield's name appears on the title page of numerous pro-monarchy texts.[49] Given Wright's own royalist sympathies and tastes, it is unsurprising that Wright instructed his son to frequent a royalist bookseller. James took his father's advice seriously and became, as the eighteenth-century historian Thomas Warton noted, "perhaps one of the first collectors of Old Plays since Cartwright."[50] Warton also pointed out that James Wright "was attached to the principles of monarchy in their most extensive comprehension; and from this circumstance he might have also derived a predilection for the theatre."[51] Whether being a royalist led to a love of theatre or a love of theatre led to royalism, both James's royalism and his interest in old plays can be traced to his father.

Wright went beyond simply advising his son about where to purchase books; on the first page of the dramatic miscellany, Wright indicated what and how his son should read: "Marke Montague Sydnam The voiage to the Levant. Herberts poems Maines and Shirleys play ffelthams resolves."[52] He saw reading as a means to increase vocabulary: "for words that are new, your English dictionary will alone suffice."[53] The final instruction Wright left his son was, "Mark Sydenham for penning epistles and imitate him. Take out of these some expressions and make common use of them upon their several occasions. See for the names of each play page 43."[54] Here, Wright advocated commonplacing: James is to look for expressions that he can use in conversation or writing. Moreover, Wright's table of contents emphasizes his intentions to excerpt from plays specifically, that is, to create a dramatic miscellany. Wright offered his own commonplaced dramatic extracts as a practical tool for self-improvement, a common feature advertised by print miscellanies.

To conclude the analysis of Wright, it seems fitting to turn to the dedicatory epistles with which he often opened his dramatic excerpts, as they offer an example of both his royalist political motivations and his desire to use dramatic extracts as a form of self-improvement. For instance, Wright excerpted from the epistle to *The Lady of Pleasure*, "If it meet with your Lordships acceptance, you shal forever by this favour oblige, / My Lord, / The most humble services / of your honourer / James Shirly."[55] These extracts from the dedications offer a model for correspondence, which can be used for self-improvement. The epistles that he chose to copy show deference to an artistic patron and a respect for patronage that reinforces notions of nobility and hierarchy, perhaps elements of an inherently royalist attitude. Wright copied excerpts from eleven Shirley plays, and generally copied at least a few lines from the epistle. The three notable times he skipped the epistle were when the dedicatee was one of Shirley's friends instead of a noble patron: *The Schoole of Complement*, dedicated to William Tresham; *The Contention for Honour and Riches*, dedicated to Edward Golding; and *The Wedding*, dedicated to William Gowre.[56] The majority of dedications Wright copied are to noble patrons, including the Earls of Rutland, Holland, and Newcastle, and Lords Berkeley and Lovelace.[57] Wright's choice of dedications reflects his interests in acquiring appropriate language to improve himself while also reinforcing the aristocratic hierarchy.

The plays from which Wright chose to excerpt and his selection of excerpts, including his particular interest in dedicatory epistles, demonstrates his royalist nostalgia. Wright chose to read not only pre-civil war theatre but also plays published when the theatres were closed. Perhaps most important, however, this manuscript demonstrates the perceived value of dramatic extracting in the mid-seventeenth century and the ways in which it could be simultaneously edifying, educational, and political. Furthermore, this manuscript reveals one of the ways that extracts circulated: by being passed along in completed manuscripts from father to son. For Wright, it was not just the act of reading and commonplacing that would be of value to his son but also the pre-selected dramatic extracts that Wright himself judiciously copied.

JOHN COTGRAVE'S *ENGLISH TREASURY OF WIT AND LANGUAGE*

Unlike Wright's royalist dramatic miscellany, John Cotgrave's *English Treasury of Wit and Language*, which contains more than 1,500 extracts from plays, is a more ambiguously political text.[58] In some cases, such as Wright's, a manuscript compiler assembled texts that support a particular viewpoint, whereas in other miscellanies, compilers sought dialogic or even contradictory texts.[59] Cotgrave's collection does not offer a single position: rather, the *English Treasury* by its polyvocal nature expresses multiple viewpoints. Cotgrave's collection of these disparate voices (of both different playwrights and different characters) puts these selected ideas in dialogue with one another. Although Cotgrave was a major proponent of theatre, his personal political views were republican, that is, pro-parliament yet anti-Protector. Understanding Cotgrave's miscellany requires reconsidering the impact of his source texts in light of changing historic circumstances.

Cotgrave defended his choice to excerpt from drama alone, unlike previous miscellanies that appropriated from primarily poetical sources: "the Dramattick Poem seemes to me (and many of my friends, better able to judge then I) to have been lately too much slighted, not onely by such, whose Talent falls short in understanding, but by many that have had a tolerable portion of Wit, who through a stiffe and obstinate prejudice, have (in neglecting things of this nature) lost the benefit of many rich and usefull Observations."[60] By calling plays "dramatic poems," Cotgrave highlighted their literary nature, making them worthy sources for commonplaces. Cotgrave asserted that theatre is a useful source of wisdom and situated his work as continuing a strong intellectual legacy: just as the playwrights "culled the choicest Flowers out of the greater number of Greeke, Latin, Italian, Spanish, and French Authors," he excerpted the "best . . . taken out of the best" for his reader.[61]

Cotgrave expressed his nostalgia by praising dramatists as "the most fluent . . . Wits that this age (or I thinke any other) ever knew."[62] He positioned his miscellany as a response to the closing of the theatres: theatre has "been lately too much slighted" and people have been prejudiced against plays. Along with his dramatic miscellany, Cotgrave published another miscellany, *Wits Interpreter* (1655), that includes a number of dramatic extracts.[63] Despite being an avid dramatic extractor and theatre lover during the interregnum, Cotgrave did not hold anti-parliamentary views.

Cotgrave has also been credited with *The Muses Mistresse: Or, A Storehouse of Rich Fancies* (1660), a political poem that touches on interregnum theatre.[64] Although the title page promises "other high Rapsodies, extracted from the choicest Wits of our Age," *The Muses Mistresse* is not a collection of extracts like *The English Treasury* or *Wits Interpreter* but rather, two complete poems. The second poem ("Upon the late *Babel Parliament*; no less pitifully then penitently Dissolv'd by the late last *Protector*, Innocent Dick *Cromwel*") discusses the 1659 third protectorate parliament and takes a republican stance: this poem trumpets the "Good Old Cause."[65] *The Muses Mistresse* points to the persistence of theatre in the interregnum, with a tone that suggests both Parliament's lack of power and, perhaps, the indomitability (and costliness) of theatre: "The *Cock-pit* holds up still for all the cost / Bestow'd on *Drakes Fleet* and the *Savage Roast* / The *Siege of Rhodes* too."[66] These lines mention Davenant's operas, *The Siege of Rhodes* (1656) and *The History of Sir Francis Drake* (1659), while also alluding to *The Cruelty of the Spaniards in Peru* (1658): the "Savage Roast" refers to the fifth entrance, when two Spaniards enter, "the one turning a Spit, whilst the other is basting an *Indian* Prince, which is rosted at an artificiall fire."[67] This gentle jabbing at Davenant's operas, compared to some of the more biting lines in the poem, reflects a nostalgia for earlier theatre. The poem's final line, "*Prynns* prating must not make them change their note" criticizes

William Prynne (noted for his anti-theatrical polemic, *Histrio-mastix*), for his attack on republicanism, *The Good Old Cause rightly stated* (1659). While Cotgrave's association with *The Muses Mistresse* and his probable involvement with parliament-friendly newspapers (including *The Court Mercurie* and *Le Mercure Anglois*) cannot be cemented with absolute certainty,[68] they align with his positive views on both parliament and theatre.

Although Cotgrave was not affiliated with the royalists, both of his works that contain dramatic extracts were published by royalists: Nathaniel Brooke published *Wits Interpreter* and Humphrey Moseley published *The English Treasury*.[69] I further discuss the importance of Moseley's play publication and his publication of dramatic extracts in relation to *Hesperides*, below. Brooke's royalist sympathies are evident in *Englands Glory* (1660), a collection of various catalogues mainly having to do with nobility and peerage, "made since his Majestie's happy Restoration."[70] John H. Astington suggests that the pieces in *Wits Interpreter* are not particularly politicized; even those extracts taken from royalist writers are removed from their political contexts. I posit that the political elements in *The English Treasury* are not absent, but altered. I further contend that the extracts do not present only one political view, but many, most of which can and should be read in relation to mid-century politics.

Cotgrave's commonplace headings and extracts show a preoccupation with the themes of Elizabethan and, primarily, Stuart drama: "Of Cuckolds," "Of the City, &c," "Of Inconstancy," and "Of Swearing, Forswearing, &c."[71] And while some of his other headings, such as "Of Warre," "Of Tyrannie, Tyrants," and "Of Rebellion and Sedition"[72] are classical commonplace headings that have been used for ages, these sections are particularly politically charged because of when they were published. For instance, the mid-century republicanism that Cotgrave espoused can be seen in "States trespasse not, Tyrants they be that swerve, / And bring upon all Empire age or death, / By making truth but onely Princes breath," from Sir Fulke Greville's *Mustapha*, an earlier play that could not purposefully comment on these later contexts.[73] Commonplace headings resituate the extracts and focus the reader on one particular idea from what can often be a nuanced source text.

Dramatic extracts gain different meaning over time and in changing historic circumstances. Extracts, like republished plays, are by their nature often situated in a new historic moment that is not the moment of originary authorship, initial performance, or first publication. Furthermore, extracts highlight particular portions of the original, which can heighten their impact. Although many of the sayings Cotgrave selected can be seen as simply sententious, others can be read as topical, and, notably, topical in relation to events that the playwrights themselves could not have foreseen.

Cotgrave's dramatic extracts reflect the turbulent time after the execution of King Charles I. In Cotgrave's miscellany, a selection from George

Chapman's *Revenge of Bussy D'Ambois* could refer to Oliver Cromwell, who by 1655 was firmly ensconced as Lord Protector of England: "Woe be to that State / Where treachery guards, and ruine makes men great."[74] Philip Massinger's words from *The Great Duke of Florence* seem to support an absolutist monarchy even while prophesying the abolishment of the weakened English monarchy: "The Prince, that pardons / The First affront offer'd to Majesty / Invites a second, rendring that power / Subjects should tremble at, contemptible."[75] Conversely, James Shirley's words from *The Gratefull Servant* oppose the divine right of kings in relation to tyrants. This extract from Shirley could not help but to conjure images of Charles's beheading in readers: "It is not breath / Can fright a noble truth, nor is there Magick / In the person of a King that playes the Tyrant, / But a good sword can easily uncharm it."[76] Shirley's lines, when applied to Charles's execution, liken the murder of a king not to sin or treason, but rather to a demystification of magic. While Chapman, Massinger, and Shirley were not themselves writing about Charles's downfall, Cotgrave's readers would likely have seen resonances with current or recently past events. These extracts from Chapman, Massinger, and Shirley point to the polyvocality of this collection; *The English Treasury* is neither a straightforwardly parliamentary nor royalist work.

Cotgrave's heading "Of Allegiance, Subjection" contains similarly self-contradictory materials. The connotations of the words in the heading itself suggest the conflicting valences of the extracts: while allegiance seems positive enough, subjection is not always positive. In Randle Cotgrave's (John's father's) French-English dictionary, "subjection" is equated with "thraldome, servitude, obedience; restraint, limitation."[77] Some of Cotgrave's excerpts extol the virtue of allegiance, such as this selection from Samuel Daniel's *Philotas*: "God gives to Kings the honour to command / To subjects all their glory to obey."[78] Other extracts suggest the limits of loyalty should be within reason: "Allegiance / Tempted too far, is like the triall of / A good sword on an Anvil, as that often / Flyes in pieces without service to the owner."[79] Another extract from *Valentinian* expresses precisely this ambivalence:

> No more, (my worthy friend) though these be truths,
> And though these Truths would ask a Reformation,
> At least a little squaring; yet remember,
> We are but Subjects, whose obedience
> To what is done, and griefe for what is ill done,
> Is all we can call ours: The hearts of Princes
> Are like the Temples of the Gods, pure incense
> (Untill unhallowed hands defile those offerings)
> Burns ever there, we must not put them out,
> Because the Priests that touch those sweets are wicked.[80]

This speaker suggests that allegiance and obedience are required, but not necessarily positive because there are past and ongoing injustices. The unclear resolution of conflicting opinions in *The English Treasury* is heightened by the multiple possible referents: concepts of allegiance and obedience could be applied not only to Charles but also to Oliver Cromwell, the Lord Protector. These extracts do not offer a clear-cut moral or political vision, but rather, highlight the instability of Cotgrave's time.

Cotgrave's selection and publication of these dramatic extracts repurposed older material and brings it to bear on present events. One of the most interesting subject headings in this collection is "Of Warre," which is not even a page and a half long (although many other subjects are equally short, the next subject in *The English Treasury*, "Of Whores," runs for five and a half pages). The snippets from plays reflect disillusionment about the effect of war: "The Wars are dainty Dreames to young hot spirits / Time and exeperience will allay those Visions."[81] Cotgrave's decontextualized extract from *Pericles* is given more credibility and sententiousness than in Shakespeare's original play; in the play, the passage is spoken by Boult when attempting to rape the virtuous virgin Marina, whereas Cotgrave's selection could be a genuine condemnation of war from the point of view of a poor soldier: "Would you have me go / To the Wars where a man may serve seven years / For the losse of a Leg, and have not money / Enough in the end, to buy him a woodden one?"[82] Although Cotgrave harvested quotations that reflect the horror of war ("all the Murthers Rapes, and thefts / Commited in the horrid lust of War"),[83] some of the extracts suggest that wars are at times necessary: "All Wars are bad, yet sometimes they do good" and "The pangs of War are like to Child-bed Throes, / Bitter in suffering, but the storm being past, / The talk, as of 'scap'd ship wrack sweet doth tast."[84] In his choice of extracts, Cotgrave does not glorify war as a noble endeavor, but perhaps his parliamentary leanings led him to believe that the English civil wars were a necessary evil. Although the plays gathered together in *The English Treasury* were written over the course of decades, Cotgrave brings them to bear on the post-civil war England.

Cotgrave's extracts comment not only on the political situation of the interregnum but also on the closure of the theatres. Under the heading "Of Playes, Players," Cotgrave's selections show the difficulty actors faced in their time:

> Players
> Were never more uncertain in their lives,
> They know not what to play, for fearfull fools,
> Where to play, for Puritan fools, nor what
> To play, for Criticall fools.[85]

These lines from Thomas Middleton's *A Mad World My Masters* were first published in 1608, but by 1655 when they reappear in *The English*

Treasury, the "Puritan fools" had closed the theatres. Cotgrave's other extracts under this subject heading point to theatre's positive effects: he cites Hamlet's attestation that criminals attending a play have be so affected that "they have proclaim'd their malefactions."[86] Cotgrave also quoted from the anonymous *Tragedy of Nero* on how theatre brings out the best in its audiences, "The shews of things are better then themselves / How doth it stir this aery part of us: / To hear our Poets tell imagin'd sights."[87] Cotgrave's opening for this section admits the shortcomings of certain performances: "We must have nothing brought now upon Stages / But Puppetry, and pyed ridiculous Anticks" but continues to say that good theatre "makes the place / Holy and sacred."[88] In the context of his dramatic miscellany, Cotgrave's choice phrases about theatre are, like his prefatory material, a justification of the value of good plays. These dramatic extracts that emphasize the significance of theatre would have been particularly pointed during the years when the theatres were closed. Cotgrave's subject heading, "Of Playes, Players," and his selected extracts highlight the power of theatre.[89] Even more important, Cotgrave's chosen genre, dramatic extracts, implicitly values plays.

By compiling *The English Treasury*, Cotgrave both valued plays and showed the worth of commonplacing from plays. Although, or perhaps because, dramatic extracting was widely practiced, it was also criticized. As early as 1598, Marston satirized Luscus, a character who "writes," "railes," "jests," and "courts" by using the dramatic extracts he had once copied into manuscript:

> Now I have him, that nere of ought did speake
> But when of playes and Plaiers he did treat.
> H'ath made a common-place booke out of plaies,
> And speakes in print, at least what ere he sayes
> Is warranted by Curtaine *plaudeties*
> If ere you heard him courting *Lesbias* eyes;
> Say (Curteous Sir) speakes he not movingly
> From out some new pathetique Tragedie?
> He writes, he railes, he jests, he courts, what not
> And all from out his huge long scraped stock
> Of well penn'd playes.[90]

In Jonson's *Volpone* (1607), the foolish Sir Politic Would-be has "none, but notes, / Drawne out of Play-bookes."[91] John Stephens ridiculed a fictional lawyer's clerk who "woes [woos] with bawdery in text; and with Jests, or speeches stolne from Playes, or from the common-helping *Arcadia*."[92] Similarly, Thomas Tomkis included a clown, Trincalo, in his play *Albumazar* who garners laughs by suggesting how he will reuse commonplaces from plays: "then will I confound her with complements drawne from the Plaies

I see at the Fortune, and Red Bull, where I learne all the words I speake and understand not."[93] One late-seventeenth century writer felt the need to begin his tract on commonplacing by refuting the anti-commonplace attitudes: "Because some make *too much ado about* collections, and lean so upon others's sentiments, that they neglect the exercise of their own judgments, . . . many have a common place against common places and cry down all collections as a useless drudgery."[94] Some critics argued that creating one's own commonplace book had value, where turning to a printed commonplace book was intellectual laziness. Cotgrave's introduction attempted to pre-empt such criticisms by presenting his book as a much-needed shortcut for people who would not be able to read all of the complete plays:

> if *Salomon* could say, That the reading of many Bookes is wearinesse to the flesh, when there were none but Manuscripts in the world: How much is that wearinesse increased since the [a]rt of Printing has so infinitely multiplyed large and vast volums in every place, that the longest life of a man is not sufficient to explore so much as the substance of them, which (in many) is but slender? Extractions therefore are the best conservers of knowledge, if not the readiest way to it.[95]

Cotgrave championed not only drama when the theatres were closed but also dramatic extracts when detractors denied their value.

Cotgrave's dramatic miscellany and his other printed dramatic extracts show that both royalists and parliamentarians contributed to dramatic extracting during the turbulent political times after the closure of the theatres—and although he does not share Wright's royalist nostalgia, Cotgrave certainly exhibits a nostalgia for the plays that were no longer being performed. *The English Treasury* was published at a time when people turned to alternative modes of theatrical engagement to fill the void left by closure of the public theatres. Cotgrave's work serves as an example not only of the timely rise of the dramatic miscellany but also as a reminder that dramatic extracting continued in printed sources (particularly miscellanies, commonplace books, and conduct guides) throughout the seventeenth century.

JOHN EVANS'S *HESPERIDES, OR THE MUSES GARDEN*

John Evans's *Hesperides, or The Muses Garden* is a commonplace book with a preponderance of dramatic extracts taken from 177 plays by 31 playwrights.[96] While this might seem like a staggering number of dramatic extracts, they are outnumbered by prose and poetic works. This commonplace book, while not a dramatic miscellany, emerges from the same cultural moment as dramatic miscellanies. *Hesperides* continues the long tradition of both manuscript and printed commonplace books that extract from drama among other literary works. Evans collected the extracts in *Hesperides*, dramatic and otherwise, from print sources and recopied them into manuscript with the intention of publishing a print miscellany. There were originally two manuscript versions of this commonplace book. The Folger Shakespeare library holds the complete edition (Folger MS V.b.93); the other was cut up by James Orchard Halliwell-Phillipps, the nineteenth-century Shakespearean scholar.[97] Evans compiled both versions, probably between 1654 and 1666.[98]

Humphrey Moseley, the publisher of *The English Treasury*, also commissioned Evans's commonplace book for publication. While *Hesperides* was never published, Moseley registered it and advertised it in his other publications.[99] Moseley's advertisement situates *Hesperides* in the tradition of earlier commonplace books that include dramatic extracts by echoing Allott's earlier title page for *Englands Parnassus* (1600), one of the first commonplace books to include dramatic works alongside more serious and respected literature. Moseley wrote that *Hesperides* is "stored with the choicest Flowers of Language and Learning," just as *Englands Parnassus* collected "the choysest Flowers of our Moderne Poets."[100]

Moseley not only made possible the culture of dramatic extracting through his play publication, he also valorized it with his publication of Cotgrave's dramatic miscellany, *The English Treasury of Wit and Language* and his commission and advertisement of *Hesperides*. Moseley was a reputable literary publisher responsible for the publication of many plays (both old and new), including the Beaumont and Fletcher folio of 1647. He published a series of books featuring contemporary royalist poets and also embarked on a project of publishing single-author play anthologies in octavo, including Brome's *Five New Playes* (1653) and Shirley's *Six New Playes* (1653), as well as short collections by Massinger, Lodowick Carlell, and Middleton.[101] David Scott Kastan credits Moseley as an inventor of English literature, publishing vernacular literature and theatrical works that would not have been considered canonical at the beginning of the seventeenth century.[102] Publishing complete plays, printing Cotgrave's dramatic miscellany, and contracting Evans's miscellany that was replete with dramatic extracts is another way he invented English literature: he published the first English print dramatic miscellany and was instrumental in the ongoing culture of mid-seventeenth-century dramatic extracting.

Moseley anticipated that people who read early modern drama would be interested in reading commonplace books: both those filled entirely with dramatic extracts, such as Cotgrave's, and also those that place extracts from theatre alongside extracts from other works. Moseley's twenty-page catalogue listed more than two hundred books available at his shop in St. Paul's, which he divided into different generic categories, including "Various Histories, with curious Discourses in humane Learning, &c," "Severall Sermons, with other exeellent [sic] Tracts in Divinity," "Choyce Poems with excellent Translations," "Incomparable Comedies and Tragedies" and "New and Excellent Romances." He announced recent publications, "Books lately Printed," as well as "Books now in the Presse, and to be Printed," as well as "These Books I purpose to Print, Deo Volente."[103] Moseley astutely marketed literature, even the classics, as a hot commodity. With his list of upcoming publications, Moseley intended to make readers want to stay up-to-date on the latest books printed. Reading extracts was one way to stay abreast of a constantly growing literary and cultural field, and Moseley's catalogue offered the most recent collections, including commonplace books like Cotgrave's *English Treasury* (1655) and Thomas Blount's *The Academie of Eloquence* (1654), as well as miscellanies such as *The Card of Courtship* (1653), and *The Marrow of Complements* (1654).

Moseley's description of *Hesperides* explains what kind of audience he expected to attract in the late 1650s. He did not highlight the prevalence of drama in Evans's work: instead, he explained that it contained "the Fruits of Philosophy, History, & Cosmography, with the sweets of Poetry."[104] While Moseley began his pitch by suggesting *Hesperides* would be of value to "grave and serious minds," which flatters potential buyers, he concluded with what is perhaps a more realistic description of anticipated readers: "and the ceremonious Courtier, the passionate Amourist with his admired Lady, may gather Rarities suitable to their fancies."[105] For Moseley, the audience for printed extracts (or, perhaps, for book buying) was primarily male, but allowed for female readers. And while dramatic extracting in manuscript flourished in the universities in the 1620s and 1630s, by the 1650s, courtiers and hopeful would-bes could easily purchase printed books that included dramatic extracts already "digested into common places."[106]

In many ways, Evans's commonplaces are, indeed, commonplace and generalized, although other extracts are quite specific. He included, for instance, selections that are proverbial and abstracted, such as two extracts from Chapman's *Bussy D'Ambois* under the heading "Life of Man": "Man is a torch borne in the winde; a dreame but of a shadow" and "Man is a tree that hath no top in cares no root in comforts."[107] These phrases lend themselves easily enough to commonplacing: in 1685, Edward Phillips repurposed the latter in his book of commonplaces to be memorized for "wooing" in *The Mysteries of Love and Eloquence*.[108] At times, Evans's commonplace headings provide context to clarify the meaning of his selections. Rather than including Richard II's line "Give me that glass, and therein will I read," Evans began with the king's "No deeper wrinckles yet? Hath sorro^w^ struck so many blows upon this face of mine & made no deeper wounds?"[109] Evans's heading, "looking glass," conjures the visuals of the performed play that add the needed context for these words.

While most of his extracts were commonplaces, Evans occasionally included others that are specific to historical moments and individuals (with a particular emphasis on the classics). One example of this specificity is an excerpt from Robert Burton's *Anatomy of Melancholy* (1621) under the heading "Libraries":

> King James in 1605, when he came to see the university Oxford, & amongst other edifices, went to see that famous library renewed by Sr Thomas bodley; in imitation of Alexander at his departure broke out into that noble speech, If I were not a K[ing] I would be an University man; And if it were so that I must be a prisoner, if I might have my wish, I would desire to have no other prison then that library, & to be chained together by so many good Authors.[110]

Generally, however, the dramatic extracts in *Hesperides* fall into the former category of lines that can be easily removed from the context of the complete work for general application.

Although they were never published, Evans's extracts had enduring value, just as Moseley predicted. Where Evans had filled an entire column with extracts related to "Death," a later reader (and, in a sense, later compiler) added the same heading to the second, blank column, and included the opening of a by-then famous Macbeth soliloquy, probably on the assumption that it was a shame Evans missed it:

> To morrow & to morrow & to morrow
> Creeps in this pretty pace from day to day
> To the last Syllable of recorded time
> And all our yesterdays have lighted fools
> The way to study death. Shakesp. Macb.[111]

This later contributor quoted from the second folio of the works, the only early print source with "study death" instead of "dusty death."[112] In the context of *Hesperides*, this second folio source text is particularly fitting; a person re-reads an old manuscript commonplace book, which, although not quite the "last Syllable of recorded time," is a tangible example of how "all our yesterdays" can help fools "study death." The commonplace book itself allows this later reader to study and comment on death by perusing carefully selected pieces of wisdom on which to ruminate and adding another pearl of wisdom. Although some people criticized the value of using pre-fabricated commonplace books, the practice persisted.[113]

FOLGER MS V.A.87, A DRAMATIC MISCELLANY

Like Cotgrave's *English Treasury* and Wright's manuscript, Folger MS V.a.87 is a dramatic miscellany dating to the closure of the theatres (comp. c. 1650).[114] Unlike other political charged manuscripts, Folger MS V.a.87 serves as an example of how compilers changed dramatic extracts to shape them into commonplaces, those pithy expressions of wisdom, which in turn makes them more applicable and usable.

The Folger Shakepeare Library Catalogue, Hamnet, and the spine of the manuscript misidentify the manuscript compiler as William How. How (which could be an abbreviation for Howard, Howell, or other names) wrote the unfinished revisions of a religious treatise that fills the first four folios of the manuscript and signed it "Willam: How:" on folio 1, but did not copy the bulk of the manuscript. Folios 4v–35 are completely filled with dramatic excerpts, possibly compiled by someone with the initials EC.[115] The manuscript continues with blank yet lined pages until the end (f. 46).

In order to make an extract more broadly applicable and commonplace, EC often omitted the names of characters. Bassanio's line, "Gratiano speaks an infinite deal of nothing, / more than any man in all Venice" becomes "He speakes an infinite deale of nothing."[116] By removing both character-specific and location-specific references, EC made Shakespeare's line more widely applicable. Similarly, EC changed "Piero's triumphs beat the ayre" to "His triumph."[117] EC not only substituted pronouns but also offered generalized synonyms at times: "our king" replaces "Renowned Edward" and "deare" substitutes for "Strotzo."[118] Sometimes, where a pronoun substitution or word replacement would not suffice, EC would mark a place to fill in another name: "Ile shunne all nicenesse; my nam's Florizell" becomes "Ile shun all nices my name = = =."[119] EC employed multiple strategies to remove character names, all with the ultimate goal of generalizing his extracts and making them more commonplace.

Beyond removing character names, EC also abstracted phrases and ideas. As an example, EC changed "th'ast raised / A storm which showers of bloud can hardly [al]lay" to "Heeres a storme showers of bloud can scarse allay" so the line could be more easily used.[120] In another case, the same substitution of "Heeres" generalizes a vivid image from *The Valiant Scot*, where "A murder'd father and a bleeding wife, / Mangled before him, would strike fire in snow" becomes "Heeres injuries would strike fire in snow."[121] By skipping a phrase that is descriptive of a scene in the play, EC distilled the line to one well-phrased yet arresting idea, the notion that something could "strike fire in snow."

The two most common changes throughout the extracts in Folger MS V.a.87 are generalizing, as discussed above, and manipulating the narrative voice, for instance, from first person to third person. Where in *The Dutch*

Courtezan Marston originally wrote, "as deare as the ayre to him," EC adapted it to, "deare as the ayre to mee."[122] The omission of names and shift in speaker at times coincide, as in this example, when the imagined speaker appropriates an action originally attributed to "My Lord Bassanio": "*I* upon more advice have sent you the ring" (emphasis added).[123] Although the compiler, in many cases, appropriated the subject position, in other cases, the quoted extract abdicates the subject position, particularly when the subject is female or unsavory. Where Mary Faugh says, "I ha made as much a your maydenhead," EC chose to copy "Whores make much of their maydenheads."[124] Examining how compilers modify the narrative voice tells us which parts of the play were attractive to readers on a personal level, while also showing how dramatic extracts could be reused.

Some of EC's changes demonstrate a clear motivation for increasing usability. In some cases, EC modernized old-sounding language: "Thou belongest" becomes "You belong."[125] It is tempting to imagine that EC adapted *The Valiant Scot*'s "'tis a favour Her betters sue for" into "Thy bed is a favor betters sue for" as a line to be put to use in courtship.[126] In the play, the "favour" is "a lawfull marriage" discussed in the third person; EC's changes make the line address a woman directly. EC's modifications in this respect are not consistent, however; he changed other lines from direct speech to indirect: "Honour is proud to be thy tytle" becomes "her title."[127] Modernizing language, changing the narrative voice, and generalizing ideas to be more commonplace are all methods for making dramatic extracts more personalized—and even, useful.

The general usefulness of dramatic extracts is perhaps measured in the marginal note EC included next to the first selections from plays in this manuscript. The marginalia reads, "I rest at your your [sic] dispose ES in the list of those you have obliged to you contemne not the name of your true and faithfull honourer EC" (f. 4v; see Figure 3.2). We do not know the exact role(s) ES or EC played in the creation of this manuscript; after all, they could be invented characters. This marginal note nevertheless shows that dramatic extracts could be applied to real-life situations, as it is adapted from two dramatic extracts. The first part appropriates a line in Marston's *The Fawne*, "I rest most dutious to your dispose"; the second part incorporates part of Massinger's dedicatory epistle that prefaced *The Great Duke of Florence*, which reads, "Accept I beseech you the tender of my service, and in the list of those you have obliged to you, contemne not the name of Your true and faithfull honorer."[128] Although EC included the Marston extract later in his manuscript with other extracts from the same play (f. 8v), the extract from the dedicatory epistle does not appear later in the manuscript. For EC, dramatic extracts could be separated from their sources, adapted, and recombined in new patterns. Folger MS V.a.87 exemplifies how abstract play extracts could

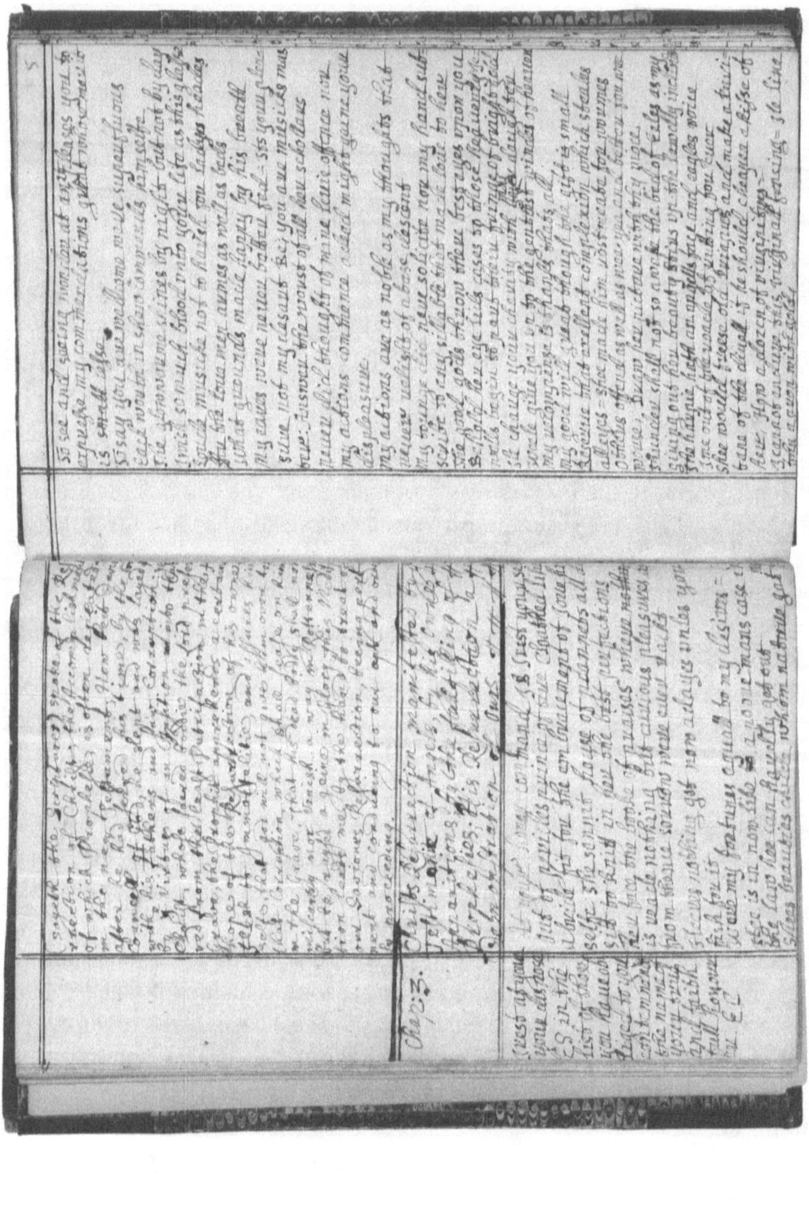

Figure 3.2 Folger MS V.a.87, f. 4v–5. By Permission of the Folger Shakespeare Library.

be altered and put to practical use, as the case of the combined line from *The Fawne* and *The Great Duke of Florence* demonstrates.

EC's dramatic miscellany also reveals how plays that we consider canonical were read and extracted alongside plays that are now rarely studied. Folger MS V.a.87 presents early modern tastes largely at odds with our modern conception of the early modern theatrical canon. EC collected extracts from plays that vary widely in date and genre. The earliest play included is Shakespeare's *Merchant of Venice*, which was written around 1596 and published in 1600; the latest published play excerpted is John Ford's *Fancies, Chast, and Noble* (1638). The plays range from comedies of manners (James Shirley's *The Gamester*) to revenge tragedies (Marston's *Antonio's Revenge*), to farce (Chapman's *Sir Gyles Goosecappe*). The plays were primarily performed in commercial theatres, with the exception of Peter Hausted's *Rivall Friends*, which was presented for King Charles and Queen Henrietta Maria at Cambridge in March 1632; and Chapman's *Caesar and Pompey*, which was likely never performed in a public theatre.[129] Dramatic miscellanies offer particularly valuable insight into the relative popularity of plays because they were compiled by readers who were interested in theatre and who had access to printed plays. (See Table 3.2 for the contents of Folger MS V.a.87.) Although it may seem evident, these wide-ranging selections in Folger MS V.a.87 remind us that early modern readers were faced with more plays than are found in our modern anthologies. Even EC's choice of Shakespeare's plays, particularly *Pericles*, might seem unexpected. Furthermore, Folger MS V.a.87 (like Wright's miscellany) serves as a reminder that readers used books that we now sometimes consider "bad quartos." Continued work on dramatic extracts can contribute to the ongoing recovery of overlooked authors and maligned editions, all while turning to manuscripts that are often ignored or under-explored.

It is not only the amount copied from each play that reveals EC's tastes but also the parts of the plays that EC selected. EC's selections from Massinger's plays reveal his preference for *The Maid of Honour* over *The Great Duke of Florence*. EC stopped copying selections from *The Great Duke of Florence* after act two scene one; he may have abandoned reading the play at this point too, turning instead to Hausted's *Rivall Friends*. Conversely, EC transcribed copious amounts from *The Maid of Honour*, including some scenes almost in their entirety. Without speech prefixes, EC's selections cannot serve as an abridgment: instead, his extensive extracts, from both *The Maid of Honour* and *Fancies, Chast and Noble*, reflect the depth of his engagement with these plays. EC, like many other early modern readers, read plays in their entirety, yet found them valuable for their parts.

In many ways, Folger MS V.a.87 exemplifies the dramatic miscellanies discussed in this chapter and the next. These miscellanies are taken from

Table 3.2 The contents of Folger MS V.a.87.

Title (Normalized)	Author	First Published	Folio(s)
Pericles	Shakespeare	1609	4v–5v
Merchant	Shakespeare	1600	5v, 6
Henry V (uses the "bad quarto")	Shakespeare	1600	5v, 6
Hyde Park	Shirley	1637	6r–v, 12v–14v
The Bondman	Massinger	1624	6v–7
Sophonisba	Marston	1606	7, 12r–v
The Raging Turk	Goffe	1631	7r–v
The Isle of Gulls	Day	1606	7v–8v
The Fawn	Marston	1606	8v–9
The Dutch Courtesan	Marston	1605	9r–v
Tragedy of Nero	Anon	1624	10–11
Antonio and Mellida	Marston	1602	11r–v
Antonio's Revenge	Marston	1602	11v–12
Hyde Park	Shirley	1637	13v–13bv
The Insatiate Countess	Marston	1613	14r–v
The Gamester	Shirley	1637	14v–17
The Valiant Scot	J. W. Gent	1637	17v–18v
The Example	Shirley	1637	18v–21v[1]
Sir Giles Goosecappe	Chapman	1606	21v
The Great Duke of Florence	Massinger	1636	21v–22v
Rival Friends	Hausted	1632	22v–24
Caesar and Pompey	Chapman	1631	24
Maid of Honour	Massinger	1632	24–30
Fancies, Chaste and Noble	Ford	1638	30–33
The Phoenix	Middleton	1607	33

[1]This page range includes f. 20br–v.

plays published both in folio and quarto, collected and individual, first and later editions, authoritative and bad quartos. EC, like Wright and Cotgrave, chose and carefully crafted his extracts. Like Wright, EC saw a value in repurposing both drama and its paratexts. EC's extracts could easily be dismissed as reductive because they abridge and generalize the original sources. We need to consider EC's extracts as reductions: not in the sense of simplifications or lessening, but in the sense of distilled concentrations. While many compilers sought out commonplaces in drama, they also changed selections from drama so it would be more commonplace.

PLUS ÇA CHANGE

This chapter has focused on dramatic miscellanies from 1642 to 1660 period, although during this period dramatic extracts continued to be copied in commonplace books, verse miscellanies, songbooks, and other manuscripts.

While this discussion so far has concentrated on the changing ways of copying dramatic extracts, that is, in dramatic miscellanies, it has elided another way dramatic extracts circulated. As in the earlier decades, the majority of dramatic extracts were songs, which were often disseminated separately from the plays. The compilers discussed in depth—Wright, Evans, EC, and Cotgrave—preferred to copy short non-musical passages. Other manuscript compilers, conversely, included a preponderance of songs, and may not have been copying from complete versions of the plays. To conclude the chapter, I gesture to the ongoing dramatic extracting that continued unchanged after the closure of theatres and point to further avenues for research.

As this section will show, the circulation of songs from plays persisted unabated after the closure of the theatres. This is perhaps unsurprising, as songs were often written separately from the play, could be easily memorized, and often appeared in songbooks and verse miscellanies. The other major point of continuity after the theatres closed is that people still turned to printed plays as a source of commonplaces. While commonplacing from plays is highlighted by the dramatic miscellanies of this period, dramatic-extracts-as-commonplaces can also be found amid non-dramatic commonplaces in traditional commonplace books that draw from diverse genres and authors.

Many of the same songs that were popular in early seventeenth-century manuscripts were still copied and recopied in mid-century manuscripts. For instance, Shirley's "Glories of our Blood and State" from *The Contention of Ajax and Ulysses*, one of the most popular songs in manuscript before the closure of the theatres, continued to circulate afterwards as well as through the Restoration and into the eighteenth century. As a nationalist anthem, the song eclipsed the dramatic work in terms of recognizability and importance.[130] This piece is still anthologized to this day.

As this chapter has demonstrated, miscellanies can provide politicized new contexts for extracts or can host generalized and abstracted extracts. Like "The Glories of our Blood and State," a pastoral song from Shirley's *The Cardinal*, "Come my Daphne, Come away," also circulated separately from the play, and is found in more than one royalist manuscript: the diary of a royalist soldier, Richard Symonds (BL MS Harley 944, copied 1645) and a collection that "reflect[s] the taste of Interregnum Royalist sympathisers" (University College London MS Ogden 42, comp. late 1650s).[131] Other popular songs, such as "Hence all you vain delights" from Middleton's (or perhaps Fletcher's) *The Nice Valour*, were also co-opted into royalist publications during the mid-century period.[132] At the other end of the continuum, songs from plays and masques were gathered into songbooks by compilers with more interest in the musical and artistic value of the pieces than their political importance, such as John Hilton's songbook, BL MS Add. 11608, or Henry Lawes's songbook, BL MS Add. 53723.[133]

Songs also continued to appear in verse miscellanies written as poems; for instance, Bodleian MS Don. d. 58 includes three Jonson songs: "Have you seene the white lillye grow" from *The Devil is an Ass*; "If I freely may discover" from *Poetaster*; and the second verse of "Still to be neat" from *Epicoene*.[134] The adapted verse from "Still to be neat" is titled "His choice" and runs as follows:

> Give me â forme, give me â face
> To which simplicitye adds grace
> Robes loose hanging, haire as free
> This sweete neglect more pleaseth me
> Then all th'adulteries of art
> those catch the eye, but these the heart.[135]

Although this version varies from the original in diction, it maintains the original message of the poem. The first poem at the top of the page is titled "wooeing stuffe"; the poem directly below is titled "Councell" and describes "She that will eate her breakfast in her bed."[136] The bottom poem on the page, "How to chuse a wife" begins, "A maiden faire I dare not wedd."[137] In this case, the second verse of "Still to be neat" contributes to a chorus of voices on similar issues: its message amplifies and is amplified by the poems that surround it. The songs in Bodleian MS Don. d. 58 are not differentiated from the poems that surround them, as is the case with many early miscellanies. Songs, both from plays and not, existed as both musical creations and poetic texts without musical contexts.

Mid-century manuscripts, like those earlier and later, reflect the interests of their compilers. The compiler of BL MS Harley 3889 was interested in Sir John Suckling's *Aglaura* and began copying the play from the beginning, but trailed off before finishing the first act.[138] Bodleian MS Don. e. 6, a mid-seventeenth-century miscellany compiled by the Cartwright family of Aynho, offers an array of material in multiple hands, including one short line from *Sejanus*: "A Passive fortitude to suffer & be silentes."[139] Below it, in a different hand, is a line from one of Jonson's poems, which varies wildly from the first in both tone and topic: "Do all that 'longs to th'Anarchy of drinke except the Duell."[140] As with earlier manuscripts, we cannot expect thematic unity or uniformity.

While this chapter has focused on dramatic miscellanies, there are dozens more manuscripts with dramatic extracts from the mid-century period that require further analysis. Moreover, the dramatic miscellanies discussed at length in this chapter can and should receive more attention: each extract can illuminate our understanding of both the text and its early readers. Dramatic miscellanies, in particular, will be of use to future editors, as they often offer longer sequences of extracts that provide particular readings of plays and give tangible evidence of how particular readers approached the text.

Mid-century dramatic extracting continued directly from earlier traditions while also changing in response to the closure of theatres and the politically charged time. Many manuscripts from this period (as well as Cotgrave's print *English Treasury*) reveal a theatrical nostalgia. If the advent of dramatic extracting in the 1590s marked drama's arrival as a form of literature, the mid-seventeenth-century development of dramatic miscellanies shows that theatre began to be seen as an important genre in its own right. As the next chapter will demonstrate, dramatic extracting, both in dramatic miscellanies and other kinds of manuscripts, continued after Charles II reopened the theatres in 1660. Analyzing these later dramatic extracts reveals that, as in earlier periods, Restoration readers and playgoers held a wide range of attitudes toward Elizabethan and Stuart drama. Chapter 4 continues to prove how the reception and meaning of an extract, a play, or writer's oeuvre changes when we consider individual readers and particular moments of reception.

NOTES

1. C. H. Firth and R. S. Rait, eds, *Acts and Ordinances of the Interregnum, 1642–1660*, 3 vols. (London: His Majesty's Stationery Office, 1911): 1.26-27.

2. Aston Cockayne, "A Præludium to Mr. Richard Bromes Playes," in *Five New Playes* by Richard Brome (1653), sig. A2. For more on the publication of plays when the theatres were closed, see David Scott Kastan, "Performances and Playbooks: the closing of theatres and the politics of drama" in *Reading, Society, and Politics in Early Modern England*, ed. Kevin Sharpe and Steven N. Zwicker (Cambridge: Cambridge University Press, 2003), 167–84.

3. For a discussion of theatre from 1642–1660, see Lois Potter, *Secret Rites and Secret Writing: Royalist Literature, 1641–1660* (Cambridge: Cambridge University Press, 1989); Nigel Smith, *Literature and Revolution in England, 1640–1660* (New Haven, CT: Yale University Press, 1994); Dale BJ Randall, *Winter Fruit: English Drama 1642–1660* (Lexington, KY: University Press of Kentucky, 1995); and Leslie Hotson, *The Commonwealth and Restoration Stage* (Cambridge, MA: Harvard University Press, 1938).

4. For examples of theatre and theatrical tropes used by Parliamentarians and for examples of actions by royalists against theatre, see Susan Wiseman, *Drama and Politics in the English Civil War* (Cambridge: Cambridge University Press, 1998); Lois Potter, "The Plays and the Playwrights: 1642–1660," in *The Revels History of Drama in English*, vol. 4, ed. Philip Edwards, Gerald Eades Bentley, Kathleen McLuskie, and Lois Potter (London and New York: Methuen, 1981), 261–306; and N. W. Bawcutt, "Puritanism and the Closing of the Theaters in 1642," *Medieval and Renaissance Drama in England* 22 (2009): 179–200. Wiseman warns against automatically associating theatre with royalism.

5. Janet Clare, *Drama of the English Republic 1649–1660* (Manchester: Manchester University Press, 2002), esp. 21. For more on songs from plays and their use in drolls, see Mary Chan's "Drolls, Drolleries, and Mid-Seventeenth-Century Dramatic Music in England," *Royal Musical Association Research Chronicle* 15 (1979): 117–73, which offers in-depth commentary on BL MS Add. 29396. For more on specific manuscripts related to drolls, see Chan's "Edward Lowe's Manuscript British Library MS Add. 29396," *Music & Letters* 59 (1978): 440–54 and "John Hilton's Manuscript British Library MS Add. 11608," *Music & Letters* 60 (1979): 440–49.

6. Although Marsh's collection was published after the Restoration, it contains pre-Restoration drolls.

7. John James Elson, ed., *The Wits, or Sport Upon Sport* (Ithaca and London: Cornell University Press and Oxford University Press, 1932), esp. 19.

8. As Smith explains, there was "a remarkable transformation of literary activity during the central years of the [seventeenth] century" (*Literature and Revolution*, 23).

9. Peter Beal, *A Dictionary of English Manuscript Terminology* (Oxford: Oxford University Press, 2010), 255.

10. A verse or poetical miscellany is "a compilation of predominantly verse texts, or extracts from verse texts" (Beal, *Dictionary*, 429). A commonplace book contains sayings and quotations that the compiler can later employ.

11. The Folger Shakespeare Library's online catalogue, Hamnet (http://shakespeare.folger.edu), labels Folger MS V.a.87 a dramatic miscellany, but no scholar has clearly defined this term.

12. For more on history of dramatic extracting and the *flores poetarum* tradition, see Hilton Kelliher, "Contemporary Manuscript Extracts from Shakespeare's *Henry IV, Part 1*," *English Manuscript Studies 1100–1700* 1 (1989): 159–61.

13. *Floures for Latine spekynge selected and gathered oute of Terence* (1534). For more information, see Chapter 1, n. 16.

14. The Folger Library catalogue, Hamnet, does not differentiate between a dramatic miscellany and anthology, so some anthologies of full-text plays, such as Folger MS V.b.222, are labeled dramatic miscellanies.

15. For more on the practice of binding full-text plays into larger volumes, see Jeffrey Todd Knight, "Making Shakespeare's Books: Assembly and Intertextuality in the Archives," *Shakespeare Quarterly* 60 (2009): 304–40 and *Bound to Read: Compilations, Collections, and the Making of Renaissance Literature* (Philadelphia: University of Pennsylvania Press, 2013).

16. The Boston Public Library includes quite a few examples of these "composite dramatic anthologies," some of which are thematically organized, like a collection of multiple editions of *Philaster* (G.3967.6) and a series of Thomas Middleton plays (G.3974.40).

17. John Marston, *The Scourge of Villanie* (1598), sig. H4.

18. For further information on Wright's life, see Stephen Wright, "Wright, Abraham 1611–1690," *ODNB* and Peter Beal, introduction to *Parnassus Biceps*, comp. Abraham Wright (Aldershot, UK: Scolar, 1990).

19. Wright's manuscript is a dramatic miscellany because it comprises primarily extracts from drama; the selections from Fuller's *Holy Wars* (ff. 101v–110v) make

up less than a quarter of the extracts, the rest of which are taken from drama. The manuscript has a modern binding.

20. Wright's manuscript is one of only a handful (such as BL MS Lansdowne 1185, discussed in Chapter 4) that contains extracts alongside commentary. John Newdigate included dramatic excerpts in his 1601 summary of Marlowe's *Edward II* (Warwickshire County Record Office, CR 136/B690). See Siobhan Keenan, "Reading Christopher Marlowe's *Edward II*: The Example of John Newdigate in 1601" *Notes and Queries* 53 (2006): 452–58. Keenan explains that Newdigate read the play (and arguably, copied dramatic extracts) for "implicitly instructive reasons" (458).

21. For a transcription of some the Shakespearean extracts in this manuscript, see James C. McManaway, "Excerpta Quaedam per A.W. Adolescentem," in *Studies in Honor of DeWitt T. Starnes*, ed. Thomas P. Harrison et al. (Austin: University of Texas Press, 1967), 117–29. For a transcription of Wright's commentary on the plays, see Arthur C. Kirsch, "A Caroline Commentary on the Drama," *Modern Philology* 66 (1968): 256–61. It is also worth reading Sasha Roberts's interpretation of the manuscript in regards to Shakespeare's diminishing popularity in the Caroline period and comments on the textual liberties Wright took with *Othello*, in "Reading Shakespeare's Tragedies of Love: *Romeo and Juliet*, *Othello*, and *Antony and Cleopatra* in Early Modern England," in *A Companion to Shakespeare's Works: The Tragedies*, ed. Richard Dutton and Jean Elizabeth Howard (Malden, MA: Blackwell, 2003), 121–22.

22. I follow Harold Love's definition of scribal publication here: Wright's miscellany is an act of user publication, which Love explains is most characteristically "the edition of one, copied by the writer for private use into a personal miscellany or 'commonplace book,'" although it always "involved a transaction between at least two individuals," in this case, Wright and his son. Love, *Scribal Publication in Seventeenth-Century England* (Oxford: Oxford University Press, 1993), 79.

23. I rely on Beal's attribution in his edition of *Parnassus Biceps*, xx–xxiv.

24. Beal, ed., *Parnassus Biceps*, sigs. E3v–E4.

25. Ibid., sig. I5.

26. Ibid., sig. A2v.

27. Arthur F. Marotti, *Manuscript, Print, and the English Renaissance Lyric* (Ithaca: Cornell University Press, 1993), 270. While this miscellany advertises Beaumont and Jonson on the title page, it also includes a poem by James Shirley ("Love's Hue and Cry," sig. Cv–C2).

28. *The Famous Tragedie of King Charles I* (1649), prologue 1–2, sig. A3. See also Wiseman, *Drama and Politics*, 66. For this and other examples, see also Nicholas McDowell, "Milton's Regicide Tracts and the Uses of Shakespeare," in *The Oxford Handbook of Milton*, ed. Nicholas McDowell and Nigel Smith (Oxford: Oxford University Press, 2009), 252–71.

29. Kirsch dates the manuscript to "approximately 1640," noting that "all of the histories and plays Wright copies from were printed before 1640; the latest work is Fuller's *History of the Holy War*, the first edition of which was published in 1639" ("A Caroline Commentary," 256). McManaway dates the composition "no earlier than 1639" and claims that Henry Shirley's *The Martyr'd Soldier* (1638) and James

Shirley's *The Royall Master* (1638) are "the last two plays to be quoted from" ("Excerpta Quaedam per A. W.," 121).

30. To establish that Wright wrote after the closure of the theatres requires showing that he worked from print sources. Wright could not have been copying from performances of the two latest plays, as neither were performed. See Alfred Harbage, *The Annals of English Drama 975–1700*, rev. S. Schoenbaum (London: Methuen, 1964), 134–35; and Dennis Flynn, "Jasper Mayne," *DLB*. It is not unreasonable to assume that Wright copied from print sources in the cases of Mayne's and Peaps's plays, as he copied from print sources for his other extracts, at times noting the page numbers and frequently copying from the dedicatory epistle.

31. Peaps, *Love In it's Extasie* (1649), sig. A2.

32. Annabel Patterson, *Censorship and Interpretation: The Conditions of Writing and Reading in Early Modern England* (Madison: University of Wisconsin Press, 1984). She explains that the popularity of pastoral in the Caroline period was "due in large part to Henrietta Maria's famous preference for pastoral as the expression of *her* personal style, and the encouragement she gave to writers to articulate that style" (147).

33. Randall, *Winter Fruit*, 187.

34. Peaps, *Love In it's Extasie* (1649), sig. A2, punctuation and spacing in the original.

35. Potter, "Plays," 265.

36. Alfred Harbage, *Cavalier Drama: An Historical and Critical Supplement to the Study of the Elizabethan and Restoration stage* (New York: Russell & Russell, 1964), 120.

37. Flynn, "Mayne, Jasper (1604–1672)," *ODNB* and "Jasper Mayne," *DLB*.

38. Mayne's title page includes the Biblical citation in Greek. Here I use the King James Bible for the English.

39. Flynn, "Mayne, Jasper," *ODNB*.

40. Mayne describes the paradox of rebelling against the king: in "our late *Civill Warres*," the "Synedrium" (collection of judges or politicians) "did enact it lawfull / Ith' *Kings* Name to take Armes against Him; And / Out of Obedience to Him to rebell" (*Amorous Warre*, 1648, sig. I).

41. Mayne's poem commending Shakespeare prefaced the 1632 Second Folio. His praise of Ben Jonson (which claims Jonson is "as *rare* / As *Beaumont, Fletcher* or as *Shakespeare* were") is found in *Jonsonus Virbius* (1638, sig. E3-F). Wright also published Mayne's praise of Jonson anonymously in *Parnassus Biceps* (1656, sigs. K-K3).

42. Edward Pudsey, discussed in Chapter 1, similarly bequeathed his manuscript commonplace book to his son, indicating its educational and personal value. See Fred Schurink, "Manuscript Commonplace Books, Literature, and Reading in Early Modern England" *Huntington Library Quarterly* 73 (2010), 466.

43. James Wright, *Country Conversations* (1694), sigs. B1v–B2.

44. Ibid., sig. B2.

45. Ibid., sig. B8v.

46. BL MS Add. 22608, f. 111 (top left-hand margin; see Figure 3.1 and Table 3.1). Henry Shirley's *The Martyred Soldier* was sold at the Marigold. Henry

Shirley has no other surviving plays. The title pages of James Shirley's plays do not announce that they were sold at the Marigold. As David Kathman notes, the Stationer's Register credits Henry Shirley with other now-lost plays, *The Dumb Bawd of Venice* and *The Spanish Duke of Lerma* ("Shirley, Henry (1591x7-1627)," *ODNB*).

47. Elizabeth Sauer, *"Paper-Contestations" and Textual Communities in England, 1640–1675* (Toronto: University of Toronto Press, 2005), 71–72. As Sauer puts it, "At a time when the printed book became identified with the corpus carrying the life and spirit of the author, *Eikon Basilike* in whole and in parts began the process of resuscitating royalism" (71). Eglesfield also published John Gauden's collection of commonplaces from *Eikon Basilike* (1649).

48. The *ESTC* lists Eglesfield as the author of both.

49. Eglesfield was involved in the publication or sale of, for instance, John Rich's *Verses On the blessed and happy Coronation of Charles the II* (1661), William Okeham's *The Preservation Of the King's Majestie's Royal Person* (1664), and the pro-theatre *Theatrum Redivivum* by Richard Baker (1662). Just before the closure of the theatres, Eglesfield published James Shirley's pastoral drama, *The Arcadia* (1640), although this was sold at the sign of the Crane rather than the Marigold.

50. Thomas Warton, ed., *Poems Upon Several Occasions, English, Italian, and Latin, With Translations, by John Milton* (London: James Dodsley, 1785), 601. Available via the Internet Archive, www.archive.org, identifier: poemsuponsevera00wartgoog. See also Theodor Harmsen, "James Wright (*bap.* 1644, *d.* 1716/17)," *ODNB*. Note that this refers to William Cartwright the younger (d. 1686), the actor, not the playwright.

51. Warton, *Poems*, 603.

52. BL MS Add. 22608, f. 69. The first writer mentioned, Montague, is the hardest to identify. Kirsch proposes Sir Henry Montagu, first Earl of Manchester (1563?–1642), the author of *Contemplatio Mortis et Immortalitatis* (1631), who was an administrator in various positions in the Stuart court ("A Caroline Commentary," 260). McManaway proposes Bishop Richard Montague (1575?–1641), who was known as the "Champion of the English Church" and published various theological tracts ("Excerpta Quaedam per A.W.," 129 n.8). Montague could also be Montague Bertie, the second Earl of Lindsey, who was imprisoned in Warwick Castle in 1642 by Parliamentarians for his royalist leanings. "Sydnam" is Humphrey Sydenham (1591–1650), known as "Silver-tongued Sydenham," who published multiple sermons. "The voiage to the Levant" is Henry Blount's travelogue *A Voyage into the Levant* (1636). Owen Felltham's *Resolves Divine, Morall, Politicall* (1623) were revised and published repeatedly.

53. BL MS Add. 22608, f. 69. In the manuscript, this reads, "for words that are nffXXff yr ffnglKsh dictionary will alone suffice." Wright used a simple substitution code: every time he uses a capital letter (such as ff for F), it is intended as the letter before it in the alphabet. Wright evidently intended his son to be able to read the cipher, as he mentions "your English dictionary." In this case, the code that Wright used is simple enough, yet it still creates a private audience for the manuscript, even if it is only an intended audience of one.

54. BL MS Add. 22608, f. 69. Here, Wright's words have been decoded, his abbreviations expanded, spelling and punctuation modernized, and one indecipherable parenthetical reference omitted.

55. BL MS Add. 22608, f. 99v; James Shirley, *The Lady of Pleasure* (1637), sig. A2r-v.

56. For a discussion of James Shirley's patrons, see David Bergeron, *Textual Patronage in English Drama, 1570–1640* (Aldershot, UK: Ashgate, 2006), esp. 203–4.

57. The notable dedication that Wright copies that was not written for a noble is the biting satirical dedication of *The Bird in a Cage* to the Puritan opponent to theatre, William Prynne. Wright's love of the theatre (as demonstrated by his dramatic miscellany) indicates why he might have enjoyed an attack on Prynne.

58. For a description of the contents of *The English Treasury*, see Gerald Eades Bentley, "John Cotgrave's *English Treasury of Wit and Language* and the Elizabethan Drama," *Studies in Philology* 40 (1943): 186–203.

59. For more on the juxtaposition of dissenting texts, see Sasha Roberts, "Women's Literary Capital in Early Modern England: Formal Composition and Rhetorical Display in Manuscript and Print," *Women's Writing* 14 (2007): 246–69.

60. Cotgrave, *English Treasury* (1655), sig. [A]3; p. [iii].

61. Ibid.

62. Ibid.

63. For a thorough discussion of the dramatic extracts in *Wits Interpreter*, see John H. Astington, "Dramatic Extracts in the Interregnum," *Review of English Studies* 45 (2003): 601–14.

64. The *ESTC* credits Cotgrave with *The Muses Mistresse*. Some earlier critics suggest the poems were written by John Cleveland, but Cleveland could not have written these poems because he died in 1658. See Eleanor Withington, "The Canon of John Cleveland's Poetry," *Bulletin of the New York Public Library* 67 (1963): 326–27.

65. Cotgrave, *The Muses Mistresse* (1660), sig. B4.

66. Ibid., sig. C.

67. William Davenant, *The Cruelty of the Spaniards in Peru* (1658), sig. C4.

68. Joseph Frank, *The Beginnings of the English Newspaper 1620–1660* (Cambridge, MA: Harvard University Press, 1961). Frank suggests that Cotgrave edited the pro-Parliament newsletter, *The Court Mercurie* (1644) as well as translated the French pro-Parliament newsletter *Le Mercure Anglois* from November 1645–1648 (102). Cotgrave's ability to translate the latter could stem from his father, Randle Cotgrave, author of one of the most popular French-English dictionaries in England.

69. See Astington, "Dramatic Extracts," for a discussion of the politics of these printers in relation to *Wits Interpreter*, esp. 610–11.

70. *Englands Glory* (1660), title page. According to the *ESTC*, Brooke both published and authored this work.

71. Cotgrave, *English Treasury* (1655), sigs. E8v, D7v, K7, S7v.

72. Ibid., sigs. T8v, T2v, R3v.

73. Ibid., sig. T2v; Fulke Greville, *Mustapha*, 5.3 (1606), sig. Z. Scene divisions from *Mustapha* are taken from the 1633 *Certaine Learned and Elegant Workes of the Right Honorable Fulke Lord Brooke*. In the 1633 edition, this line, "States trespasse not," is highlighted as a commonplace by italics.

74. Cotgrave, *English Treasury* (1655), sig. T3; George Chapman, *Revenge of Bussy D'Ambois* (1613), sig. H2.

75. Cotgrave, *English Treasury* (1655), sig. R4; Philip Massinger, *The Great Duke of Florence* (1636), sig. I3r–v.

76. Cotgrave, *English Treasury* (1655), sig. H7; James Shirley, *The Gratefull Servant* (1630), 54.

77. Cotgrave, *English Treasury* (1655), sig. B4v; Randle Cotgrave, *A Dictionarie of the French and English Tongues* (1611), sig. Eeee6v–Eeee7.

78. Cotgrave, *English Treasury* (1655), sig. B5; Daniel, *Philotas* 1677–78 (in *Certaine Small Poems Lately Printed*, 1605), sig. E6. Line numbers for Daniel's plays are taken from Alexander B. Grosart, ed., *The Complete Works in Verse and Prose of Samuel Daniel*, vol. 3: The Dramatic Works (Printed for Private Circulation, 1885).

79. Cotgrave, *English Treasury* (1655), sig. B4v; Massinger, *The Great Duke of Florence* (1636), sig. E2v.

80. Cotgrave, *English Treasury* (1655), sig. B5; John Fletcher, *Valentinian*, in *Comedies and Tragedies* (1647), 1.3, sig. Aaaaaaa2, p. 3 (the folio is not paginated consecutively).

81. Cotgrave, *English Treasury* (1655), sig. T8v; Fletcher, *Rule a Wife And have a Wife* (1640), sig. A3.

82. Cotgrave, *English Treasury* (1655), sig. V; Shakespeare, *Pericles* 4.6.17-73 (1609), sig. H2, paraphrased and adapted as verse.

83. Cotgrave, *English Treasury* (1655), sig. V; John Webster, *The White Divel* 4.1.8-9 (1612), sig. G. All line numbers from Webster's plays are taken from René Weis, *John Webster: "The Duchess of Malfi" and Other Plays* (Oxford: Oxford University Press, 1996).

84. Cotgrave, *English Treasury* (1655), sig. V; the first extract is a paraphrase from Thomas Dekker, *The Second Part of the Honest Whore* (1630), sig. F4; the second is from J. W., Gent., *The Valiant Scot* (1637), sig. H4.

85. Cotgrave, *English Treasury* (1655), sig. Qr-v; Middleton, *A Mad World My Masters* (1608), sig. G4v.

86. Cotgrave, *English Treasury* (1655), sig. Qv; Shakespeare, *Hamlet* 2.2.592.

87. Cotgrave, *English Treasury* (1655), sig. Qv; *The Tragedy of Nero* (1624), sig. E1v.

88. Cotgrave, *English Treasury* (1655), sig. Q; Chapman, *Revenge of Bussy D'Ambois* (1613), sig. C1v.

89. Cotgrave, *English Treasury* (1655), sig. Q.

90. John Marston, *Scourge of Villanie* (1598), sig. H4, "Satire xi," ll. 41–51.

91. Jonson, *Volpone* 5.4.41-42 (1607), sig. M2.

92. Stephens, *Satyrical Essayes Characters and Others* (1615), 276. For more accounts of people commonplacing from plays, see Tiffany Stern, *Making Shakespeare: From Stage to Page* (London: Routledge, 2004), 20–21. Adam Smyth summarizes the portrayal of "printed miscellanies supplying tired lines for tired wits" in various seventeenth-century plays, including William Cavendish's *The Triumphant Widow*, Thomas Forde's *Love's Labyrinth*, and Richard Brome's *A Jovial Crew* (29–31). Smyth, *"Profit and Delight": Printed Miscellanies in England, 1640–1682* (Detroit: Wayne State University Press, 2004).

93. Thomas Tomkis, *Albumazar* (1615), sigs. C4v-D.

94. Earle Havens, ed., *"Of Common Places, or Memorial Books": A Seventeenth-Century Manuscript from the James Marshall and Marie-Louise Osborn Collection* (New Haven, CT: Beinecke Rare Book and Manuscript Library, 2001), 1.

95. Cotgrave, *English Treasury* (1655), sig. [A]2v; p. [ii].

96. Folger MS V.b. 93, title taken from the Folger Shakespeare Library's Hamnet catalogue (shakespeare.folger.edu). For a detailed discussion of *Hesperides*, see Tianhu Hao, "*Hesperides*, or the Muses' Garden and its Manuscript History," *The Library*, 7th ser., 10 (2009): 372–404, based on an unpublished dissertation ("*Hesperides, or the Muses' Garden:* Commonplace Reading and Writing in Early Modern England," PhD diss., Columbia University, 2006). These numbers are taken from Hao, diss., Appendix IV, 200–2. Unless otherwise noted, references to Hao are to her *Library* article. This manuscript has also been discussed by Gunnar Sorelius, "An Unknown Shakespearian Commonplace Book," *The Library*, 5th ser., 28 (1973): 294–308.

97. The majority of the fragments Halliwell-Phillipps cut up can be found in Folger MSS V.a.75, V.a.79, and V.a.80 as well as in the extensive collection of Halliwell-Phillipps notebooks in the Shakespeare Birthplace Trust Record Office.

98. Hao suggests that one version was completed in the two-year period 1655–1656 ("*Hesperides*," 374–75).

99. Hao, "*Hesperides*," 382. For the Stationer's Register, see August 16, 1655 in G. E. B. Eyre, ed., *A Transcript of the Registers of the Worshipful Company of Stationers from 1640–1708 AD*, 3 vols. (London: privately printed, 1913–14), II.8.

100. "Books Printed for Humphrey Moseley" advertisement number 341, sig. B7v, bound with Edmund Waller, *Poems, &c.* (London: Humphrey Moseley, 1645), shelfmark Bodleian don. f. 144; Allott, *Englands Parnassus* (1600), title page.

101. Marotti, *Manuscript, Print, and the English Renaissance Lyric*, 260; Lindenbaum, "Humphrey Moseley," *DLB*; Paulina Kewes, "'Give me the Sociable Pocket Books': Humphrey Moseley's Serial Publication of Octavo Play Collections," *Publishing History* 38 (1995): 5–21.

102. David Scott Kastan, "Humphrey Moseley and the Invention of English Literature," in *Agent of Change: Print Culture Studies after Elizabeth L. Eisenstein*, ed. Sabrina Alcorn Baron, Eric N. Lindquist and Eleanor F. Shevlin. (Amherst, MA: University of Massachusetts Press, 2007), 105–24.

103. "Books Printed for Humphrey Moseley," bound with Edmund Waller, *Poems, &c.* (London: Humphrey Moseley, 1645), shelfmark Bodleian don. f. 144. There are multiple examples of Moseley's book-lists that market *Hesperides* being bound with full-text plays, such as James Shirley's *Six New Playes* (1653, shelfmark All Souls College Library, Great Library Gallery, pp. 15.13) and Middleton's *No Wit, No Help Like a Woman's* [title normalized] (1653, shelfmark BL Ashley 1160). The lists are not identical.

104. "Books Printed for Humphrey Moseley" advertisement number 341, sig. B7v, bound with Edmund Waller, *Poems, &c.* (London: Humphrey Moseley, 1645), shelfmark Bodleian don. f. 144.

105. Ibid.

106. Ibid., advertisement number 193, sig. a7v. Rather than highlight that the extracts in *The English Treasury* were "Collected Out of the most, and best of our

English Drammatick Poems," Moseley skipped that part of the title page and instead chose to highlight in his book-list that the extracts were "digested into common places." The title page continues by suggesting that these digested extracts are "For Generall Use." See also Peter Beal, "Notions in Garrison: The Seventeenth-Century Commonplace Book," in *New Ways of Looking at Old Texts: Papers of the Renaissance English Text Society, 1985–1991*, ed. W. Speed Hill (Binghamton: Renaissance English Text Society, 1993), 131–47.

107. Folger MS V.b. 93, p. 460; Chapman, *Bussy D'Ambois* (1607), sigs A2, I1v.

108. Phillips, *Mysteries of Love and Eloquence, or The arts of wooing and complementing as they are manag'd in the Spring Garden, Hide Park, the New Exchange . . .* (1685) sig. Bb6.

109. Folger MS V.b. 93, p. 467; Shakespeare, *Richard II* 4.1.276–79 (1616 folio), sig. D2v.

110. Folger MS V.b. 93, p. 458; Burton, *The Anatomy of Melancholy* (1621), sig. Z1v-Z2.

111. Folger MS V.b. 93, p. 184; Shakespeare, *Macbeth*, 5.5.19–23 (1632 folio), sig. PP1v.

112. Shakespeare, *Macbeth* 5.5.23 (1632 folio), sig. PP1v.

113. Beal, "Notions in Garrison," esp. 139, 147.

114. As this manuscript was likely compiled seriatim (there are no blank spaces between plays and extracts), compilation began around 1637–1638. See Table 3.2.

115. Folger MS V.a.87, f. 4v margin. For ease of reference, I will call this compiler EC and use masculine pronouns.

116. Folger MS V.a.87, f. 5v; Shakespeare, *The Merchant of Venice* 1.1.114–16 (1616 folio), sig. O4v.

117. Folger MS V.a.87, f. 11; Marston, *Antonio and Mellida* (1602), sig. B2v.

118. Folger MS V.a.87, ff. 17v, 12; *Valiant Scot* (1637) sig. A3. and Marston, *Antonio's Revenge* (1602), sig. E2.

119. Folger MS V.a.87, f. 11; Marston, *Antonio and Mellida* (1602), sig. C.

120. Folger MS V.a.87, f. 17v; *The Valiant Scot* (1637), sig. B3v.

121. Folger MS V.a.87, f. 18; *The Valiant Scot* (1637), sig. E4.

122. Folger MS V.a.87, f. 9v; Marston, *The Dutch Courtezan* (1605), sig. C4v.

123. Folger MS V.a.87, f. 6; Shakespeare, *The Merchant of Venice* 4.2.6 (1616 folio), sig. Q.

124. Folger MS V.a.87, f. 9v; Marston, *The Dutch Courtezan* (1605), sig. C2v.

125. Folger MS V.a.87, f. 8v; Marston, *The Fawne* (1606), sig. B1v.

126. Folger MS V.a.87, f. 17v; *Valiant Scot* (1637), sig. A4v.

127. Folger MS V.a.87, f. 10; *The Tragedie of Nero* (1624), sig. A3v.

128. Marston, *The Fawne* (1606), sig. B2; Massinger, *The Great Duke of Florence* (1636), sig. A3v.

129. Lauren Mills, ed., introduction to *The Rival Friends* by Peter Hausted (Bloomington: Indiana University Press, 1951), xi. Chapman claims in his dedicatory epistle that *Caesar and Pompey* "never toucht it at the Stage" (1631), sig. A3.

130. For a list of manuscript and print sources of the song, see *CELM*; the Folger Shakespeare Library's *Union First Line Index of English Verse: 13th–19th Century*

(bulk 1500–1800), firstlines.folger.edu; Abigail Williams, ed., Digital Miscellanies Index, Bodleian Library, University of Oxford, http://digitalmiscellaniesindex.org; and Adam Smyth, "An Online Index of Poetry in Printed Miscellanies, 1640–1682," *Early Modern Literary Studies* 8 (2002): 1–9, http://purl.oclc.org/emls/08–1/smyth.htm, index now available here: http://tinyurl.com/3xadpbd.

131. *CELM*. See *CELM* for a list of further manuscripts that contain this song. Smyth mentions songs that parody "Come my Daphne" (*"Profit and Delight,"* 96–97). For a list of print sources that contain this song, including James Shirley's *Poems* (1646), see Gordon J. Callon, ed., *William Lawes: Collected Vocal Music* (Middleton, WI: A-R Editions), 2.122.

132. Wiseman, introduction to *The Nice Valour; or, the Passionate Madman* in *Thomas Middleton: The Collected Works*, ed. Gary Taylor and John Lavagnino (Oxford: Clarendon, 2007), 1679. *CELM* lists a staggering forty-five extant seventeenth-century manuscripts that contain this song, dating from the 1620s to the late seventeenth century (B&F 112–53). A handful of manuscripts (Christ Church, Oxford MS Mus. 350, pp. 64–65; Bodleian MS Mus. Sch. F. 575, f. 7v; BL Egerton MS 2013, f. 3v) include musical settings for the song.

133. See Chan, "John Hilton's Manuscript." Hilton's songbook includes songs from masques and plays by Beaumont and Fletcher, Jonson, James Shirley, and Thomas Randolph. Lawes's songbook includes songs from plays and masques by Jonson, William Cartwright, Beaumont and Fletcher, and Sir John Suckling, as well as the songs from Milton's *Comus*.

134. Bodleian MS Don. d. 58, f. 26v, f. 29, and f. 14, respectively.

135. Bodleian MS Don. d. 58, f. 14; Jonson, *Epicoene*, 1.1.77-82 (1616 folio), sig. Yy2v.

136. Bodleian MS Don. d. 58, f. 14. This poem, sometimes attributed to Matthew Mainwaring, was first printed in *Witts Recreations* (1640) and appears in many verse miscellanies—see the Folger *Index*.

137. Bodleian MS Don. d. 58, f. 14. The poem was first printed in Thomas Deloney's *The Pleasant Historie of John Winchcomb* (1619), which appeared in multiple editions over the first half of the seventeenth century.

138. The compiler does not include the prologue to the court or to the king (both of which were included in the printed editions of 1638 and 1646 and the full-text play in BL MS Royal 18 C. XXV). This version in BL MS Harley 3889 ends in the middle of the first soliloquy (by Ziriff-as-Zorannes) at "poorely to fare, till thyne owne propter [sic] strength" (f. 31v). This, furthermore, ends mid-sentence: perhaps the compiler intended to continue copying.

139. Bodleian MS Don. e. 6, f. 2v; Jonson, *Sejanus*, 4.294-95 (1605), sig. I2. Information on the manuscript taken from *CELM*.

140. Bodleian MS Don. e. 6, f. 2v; Jonson, "On the Townes Honest Man," *Epigrams* 115.12-13 (1616 folio), sig. Yyyv.

Chapter 4

Re-Presenting and Re-Reading the Renaissance

Restoration Extracts from Renaissance Plays, 1660–1700

When King Charles II reopened the theatres in 1660, there were no new plays immediately on hand, so managers and actors re-staged the old plays from the first half of the century. Initially, these plays were performed unrevised, but there soon arose a cottage industry of adapting Renaissance drama.[1] The frequent and popular adaptations of Renaissance plays reflect the continued interest in earlier drama and show that these plays had not calcified into untouchable classics: rather, plays continued to be seen as pliable texts that could be appropriated and used. Playwrights' adaptations function as a large-scale and public counterpart to the dramatic extracting that continued in this period. Although scholars have analyzed many of the theatrical adaptations of Renaissance plays in the Restoration, the responses of individual play-readers and audience members to pre-1642 plays as registered by their dramatic extracts have not yet been investigated. This chapter considers how readers and audiences from 1660–1700 read and saw plays that were written before the 1642 closure of the theatres.

The reopening of the theatres was a momentous event that in many ways altered how people read earlier plays, although, paradoxically, in other cases dramatic extracts continued to circulate just as they had in the earlier seventeenth century. During the Restoration, extracting from Renaissance plays continued unabated in commonplace books, verse miscellanies, and songbooks. For readers and audiences copying selections from plays, however, these pre-1642 plays were no longer the latest new things. Revivals, fresh adaptations, and republications remained steadily popular, but as early as 1670, new plays were emerging and competing with reworkings of old plays both in theatres and booksellers' stalls.[2] Late seventeenth-century dramatic extracting, then, reflects how readers compared early plays and masques to the new.

Dramatic extracts from late seventeenth-century manuscripts reveal a gamut of responses to Renaissance plays as wide-ranging as those from earlier in the century. These later responses are particular to the historic moment when Renaissance plays could be compared to Restoration plays. As this chapter will demonstrate, some readers preferred new Restoration plays to their Renaissance counterparts. Indeed, many manuscripts from this period include selections from Restoration plays without any reference to earlier plays, although they are outside the scope of this study.[3] For other readers, there was a continued nostalgia for Renaissance plays as superior to Restoration plays. Chapter 5 offers an extended discussion of the tastes of one particular compiler, Archbishop William Sancroft, who falls into the latter category.

Just as the appearance of new material (from adaptations to fresh plays) affected readers' opinions of earlier plays, it also changed the contexts for dramatic extracting. Dramatic extracts from Renaissance plays were often copied alongside those from Restoration plays. Some manuscript compilers turned to the latest play publications, which included both republications and adaptations. New prologues and epilogues were added for play revivals and republications, and sometimes published separately from the play altogether. The expansion, expurgation, and alteration of earlier plays not only offered new material to be extracted; it also provided a new context for extracting where readers had the choice to turn to an earlier play, a republication, an adaptation, or an entirely new play.

Many dramatic extracts from earlier plays in late seventeenth-century manuscripts reflect John Dryden's ascendancy both as a playwright and a critic—and this discussion doesn't even touch on the circulation of extracts from Dryden's plays themselves that appeared without mention of earlier plays. The late seventeenth-century readers analyzed here copied extracts from pre-1642 plays, but many also wrote about reading Dryden's plays and or transcribed selections from his plays and criticism. Dryden's *Essay of Dramatick Poesie* (1668) praised earlier theatre, while holding it to new critical standards: Dryden could have influenced many readers to turn to earlier plays and consider them afresh.

This chapter presents particular moments of play reading as registered in late seventeenth-century verse miscellanies, songbooks, commonplace books, and one dramatic miscellany. The first commonplace book that this chapter examines, John Abbott's, establishes how one reader purposefully approached plays as a source of commonplaces, entering a decades-old tradition. Abbott's commonplaces can decontextualize the extracts from their original moment in the plays, but they also indicate that he read and understood the play in its entirety; that is to say, his extracts are paradoxically separate from and connected to the play.

Among the most frequently decontextualized extracts, songs from Renaissance plays continued to circulate in late seventeenth-century songbooks and verse miscellanies. The analysis of songs from Renaissance plays takes two approaches: the first involves investigating many songs in one particular late-seventeenth manuscript, and the second requires examining individual songs in multiple manuscripts. Both approaches yield different results, illustrating the need for continued reconsiderations of dramatic extracts from multiple perspectives. This discussion of songs necessarily focuses on the material texts that are left, but songs circulated orally in ways that their print and manuscript traces can only hint at.

While the first part of this chapter shows the continued circulation of extracts and songs from plays in commonplace books, verse miscellanies, and songbooks, the latter section focuses on four manuscripts with attitudes particular to the Restoration. As these manuscripts demonstrate, commonplacing remained a crucial part of education in the late seventeenth century. The first of these manuscripts, BL MS Sloane 161, illustrates the social circulation of plays through book lending and play reading. The second and third, PD's Bodleian MS Eng. misc. c. 34 and William Deedes's Folger MS V.a.226, showcase readers who preferred Restoration plays to their earlier counterparts, in sharp contrast to the fourth, BL MS Lansdowne 1185, a dramatic miscellany that reveals one reader's Shakespearean nostalgia. Both PD and the Lansdowne compilers provide early examples of literary criticism.

The late seventeenth century presented play-readers and playgoers with a choice of texts particular to that moment, while also offering new historic and political contexts in which readers approached plays. As the final manuscripts examined in this chapter reveal, Restoration readers were a new generation who turned to older plays for a variety of reasons. For instance, one reader, John Muddyclift, depoliticized Sir Philip Sidney's much earlier *The Lady of May*, although he also copied very political elements from Ben Jonson's roman tragedies. The Restoration, with its new theatrical aesthetics, repurposing of earlier plays, and changing political contexts, offers scholars a wealth of archival material about reading earlier plays, much of which has yet to be considered by theatre historians or literary critics.

LATE SEVENTEENTH-CENTURY COMMONPLACE BOOKS, SONGBOOKS, AND VERSE MISCELLANIES

This section begins by touching on several commonplace books, before turning to songbooks and verse miscellanies and leading to a discussion of songs from Shakespeare's *The Tempest*. Late seventeenth-century commonplace books and miscellanies exhibit the same range of textual engagement as their earlier counterparts. At times, readers self-consciously extracted, purposefully engaging in the existing commonplacing and extracting tradition. For instance, one anonymous late seventeenth-century compiler chose to copy what is now the most famous sententious speech in drama: Polonius's advice to his son Laertes in *Hamlet*.[4] Literary critics are divided on the interpretation of this passage: is Polonius's advice to be taken earnestly? Is he a fool who can offer nothing but borrowed wit? Even if his words are hackneyed, do they possess a seed of truth? The late seventeenth-century extracts in University of Chicago MS 824 do not reveal what the manuscript compiler thought of Polonius, but this anonymous reader certainly recognized that the importance of this part of Shakespeare's play lies in its commonplace nature. Titled "Advice to a Young man" in the manuscript, like in the play, these apothegms can be taken at face value or as an object of ridicule.[5] Most important for the context of this study, as this manuscript and the following example show, Restoration readers recognized that commonplaces were integral parts of drama that playwrights purposefully inserted and intended as key points to be taken by readers. Indeed, by giving Polonius a series of commonplaces, Shakespeare himself calls attention to the commonplace tradition.

The complete text of the Polonius extracts in University of Chicago MS 824 run as follows:

> Advice to a Young Man
> Give thy thoughts noe tongue,
> nor any Unproportione'd thought his Act
> Bee thou Familliar, but by noe meanes vulgar:
> those Friends thou hast & their Adoption tryed,
> Grapple them unto thy soule with Hoopes of steele:
> But doe not dull thy Palme with Entertainment
> of each new hatcht; unfledg'd Courages: beware
> of entrance to a Quarrell, but being in
> bear't that the oppose may beware of thee;
> Give every man thy eare, but few thy voice
> take each mans Censure, but reserve thy Judgement
> Neither a borrower nor a Lender bee,
> for Lone oft loses both it selfe & Friend,
> and borrowing Dulls the edge of Husbandry
> to thine owne selfe be true ./
>
> Sh:[6]

In the play, Polonius instructs his son to memorize these adages: "these few precepts in thy memory / Look thou character" (1.3.58-59). Polonius's words are, indeed, a series of precepts that can be heeded or ignored. This manuscript compiler chose to copy the bulk of them, but skips the passage about advice on how to dress and how they dress in France, "Costly thy habit as thy purse can buy, / But not expressed in fancy, rich, not gaudy, / For the apparel oft proclaims the man, / And they in France of the best rank and station / [Are] of a most select and generous chief in that" (1.3.70–74). By omitting Polonius's blessings on his son and his editorializing, "This above all," this compiler did not present the speech of a character, but rather, like Polonius himself, a slew of aphorisms. While modern readers and audiences can dismiss Polonius for regurgitating clichéd commonplaces, this manuscript compiler chose only his words from all of *Hamlet*—no "to be or not to be" for this reader. Whether Shakespeare's Polonius bears mocking like John Marston's Luscus or Jonson's Sir Politic Would-Be (who "speaks in print" and has "none but notes / drawn out of playbooks" respectively),[7] this reader offers Polonius's speech without negative judgment, and perhaps, even favorably, by restoring his parroted words to their generalized, commonplace, and applicable nature. University of Chicago MS 824 presents Polonius as a repository of wisdom: more than a century later, Edward Fitzgerald would do the same by titling his nineteenth-century book of proverbs *Polonius: A Collection of Wise Saws and Modern Instances*.[8]

While dramatic extracts are often decontextualized in commonplace books and miscellanies, Bodleian MS Rawl. D. 954 (c. 1670s) presents one university reader, John Abbott, who read plays thoughtfully, pointed to the extracts' original context, and also shaped the pieces to be more easily read without the full context. Abbott's extracts, while physically separate from the full-text play, are still connected to the themes and characterizations of the original. Abbott copied selections from William Cartwright's plays and the anonymous *Caesar's Revenge* (*Caesar and Pompey*). Abbott's commonplace book, possibly compiled while he attended Oxford, reveals that his dramatic extracting was motivated by early modern education practices. Abbott's manuscript begins with a prose extract about how to copy commonplaces (ff. 4–12) from John Brinsley's pedagogical guide, *Ludus Literarius* (1612), which suggests that Abbott approached the practice with deliberation. The manuscript then continues with extracts from Latin and English works.[9] The last ten leaves are upside down and contain numbered Greek "Adagia" and some neatly written algebra problems. Abbott's manuscript exemplifies the close contexts of adages, extracts, commonplaces, and pedagogy by linking them in one volume.

Abbott's extracts from seventeenth-century drama self-consciously participate in the history of commonplacing described in Chapter 1. The manuscript opens with selections from Chapter 13 of Brinsley's pedagogical guide about commonplaces (which Brinsley calls "Theames"): "The Art of making Theames full of good matter & with Judgment."[10] Brinsley explained why extracting is a valuable undertaking: "The principall end of making Theames I take to be this, to furnish Schollers with the choicest matter that they may therby learne to understand speak or write" and to "worke in your selfe a greater love of the vertuous & hatred of the vice."[11] Abbott's dramatic extracts follow Brinsley's advice, as he selected the "choisest matter" from each play, presumably as way to educate and improve himself. Abbott also copied selections from William Basse's often-republished *A Helpe to Discourse* (discussed at more length in Chapter 6) and Obadiah Walker's *Of Education* (1673), two texts with explicit educational aims. For Abbott, extracting from Renaissance drama was a normal and expected part of education, as was his reading of the other classical and religious texts from which he copied. Although, as Chapter 1 demonstrates, a century earlier it would have been uncommon to transcribe sections from contemporary or even old plays, by the late seventeenth century, dramatic extracting was a standard practice, albeit one that was undertaken in widely varying circumstances for a gamut of reasons, as the many examples in this chapter establish.

Abbott's extracts and titles demonstrate his understanding of the speeches' original contexts; his titles offered him a shorthand for remembering what happened in the play. Abbott extracted a speech from Cartwright's *The Royall Slave*, "To accuse or Gods or men's the part of him," adding the title "The speech of Cratander when he—heard the sentence of his death after he had been pardon'd."[12] Although more than a dozen manuscripts contain extracts from Cartwright's plays, the majority of these extracts are songs (at times set to music), prologues, and epilogues.[13] Abbott's extract, which has not yet been catalogued or discussed, is an important addition to these other extant extracts and paratexts precisely because it refers back to the complete work. These lines both capture one of *The Royall Slave*'s most emotional moments and, paradoxically, could be taken as any execution speech. Gallows speeches featured common generic characteristics that could often be interchangeable.

With his other Cartwright extracts, all from *The Siedge: Or, Love's Convert*, Abbott identified the play but also shaped the extracts so they could be understood without the context of the plot or character. Abbott combined two responses by Euthalpe, Leucasia's handmaid:

> [TLN 1188-90] That I am a woman cannot take
> of[f] from virtuous deeds; my soule's as Male
> as yours; ther's no sex in the Mind.
> [TLN 1212-13] He scarce breath, except it be to let
> a sigh at Liberty.[14]

Abbott shaped the piece to stand grammatically on its own, elided Euthalpe's initial response to an interlocutor, and removed the parts of the speech that specifically refer to the events of the play. Rather than point to particular characters (like the Cratander mention a page earlier), these extracts offer a generalized comment on women's equality and a description of a melancholic man.

Unlike the clearly labeled selections from Cartwright's plays, Abbott included two pages with unattributed extracts from *Caesar's Revenge* (the anonymous play also called *Caesar and Pompey*, not to be confused with the George Chapman play of the same title). The first passage, "This between Princes doth contention bring," is titled "Wealth" so that the pronoun "This" would be clear to the reader.[15] On the page verso, a series of extracts about Cleopatra's beauty are given without comment or context. Virtue, melancholy, wealth, and beauty: for Abbott, these "Theames" were important not only because they appeared in drama, but also because he valued them as part of his education. The University of Chicago manuscript and Abbott's miscellany show how early readers both took existing commonplaces from plays and shaped other extracts into commonplaces.

Commonplaces from plays never ceased to interest seventeenth-century manuscript compilers, but as with earlier periods, songs continued to be among the most popular dramatic extracts in verse miscellanies, songbooks, and even (as manuscript additions in) printed books. For instance, in one case, sometime between 1653 and the early 1660s, someone copied a musical setting of Sir John Suckling's "Why so pale and fond wan lover," the most popular song from *Aglaura*. This setting is bound with John Playford's printed *Select Musicall Ayres and Dialogues* (1653), which includes yet another song from *Aglaura*, "No, no, faire Heretick."[16] This volume demonstrates the interrelation of print and manuscript as well as the integration of songs from dramatic sources with non-dramatic songs. "Though I am young and cannot tell" from Jonson's *The Sad Shepherd* faces the non-dramatic "My Clarissa, thou cruell fair"; the two are not differentiated, as Playford prints only the composer's name, and not the poet, lyricist, or reference to the source text.[17] The ongoing publication of unattributed songs from Renaissance plays undoubtedly contributed to their appearance in manuscript, or, in this case, to a manuscript addition to a printed source.

The Killigrew Miscellany exemplifies the continued, and perhaps increasing, importance of songs from plays during the Restoration.[18] This late seventeenth-century verse miscellany includes songs from plays by Francis Beaumont and John Fletcher, Jonson, Suckling, Shakespeare, and other Renaissance writers alongside songs from later plays by Dryden, Aphra Behn, Charles Sedley, Thomas Shadwell, Thomas Southerne, and others.

Many of the songs from plays in this manuscript were popular in both verse miscellanies and songbooks, such as Suckling's "Why so pale and wan fonde lover" (*Aglaura*) and Nathaniel Lee's epithalamium from *Caesar Borgia*, "Blush not reder then the morning."[19] Although this manuscript includes some poems, the compiler favored songs and lyrics, sometimes simply offering the title "Song," but frequently leaving the pieces untitled. Some of the pieces from early seventeenth-century plays in this manuscript may have been copied because of revival performances, such as "Why so pale" from Suckling's *Aglaura*, but others, such as "Beauties, have you seene a toy" from Jonson's *The Haddington Masque*, were not recently performed.[20] Many of the lyrics in this manuscript circulated in print miscellanies, and so may not have been copied solely because of their theatrical origins.[21] The scant scholarly attention this manuscript has received began because it was suggested that it might have been written by Thomas Killigrew, the playwright and theatre manager, although this has since been disproven.[22] The desire to associate this manuscript with a theatrical figure is understandable because of the prevalence of songs from plays, both old and new. As this book shows, there was a larger readership (beyond players, playwrights, composers, and managers) of both plays and miscellanies with dramatic material.

Another late seventeenth-century verse miscellany, Bodleian MS Rawl. poet. 65 (c. 1680s) exemplifies how songs from plays were not necessarily gathered by a compiler interested in their theatrical provenance. Along with a number of poems by Katherine Philips (the Matchless Orinda), this verse miscellany contains songs from both Renaissance and Restoration plays, as well as a song from Restoration adaptations of earlier plays, in this case, a song from William Davenant's operatic adaptation of *Macbeth* (1664; f. 27v). On one opening, a song from Dryden's *Secret-Love, or the Maiden-Queen* (1668) faces a song from James Shirley's *The Cardinal* (1652).[23] With songs from plays by Jonson, Davenant, Beaumont and Fletcher, and other dramatists, it might seem natural to conclude the compiler of this manuscript read plays. These songs, however, are copied without music and with no reference to their musical nature or dramatic sources: Shirley's song is labeled "Ignot," that is, unknown. Shirley's "Come, my Daphne, come away" is found in many songbooks and verse miscellanies of the mid- to late seventeenth century—before it was included in *The Cardinal*, it appeared in Shirley's *Poems &c* (1646).[24] Jonson's song "If I freely may discover" from *Poetaster* (1601), also found in Bodleian MS Rawl. poet. 65 (twice, ff. 27, 35v), circulated widely in manuscript throughout the century, often without music. Although Jonson's and Shirley's songs were disassociated from their source texts decades earlier than Davenant's and Dryden's songs, the compiler of Bodleian MS Rawl. poet. 65 treated both the same, giving each without reference to their source, author, or, indeed, music. We might now think of certain songs only in reference to their theatrical provenance, but in the late seventeenth century these texts circulated separately from their plays. This is the early modern equivalent of hearing "Magical Mister Mistoffelees" and not thinking of the musical *Cats*.

Folger MS V.a.169 embodies the link between print miscellanies and songbooks of the time because of its close relation to John Playford's *Select Musical Ayres and Dialogues*. This manuscript was likely compiled by James Bateman and Robert Pierrepont in the 1650s, who were at the time two students at Emmanuel College, Cambridge; thirty years later, the manuscript came into the hands of John Oldham, the poet.[25] Many of the songs in the manuscript could have been taken from Playford's songbook. Although Playford's songbook includes music, the songs in the manuscript were copied without music. The one song in this manuscript with theatrical connections is "Fine young folly though you were" from William Habington's *The Queene of Arragon*, which like the rest of the non-theatrical songs, was also printed in Playford's songbook.[26] Playford includes Habington's song in three-part vocal harmony with no reference to Habington or the play; instead, as with the other songs in Playford's book, the composer (William Tompkins) is noted. Although Habington's song was originally published with music, it eventually joined other songs printed only as lyrics in late seventeenth-century verse miscellanies.

Bateman and Pierrepont's (later Oldham's) manuscript, then, offers a tantalizing handwritten counterpart to the printed miscellanies of the mid- to late seventeenth century by showing how songs could be copied from sources without music. Separating songs from their music does not necessarily mean that their tunes were lost and these songs became poems: many summer camp songbooks have been passed down generations with no score, yet the tunes are still well known. If Bateman and Pierrepont knew the tune when they copied the lyrics, did Oldham when he later read the text? Did Bateman, Pierrepont, or Oldham recognize Habington's song as dramatic? Habington's song, decontextualized in Playford's music book, copied again by Bateman or Pierrepont, and later presumably read by Oldham, offers one of the more straightforward cases of textual transmission, but still raises more questions than it answers. Oldham's signature demonstrates that educated readers and writers turned to verse miscellanies, which could offer judiciously curated complete texts. A song from a play did not have to be primarily identified as "from a play." Rather, these extracts were not always perceived as extracts, but instead, as complete ideas and works of art unto themselves.

Songs from plays, as Tiffany Stern reminds us, "often circulated in a different way from—and so 'outside'—playbooks."[27] Bodleian MS Rawl. poet. 65, the Killigrew miscellany, and Folger MS V.a.169 are just a few examples of this kind of circulation. Stern also points out that songs were often composed separately from the play—even when they were written by the playwright (consider, for instance, Shirley's "Come, my Daphne," which he published as a poem and later recycled in his play). In many cases, we do not have the original settings (or even lyrics) to early modern songs from plays precisely because the songs were separate from the plays, and not always published. One seventeenth-century composer, Edward Lowe (c. 1610–1682), compiled multiple music manuscripts, from the Caroline period until his death in 1682. Lowe was both a professor of music at Oxford and one of the organists at the Chapel Royal. Although the majority of Lowe's manuscripts contain primarily religious music or instrumental music, others include multiple songs from Renaissance plays. In BL MS Add. 29396, for instance, Lowe copied secular vocal songs from about 1636 through to the early 1650s.[28] Mary Chan suggests that the very first songs copied into this manuscript were of dramatic origin: "Come from the Dungeon to the Throne" from Cartwright's *The Royall Slave* and "Hayle thou great Queene" from William Strode's masque *The Floating Island*.[29] The latter's theatrical provenance is highlighted by Lowe's title, "In Dr Strodes Play used before the Kinge."[30] Lowe continued including dramatic songs throughout the interregnum, including "Tis late & Cold stirr up the fyre" from Beaumont and Fletcher's *The Lovers Progres[s]*.[31] After the Restoration, Lowe (or someone with a similar hand) added settings for songs from the Dryden-Davenant adaptation of Shakespeare's *Tempest*, including "Full fathom five thy father lys" and "Where the bee sucks there suck I."[32] With his decades-spanning manuscript, Lowe exemplifies how new settings of songs from plays circulated at times without reference to the full play (as with the Shakespearean songs), and other times, with particular mention of their dramatic origins (as with "Hayle thou great Queene").

This section has looked at different approaches to dramatic extracting in order to show how extracts can be severed from their original text or, conversely, can refer specifically to those texts. The manuscripts discussed here reveal that some late seventeenth-century readers self-consciously participated in the commonplacing tradition by turning to earlier plays and songs. The examples here, particularly Abbott's commonplace book and instructional guide and the University of Chicago manuscript with Polonius's speech, offer examples of readers actively participating in commonplace culture, where the verse miscellanies and songbooks offer examples of the ubiquitous circulation of songs from plays. This section has only touched on some representative commonplace books, verse miscellanies, and songbooks: the next part of this chapter will touch on more of these primary sources that contain Shakespearean extracts. As Peter Beal's *Catalogue of English Manuscripts* (*CELM*) attests, there are many more manuscripts to be considered—and librarians, archivists, and researchers will certainly continue to discover even more examples. The next section of this chapter demonstrates the complicated textual lineage of songs from plays, which is, of course, further complicated by their oral circulation as well.

The most popular Shakespearean songs in mid- to late seventeenth-century songbooks and verse miscellanies were those from *The Tempest*—which is perhaps unsurprising, as *The Tempest* is often billed as Shakespeare's most musical play. Currently, *CELM* lists ten copies of "Where the bee sucks, so suck I" dating from the 1640s–1720s. Many manuscripts that include "Where the bee sucks," like Edward Lowe's songbooks discussed above, also include "Full fathom five thy father lies."[33] Versions of these songs from Dryden and Davenant's adaptation (1670), Shadwell's opera (1674), and Henry Purcell's score (c. 1695) circulated in manuscript at the same time as Robert Johnson's initial setting. It was not simply the continued adaptation of these plays that led to the songs' popularity in manuscript: these songs, particularly "Where the bee sucks," were often published in print songbooks and miscellanies from 1659–1689.[34] Indeed, the market for songs from plays was such that in 1674, a short leaflet, *Songs and Masques in the Tempest* was published.[35] *The Tempest*, with its adaptations, revivals, republications, and spoofs, was part of the theatrical, musical, and literary culture of the late seventeenth century. The abundance of dramatic extracts from *The Tempest* in both print and manuscript both signal and contribute to its cultural currency.

While Lowe's secular vocal songbook illustrates how theatrical songs were sometimes associated with their plays (discussed above), his other songbooks participate in the social circulation of songs from plays. Lowe compiled three related partbooks with songs from plays and masques. The first partbook (*cantus primus*) is at Edinburgh University Library (MS Dc. 1.69), the *cantus secundus* is in Bodleian MS Mus. d. 238, and the *cantus bassus* is now lost.[36] This songbook includes two different settings than BL MS Add. 29396 for Shakespeare's songs, "Full fathome five" and "Wher the Bee sucks."[37] Lowe attributed them both to Robert Johnson, and included "3 stanza's more to—Wher the Bee sucks."[38] The careful ascriptions clearly point to how songs from plays could be passed from person to person: "This I had of Madam Trumball at Chalfont. 27 Sept 1676." We can only speculate whether Madam Trumball sang the song and Lowe wrote the music by ear, or she provided him with the sheet music. If Trumball provided Lowe with the sheet music, it was perhaps a single piece of paper that has now been lost. What the ascription reveals, however, is that friends passed songs along to interested friends. Lowe's musical source, Madam Trumball, was possibly Katherine (or Elizabeth) Trumbull (d. 1704), wife of Sir William Trumbull, a lawyer and government official.[39] Lady Trumbull was the daughter of Sir Charles Cotterell, master of ceremonies at court and part of Katherine

Philips's literary coterie.[40] The circulation of extracts, particularly songs, from earlier plays was not separate from other literary production and transmission; rather, it was part of the norm.

Beyond indicating their social circulation, the additional verses to "Where the bee sucks" show how songs from plays were updated to apply to particular circumstances. The additional verses include both broad descriptions of fairies and drinking as well as particular and topical references, such as Charles II's notorious womanizing:

> I bath in Rose dew, & ne're fayle
> to breakfast in the milkinge payle.
> With the Kinge I sitt & sine
> tast his meate, & drinke his wine
> Court & Kisse his Concubine.
> Merrily merrily voide of all care
> Shall I live now, & as free as they ayre
> Spight of Dick I dance & play
> With the Lady of the May.
> Numps his Malmsye nose I'le ply
> tickle Maudlins spirit Eye
> Buz in Rogers Eare I cry.
> Merrily merrily now here now ther
> This side & that side & Every wher
> But in Autumne I as Cupid
> & God Bacchus blinde & stupid
> On the glasses brim I hopp
> Sippinge still, till from the topp
> to the bottom downe I dropp.
> Merrily merrily there yet I lye
> I drinke, & am drunk, & dead drunk I dye.[41]

The names in the second verse are topical references: Dick is likely Richard Cromwell, who succeeded his father, Oliver, as Lord Protector for less than a year in 1658–1659.

Although Lowe received this manuscript with the additional verses to "Where the bee sucks" in 1676, his other note, "thes supposd to bee made my Mr Smith secretary to the Archbishop of Canterbury," pushes their date of composition back a few years and proves that even these additional topical verses were of interest beyond their initial moment of creation.[42] Miles Smith, secretary to Archbishop Gilbert Sheldon, died in 1671.[43] Smith's only known publication, *The Psalms of King David Paraphrased, And turned into English Verse, according to the common Metre, As they are usually sung in Parish Churches* (1664), indicates his interest in creating verse to be sung.

Like poems and other dramatic extracts, songs from plays were ultimately social and changeable.

Songs from plays by Shakespeare and his contemporaries were often copied from intermediate print sources. Although it was not revived and adapted to the extent of the songs from *The Tempest*, "Lawn as white as driven snow" from *The Winter's Tale* can be found in a handful of late seventeenth-century manuscripts. The songs from *The Tempest* and "Lawn as white as driven snow" were published separately from the original plays, when many other Shakespearean songs were not.[44] The publication of the songs both with music (new and old) and as poems gave manuscript compilers access to some of Shakespeare's songs, if not others. Folger MS V.a.409 illustrates this point: many of its songs are also found in John Hilton's *Catch that Catch can* (1652, with later republications).[45] Both Folger MS V.a.409 and Hilton's printed songbook include "Come lets away to the Taverne I say," from Suckling's *The Sad One* but with two extra lines at the end.[46] Similarly, both contain Hilton's setting for "What shall he have that kild the deere" from *As You Like It*.[47] The separate publication of songs from plays, unsurprisingly, made them more accessible to readers and easier to copy into manuscripts. Furthermore, songs circulated as oral texts and remembered texts that readers could bring to mind when they saw printed songs.

Songs and extracts from old plays, like their republication and their adaptations, reveal the continued cultural currency of Renaissance plays in the late seventeenth century. Moreover, when people copied songs from earlier plays such as *The Tempest*, they had a choice of source text and versions. The proliferation of late seventeenth-century extracts indicates the range of choices readers had for their source-materials, from original texts, republications, and intermediate print and manuscript sources, not to mention the potential oral transmission of songs. This chapter's next example demonstrates how drama circulated in everyday life not just through social transmission of extracts (that is, passing from one person to another as from Madam Trumball to Edward Lowe) but also through social reading practices.

MAKING MEANING IN BL MS SLOANE 161

John Muddyclift's diary and miscellany, BL MS Sloane 161, offers an example of social play reading and the public circulation of dramatic texts. Muddyclift's extracts, like those of Archbishop Sancroft discussed in the following chapter, highlight how one person could approach printed plays differently, by copying from recently published works and seeking out old editions, or by choosing highly political selections in some cases while completely eliding the political material in others.

Muddyclift (or Muddiclift, 1651–1690) was an Englishman who, while studying medicine in Utrecht in 1670, copied dramatic extracts in English that are now bound with his primarily Latin diary.[48] A typical diary entry discusses reading for pleasure, studying, attending lectures, and eating and walking with friends and family members.[49] After the diary comes a booklist (f. 19) and a ripped page with a fragment from Sir Thomas Browne's "As when the labouring sun hath wrought his track," from section 32 of *Religio Medici* (f. 20). The manuscript concludes with various excerpts from dramatic works: a Restoration Comedy, Shadwell's *The Miser* (f. 21); two Renaissance Roman tragedies, Jonson's *Catiline* (ff. 22–26) and *Sejanus* (f. 28); and an Elizabethan courtly entertainment, Sidney's *The Lady of May* (ff. 29–30). Muddyclift's manuscript is particularly important because it includes both dramatic extracts and a description of him reading a play with another person.

Muddyclift's diary links social play reading to seduction. On October 3rd, 1672, Muddyclift wrote about reading Dryden's newly published *The Conquest of Granada*.[50] Muddyclift reported, "I was reading for two hours in a bedroom with Mrs. Elizabeth Cleyton in tragecom[edy] the Conquest of Granada."[51] Muddyclift described reading alone with Elizabeth Cleyton, wanting to kiss her—and more. As he explained in his diary entry, his Aunt Gooche was not happy that he was reading upstairs with a woman. According to Muddyclift, Elizabeth was upset to be parted and exclaimed, "Tis {so long} before we can get ? fa{mil}r together!" (f. 18; see Figure 4.1). When describing play reading, Muddyclift at times used Greek letters to conceal the more titillating words ("about kissing," "joined together"), but other times used them for more mundane words ("so long," "while I was reading").[52] Muddyclift's use of Greek characters would not have fooled an educated reader. His use of Latin and Greek, however, might have stopped a woman, such as his Aunt Gooche, from reading his diary.

In describing play reading as a kind of seduction, Muddyclift's shift between the Latin alphabet and the Greek alphabet might also leave a reader stymied and his use of sentence fragments leaves readers filling in the blanks. Muddyclift's terse fragments are punctuated with question marks, perhaps demonstrating a shocked pleasure, or exclamation points, expressing excited urgency: "It must be noted how to be intimate? Also innocent? With the hands?" (f. 18; see the antepenultimate line of Figure 4.1). Reading *The Conquest of Granada* with a woman was not simply a social activity, but one that could lead further: "afterwards intimacy?" (f. 18). Muddyclift presented the act of reading a play as an act of foreplay: "With her very own eyes ... turned intently on {me while I was reading}, I would have gone to bed" (f. 18). Muddyclift described the intimate relationship a play-reader has when performing to an audience of one.

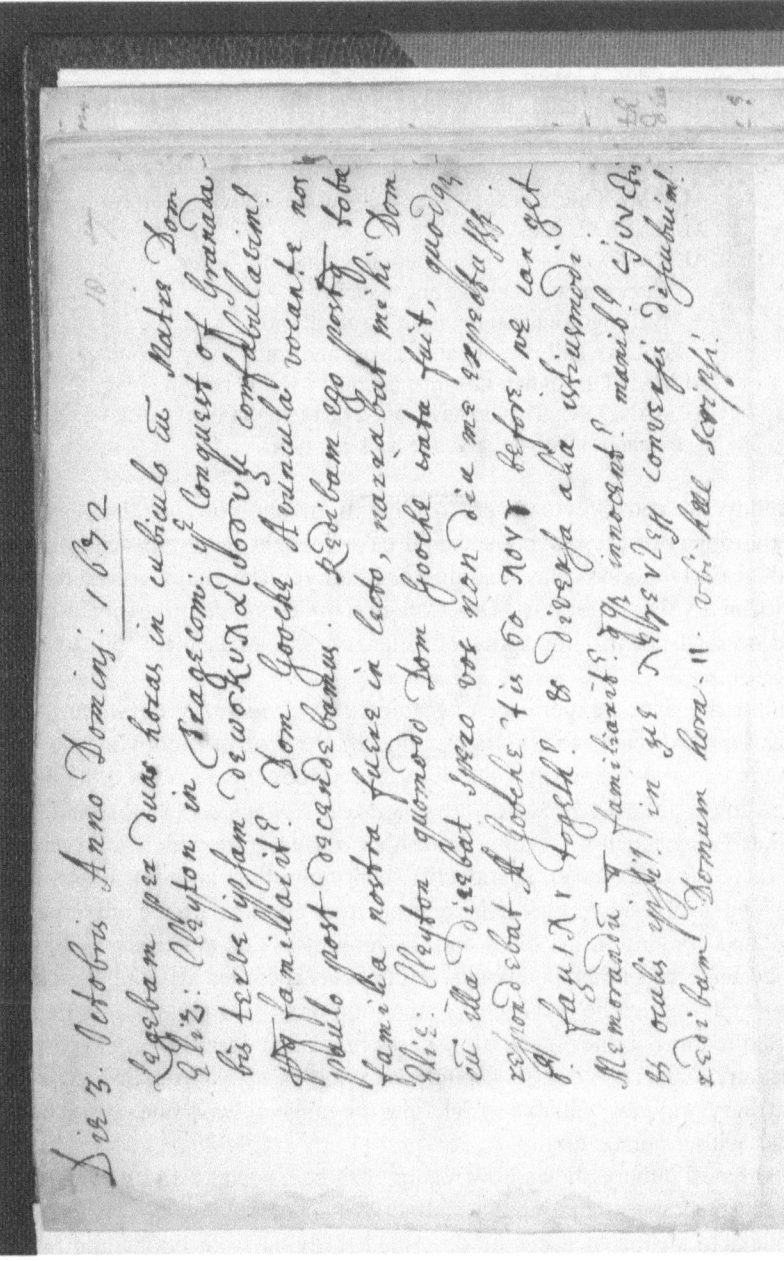

Figure 4.1 © The British Library Board. BL MS Sloane 161, f. 18, top.

Muddyclift's description suggests that the young couple read the play aloud. Did one (Muddyclift, perhaps) read aloud while the other listened? Did they take turns speaking the different parts? It is tempting to imagine two young lovers, filled with intense undercurrents of desire, reading a scene in the voice of Dryden's lovers:

> ALMANZOR. You are— [angrily
> ALMAHIDE. —I know I am your Captive, Sir.
> ALMANZOR. You are—you shall—and I can scarce forbear
> ALMAHIDE. Alas!
> ALMANZOR.—'Tis all in vain; it will not do: [aside.
>   I cannot now a seeming anger show:
>   My Tongue against my heart no aid affords,
>   For Love still rises up and chokes my words.
> ALMAHIDE. In half this time a tempest would be still.
> ALMANZOR. 'Tis you have rais'd that tempest in my will,
>   I wonnot love you, give me back my heart.[53]

If Muddyclift and Cleyton were reading from one copy of the play, the material object of the playbook would have brought them physically closer together. Early modern play reading, for Muddyclift, perhaps moved beyond the social to the flirtatious. *The Conquest of Granada*, like other plays, could be read not just for solitary edification and amusement, but to build relationships.

Unlike the shared experience of reading *The Conquest of Granada*, Muddyclift reported reading *Catiline* by himself. He described copying the very dramatic excerpts found after the diary. As Muddyclift recounted, he began by reading a little in Browne's *Pseudodoxia Epidemica* (1646), and then continued after lunch by reading Jonson's *Catiline*, from which he excerpted until three o'clock (f. 4v). Muddyclift spent more than an hour transcribing selections from a single play. His excerpts from *Catiline* are the only ones he mentioned copying in his diary and the longest in this manuscript—though he may have had other notebooks. Muddyclift recorded reading Fletcher's plays, implying that he had access to the folio or to multiple quartos. He also reported reading lighter material, such as plays and *Merry Drollery*, a print miscellany.[54] Because it offers multiple examples of play reading, Muddyclift's diary provides valuable insight into the range of ways one person could interact with dramatic text.

Muddyclift's diary shows how reading can be a social activity even when undertaken alone, as marginalia, extracts, and notes could be written with the intent to share. At times he described studying from books and taking notes: "Legebam paucula in Medecina Regij & quo nonnulla annotabam" ("I was reading a little in *Royal Medicine* & there taking a few notes").[55]

Note-taking, however, was not only for personal gain, as students and faculty shared their notes in the university setting. His advisor, Isbrand van Diemerbroeck, shared notes with Muddyclift: "postea legebam Notas Dom Diemibrokij in Johnstonum"—after, I was reading Master Diemerbroeck's notes on Johnston" (f. 9v). The university environment fostered social reading through note sharing.

Muddyclift's book-list and diary demonstrate his interest in a variety of genres (plays, religious works, medical manuals) spanning periods (classical, medieval, Renaissance, contemporary late seventeenth-century texts), but the majority of extracts appended to his diary are from English plays. The first dramatic extract following the diary is from Shadwell's *The Miser* (1672), a translation of Molière's *L'Avare* (1667). Like the *Conquest of Granada*, Muddyclift likely read *The Miser* soon after its initial publication in 1672. The excerpt from Shadwell's play is a four-stanza song about a fellow who meets a maid in the woods suffering with greensickness, that peculiar early modern affliction of young virgins that could only be cured by sex:

> As I walk'd in the woods one evening of late
> A lass was deploring her hapless estate
> Shee sigh'd and shee sob'd ah wreched shee said
> Will no youth come succour a languishing maid
> Shall I still sigh and cry, and look pale & wan
> And languish for ever for want of a man.
>
> At first when I saw a young man in the place
> My colour would fade and then flush in my face
> My breath would grow short and I shiver'd all o're
> I thought 'twas an Ague but alas it was more
> Fore e're since I've sigh'd and doe what I can
> I find I must languish for want of a man
>
> When in bed all the night I weep on my Pillow
> To see others happy, while I weare the Willow
> I revenge my selfe ~~my~~ on the innocent sheet
> Where in rage I have often times made my teeth meet
> But all this won't serve let me doe what I can
> I find I must languish for want of a man.
>
> Now all my fresh colour deserted my face
> And let a pale greenness succeed in the place
> I pine and grow faint and refuse all my meat
> And nothing ^but^ chalk, Lime or Oatmeal can eat
> But in my despair I'le die I can
> And languish no more want of a man[56]

Alongside these lyrics, Muddyclift wrote Shadwell's name and the title of the play in the left-hand margin. This excerpt is headed with the number 2; since the page before it is torn, there was likely one or more missing page that contained similar dramatic extracts or songs. The greensickness song from *The Miser* easily stands alone, and holds a certain appeal when taken entirely out of context of the play. In the play, it is not integrally related to plot or character; rather, it is a "little Countrey song" that is "a little too wanton" that Cheatly sings to "stirr up these Girles."[57] Perhaps the erotic moments in Muddyclift's diary explain his interest in a song about a woman who "must languish for want of a man."

Muddyclift's play reading was influenced by recently printed plays, including republications of earlier plays. Muddyclift copied extracts from the 1669 edition of *Catiline*, including the prologue to the 1668 performance, "to be Merrily spoaken by Mrs Nell Guin: in an Amazonian habit."[58] His selections from *Catiline* are essentially an abridgment, although one that heightens the Machiavellian impact of the play. He centered on Catiline and Cethagus, cutting the involvement of many other characters. Muddyclift's expurgations left a focus on the conspirators and their effect on the Roman government. After briefly quoting Gwyn's prologue, Muddyclift began with Sylla's first fifteen lines. Muddyclift's abridged *Catiline*, then, still opens with an ominous sense of foreboding, as Sylla has come "like a Pestilence that should display / Infection through the world."[59] After including much plotting from Catiline and Cethegus, Muddyclift excerpted Cicero's speech bemoaning Rome's sickness. Muddyclift's version ends with Petreus relating Catiline's fall in battle and Cato's remark, "A brave bad dea^th^. / Had this bin honest now, and for his country / As 'twas against it, who had e're fallen greater?"[60] Even while relating Catiline's deserved death, Petreus and Cato begrudgingly admire Catiline's ambition. Muddyclift concluded this interchange with "The End," not allowing Cicero to finish the play by bringing the audience's focus on the uneasy political peace now in Rome. Concluding with Cato's comments about Catiline's fall links the ending of this play more directly to the material from *Sejanus His Fall* that follows and shows that Muddyclift recognized the similar preoccupations in both plays.

After pages of extracts from *Catiline*, Muddyclift excerpted only one part-speech from *Sejanus*. While his extracts from *The Miser* and *Catiline* were both taken from recently (re)published plays, Muddyclift must have used an earlier edition of *Sejanus*, which was not republished after the Restoration.[61] Although he copied less from *Sejanus* than he did from *Catiline*, Muddyclift was attracted to similar themes in both of Jonson's plays: power, fate, and treachery. In the last act of the play, Sejanus expresses his self-doubt and anxiety at losing his position of power—"How vaine, and vile a passion is this fear?"[62]—and then discusses how fear makes men behave poorly.

Muddyclift's extract begins mid-speech with Sejanus addressing the gods haughtily,

> Sejanus speaks.
> ——by you that fooles call gods
> Hang all the skie with your prodigious signs
> Fill earth with monsters, drop the scorpion down
> Out of the Zodiack, or the fiercer Lyon
> Shake off the loos'ned globe from her long hinge
> Rowle all the world in darkness: and let loose
> Th'inraged winds to turne up groves & townes
> When I do feare againe; let me be struck
> With forked fire and unpittyed dye
> Who fears is worth of calamity.[63]

Muddyclift omitted Sejanus's admissions of weakness and only portrays him tempting the gods and rejecting future fear. By copying this speech without the initial discussion of fear, Muddyclift presented a portrayal of Sejanus that is even more hubristic and Machiavellian than he appears in the play.[64] Muddyclift's single extract from *Sejanus* functions like his extracts of *Catiline*; it highlights the importance of the title character and presents him as a power-hungry politician.

The political relevancy of *Catiline His Conspiracy* to Jonson's day has been discussed as widely as Jonson's intended interpretation of *Sejanus His Fall*.[65] Muddyclift, however, likely did not associate these plays to one particular bygone event, such as Guy Fawkes's Gunpowder Plot, or the rise and fall of the Earl of Essex (Robert Devereux), or the trial of Sir Walter Raleigh. Rather, Muddyclift could have read these plays in relation to the contemporary events of the early 1670s, when politics in England were just as secretive and alliance-based as in the Rome described in *Catiline* and *Sejanus*.[66] When Muddyclift read Jonson's plays, the powerful advisors in Charles's court known as the CABAL ministers (Thomas **C**lifford, Baron Clifford of Chudleigh; Henry Bennet, Earl of **A**rlington; George Villiers, Duke of **B**uckingham; Anthony Ashley Cooper, Baron **A**shley; and John Maitland, Duke of **L**auderdale) were seen as colluding over important decisions, while also conspiring against one another and vying for authority. Although the particular current events and intrigues changed in the seventy years between when Jonson wrote his Roman tragedies and when Muddyclift read them, the enduring themes of royal favorites, tyranny, and conspiracy would have resonated in Muddyclift's time.

Unlike the political valences that Muddyclift's extracts from *Catiline* and *Sejanus* retain, his selections from Sidney's *The Lady of May* depoliticize the original masque. Furthermore, Muddyclift's extracts from *The Lady of May* are not taken from a recent publication.[67] Sidney designed *The Lady of*

May to be performed for Queen Elizabeth in 1578 or 1579. The performers stopped the queen as she walked through the gardens in Robert Dudley, Earl of Leicester's estate at Wanstead to ask her to choose between two suitors, the forester Therion and the shepherd Espilus, who vie for the hand of the May Lady. The queen chose the shepherd Espilus as the winning suitor.

Though scholars are not unanimous in their appraisal of the political nuances of the masque, it is universally acknowledged that Sidney's entertainment, including Elizabeth's responses, was not an aesthetic diversion, but rather, profoundly political.[68] Muddyclift's apolitical excerpts, then, are particularly interesting when taken from such a political text and placed next to the politically charged extracts from *Catiline* and *Sejanus*. As with the other masques discussed in Chapter 2, the scholarly preoccupation has been in understanding *The Lady of May* in its original performed contexts.[69] As Muddyclift's extracts demonstrate, however, he did not share our modern concerns with Sidney's intentions, the original staging, and the audience reception. Muddyclift's excerpts from *The Lady of May* are best read in light of his diary entries, which position him as a polyglot interested in wordplay. The extracts from *The Lady of May* in BL MS Sloane 161 are speeches by Rombus, who mediates the debates between both sides. Instead of focusing on the deeply political occasions of this entertainment, Muddyclift excerpted the lines of a stock character, the incompetent academic.

Muddyclift's excerpts from Sidney's entertainment reveal that his interest lay not in the Elizabethan politics but in academic humor. Muddyclift's manuscript contains all of Rombus's speeches from the print editions, save two.[70] Muddyclift was evidently most interested in Rombus's Latin malapropisms, that is, his role as the comedic pedant figure, similar to Holofernes in *Love's Labour's Lost*. Rombus misuses Latin and quotes from classical authors, including Cicero and Virgil. Muddyclift's diary and book-list indicate his familiarity with classical authors, as would have been expected of a late seventeenth-century student. Katherine Duncan-Jones notes that this entertainment "is characterized by a particularly academic kind of humor, reminding one that his [Sidney's] education had only just been completed."[71] Sidney's "particularly academic" entertainment appealed to Muddyclift, who likely copied this extracts when he too had just graduated from university.

By copying only the parts of *The Lady of May* that do not relate to Queen Elizabeth (or to Leicester and the suitors), Muddyclift removed the masque from the original occasion of its performance. When this performance was included in print versions of *Arcadia*, it bore the title:

> Her most excellent Majestie walking in Wansted Garden, as she passed downe into the grove, there came suddenly among the traine, one apparelled like an honest mans wife of the contrey; where crying out for justice, and desiring all

the Lords and Gentlemen to speake a good word for her, she was brought to the presence of her Majestie, to whom upon her knees she offered a supplication, and used this speech.[72]

This title invokes the occasional nature of this performance by twice naming the Queen's Majesty, by directly mentioning the place, and by giving the reader ample context (of visual cues, costume, and set-up).[73] Muddyclift's title indicates that he is not interested in the circumstances in which it was presented; he labeled the extracts "The speech of Rombus a schoolmaster" (f. 29). Muddyclift's extracts remove all reference to the original performance, and instead present a more general sketch of a stock character, one who would particularly interest a scholar and a polyglot. The context of these excerpts offers us an insight into Muddyclift's motives. As a voracious reader who was active in manuscript culture, who read and excerpted from plays, and who enjoyed playing with language in his own diary entries, Muddyclift was drawn to Rombus's speeches.

Ultimately, BL MS Sloane 161 offers a snapshot of John Muddyclift's life as a medical student in Utrecht and recent graduate returned to England who loved reading. In his diary, Muddyclift explained how he read plays: at times, aloud with a woman in his bedroom, at other times, alone while copying extracts. Muddyclift described reading many different kinds of works in his diary: scientific texts, philosophical tracts, print miscellanies, and others. Yet, of all the works Muddyclift read, the dramatic extracts are the only extracts or notes of his that survive. Most likely, however, the extracts were stored with his diary and his other notes on scientific or theological topics were written in other gatherings, perhaps kept elsewhere, or even passed along to friends. If he kept them alongside his diary, Muddyclift signaled their private importance to him. If a later reader bound Muddyclift's dramatic extracts and booklist with his diary, it indicates their continuing value to someone beyond the original copyist. By being bound with his diary, these extracts define Muddyclift's life as much as the Hippocratic oath he took and copied. It is this personal nature of dramatic extracts, the individual selection and copying, that makes the new contexts in which we find these extracts and the historical and cultural milieux in which they were copied so important to analyze.

The final manuscripts discussed in this chapter reveal a framework for reading early modern plays in the Restoration that did not exist before 1660. After 1660, a choice to turn to pre-1642 plays could reflect a deliberate decision to read older works rather than the latest new publications. Unsurprisingly, we have extracts from readers who preferred the older plays (exhibiting a nostalgia similar to Abraham Wright's, discussed in Chapter 3, or Archbishop Sancroft's, discussed in Chapter 4), but also from individuals who read earlier plays but found they did not meet the standards of the Restoration stage.

In short, dramatic extracts from the late seventeenth century reflect the changing theatrical landscape of the Restoration stage.

RESTORATION PREDILECTIONS IN BODLEIAN MS ENG. MISC. C. 34 AND FOLGER MS V.A.266

For twenty-first-century readers, Shakespeare has gained a glow from history, but for PD, the compiler of Bodleian Eng. misc. c. 34, the newer plays gleamed brighter than those by Shakespeare and his contemporaries. Although Bodleian MS Eng. misc. c. 34 has been briefly discussed in relation to its Shakespearean extracts, this miscellany has been overlooked as a key example of seventeenth-century reader response, particularly in relation to early modern plays. There is only one scholarly article that discusses Bodleian MS Eng. misc. c. 34, which reflects our own twentieth- and twenty-first-century preference for Shakespeare's plays over those of his contemporaries and not the tastes of the original manuscript compiler.[74] With its at times trenchant commentary, Bodleian MS Eng. misc. c. 34 has the potential to be as important to early modern literary reception as Samuel Pepys's diary is to the discussion of Restoration audience response.

In the late 1680s, an anonymous reader, PD, copied extracts from and notes about the material he read into his commonplace book, Bodleian MS Eng. misc. c. 34.[75] PD extracted from a wide array of works, ranging from classical authors (including Aristotle and Cicero), to historical tracts (such as notes on the trial of Sir Walter Raleigh), to religious pieces (including Bishop Gilbert Burnet's multi-volume *History of the Reformation of the Church of England*, vol. 1, 1681). PD also included numerous extracts from and commentary on many Restoration plays, such as Behn's *The Emperor of the Moon* (1687), William Wycherley's *The Plain-Dealer* (1677) and Dryden's *Marriage A-la-Mode* (1673).[76] PD's commentary and extracts highlight his preference for Restoration drama over Renaissance drama; Restoration plays far outnumber Renaissance plays in the manuscript. PD extracted from only four pre-Restoration playwrights: Shakespeare, Jonson, Richard Brome, and Suckling, and of these, he copied most from Suckling and Shakespeare. In 1688, PD copied dramatic extracts into his miscellany along with a few notes on the plays.

PD's commentary reveals that he preferred the witty banter of Restoration plays to the earlier Renaissance plays, but he did not find the Renaissance plays without merit. Although it might surprise today's readers, PD approached Suckling's collected works (*Fragmenta Aurea*) the same way he approached Shakespeare's collected plays (fourth folio, 1685)—he valued their dramatic and literary contributions similarly. He extracted from and commented on both, devoting two and a half pages to Shakespeare and just over three to Suckling. PD offered nuanced reactions to a handful of Shakespearean plays: for instance, although he found *Othello* "very serious, & full of good thoughts, the Plott regular & Tragical," he would have preferred "a greasy Cook" to add wit instead of Iago and Roderigo (f. 60v).[77] Conversely, he did not approve of the low-class characters in *The Merry of Wives of Windsor*: "their witt & language & conversation so plain, that 'tis scarce worth reading" (f. 60). PD's harshest comment about Suckling (that *The Goblins* is "confused," f. 101v) is hardly a criticism at all compared to his views of Shakespeare.

Taken alongside his relatively extensive engagement with Shakespeare and Suckling, PD only cursorily considered Jonson and Brome. The Jonson extract, "Two lips wagging & never a wise word," attributed to "B. Johnson," is just a single extract rather than a collection of multiple extracts with summary and commentary.[78] This single line offers no proof that PD read *Cynthia's Revels*; it may have been passed along orally or copied from an intermediary source. "Two lips wagging" only appears in the folio version of *Cynthia's Revels*, yet we have no examples of PD copying from any Jonson save for this quip. Compared to his relative disinterest toward Jonson, his general praise for Suckling, and his mixed opinions about Shakespeare, PD's remarks about Brome's *The Northern Lasse* (1632) are unmitigatedly excoriating: "The plott is tedious, and not pleasant when disclosed: Ther's as little of any Comicall humour in the play, as instruction. then for witt & language no body aims at it but bully Anvile, as dull a jester as ever trod the stage" (f. 28). For PD, Brome's play falls short of the Horatian ideal of theatre that pleases and instructs, while also lacking repartee. In their time, Brome disdained Suckling as a courtier-playwright, but half a century later, PD clearly favored Suckling over his literary rival.[79]

PD's interest in Wycherley parallels his interest in Jonson. For this reader, it is not the wisdom of the "sentences" that has value, but sharp descriptions or witty rhetoric. Unlike the single extract from *Cynthia's Revels*, PD chose multiple extracts from Wycherley, which were primarily incisive insults, such as "An ill peice of daubing in a rich frame" and "As proud as a churchman's wife."[80] After reading the play for such acerbic remarks, PD returned to the dedicatory epistle to copy one more phrase, "A double meaning saying." PD's final extract from Wycherley reveals his interest in plays as a source of wordplay.

Considering PD's fascination with "wit," it is unsurprising that he gravitated to comedies. PD's predilections are, in this case, particularly reflective of his time, as the currency of Restoration comedies was wordplay. Even these texts could be found lacking, however—PD's criticism of Behn's *The Emperor of the Moon* suggested that the play contained "some comicall passages which may raise delight & more laughter, but little witt or language or humour to give it a true value" (f. 20). PD's genre-oriented criticism is most notable in his treatment of *Measure for Measure*, which he deemed "something to serious for a Comedy" (f. 59v). In many cases, PD's observations can hardly be faulted—*Measure* continues to be considered a "problem play" today. PD's commentary on Restoration plays, and his praise of Dryden in particular, show the yardstick by which he measured Shakespeare's plays. Even his criticism of *The Emperor of the Moon* rests on generic grounds: PD admits that Behn's play "hath extravagance enough to make it a farce" (f. 20). For PD, farces and problem plays (and the city comedy of *The London Prodigal*) were not of the same caliber as Restoration comedies—though Restoration comedies did not entirely escape his censure.

In gauging PD's tastes, it is important to consider not only his commentary, but the kinds of plays he commented on: this manuscript suggests that he interacted with far more Restoration plays than Renaissance plays. In general, PD's commentary on Restoration plays tends to be longer. He would often include three sections in his response to each play: a plot summary, a series of extracts (or "sentences" as he often titled them), and his commentary (or "censure"). In a few rare cases, PD presented the plot without commentary, as with *The Mistaken Husband*. Conversely, with Shakespeare's plays, PD did not bother to offer a synopsis, and, as with *Merry Wives*, at times offered only a brief scathing review.

As You Like It and *Othello* are the only two Shakespearean plays from which PD gathered extracts. Predictably, in his extracts from *As You Like It*, PD focuses on some of the play's sharper banter. PD merged some of Rosalind's clever retorts to Orlando into one speech:

> I had rather be woo'd by a snail than you: for tho he comes slowly yet he brings his house upon his back & that's a better jointure than you can make me. besides he brings his horns along with him which such as you are fain to be beholding to your wifes for, but he comes armed with his fortune & prevents the slander of his wife. Act. 4. S. 1.[81]

His only other selection from *As You Like It* was Touchstone's "I am never aware of my witt till I break my shins against it. Act. 2. Sc. 4."[82] The extracts from *As You Like It* clearly reflect PD's self-expressed interest in wit and badinage, perhaps even more strikingly than his commentary on *Much Ado*: "Seignior Benedict & Madam Beatrice are very diverting characters, witty, well-humoured, against marriage, given to raillery quick at Repartee" (f. 59v). While not all manuscript compilers provided notes on their play reading, PD's reviews reinforce the opinions presented in his extracts, namely, that he read Shakespeare's comedy for the wordplay.

While some of his selections from *Othello* might be considered more traditionally sententious, PD's only excerpts from this Shakespearean tragedy are, like those from *As You Like It*, primarily focused on pithy phrases and cunning turns-of-phrase. PD's first extract from *Othello*, "the robbed that smiles steales something from the theif," exemplifies the kind of wisdom that is typical of commonplaces (or *sententiae*).[83] PD's following quotations, however, such as "My services shall out-tongue his complaints" are less proverbial and more valuable for their adept phrasing.[84] Indeed, PD's longest (and final) *Othello* passage is Iago's misogynist "She that was ever fair & never proud" speech, which is notable for its rhymed rhetorical turns.[85] PD's extracts from *Othello* both highlight the play's popularity in the Restoration and follow the turn for miscellanies to focus on lighter material, rather than only including religious and educational texts.

PD's miscellany offers not only extracts from and commentary on a number of plays; he also extracts from critical material, that is, Dryden's paratextual matter from *The Conquest of Granada*. In the epilogue to *The Conquest of Granada*, Dryden criticized Renaissance playwrights. In performance, the epilogue was poorly received, but instead of omitting it from the printed version, Dryden wrote a "Defence of the Epilogue: Or, An Essay on the Dramatique Poetry of the last Age" that was published in both the 1672 and 1673 editions of the play. Below his extracts from Jonson and Wycherley, PD copied extracts from both the "Defence of the Epilogue" and the dedicatory epistle of the play. Here, PD chose some parts of Dryden's more general commentary such as "To observe errors is a great step to the correcting them [sic]."[86] PD translated some of the quotations Dryden borrowed from classical authors: "Use is the great arbitrator of wordes and master of languages" and "Tis allowed to some that are eminent for eloquence, to apply received words to a new signification."[87] Whether or not PD felt himself "eminent for eloquence," he found at least some Renaissance plays eloquent enough to serve as sources for extracts.

PD both read and wrote commentary on the relation between Renaissance and Restoration plays. In Dryden's epilogue to the second part of *The Conquest of Granada*, he claimed that Restoration plays are held to a higher standard than earlier works. "Fame then was cheap," as he puts it, "were they now to write when Critiques weigh / Each Line, and ev'ry word, throughout a Play, / None of 'em, no not *Jonson*, in his height / Could pass."[88] Dryden's "Defence of the Epilogue" elaborates on this theme: "let any man who understands English, read diligently the works of Shakespeare and Fletcher; and I dare undertake that he will find, in every page either some *Solecism* of Speech, or some notorious flaw in Sence: and yet these men are reverenc'd when we are not forgiven."[89] For Dryden, earlier poetry had "not arriv'd to its vigor and maturity"; by implication, contemporary plays were both vigorous and mature.[90] Dryden's "Defense" contains both broad criticisms of Renaissance plays and usage guidelines for writers. PD was interested in both the epilogue and its defense, as well as Dryden's classical precedents such as the three unities. Although he did not copy the above selections from Dryden, PD's dramatic extracts mirror Dryden's opinions; PD chose to copy from more Restoration plays than Renaissance.

Along with the assorted "sentences" from the "Defence of the Epilogue," PD gathered Dryden's particular comments on Renaissance plays, with the marginal note, "Of Playes." PD paraphrased, "Ben Johnson in his character of Asper personates himself. . . True-witt in the silent woman is his masterpeice__ Shakespear shewd the best of his wit in Mercutio & Fletcher in Don John."[91] We cannot tell if PD read these plays himself as he did not leave any of his own commentary or notes; nevertheless, he clearly valued Dryden's opinion about earlier theatre.

That PD's Bodleian MS Eng. misc. c. 34 has gone mostly unremarked even in discussions of Shakespeare's reception history emphasizes the need for further research in the field of early modern drama and manuscript studies. There are hundreds of manuscripts that contain extracts from and commentary on early modern drama, most of which have been overlooked to date. By considering seventeenth-century mentions of early modern plays both on a macro level and on a micro level, we will come to a new understanding of both the plays themselves and the contexts in which they circulated. In this case, PD's miscellany supports the hypothesis that in the Restoration, Shakespeare's cultural currency was not as an English icon, but as a playwright like any other; furthermore, this manuscript reveals how early modern play-readers engaged with literary critics while also formulating critical opinions of their own.

Around 1690, another avid play-reader, William Deedes (1660–1738), shared PD's predilection for Restoration plays.[92] Deedes compiled Folger MS V.a.226, a dramatic miscellany taken entirely from plays. Deedes's title for his table of contents shows that he purposefully created a dramatic miscellany: "The Names of the Plays quoted in this Booke."[93] He copied series of extracts of varying length from thirteen plays, including plays by Dryden, Shadwell, and Roger Boyle, Earl of Orrery.[94] Deedes's miscellany shows the importance of adaptation to the late seventeenth century, as it includes, among others, selections from Orrery's *Mustapha*, Shadwell's *Timon of Athens*, and Dryden's *Oedipus*. In a Restoration-heavy manuscript, Deedes included one exception: John Denham's *The Sophy*, the only play represented in this manuscript that was written and performed before the year of his birth. *The Sophy* was one of the last plays to be performed before the theatres were closed in 1642.[95] Deedes's extracts from *The Sophy* are taken from one of the play's reprints with Denham's other poetry, yet Deedes set out to compile a dramatic miscellany—he either skipped the poetry altogether, or copied poetic extracts and poems into another manuscript.[96]

Deedes sorted his extracts; his dramatic miscellany is actually two volumes, with different extracts from the same plays: volume one focuses on valor, happiness, virtue, and destiny, whereas volume two is dedicated to the theme of love. When reading *The Sophy*, Deedes gravitated to commonplace selections about rulership, courage, ambition, and reputation to fill six and a half pages in volume one (pp. 33–39); in volume two, he filled only half a page with two passages from *The Sophy* about love and beauty (p. 44). Deedes's selections from *The Sophy* range from short commonplaces, such as "Judgment is more essential in a General then Courage," to two long speeches in act four about kingship and religion.[97] Denham wrote his royalist play on the eve of civil war, but Deedes copied the extracts well after the outcome had been decided.

Deedes's selections from *The Sophy* tend to sympathize with difficulties faced by rulers. Deedes's extracts, for instance, show how rulers do not know who to trust:

> 'Tis the fate of Princes, that no knowledge
> Comes pure to them, but passing through the eyes
> And ears of other men, it takes a tincture
> From every channel; and still bears a relish
> Of Flattery of private ends.[98]

Deedes parroted Denham's injunction that Kings must not listen to their subjects' unrest: "Those Kings whom envy or the Peoples murmur / Deters from their own purposes deserve not, / Nor know not their own greatness."[99] The extracts highlight the potential danger for kings, "The greatest heights are near the greates [sic] precipice," but offer hope that rulers can avoid downfall through wisdom: "Greatness we owe to Fortune or to Fate; / But wisdom only can secure that state."[100] Deedes blithely repeats Denham's claims that "Poor Princes" carry the weight of the world on their shoulders, where others can live in the "happiness of poverty."[101] Denham distanced his critique of religious zealotry by setting his play in faraway Persia, but Deedes's selections, because of their abstract, commonplace, and at times, preachy nature are held as universal claims that must apply to England.

Deedes, like others who compiled dramatic miscellanies, engaged with plays as printed texts. He copied his selections from the plays seriatim. The print presentation of plays seems to have influenced both the texts he read and the texts he extracted. For instance, he read four plays by Orrery that were published in one volume (although it is possible that he read them in two double-play editions as his arrangement follows the order of the double-play editions: *The Black Prince* and *Tryphon* followed by *Henry the Fifth* and *Mustapha*).[102] It was not just the contents of the anthologies but also the typography that influenced Deedes, who frequently copied passages marked by commonplace markers from Richard Fanshawe's translation of *Il Pastor Fido* (*The Faithfull Shepherd*, 1647).[103] The continued presence of commonplace markers in late seventeenth-century printed plays reinforces the ongoing importance of dramatic extracting. If the impulse to collect dramatic miscellanies began after the closure of the theatres in 1642, by the time Deedes compiled his manuscript (around 1690), dramatic miscellanies were not, by default, associated with nostalgia. Being born in 1660, Deedes would not remember a time when, to use an anachronistic metaphor, the theatres were dark. Deedes's dramatic miscellany reveals the continuing impulse to copy from new plays; whereas the final manuscript discussed in this chapter, BL MS Lansdowne 1885, shows that old plays did not lose their allure.

BL MS LANSDOWNE 1185: A SHAKESPEAREAN MISCELLANY

Contrary to PD's and Deedes's penchants for Restoration drama, the compiler of BL MS Lansdowne 1185 (compiled c. 1700, chronologically the latest manuscript discussed in this chapter), preferred Renaissance plays. This dramatic miscellany foreshadows the eighteenth century's changing attitudes toward English Renaissance drama by demonstrating its compiler's preference for Shakespeare compared to other playwrights. Like the dramatic miscellanies that emerged in the civil wars and interregnum, BL MS Lansdowne 1185 exhibits nostalgia for the drama of an earlier period. The compiler chose to extract from Shakespeare alone, and not the many other published Renaissance or Restoration dramatists.[104] Furthermore, rather than turning to more recent Shakespearean adaptations, such as Nahum Tate's *The History of King Lear* (1681) or Colley Cibber's *Richard III* (1699), the compiler opted to quote from the original plays.

Copying from a folio edition of Shakespeare's plays, the Lansdowne compiler did not extract from every work therein; he chose selections from a variety of plays, including histories, comedies, and problem plays or romances, which suggests his literary preferences.[105] It may come as a surprise to modern readers that the Lansdowne compiler ignored most of what are now considered Shakespeare's major tragedies: there are no extracts from *Hamlet*, *King Lear*, *Othello*, *Romeo and Juliet*—and there is but one phrase from *Macbeth* that does not reflect the plot, theme, or characters of the play. As opposed to being drawn to Shakespeare's tragic heroes, the Lansdowne compiler preferred historical portraits. Based on the number and length of extracts, *King John* and *Antony and Cleopatra* were favorites, whereas *Troilus and Cressida* and *The Tempest*, although still represented, were less appealing.[106]

Ultimately, however, as a purely Shakespearean dramatic miscellany, BL MS Lansdowne 1185 highlights the compiler's preference for the bard's plays. Perhaps the Lansdowne compiler had other single-author dramatic miscellanies, or even miscellanies drawn from multiple playwrights; if so, these have been lost or not identified, and as such, can only be a topic for conjecture.

Instead of transcribing short, sententious passages, the Lansdowne compiler chose longer selections, giving marginal notations that indicated his interest in the plays and that offer an early example of literary interpretation.[107] This literary interpretation manifests both in the opening page of thematically linked extracts and in the marginalia. The marginalia in this dramatic miscellany functions in multiple ways: at times, it links the extract to a specific moment in the play, whereas, at other times, it generalizes the extract to apply as an abstract concept. Furthermore, the marginalia shows the compiler's biases while pointing out themes linked in the plays.

The compiler of BL MS Lansdowne 1185 chose to start the manuscript with commentary on Shakespeare's plays, noting that "Shakespears Descriptions are stronger and more natural than any of the other Poets, who generally describd with too stiff and learned a manner, and often not to be understood by those that are unacqueinted with the fiction of Poetry" (f. 2). The compiler continued, "His [Shakespeare's] frequent and various descriptions of the Morning and Evening" are "different according to the different views of Nature" (f. 2). This praise of Shakespeare is followed by five excerpts describing dawn or dusk, from *Macbeth*, *1 Henry IV*, *Richard II*, and *Richard III*:

[*Macbeth* 3.3.5-8] The West yet glimmers with some streaks of Day
Now spurres the latest Traveller apace
To gain the timely Inn. [*Macbeth* 3.2.50-51] Light thickens and the Crow
Makes wing to th' rookie woode
[*1 Henry IV* 5.1.1-2] How bloodily the Sun begins to peer
Above yon busky Hill __
[*Richard II* 3.2.42] He fires the proud tops of the Eastern pines
Richm: Of the Evening promising a fair Day Rich: 3. 201.
[*Richard III* 5.3.19-21] The weary Sun hath made a golden set
And by the bright track of his fiery carr
Gives token of a goodly day to morrow. (f. 2)

Had he written out his observations more fully, this compiler's effort to marshal similar imagery would be comparable to some veins of early twentieth-century Shakespearean scholarship, in that the compiler gathered multiple pieces of textual evidence in order to discuss a theme in Shakespeare's plays.

The Lansdowne compiler did not continue copying evidence from multiple plays, but, like the other dramatic miscellanies discussed in Chapters 3 and 5, proceeded by collecting extracts organized by play (see Table 4.1).

Table 4.1 Shakespearean extracts in BL MS Lansdowne 1185.

Play	Selection(s)	Folio(s)
Macbeth	**3.3**.5–8; **3.2**.50–51	2
1 Henry IV	**5.1**.1–2	2
Richard II	**3.2**.42	2
Richard III	**5.3**.19–21	2
Richard III	**5.3**.85–86, 87–90, 97–99, 108–17, 53–58, 63–65, 68–74; **5.1**.7–8	2v–3
King John	**2.1**.241–56, 283–86	3v
All's Well That Ends Well	**1.1**.64–68, 92–98, 135–36, 138–41, 145–49, 154; **1.2**.19–21, 26–31, 36–45, 52–61; **1.3**.32–37, 204–07; **2.1**.30–33, 165–66; **3.2**.105–09	4–5
2 Henry IV	**4.5**.65–74, 169–73, 213–15; **4.4**.122–25; **5.1**.43–51, 80–84	5v–6
Coriolanus	**3.2**.9–13; **1.1**.172–73, 90–96, 204–09; **2.1**.70–73; **3.2**.73–77	6v–7
Troilus and Cressida	**3.3**.80–87	7v
King John	**2.1**.65–78, 288–90, 307–08, 314, 328–29, 437–40, 461–66, 587–96; **3.1**.22–23, 19–21, 53–61, 114, 116–26, 131, 133?, 149–54, 161–71; **3.3**.19–47, 52–54, 59–68; **3.4**.76–89, 93–97; **4.3**.25–34; **3.4**.144, 153–59, 3.4.107–09; **4.1**.13–20, 24–25, 28–31, 40–48; **4.2**.182–201, 208–09, 211–14, 219–27, 231–35; **4.3**.107–10; **5.1**.46–53; **5.2**.45–48; **5.5**.22–25; **5.7**.41–47	7v–14
Love's Labour's Lost	**1.1**.84–87; **2.1**.66–77; **3.1**.180–85, 196–97; **5.2**.69–76, 397–99, 363–6, 480–81, 842–46, 852–54, 858–63, 581–84, 410–11	14v–16
The Merchant of Venice	**1.1**.74–85, 88–92, 114–15, 122–25, 153–57; **1.3**.106–29; **2.5**.28–36; **1.8**.12–22;	

(Continued)

Table 4.1 Shakespearean extracts in BL MS Lansdowne 1185. (*Continued*)

Play	Selection(s)	Folio(s)
	2.8.46–49; 2.9.41–49, 93–94; 3.2.74–89, 104–05, 175–83, 243–47, 251–52, 292–94; 3.3.4–5; 3.4.11–24; 4.1.268–72; 5.1.71–79, 83–88	
Much Ado About Nothing	5.1.31–32; 5.1.7, 9–15, 17–24, 26–31, 34–38, 74–76; 3.1.7–11; 1.1.298–30; 2.1. 175–81,137–41; 3.1.49–56	20–21v
Merry Wives of Windsor	1.3.43–47, 58–68, 71–74, 88–89, 91, 93; 1.4.8–15, 146–48, 151, 154–60; 2.1.22–28, 222–29; 2.2.12–14, 44–45, 47–78, 88–91, 94–122, 191–92, 194–99, 221–29, 231–35, 245–51, 281–83; 3.5.9–16, 89–93, 112–17; 4.2.2–6; 3.1.~~103–5~~	21v–25
The Tempest	2.1.83–87, 89–92, 115–22, 138–40; 3.1.39–46, 81–82	25v–26
Antony and Cleopatra	1.1.1–6, 8–9, 15, 29–32, 36–37, 44–47; 1.2.95–98, 107–9, 123–26, 183–6; 1.3.3–5, 47–49; 1.4.4–7, 12–14, 25–29, 41–44, 56–69; 1.5.18–20, 27–32, 42–47, 53–61, 74–75; 2.1.11–16, 20–26, 32–34; 2.2.8–9, 19–22, 72–82, 107–10, 153–57, 176–77, 234–38; 2.3.4–7, 20–22, 29–34, 19–23; 2.7.122–31, 106–8, 110, 113–27; 3.1.17–27, 30–34; 3.2.7–8; 3.3.11–22, 23–24, 29–34, 23–24; 3.11.7–12, 15–19, 21, 61–65, 69–71, 72–74; 3.13.6–8, 29–37, 42–43, 111, 112–14, 116–20, ~~121–22~~, 177–84, 196–97; 4.2.44–45; 4.5.7–9, 12–17; 4.7.7–8, 9–10; 4.15.41 4.8.17–18, 18–21, 33–35; 4.12.6–9, 18, 20–24;	26v–36

(*Continued*)

Table 4.1 Shakespearean extracts in BL MS Lansdowne 1185. (*Continued*)

Play	Selection(s)	Folio(s)
	4.14.5–6, 62–66, 72–75, 83–84, 134–138; **4.15**.24, 27–29, 41–42, 51–59, 65–68; **5.1**.32–34; **5.2**.51–57, 86–87, 122–24, ~~134~~, 134–36, 185, 190–91, 193–194, 207, 209–13, 214–20, 238–41, 294–96, 315–16, 346–48	
Twelfth Night	**1.1**.4–7, 36–41; **1.3**.~~25~~, 25–27, 92–94, 132–33, 134–35; **1.4**.16–18, 21–22; **1.5**.32–35, 36, 83–89, 84–96, 146–49, 170–76, 204, 206–7, 214–17, 230–32, 236–49, 254–56; **2.3**.89–91, 190–91; **2.4**.2–6, 22–24, 110–15; **2.5**. 16–20, 58–60, 65–66, 68–71, 77–81, 86–87, 149–52, 160–63, 170–72, 175–78; **3.1**.60–63, 65–66,145–8; **3.2**.41–42, 44–46, 48–49; **3.4**.176–82, 188–89, 193–95, 231–40, 246–51, 266–68, 283–86, 354–57, 390–91, 361–63, 365–66; **4.2**.6–8; **4.3**.11	

Note: The selections are given in the order they are copied in the manuscript. A strikethrough in the line number indicates that the line is crossed out in the manuscript. I am able to provide line numbers for all extracts because BL MS Lansdowne 1185 is the only all-Shakespearean dramatic miscellany discussed in this book.

The compiler, it seems, began transcribing selections from *Richard III* about morning and evening from act five scene three, but then continued to copy a particularly moving passage, Richmond's prayer for victory, "O thou whose captain I account my self / Look on my forces with a gracious eye."[108] After abandoning his search for themed extracts, the compiler turned to how both Richmond and Richard prepared for battle. The extracts in BL MS Lansdowne 1185 present Richmond as a pious, brave, and solitary figure, whereas Richard is presented as an insecure man who relies heavily on his subordinates. The compiler presents Richard's final words as "Give me a bowle of Wine / I have not that Alacrity of spirit / Nor cheere of Mind that I was wont to have."[109] Rather than copying short commonplaces to be reused, the Lansdowne compiler often included clear speech prefixes and stage directions, such as "Richmond alone" (f. 2v). The opening pages of the BL MS Lansdowne 1185 reveal a compiler interested in the plays for themes and imagery; the later pages further highlight his investment in characterization.

The Lansdowne compiler concluded his extracts from *Richard III* not with a focus on Richard or Richmond, but rather, with Buckingham's words as he is led to his execution. In the manuscript, he wrote: "Buckingham going to Execution / Gray Vaughn and River / If that your moody discontented Souls/ Do thru the clouds behold this present hour."[110] The first line, "Buckingham going to Execution," paraphrases the stage direction, "Enter Buckingham with Halberds, led to Execution," and clearly situates the piece in relation to the play and Buckingham's character.[111] The second line abridges the opening of Buckingham's speech, which in the full play reads, "*Hastings*, and *Edwards* children, *Gray* and *Rivers*, / Holy King *Henry*, and thy faire Sonne *Edward* / *Vaughan*, and all that have miscarried / By under-hand corrupted foule injustice."[112] This abridgment crystallizes Buckingham's regret so that, instead of referring to all of his misdeeds with Gloucester, he instead focuses on three men he unduly executed. As Hastings warned Catesby, "O monstrous, monstrous! and so it falls out / With Rivers, Vaughan, Grey: and so 'twill doe / With some men else."[113] With only a few lines, the Lansdowne compiler captured Buckingham's karmic downfall.

Unlike the extracts from *Richard III*, which are carefully situated in relation to the play, the next extracts from *All's Well that Ends Well* are rarely attributed to characters, and instead, have topical headings and marginal notes, such as "Of Greif," "Of Love," "Of Virginity," and "Character of a courtier" (f. 4r-v). The last, the "Character of a courtier" is the longest and most sustained passage from *All's Well* and comprises many of the King's thoughts about Bertram's father, shaped into a cohesive monologue and compelling character sketch. This passage, however, is abstracted from the play as the speaker is unnamed and the subject changed from a particular individual (Bertram's father) to a generalized and indefinite subject, "a courtier." The compiler offered only speech prefixes to clarify a short passage of dialogue about marriage between the Countess and the Clown. The compiler contextualized just one passage in relation to the play, "Helena in love with her mistress's son": "thus Indian like / Religious in mine error I adore / The Sun that looks upon his Worshipper / But knows of him no more."[114] The excerpted passages offer two contrasting views of love, marriage, and virginity: the earnest, ideal emotions expressed by Bertram and (predominantly in this manuscript) Helena, are juxtaposed with Parolles and the Clown's cynical but pragmatic comments.

Many of the other extracts from comedies in BL MS Lansdowne 1185 function similarly to those from *All's Well that Ends Well* in that they are given with generalized subject headings. For *Love's Labour's Lost* and *Much Ado About Nothing*, as with *All's Well*, the compiler offered few speech prefixes. Instead, he noted the topic of the passage, often focusing on similar themes, such as "Of ~~Cupid~~ Love," "Of Men of Wit in Love," "Of Love," and

"Of Love in a Soldier" (ff. 15, 21). Other headings and marginal notes similarly clarify the subject matter: "Of Study," "Of a vain fellow," or "a comon flatterer is a favourite" (f. 14v, 15v). The Lansdowne compiler did not remove the characters' proper names or specifics from the speech, as, for instance, the compiler of Folger MS V.a.87 did. Instead, the Landsowne compiler at times pairs conceptual subject headings, such as "Of a proud woman," with concrete moments from or characters in the plays, in this case, "Nature never framd a womans Heart / Of prouder stuff than that of Beatrice."[115] Although many of the dramatic extracts in BL MS Lansdowne 1185, particularly from the comedies, include broad thematic headings, the compiler did not seek to actively suppress the specifics of the plays.

In contrast with the majority of comedic extracts in BL MS Lansdowne 1185 that focus on love and wit, many of those from *The Merchant of Venice* pessimistically focus on money and class. Beginning with Gratiano's imploring Antonio to lighten up, the opening extracts set a bittersweet tone, as Antonio replies, "I hold the World but as the World, Gratiano, / A stage where every man must play a part / And mine a sad one," headed, "Of Worldly Care."[116] Many of the other headings present a similarly negative outlook: "Of Affected Gravity & Wisdom," "Of Impertinence," "Of living above ones circumstances," "Of the parting of the Friends," and "Death an advantage to the miserable" (ff. 16v, 18, 19v). Even seemingly neutral headings are paired with pessimistic extracts: for instance, the compiler wrote "Of friendship" next to Antonio's

> You know me well and herein spend but Time
> To wind about my Love with Circumstance
> And out of Doubt you doe to me more wrong
> In making question of my uttermost
> Than if you had made Waste of all I have.[117]

While the manuscript includes some uplifting extracts and headings, notably Lorenzo's musings on music, BL MS Lansdowne 1185 presents *The Merchant of Venice* as darker than the other comedies.

Although the Lansdowne miscellany includes many extracts from *Merchant* about money, Shylock is not presented as the main character. Even when quoting his words or descriptions of him, the compiler portrayed Shylock as a caricature of a money-lender. Diverging from his format for extracts from the romantic comedies, the Lansdowne compiler included speech prefixes to a number of extracts from *The Merchant of Venice*, including the repeated prefix "Jew" for Shylock, a prefix not found in the compiler's print source (f. 17r–v et passim). The Lansdowne compiler labels Shylock a miser: "Advice of an Old Miser to his daughter against seeing Masks," "A miser rob'd by his Daughter" (f. 17v). One of the longest extracts in this entire manuscript is

Shylock's speech that begins "Signior Antonio many a time and oft / In the Ryalto you have rated me / About my moneys and my usances," headed "Usurer ~~on~~ lending to the men that abasd and ridiculd him."[118] The compiler also includes the famous "My Daughter O My Ducats" speech, but not Shylock's request for a pound of flesh, nor his famous "if you prick us, do we not bleed," monologue, nor the concluding courtroom drama.[119] Rather, the two pages of extracts from and about Shylock are outweighed by the other extracts, many about Bassanio's monetary problems and Antonio's melancholy.

The Lansdowne compiler presented abstract themes from the plays, passages directly linked to particular moments in Shakespeare's work, and intertextual comparisons between Shakespeare's plays. Furthermore, he compared *1 Henry IV* to a non-Shakespearean work. The Lansdowne compiler likened one of Falstaff's observations to Jean de la Bruyère's:

> Fal: O it is much that a Lye (with a slight oath) and a
> Jest with a sad countenance will doe with a fellow that
> never had the Ache in his shoulders. / This is ~~like~~ upon
> the same foundation with Bruyere who says that Men
> in ~~good~~ ^fell^ health and affluent circumstances will laugh at
> a Dwarfe Monkey or a wretched Tale. Men less happy
> never laugh but to the purpose[120]

Here, the compiler pointed his reader (or himself) to an intertext, in this case, Bruyère's *Caractères*.[121] Bruyère's work is a series of descriptions of different types of people. Falstaff's speech is about how it is easier to make a rich and carefree man laugh, in this case, particularly Prince Henry, than a working man. This intertext comes from Bruyère's section "of the great" with the same underlying meaning.[122] This marginalia indicates how the Lansdowne compiler read Shakespeare's plays thematically but did not consider them in a vacuum. Here, the Lansdowne compiler drew a comparison without fretting about who influenced whom.

This dramatic miscellany offers an example of proto-literary criticism, that is, dramatic extracts used not as commonplaces or sayings to improve one's speech, but rather, dramatic extracts that reflect the larger themes and ideas of the plays. Taken together, the thematically linked dramatic extracts, the generalized and specific marginalia, and the references to other works present different interpretations of each play. By gathering generalized extracts from the romantic comedies as well as character and moment-specific extracts from the history plays, the Lansdowne compiler used dramatic excerpting to facilitate different styles of literary criticism. In BL MS Lansdowne 1185, extracts and marginalia serve as a means of interpretation, by linking themes across Shakespeare's plays and by comparing Shakespeare's work to other writers'. Overall, this dramatic miscellany reveals why readers turned to Shakespeare's plays a hundred years after their initial publication and performance: they were both accessible texts that related to current situations as well as compelling historic tales.

Who read Renaissance plays in the late seventeenth century? John Muddyclift, a medical student, sometimes with his companion Elizabeth Cleyton; John Abbott, at St. John's College, Oxford; PD, perhaps studying in the Inns of Court;[123] and, perhaps most important, crowds of now-anonymous readers who copied reams of extracts from plays and passed along material from and related to plays. These anonymous manuscripts, including the Shakespearean miscellany, BL MS Lansdowne 1185, provide tangible and often-overlooked evidence of early readers.

The late seventeenth century offers particularly tantalizing examples of social reading, from descriptions of reading plays together to jotted notes that show how songs passed from one person to another. In many ways, late seventeenth-century play reading as registered in dramatic extracts continued and built on the patterns of the earlier periods: readers still looked to drama as a source of *sententiae*. Songs continued to be among the most popular extracts, although of course, they were not always taken from the play itself, but rather, circulated alongside the play. As Chapter 2 demonstrated, some readers turned to masques for reasons other than their original political impact: the apolitical extracts from *The Lady of May* exemplify how later readers would find different meaning in occasional drama. Muddyclift's Jonsonian extracts trace a parallel path and highlight how, similarly, plays changed their meanings over time and to new readers. The Lansdowne Shakespearean miscellany and Sancroft's dramatic miscellany discussed in Chapter 5 prove that even after the theatres were reopened, readers and playgoers continued to copy books of the kind begun when the theatres were closed: commonplace books and miscellanies with selections taken primarily from plays.

The manuscripts considered in this chapter remind us that dramatic extracts do not exist in a vacuum—even when they are copied into a dramatic miscellany. Readers added marginal comments and new titles, and changed what they copied. Some readers, like PD, included extracts along with synopses and reviews. Others, such as Muddyclift, not only copied extracts but also described the acts of play reading and note-taking.

Significantly, late seventeenth-century readers, like their earlier counterparts, saw plays as changeable and modular texts that could be taken apart, recopied, and reused. One of the main reasons these texts are important is because they preserve, in part, what early modern readers and audiences chose to copy. By the Restoration, readers and audiences had even more dramatic material at their fingers and before their eyes, from new plays and adaptations to republications and revivals. For Restoration audiences, pre-1642 plays were dated and could be compared to newer works. Unsurprisingly, late seventeenth-century readers exhibit a range of responses, tastes, and attitudes. Researching dramatic extracts does not attempt to create a monolithic theatre history, but rather, considers these varied and nuanced responses in order to demonstrate the polysemous meanings of early modern plays.

NOTES

1. See Emmet L. Avery and Arthur H. Scouten, introduction to *The London Stage*, vol. 1, ed. William Van Lennep (Carbondale, IL: Southern Illinois University Press, 1965). On the taste for old plays and adaptations, see esp. cxii and cxxix. See also Nancy Klein Maguire, *Regicide and Restoration: English Tragicomedy, 1660–1671* (Cambridge: Cambridge University Press, 1992), esp. Chapter 2.

2. Michael Dobson, "Adaptations and Revivals," in *The Cambridge Companion to English Restoration Theatre*, ed. Deborah Payne Fisk (Cambridge: Cambridge University Press, 2000), 41.

3. For instance, BL MS Sloane 1487 contains extracts from Elkanah Settle's *Cambyses* (pub. 1671, f. 7v) and John Dryden's *Tyrranick Love* (pub. 1670, ff. 7v–8), but not earlier plays. See *CELM* for further manuscripts with extracts from Restoration plays.

4. University of Chicago MS 824, f. 113. Extracts copied c. 1684.

5. Ibid.

6. University of Chicago MS 824, f. 113; *Hamlet* 1.3.59-69, 75-77, 78. Note that this manuscript does not clarify the "lone" [loan]/"love" crux as the handwriting could be read either way. Much of this passage is highlighted by commonplace markers in Q1, which reinforces its sententious (and worth memorizing) nature; this compiler, however, could not have used Q1, which offers a shortened version of Polonius's speech that skips, for instance, "neither a borrower nor a lender be."

7. For an extended discussion of Luscus, Sir Politic Would-Be, and their ilk, see Chapter 3. John Marston, *The Scourge of Villanie* (1598), sig. H4; Ben Jonson, *Volpone* 5.4.41-42 (1607), sig. M2.

8. Edward Fitzgerald, *Polonius: A Collection of Wise Saws and Modern Instances* (London: William Pickering, 1852).

9. Abbott copied from Brinsley's chapter on "making Theames full of good matter, in a pure stile, and with judgment." This section begins with Brinsley exhorting the reader to consider the purpose of copying commonplaces: "You are to consider what is the end & purpose of your making Theames" (f. 4). The essayist believes that the purpose of making themes is "to furnish Scollers with the choisest matter" and "therby learn to understand speake or write" on any topic that often arises in conversation. Brinsley sees commonplaces as both written and oral tools requisite for succeeding in school and in life.

10. Bodleian MS Rawl. D. 954, f. 4, (the tract continues from ff. 4–12); Brinsley, *Ludus Literarius* (1612), sig. Z2v. Chapter 13 runs from sig. Z2v–Bb3v.

11. Bodleian MS Rawl. D. 954, f. 4; Brinsley, *Ludus Literarius* (1612), sig. Z3v–Z4.

12. Bodleian MS Rawl. D. 954, f. 47v; William Cartwright, *The Royall Slave* 5.6, TLN1535-1546 (1639), sig. H3. Through line numbers for Cartwright's works are from G. Blakemore Evans, ed., *The Plays and Poems of William Cartwright* (Madison: University of Wisconsin Press, 1951).

13. Bodleian MS Rawl. poet. 172 and BL Egerton 2527, for instance, both contain multiple versions of the epilogue and prologue for *The Royall Slave* (when performed at Hampton Court and when performed at the University).

14. Bodleian MS Rawl. D. 954, f. 48; Cartwright, *Love's Convert* 3.4 (in *Comedies, Tragi-Comedies,* 1651), sig. I8.

15. Bodleian MS Rawl. D. 954, f. 27; *Caesar and Pompey* (1607), sig. C3.

16. Bodleian MS Wood 397. "No, No fair Heretick," Playford, sig. D2v. The title page has a handwritten name (Ant. Wood) and date (1664) added. Lawes's dedicatory epistle is dated, in manuscript, "Jan: 13: 1666/7."

17. Playford, *Select Musicall Ayres*, sigs. Ff2v-Gg2.

18. University of Texas at Austin MS (Killigrew, T.) Misc. B Commonplace book. See *CELM* and the Folger Shakespeare Library's *Union First Line Index of English Verse: 13th–19th Century (bulk 1500–1800)*, firstlines.folger.edu, for a more detailed list. See also Nancy Cutbirth, "A Seventeenth-Century Commonplace Book: Indexes to the Manuscript and an Edition of the First Hundred Poems," PhD diss., University of Texas, 1974. For more on songs from Restoration plays, see Spink, *English Song: Dowland to Purcell* (London: B. T. Batsford, 1974), especially Chapter 2.

19. Killigrew MS, f. 29 and p. [xxiv]; Sir John Suckling, *Aglaura* (1638), sig. G2; Lee, *Caesar Borgia* (1680), sig. F4.

20. Killigrew MS, ff. 59–60; *The Haddington Masque* (in *Workes*, 1616), Iiii6v.

21. Adam Smyth notes that of the 406 poems (including songs from plays) in the manuscript, 147 appear in print miscellanies (119). For instance, Francis Beaumont and John Fletcher's "How shall I pine for love?" from *The Maid in the Mill* (Killigrew MS, f. 54v) appeared in *The Marrow of Complements* (1655) and *The New Academy of Complements* (1669), among others. Smyth,*"Profit and Delight": Printed Miscellanies in England, 1640–1682* (Detroit: Wayne State University Press, 2004).

22. See Cutbirth, "A Seventeenth-Century Commonplace Book," and Cutbirth, "Thomas Killigrew's Commonplace Book?" *Library Chronicle of the University of Texas* 13 (1980): 31–38.

23. Bodleian MS Rawl. poet. 65, ff. 29v–30. For a list of the many songs from plays by William Davenant, Jonson, Beaumont and Fletcher, and Dryden, see *CELM*.

24. James Shirley, "Strephon, Daphne," *Poems &c* (1646), 24.

25. P. F. Hammond, "A Commonplace Book Owned by John Oldham," *Notes & Queries* 26 (1979): 515–18.

26. Folger MS V.a.169 II, f. 20r-v; Playford, *Select Musicall Ayres and Dialogues*, book III, sig Ii; Habington, *The Queene of Arragon* (1640), sig. I2v-I3.

27. Tiffany Stern, *Documents of Performance in Early Modern England* (Cambridge: Cambridge University Press, 2009). 124.

28. Mary Chan, "Edward Lowe's Manuscript British Library Add. MS 29396: The Case for Redating," *Music & Letters* 59 (1978): 441. I follow the dating proposed by Chan. See also Elise Bickford Jorgens, ed., *English Song 1600–1675: Facsimiles of Twenty-six Manuscripts and an Edition of the Texts* (New York: Garland, 1987), vol. 5.

29. Chan, "Edward Lowe's Manuscript," esp. 444–46; BL MS Add. 29396, f. 15r-v; *The Royall Slave* (1639), sig B3v; William Strode, *The Floating Island* (1655), sig. C2.

30. BL MS Add. 29396, f. 15v; Strode, *The Floating Isle* (1655), sig. C2.

31. BL MS Add. 29396 f. 39v; Beamont and Fletcher, *The Lovers Progres* (1647 folio), sig. Lll2.

32. BL MS Add. 29396, f. 110r-v; Dryden and Davenant, *The Tempest* (1670), sigs. D1v and M.

33. Edward Lowe's songbooks: Bodleian MS Mus. d. 238 and BL MS Add. 29396. See also Folger MS V.a.411, a manuscript songbook that includes music for *The Tempest*.

34. "Where the bee sucks" appeared in John Wilson's *Select Ayres and Dialogues* (1659), sig. BBv; *Cheerfull Ayres or Ballads* (1660), Cantus Primus, sigs. B4v-C; John Hilton's *Catch that Catch can* (1667), sigs. R3v-R4; *The New Academy of Complements* (1669), H6v-H7; *Windsor-Drollery* (1671), sig. K3v; John Playford's *The Musical Companion* (1673), sigs. Z3v-Z4; *The Wits Academy* (1677), sig. B2 (p. 27; signatures not consecutive); *The Academy of Complements* (1684), sig. M3v; and *The Theatre of Complements* (1689), sig. K12v.

35. See James McManaway, "Songs and Masques in the Tempest," rpt. in *Studies in Shakespeare, Bibliography, and Theatre* (New York: Shakespeare Association of America, 1969), 131–53. For more on the response pamphlet and Thomas Duffet's *The Mock Tempest* (1674), see Charles Haywood, "The Songs & Masque in the New Tempest: An Incident in the Battle of the Two Theatres, 1674," *Huntington Library Quarterly* 19 (1955): 39–56.

36. See Peter Walls, "New Light on Songs by William Lawes and John Wilson," *Music and Letters* 57 (1976): 55–64. See also Jorgens, *English Song*, 8.vi and John P. Cutts, "Seventeenth-Century Songs and Lyrics in Edinburgh University Library Music MS Dc. 1. 69" *Musica Disciplina* 13 (1959): 169–94.

37. Edinburgh University Library MS Dc. 1.69, pp. 87–88. These pages, Birmingham Central Library MS 57316, were originally pp. 87–88 of Edinburgh University Library MS Dc. 1.69. Page 88a is a sheet without staff markings. See Cutts, "Seventeenth-Century Songs and Lyrics."

38. Edinburgh University Library MS Dc. 1.69, p. 88a (Birmingham Central Library MS 57316).

39. A. A. Hanham, "Sir William Trumbull (1639–1716)"; Mary E. O'Connor, "Dormer, [née Cottrell] Anne"; and Roderick Clayton, "Cotterell [Cottrell], Sir Charles," *ODNB*. These sources disagree on Lady Trumbull's name; O'Connor's article recognizes the confusion.

40. Clayton, "Cotterell, Sir Charles," *ODNB*. For more on this particular coterie, see Paul Trolander and Zeynep Tenger, "Katherine Philips and Coterie Critical Practices," *Eighteenth-Century Studies* 37 (2004): 367–87.

41. Edinburgh University Library MS Dc. 1.69, p. 88a (Birmingham Central Library MS 57316).

42. Edinburgh University Library MS Dc. 1.69, p. 88a (Birmingham Central Library MS 57316).

43. John Tiller, "Smith, Miles (*d.* 1624)," *ODNB*.

44. "Lawn as white as driven snow" is found in John Wilson's *Cheerfull ayres or ballads* (1660) and *The New Academy of Complements* (1669).

45. The date of Folger MS V.a.409 is unclear. While the Folger Shakespeare Library's online catalogue, *Hamnet* (http://shakespeare.folger.edu), offers c. 1625 as the date, the card catalogue (echoed by *British Literary Manuscripts Online*, Gale Cengage, Gale Document Number MC4400003129) suggests c. 1650, which seems more reasonable given the manuscript's close relation to Hilton's published work. *CELM* offers the most judicious estimate: mid-late seventeenth century.

46. Spelling from the manuscript version; the printed versions reads, "Come, come away, to the Tavern I say." Folger MS V.a.409, f. 5; *Catch that Catch can* (1667), sig. F; *The Sad One* (in *The Last Remains of Sir John Suckling*, 1659), sig. G4v. The manuscript also includes another song that appears in Suckling's *The Goblins* (in *Fragmenta Aurea*, 1646, sig. B5v), "Round a Round a Round a Round," f. 3.

47. Folger MS V.a.409, f. 17; *Catch that Catch can* (1667), sig. H2v. The song from *As You Like It*, while noted in the Folger *Union First Line Index*, is not yet listed in *CELM*.

48. By 1671, Muddyclift had returned home to England. Although the British Library catalogue lists Thomas Gooche as the compiler, likely because the manuscript itself says "Lent Couz. J. Gooche, January 1672/3" on the first page, Kees van Strien has correctly identified Muddyclift as the compiler. Utrecht University's *Digitaal Album Promoturum* (dap.library.uu.nl) records that Muddyclift graduated in October 1670 after completing a thesis, *De Aploplexia*, under Isbrand van Diemerbroeck. See Kees van Strien, "Britse studenten in Utrecht omstreeks 1660–1710," *Jaarboek Oud-Utrecht* (1997): 206–30. Van Strien also briefly discusses Muddyclift's reading habits as it relates to his medical training, although he does not mention the dramatic extracts in this manuscript.

49. The diary has received some scholarly attention for its memorable descriptions of dissecting a cow eye and a dog: see Hervé Jamin, *Kennis als opdracht: De Universiteit Utrecht 1636–2001* (Utrecht: Utrecht Universiteit, 2001), 62, and van Strien, "Britse studenten," 224–26.

50. Part one of *The Conquest of Granada* was performed in 1670, part two followed in 1671, and both parts were first published together in 1672.

51. BL MS Sloane 161, f. 18, translated from Latin. My thanks to Jaime Goodrich for all Latin translations from this manuscript. Note that BL MS Sloane 161 f. 18 is all translated from Latin (and at times transliterated from Greek). For the language in BL MS Sloane 161, {curly brackets} denote something written in the Greek alphabet and [square brackets] denote an editorial addition or expansion of a short form.

52. Although he wrote mainly in Latin with some English interspersed, Muddyclift used Greek letters multiple times in his diary, mostly to conceal proper names.

For instance, Muddyclift mentioned looking at widow γαλλιαρδ [Galliard] (f. 15). Muddyclift was not always consistent in his use of the Greek alphabet to hide a name, though. He first mentions talking with Anna Pleσαντς (f. 15v), then Anna Ρλεασαντς (f. 15v, lower), and later gives her full last name as Pleasans (f. 16) and Pleasants (f. 16v, lower). Like his use of Greek characters to hide meaning, Muddyclift used Dutch to describe an erotic dream (f. 17) and also wrote a page in code or shorthand (f. 7).

53. Dryden, *The Conquest of Granada* Part I (1672), sig. D2v-D3.

54. *Merry Drollery . . . the First Part* and *The Second Part of Merry Drollery* were first published in 1661. In 1670, *Merry Drollery, Complete* appeared.

55. BL MS Sloane 161, f. 9v; Arthur Johnston *Medici Regii* (1632).

56. BL MS Sloane 161, f. 21; Shadwell, *The Miser* (1672), [2.1], sigs. E3v-E4.

57. Shadwell, *The Miser* [2.1] (1672), sigs. E3v-E4.

58. BL MS Sloane 161, f. 22; Jonson, *Catiline His Conspiracy* (1669), sig. A2. Muddyclift adds Nell Gwynn's last name. Gwynn was the famous mistress of Charles II.

59. BL MS Sloane 161, f. 22; Jonson, *Catiline* 1.1.14-15 (1669), sig. B.

60. BL MS Sloane 161, f. 27; Jonson, *Catiline* 5.5.269-71 (1669), sig. M4v.

61. In *Roscius Anglicanus, Or, An Historical Review of the Stage From 1660–1706* (1711), John Downes lists *Sejanus*, like *Catiline*, as one of the "Principal Old Stock Plays" performed after the Restoration, but we have no details of performance.

62. Jonson, *Sejanus* 5.383 (1605), sig. L3.

63. BL MS Sloane 161, f. 28; Jonson, *Sejanus* 5.390-99 (1605), sig. L3.

64. For a further discussion of Sejanus as a Machiavellian character, see Jonathan Dollimore, *Radical Tragedy: Religion, Ideology, and Power in the Drama of Shakespeare and his Contemporaries*, 3rd ed. (Durham: Duke University Press, 2004) esp. 134–38.

65. For instance, in *Jonson's Romish Plot: A Study of "Catiline" and Its Historical Context* (Oxford: Clarendon Press, 1967), Barbara De Luna argues that *Catiline* can be read as a direct commentary on the Gunpowder Plot. Blair Worden contends that Jonson's political meaning can be determined from his use of classical sources in "Politics in *Catiline:* Jonson and his Sources," in *Re-Presenting Ben Jonson: Text, History and Performance*, ed. Martin Butler (Basingstoke: MacMillan, 1999), 152–73. Philip J. Ayres links *Sejanus* to the downfall and trial of Walter Ralegh in "Jonson, Northampton, and the 'Treason' in *Sejanus*" *Modern Philology* 80 (1983): 356–63. Matthew Wikander and Peter Lake both suggest that *Sejanus* references multiple political and historical events. See Matthew Wikander, "'Queasy to be touched': The World of Ben Jonson's *Sejanus*," *Journal of English and Germanic Philology* 78 (1979): 345–57 and Peter Lake, "From *Leicester his Commonwealth* to *Sejanus his Fall*: Ben Jonson and the politics of Roman (Catholic) virtue," in *Catholics and the "Protestant Nation": Religious Politics and Identity in Early Modern England*, ed. Ethan H. Shagan (Manchester: Manchester University Press, 2005), 128–61.

66. For an example of how readings of *Sejanus* changed in the 1620s when George Villiers, the Duke of Buckingham rose as James's favorite, see Annabel Patterson, *Censorship and Interpretation: The Conditions of Writing and Reading in Early Modern England* (Madison: University of Wisconsin Press, 1984), 50–58.

67. When Muddyclift wrote his diary, there were multiple print sources, yet no recently published versions of *The Lady of May*. In *The Poems of Sir Philip Sidney* (Oxford: Clarendon, 1962), William A. Ringler persuasively asserts that BL MS Sloane 161 was copied from a print source by comparing it to Sir Philip Sidney's eccentric orthography (361). *The Lady of May* was first published in Ponsonby's 1598 collection of Sidney's works (*The Countess of Pembrokes Arcadia. Written by Sir Philip Sidney Knight. Now the Third Time published, with sundry new additions of the same Author*). It was reprinted along with the *Arcadia* in 1599, 1605, 1613, 1621, 1622, 1623, 1628, 1629, 1633, and 1638. Later editions (1655, 1662, 1674) of the *Arcadia* do not include *The Lady of May* and instead introduce James Johnstoun's Supplement, which includes a dedication to King James.

68. In his introduction to the entertainment, Arthur F. Kinney claims that "*The Lady of May* is as much propaganda as pageant" (*Renaissance Drama: An Anthology of Plays and Entertainments*, [Malden, MA: Blackwell, 1999], 37). In *Pastoral: Mediaeval into Renaissance* (Ipswich, UK: D. S. Brewer, 1977), Helen Cooper argues that Sidney presented the queen with a thinly veiled choice of suitors: Robert Dudley, Earl of Leicester (Therion) and Christopher Hatton (Espilus) (149–50). While rejecting one political reading of the masque, Robert E. Stillman nevertheless argues for its inherent topicality: "I do not deny that *The Lady of May* has a topical relevance; what I deny is that we have any certainty about what that topical relevance is"—see "Justice and the 'Good Word' in Sidney's *The Lady of May*," *Studies in English Literature 1500–1900* 24 (1984): 25n.5.

69. See especially Stephen Orgel, "Sidney's Experiment in Pastoral: *The Lady of May*," *Journal of the Warburg and Courtauld Institutes* 26 (1963): 198–203 and Louis Adrian Montrose, "Celebration and Insinuation: Sir Philip Sidney and the Motives of Elizabethan Courtship," *Renaissance Drama* 8 (1977): 3–35.

70. In the first omitted speech, "Do not think, sweet and gallant lady" (15), Rombus speaks no Latin. In the second omitted speech, "*Bene bene, nunc de questione prepositus*," Rombus immediately translates his only Latin interjection: "that is as much as to say, as well well, now of the proposed question" (31). Line numbers are taken from Katherine Duncan-Jones and Jan van Dorsten, eds., *Miscellaneous Prose of Sir Philip Sidney* (Oxford: Clarendon, 1973).

71. Duncan-Jones and van Dorsten, *Miscellaneous Prose*, 17.

72. *The Lady of May* (in *The Countess of Pembrokes Arcadia*, 1598), sig. Bbb3v. Other editions will have different spellings and signature numbers.

73. For a discussion of the importance of setting in *The Lady of May*, see Helen Cooper's "Location and Meaning in Masque, Morality and Royal Entertainment," in *The Court Masque*, ed. David Lindley (Manchester: Manchester University Press, 1984), 135–48.

74. For a discussion of the manuscript, particularly as it relates to Shakespeare, see G. Blakemore Evans, "A Seventeenth-Century Reader of Shakespeare" *Review of English Studies* 21 (1945): 271–79. For a transcription and analysis of the Suckling extracts, see Estill, "A Late Seventeenth-Century Reader of John Suckling," *Opuscula: Short Texts of the Middle Ages and Renaissance* 2.5 (2012): 1–10, http://hdl.handle.net/10515/sy5sn01m2, from which some of this discussion is taken.

75. Following Evans, I refer to the reader as "PD" and use masculine pronouns, although these are likely not the actual initials of our anonymous reader.

76. For instance, PD criticized John Lacy's *Sir Hercules Buffoon*, beginning his censure with, "The play is very far from being a good one" (f. 73v). He opened his consideration of Nathaniel Lee's *The Princess of Cleve* (1681) by noting, "The Serious Scenes of this play are well writ. A Jealous Husband painted in the Prince of Cleves" (f. 118). See Evans, "A Seventeenth-Century Reader," for a few other examples of PD's commentaries and a complete list of the plays from which he extracted.

77. For a complete transcription of PD's Shakespearean extracts and commentary, see Evans, "A Seventeenth-Century Reader."

78. Bodleian MS Eng. misc. c. 34, f. 121. The extract also appears, crossed out, on f. 119v. Jonson, *Cynthia's Revels* 5.3.82-83, repeated 5.4.393-94 (1616 folio), sigs. V6, X5.

79. For more Richard Brome and Suckling, see Brome's "Upon Aglaura Printed in Folio" in Thomas Clayton, ed., *The Works of Sir John Suckling: The Non-Dramatic Works* (Oxford: Oxford University Press, 1971, 201–2); and John Freehafer, "Brome, Suckling, and Davenant's Theater Project of 1639," *Studies in Literature and Language* 10 (1968): 367–83.

80. Bodleian MS Eng. misc. c. 34, f. 121. Wycherly, *The Plain Dealer* (1677), sigs. D2, D4.

81. Bodleian MS Eng. misc. c. 34, f. 60v; adapted from *As You Like It* 4.1.51, 54-57, 59-62 (1623 folio) sigs. R4v-R5.

82. Bodleian MS Eng. misc. c. 34, f. 60v; *As You Like It* 2.4.58-59 (1623 folio) sig. Q5.

83. Bodleian MS Eng. misc. c. 34, f. 60; *Othello* 1.3.208 (1623 folio) sig. ſſ5v [2s5v].

84. Bodleian MS Eng. misc. c. 34, f. 60; *Othello* 1.2.18-19 (1623 folio) sig. ſſ4v [2s4v].

85. PD copied Iago's speech but omitted the "She that in wisdom never was so frail / To change the Cod's head for the Salmon's Tail" couplet whose (likely sexual) meaning has troubled modern scholars. Bodleian MS Eng. misc. c. 34, f. 60; *Othello* 2.1.148-54, 56-57 (1623 folio) sig. tt. See Sancroft's similar extract discussed in Chapter 5.

86. Bodleian MS Eng. misc. c. 34, f. 121; Dryden, "Defence" (in *Conquest of Granada*, 1672), sig. X2.

87. Bodleian MS Eng. misc. c. 34, f. 121; Dryden, "Defence" (in *Conquest of Granada*, 1672), sigs. X4v-Y. The original quotations, which Dryden cites, are from Horace: "Quem penes, arbitrium est, & jus & norma loquendi" and "Dixeris Egregié, notum si callida verbum, Reddiderit junctura novum."

88. Dryden, *Conquest of Granada*, epilogue to part two (1672), sig. V4.

89. Dryden, "Defence" (in *Conquest of Granada*, 1672), sig. X2.

90. Ibid.

91. Bodleian MS Eng. misc. c. 34, f. 120; Dryden, "Defence" (in *Conquest of Granada*, 1672), sigs. Y2r-v.

92. The Folger Shakespeare Library's catalogue, Hamnet, claims this was William Deedes born in 1660. This is likely William Deedes (1660–1738) who attended the Merchant Taylors' school, earned his BA from Lincoln's College and became a medical doctor, settling in Canterbury. See Charles J. Robinson, *A Register of the Scholars Admitted in Merchant Taylors' School*, vol. 1 ([London]: Farncombe & Co., 1882), 288.

93. Folger MS V.a.226, f. 1. Note that Deedes paginated his manuscript on rectos only: here, I give folio numbers for pages preceeding Deedes's pagination.

94. The plays excerpted are, in the order they appear, Roger Boyle, the Earl of Orrery's *The Black Prince*, Orrery's *Tryphon*, Orrery's *Henry the Fifth*, Orrery's *Mustapha*, Fanshawe's translation of *Il Pastor Fido*, Dryden's *The Indian Emperor*, Dryden's *The Conquest of Granada*, parts one and two, Dryden's *Aureng-Zebe*, John Denham's *The Sophy*, Dryden's *Oepidus*, Shadwell's *Timon of Athens*, and Dryden's *Rival Ladies*.

95. See the *Database of Early English Playbooks*, ed. Alan B. Farmer and Zachary Lesser, University of Pennsylvania, deep.sas.upenn.edu, for more information. Henry Herbert licensed the play to be performed in 1642; the play's title page announces, "As it was acted at the Private House in Black Friars by his Majesties Servants."

96. Deedes used either the 1671 or 1684 edition of *Poems and Translations with the Sophy*, as he writes, "Morpheus the humble God" (vol. 1, p. 38), where the earlier print editions and read, "Somnus the humble God" (1642, sig. G3; 1668, sig. Ff4).

97. Folger MS V.a.226 vol. 1, p. 33; Denham, *The Sophy* (1671), sig. Aa3v. The speeches, presented as one block of text begin "Poor Princes, how are they misled?" and "Nor is this is all." They appear in Folger MS V.a.226, vol. 1, pp. 35–37; Denham, *The Sophy* (1671) sig. Dd1v–Dd2v. Note that Deedes left versos blank.

98. Folger MS V.a.226 vol. 1, p. 33; Denham, *The Sophy* (1671), sig. Aa4.

99. Folger MS V.a.226 vol. 1, p. 34; Denham, *The Sophy* (1671), sig. Cc2v.

100. Folger MS V.a.266 vol. 1, p. 35; Denham, *The Sophy* (1671), sigs. Dd1 and Cc8.

101. Folger MS V.a.266 vol. 1, pp. 35 and 38; Denham, *The Sophy* (1671), sigs. Dd1v and Ff3v.

102. The double-editions are *Two New Tragedies: The Black Prince, and Tryphon* (1669) and *The History of Henry the Fifth and the Tragedy of Mustapha, the son of Solymon the Magnificent* (1668). These were combined for *Four New Plays* (1670).

103. The commonplaces markers published in the 1647 edition of *Il Pastor Fido* remain in the 1664 and 1676 republications.

104. BL MS Lansdowne 1185 is a dramatic miscellany containing only Shakespearean material. The Shakespearean extracts (ff. 1–40) and difficult-to-date classical extracts (ff. 42–59) are followed by a copy of George Savile Lord Halifax's *Advice to a Daughter* (1688, ff. 60–71v) and a copy of Dryden's "The Flower and the Leaf," a middle English poem that was attributed to Chaucer in the sixteenth and seventeenth centuries, which Dryden reworked for publication in *Fables, Ancient and Modern* (1700, ff. 83-end). The dramatic extracts are on different paper than the classical extracts and the rest of the manuscript; this manuscript was probably copied

in separate parts and bound together at a later date. The dramatic miscellany section of BL MS Lansdowne 1185 (ff. 1–40) dates to the late seventeenth century or early eighteenth century.

105. The page numbers included sporadically indicate that the compiler was working from the 1632 Second Folio.

106. For a reading of the moralizing tone of the excerpts from *Antony and Cleopatra* see Roberts, "Reading Shakespeare's Tragedies of Love," esp. 118–19.

107. In her brief discussion of BL MS Lansdowne 1185, Roberts argues that "when gathering quotations from *Antony and Cleopatra* the compiler appears to have had an interest in plot" because of his marginal notations such as "Anthonys shame and generosity after the battle" (f. 31v), "Anthony persuading his freed man to kill him" (f. 34) and "Cleop. Dying" (f. 35v) ("Reading Shakespeare's Tragedies of Love," 118). Roberts also argues that the compiler selected quotations relating to character, particularly regarding "Antony's dissolute lifestyle," with marginal notations such as "Of Anthony's blushing" (f. 26v), "Of Anthony's Effeminacy" (f. 27v), "His untimely Negligence" (f. 27v) and others. Sasha Roberts, "Reading Shakespeare's Tragedies of Love: Romeo and Juliet, Othello, and Antony and Cleopatra in Early Modern England," in A Companion to Shakespeare's Works: The Tragedies, ed. Richard Dutton and Jean Elizabeth Howard (Malden, MA: Blackwell, 2003), 119.

108. BL MS Lansdowne 1185, f. 2v; Shakespeare, *Richard III* 5.3.108 (1632 folio), sig. V3.

109. BL MS Lansdowne 1185, f. 3; Shakespeare, *Richard III* 5.3.63 (1632 folio), sig. V3.

110. BL MS Lansdowne 1185, f. 3. Shakespeare, *Richard III* 5.1.7-8 (1632 folio), sig. U2v.

111. Shakespeare, *Richard III*, 5.1.1 s.d. (1632 folio), sig. U2v.

112. Shakespeare, *Richard III*, 5.1.3-6 (1632 folio), sig. U2v.

113. Shakespeare, *Richard III*, 3.2.64-67 (1632 folio), sig. T2v.

114. BL MS Lansdowne 1185, f. 5. Shakespeare, *All's Well*, 1.3.204-7 (1632 folio), sig. V2v.

115. BL MS Lansdowne 1185, f. 21v; Shakespeare, *Much Ado* 3.1.49-50 (1632 folio), sig. K1v.

116. BL MS Lansdowne 1185, f. 16; Shakespeare, *Merchant* 1.1.79-81 (1632 folio), sig. O4.

117. BL MS Lansdowne 1185, f. 16v; Shakespeare, *Merchant* 1.1.154-57 (1632 folio), sig. O4v.

118. BL MS Lansdowne 1185, f. 17; Shakespeare, *Merchant* 1.3.106-129 (1632 folio), sig. O5v.

119. "My Daughter O My Ducats," BL MS Lansdowne 1185, f. 17v; *Merchant of Venice* 2.8.6-22 (1632 folio), sig. P2. Not in the manuscript: "If you prick us," (3.1.64+) and "The quality of mercy is not strained" (4.1.184+).

120. BL MS Lansdowne 1185, f. 6r-v; Shakespeare, *2 Henry IV* 5.1.81-83 (1632 folio), sig. h5v.

121. Bruyère, *Les Caractères ou Les Moeurs de ce siècle* (1688), translated into English as *The Characters, or, The Manners of the Age* (1699). Here, the compiler

paraphrases some and then cites the last sentence of the English translation verbatim. Cf. *The Characters*, sig. O7v.

122. Bruyère, *Characters* (1699), sigs. O3–P5v.

123. Although we have little evidence about PD's identity, Evans offers this imagined description: "If I were tempted to guess a little further, I might think of him as a young man lately down from the University, putting in his two years at the Inns of Court, before he returns to the country, heir apparent to his father's onerous duties as Justice of the rural Quorum, though not, in the words of the penetrating Dorothy Osborne, of the 'sort of them whose aim reaches no further than to be Justice of the Peace and once in his life High Sheriff, who reads no books but statutes. . . .'" ("Seventeenth-Century Reader," 273).

Chapter 5

Archbishop Sancroft, Play-Reader and Collector of Dramatic Extracts

Archbishop William Sancroft (1617–1693) was an especially prolific manuscript compiler who copied thousands of extracts from a range of texts into a plethora of manuscripts on almost every topic imaginable. In Sancroft's own borrowed words, "Borrowed witt is learned theft"—although he also notes that "Wealth is better than fitt Witt."[1] Sancroft himself was rich in appropriated wit, which he copied out of insatiable intellectual curiosity. Chapter 4 offered an overview of the multiple ways dramatic extracts circulated during the Restoration; in this chapter, I focus on Sancroft's manuscripts and their cultural and literary contexts as a way to understand the means and reasons one individual read, adapted, and used play-texts. Sancroft's manuscripts exemplify many of the trends in dramatic extracting introduced in other chapters: extracts that circulate in separates, self-contained extracts that appear as poems in verse miscellanies, the rhetorical value of dramatic extracts, dramatic miscellanies replete with selections from plays, recontextualized and decontextualized dramatic material, and a Restoration nostalgia for Renaissance theatre. I examine the different types of manuscripts in which Sancroft copied dramatic excerpts, with particular attention to his treatment of sources, the layout and appearance of the extracts, and the material surrounding the dramatic extracts. Sancroft's selections reveal his taste in plays, his perception of the Shakespearean canon, and his multiple modes of participation in the manuscript circulation of drama. By removing the extracts from the context of their plays, Sancroft gave the words new meanings while also putting these extracts in dialogue with other texts.

Sancroft privileged Shakespeare over John Fletcher, Ben Jonson, and other early playwrights; overall, he preferred Renaissance drama to Restoration drama. Sancroft's extracts suggest that seventeenth-century readers were aware of the issues of collaborative authorship, play attribution, and canon formation. While making claims about Sancroft's tastes and interests in the plays, I argue that the types of manuscript in which he chose to place his extracts, the contexts of each manuscript, and the way Sancroft copied each extract reveal that one compiler can have multiple ways of reading and appropriating early modern drama. Sancroft borrowed and adapted dramatic extracts as a source of wit, a means of aesthetic appreciation, and as rhetorical exemplars. Sancroft's dramatic excerpts show how valuable this archival evidence can be to our understanding of early modern reader response by raising questions of literary canon, personal taste, value of theatre, and conception of genre.

Sancroft copied excerpts into commonplace books and verse miscellanies from print editions of Renaissance and Restoration plays (including all of Shakespeare's plays, as well as plays by Fletcher, John Webster, Thomas Middleton, William Davenant, and others). Sancroft both gathered dramatic extracts written by others and harvested his own passages from plays; at times, he differentiated drama from other sources and, in other instances, he elided generic differences; he both paraphrased and quoted directly; he titled and ascribed certain extracts but not others. To contextualize Sancroft's dramatic excerpting, I begin by offering a brief biography and a short sketch of the turbulent times in which Sancroft lived.[2]

SANCROFT'S LIFE AND LIBRARY

Sancroft is best known as the non juring Archbishop of Canterbury whose political and religious stance during the tumultuous late seventeenth century earned him both praise and censure. Upon his death, Thomas Wagstaffe praised him for "the Greatness of his Mind and the steadiness of his principles"; later historians remember him as "a retiring disposition in a revolutionary age," "the very model of nonjuring self-sacrifice and resolution," or, in short, a "man of God."[3] Helen Carron's examination of Sancroft's library adds to Sancroft's reputation by discussing him as a bibliophile.[4] As this chapter title suggests, Archbishop Sancroft also needs to be considered as a collector of dramatic extracts, a multifaceted designation that encompasses his roles as academic, manuscript compiler, theatre enthusiast, discerning reader, rhetor/writer, and literary analyst.

Sancroft was born on January 30th, 1616/17 in Fressingfield, the second son of Margaret (née Butcher/Boucher) and Francis Sancroft. He earned his BA in 1637 and his MA in 1641 from Emmanuel College in Cambridge; just after he took holy orders and began his academic career, the Civil War broke out. Sancroft was a royalist, but survived the Civil War because he neither fought nor openly voiced his opinions. When Parliament executed

King Charles I, Sancroft transferred his allegiance to Charles II. During the early 1650s, Sancroft remained out of the public eye in Fressingfield and London.[5] In 1657, he travelled to the continent, visiting the Low Countries and Italy. As Chapter 3 demonstrated, it was after the closure of the theatres that some manuscript compilers began compiling dramatic miscellanies as an expression of their royalist leanings. Although Sancroft's dramatic miscellany dates from later in his life when the theatres had been reopened, he was similarly motivated by his nostalgia for Renaissance theatre.

Returning to England in 1660, Sancroft soon became a favorite of both King Charles II and Gilbert Sheldon, the Archbishop of Canterbury from 1663–77. Sancroft was appointed to be one of the king's chaplains in 1661, was created the Dean of York in January 1664, and was made Dean of St. Paul's in November 1665. Sancroft's initial years as the Dean of St. Paul's were marked by his illness, the 1665 great plague of London, and the 1666 great fire of London.[6] Sancroft preached a sermon about the great fire of London in 1666, published (at the king's behest) as *Lex Ignea [Burning Laws], or The School of Righteousness*.

After Archbishop Sheldon died in 1677, and with the approval and help of King Charles II, Sancroft became the Archbishop of Canterbury, the clerical head of the Church of England. Sancroft's ascension to primate of the Anglican Church came during a rocky period. There was a growing English Catholic population and certain nobles openly converted to Catholicism; Charles himself was suspected to be a Catholic. Charles's international policies involved treaties with Catholic nations, and he attempted to give Catholics some religious freedoms in England. Sancroft unsuccessfully attempted to convert Charles's brother and heir, James, from Catholicism to Anglicanism.

The fear of having a Catholic monarch led to the exclusion bill (which Sancroft voted against) that attempted to disinherit James. In 1685, when Charles died, Sancroft officiated at James's coronation, although he did not perform communion. As king, James II attempted to create religious tolerance in England, but Sancroft, a staunch Church of England proponent, did not support James's reforms. In 1688, James ordered his second declaration of liberty of conscience to be read aloud in churches. Sancroft and six other bishops wrote a petition to King James against the declaration.[7] James had the seven bishops thrown in the tower of London and tried for sedition. The judges declared the seven men not guilty, so James dismissed half of the judges from the bench a week later. Later the same year, William of Orange circulated a Protestant manifesto. Sancroft denied inviting William of Orange into England, although he did not refute William's religious views.[8] Sancroft was prepared to declare James unfit to rule—on the grounds that James's rule was despotic and he had denied the Church of England—and to invite William to govern as regent of the country, but Sancroft did not support the Convention Parliament that declared William the King of England.

After William and Mary ascended to the throne, Sancroft refused to swear the oath of fealty to William because he had already sworn an oath of fealty to James, and James was not yet dead. As a nonjuror, Sancroft had his archbishopric suspended and he was deprived of his office in February 1690. Sancroft's removal from office, as well as that of five other bishops and around 400 other clergymen, sparked the decades-long nonjuring schism. To defend himself, Sancroft co-authored *A Vindication of the Arch-Bishop And Several other Bishops* (1690), in which they declared their innocence against slander: "we utterly deny and disavow all Plots charged upon us."[9] John Tillotson replaced Sancroft as Archbishop of Canterbury, although Sancroft awkwardly did not vacate Lambeth Palace and had to be removed. During this time, Sancroft continued expanding his personal and scholarly notes.[10] After a few more weeks in London, Sancroft retired to Fressingfield on August 3rd, 1690. Although he entertained visitors, he removed himself from public and political life.[11] He continued reading, writing, attending chapel, and leading a quiet life until he died on November 23rd, 1693.

A few important elements of Sancroft's biography relate to his dramatic excerpts. He was probably exposed to theatre during his years at Emmanuel College; his manuscripts reveal his interest in both Latin and academic plays. The closure of the theatres precipitated in some a nostalgia for pre-war theatre: Sancroft was not an exception with his preference for Shakespeare and his contemporaries. Although many of Sancroft's dramatic excerpts are not overtly religious, some are, such as those from *Measure from Measure* discussed later in this chapter.

Sancroft left a profusion of books and manuscripts. In his will, Sancroft bequeathed more than 6000 books to Emmanuel College, Cambridge.[12] Sancroft's books, like his manuscripts, signal the range of his interests: he collected "liturgical works, classical authors, and books on theology, church history, natural sciences, medicine, mathematics, astronomy, philosophy, law, history, geography, and literature."[13] Sancroft's library is not entirely represented in Emmanuel College.[14] For instance, the works of Edmund Spenser, Jonson, and Shakespeare are not represented in these volumes, but the Archbishop read all of these authors, as extracts from their works appear in Bodleian MS Sancroft 29—it is possible, however, that Sancroft borrowed some books. Other books from Sancroft's library were left at Fressingfield for his family, possibly including these dramatic and literary works, and many of these books were sold.[15]

Given Sancroft's voracious reading habits and compendious extracting, it is perhaps not unusual to find so many dramatic extracts among his manuscripts. Sancroft's manuscripts include letters (both written by him and addressed to him), commonplace books, copies of works in different genres, and even catalogues of other people's manuscripts.[16] Sancroft both saved and transcribed original letters by people of note as well as important ecclesiastical and civil documents. As George D'Oyly, a nineteenth-century biographer, remarked,

> He was particularly diligent as a transcriber. It appears to have been his constant habit to transfer to his common-place books, with the most persevering industry, copious extracts from the printed or manuscript works which he perused.... It has been said that no person ever transcribed so much with own hand: it is certain that he displayed a patient industry of research which has not often been exceeded; and, as his collections were made with judgment as well as industry, they abound with much valuable and important matter.[17]

Before his death, Sancroft was preparing Archbishop William Laud's diary for publication, a task he had begun (at Archbishop Sheldon's request) nearly thirty years earlier.

This chapter focuses on Sancroft's manuscripts that include dramatic extracts. These manuscripts can be categorized based on the contexts in which the extracts appear: amid poetry (Bodleian MSS Tanner 306 and Sancroft 53), prose (Bodleian MSS Sancroft 97 and 18), or primarily drama (Bodleian MS Sancroft 29). As a composite volume that Sancroft did not compose, but that he collected, Bodleian MS Tanner 306 requires that we consider the circulation of dramatic extracts as separates—those single sheets of paper, often folded, that contain one text or a group of related texts—rather than only considering the act of copying from a play or masque.[18] In Bodleian MS Sancroft 53, a verse miscellany, Sancroft selected dramatic extracts as complete and self-contained poems that were typographically differentiated from the surrounding text in his sources. Sancroft's prose miscellanies (Bodleian MSS Sancroft 97 and 18) exhibit his interest in drama as a source of commonplaces and wit, as well as his engagement with both older books and recent publications. Bodleian MS Sancroft 29, Sancroft's dramatic miscellany, like his prose miscellanies, demonstrates Sancroft's particular interest in reading drama to find well-turned phrases, but also reveals his broader tastes, his view of the Shakespearean canon, and his take on Francis Beaumont and John Fletcher's joint authorship. Sancroft placed dramatic extracts alongside classical and religious extracts, and, at times, pointed to the similarities between them. His manuscripts suggest that dramatic literacy was important for a late seventeenth-century educated man.

THE CIRCULATION OF DRAMATIC EXTRACTS AS SEPARATES IN BODLEIAN MS TANNER 306

Bodleian MS Tanner 306 stands out from the other manuscripts discussed in this chapter because it is not written in Sancroft's hand.[19] Sancroft did not transcribe these composite volumes; rather, he gathered together the poems, plays, letters, and other material. Bodleian MS Tanner 306 comprises two folio volumes made up of different sizes of papers in multiple hands about all manner of topics in various genres. Its contents were once multiple individual manuscripts until they were collected and bound into two volumes. These aggregations assemble a range of material from selections probably copied in the late sixteenth century to poems and letters dated from the early eighteenth century. Sancroft likely gathered the papers in all of volume one and much of volume two.[20] Along with the letters and poems can be found printed works and ballads,[21] as well as four types of dramatic documents gathered in this manuscript: complete plays, play fragments, dramatic extracts, and poems related to dramatic works. Bodleian MS Tanner 306 offers a glimpse of how dramatic excerpts circulated as separates.

MS Tanner 306 shows how both full-text plays and extracts were presented in unbound manuscripts as complete unto themselves. This composite volume begins with two full copies of George Ruggle's *Ignoramus*, a Latin play that was performed at Clare College, Cambridge in 1615.[22] Following *Ignoramus*, Sancroft included another Latin university play, Thomas Legge's *Richardus Tertius*, labeled, "Acted / In St Johns Hall [Cambridge] before the Earle of Essex / 17 March. 1582."[23] These Latin plays are written in neat hands on folio-size pages with very few corrections. Sancroft actively collected Latin plays: he owned a third copy of *Ignoramus* (Bodleian MS Rawl. D. 1361, ff. 129–175) as well as a complete copy of John Rickett's *Byrsa Basilica* (c. 1633; Bodleian MS Tanner 207). Along with these two complete Latin plays, Bodleian MS Tanner 306 contains part of yet another Latin play, *Locus, Corpus, Motus* (c. 1604/5, f. 240r-v). This is not a dramatic excerpt, but rather, a play fragment: this page likely used to be part of a complete play, but was torn apart from the rest. Dramatic excerpts and fragments preserve part of a play, but, as discussed in the introduction, represent different intentions by the compiler. Extracts are purposefully selected by the copyist.

The dramatic excerpts in Bodleian MS Tanner 306 are fortunes from Jonson's *The Gypsies Metamorphosed*, found on a simple bifolium (a sheet folded in half to produce four pages) along with two poems associated with the performance.[24] This particular separate in Bodleian MS Tanner 306 is a group of linked texts, all copied in the same hand, beginning with four dramatic extracts (the fortunes for the Lord Keeper, the Lord Duke, the Lord Treasurer, and the Lord Chamberlain) followed by two poems by King James

I written in honor of his visit to Buckingham's estate in 1621 where he saw *The Gypsies Metamorphosed* performed.[25] The last page is simply labeled "Verses & toyes 1621" (f. 253v). Second copies of James's poems, "Yf ever in the aprill of my daies" and "The heavens, that wept perpetually before," appear together on a different piece of paper bound into Bodleian MS Tanner 306 (f. 246). The other instance of James's poems, titled "Verses made by the king his majestie when he was at Burghley house: intertayned by the Marques of Bucchingham" in this manuscript, specifically links the poems to the performance of an entertainment, but is not accompanied by dramatic extracts.[26] Dramatic extracts, like poems about plays, could circulate in related groups when copied as separates.

The existence of dramatic extracts in this separate suggests that other dramatic extracts also circulated on loose pieces of paper. Manuscript separates do not have a high survival rate because they were passed from person to person and most remained unbound. The *Gypsies Metamorphosed* separate in Tanner 306 probably had a wider circulation and was seen, read, and perhaps copied or memorized by other readers before Sancroft gathered it into his composite volume. This separate shows that, as with poems, we cannot always trace a clear lemma of transmission, not just because of oral communication, but also because of the ephemeral nature of some original texts. By collecting this sheet of paper and not sending it on, Sancroft preserved what could have otherwise been lost. Indeed, Bodleian MS Tanner 306 contains the only known copy of a speech welcoming Queen Elizabeth to Wimbledon in 1599. Marion Colthorpe compares this speech, "Most noble prince I am porter," to others given by porters in the entertainments at Kenilworth (1575) and Cowdray (1591) and suggests that this speech may have been part of a longer entertainment.[27] Sancroft accumulated and preserved documents about early theatrical events, which provides scholars with evidence they would otherwise lack. Given the low survival rate of manuscript separates, we can now only conjecture about how frequently dramatic extracts were copied onto single pages or small page groupings.

Another late seventeenth-century composite volume, BL MS Harley 6947, like Bodleian MS Tanner 306, similarly includes dramatic material in separates that might otherwise have been lost. Humfrey Wanley (1672–1726), who catalogued much of the Harleian library, gathered and bound these pages, spanning multiple decades, languages, and genres. BL MS Harley 6947 contains a range of dramatic material, including extracts, plots, arguments, and prologues. Wanley collected a separate with plots from Margaret Cavendish plays, *The Sociable Companions* (here titled "The Sociable Cavaliers," f. 337r-v), *The Bridals* (f. 338r-v), and *The Presence* (here titled "The Court," f. 339r-v).[28] Other single pages in this manuscript include an argument for Jonson's *Masque of Queens* (f. 143r-v) and the prologue to

John Dryden's *The Rival Ladies* (f. 264).²⁹ One separate, likely copied in the early eighteenth century, includes extracts from *A King and No King* with the play's title and the clear intent to provide only extracts and not the whole play: "Part of the 3rd Act"; "Part of the 4th Act" (ff. 163–64v). These extracts were, as *CELM* notes, once "folded as a letter or packet," showing how easily they could have passed from person to person. Sancroft is valuable to our understanding of dramatic extracts not only because he himself copied so many selections from plays but also because, like Wanley, he preserved documentation of the transmission of selections from plays.

Sancroft's and Wanley's aggregate manuscripts demonstrate that dramatic extracts circulated as separates: they were not always copied directly from the plays themselves. The copyist of the self-contained fortunes from *The Gypsies Metamorphosed* might never have seen or read a complete version of the play. Separates could be copied from other separates, as was often the case for newsletters. The appearance of dramatic extracts in separates in Bodleian MS Tanner 306 shows that at least one writer deemed these pieces worthy of passing on to other readers. This bound collection of poetry, letters, songs, and other ephemera offers an example of the transmission of longer, self-contained extracts from plays. Unlike extracts that were copied directly from complete plays by an individual for personal edification, these extracts were copied by readers who intended to share them. Dramatic extracting could be undertaken in isolation, but was also part of the social reception of literature.

DRAMATIC EXTRACTS IN SANCROFT'S VERSE MISCELLANY, BODLEIAN MS SANCROFT 53

In Bodleian MS Sancroft 53, like Bodleian MS Tanner 306, Sancroft gathered poems with excerpts from plays, but rather than collecting already-written pages, the archbishop copied MS Sancroft 53 himself.³⁰ Bodleian MS Sancroft 53 is a comparatively small manuscript (6" × 4") written entirely in Sancroft's hand. Sancroft continued to write in this manuscript until close to his death in 1693.³¹ Bodleian MS Sancroft 53 is primarily a verse miscellany, containing dramatic extracts that look like non-dramatic poems: a reader unfamiliar with the source texts would be unable to differentiate between the selections from Shakespeare's plays and the poetry by John Donne, Edmund Waller, John Harington, and others. Many of the poets Sancroft chose—such as Richard Brome, Charles Sedley, and Thomas Shadwell—were also known for their dramatic works. The presence of dramatic extracts written as poems in Bodleian MS Sancroft 53 illustrates the liminal generic status of dramatic extracts. They are, by nature, microcosms for larger dramatic works, although they can also be self-contained as poems and create meaning without reference to the absent dramatic whole.

Besides representing dramatic extracts as poems, Bodleian MS Sancroft 53 further highlights the blurred boundaries between dramatic extract and poem by including dramatic extracts alongside poems and poems related to plays. Brome's excoriating "Upon Aglaura printed in Folio" serves as a notable example of the latter (pp. 26–27). Brome's poem would have appealed to Sancroft because of the subject matter: a play, a physical playbook, and the act of reading plays. Sancroft himself read Sir John Suckling's *Aglaura*, as well as Brome's *Jovial Crew*; he extracted from these plays and others in his dramatic miscellany, discussed later in this chapter. "Upon *Aglaura* Printed in Folio" is not just a poem by a playwright about a play; it was also published with Brome's *Five New Playes* (1659). Bodleian MS Sancroft 53 includes other poems that were published with plays, such as "We must resign: Heaven his great soul doth claim," included in Waller's 1690 edition of *The Maid's Tragedy*.[32] Like other verse miscellanies, Bodleian MS Sancroft 53 shows how dramatic extracts can at times be indistinguishable from poems.

Just as the Restoration verse miscellanies explored in Chapter 4 show, at times, Sancroft's selection of playbooks was influenced by Restoration revivals and republications of Renaissance plays. In the later seventeenth century, writers revivified old plays by adding new prologues and epilogues. Although Sancroft copied dramatic extracts in multiple manuscripts, it is only in his verse miscellany that he included prologues and epilogues. These poetic paratextual materials, like poems and songs, are self-contained pieces that circulated both with their plays and alone in print and manuscript. Sancroft copied Charles Sackville, Earl of Dorset's epilogue to the c. 1670 revival of *Every Man in his Humour*. Sackville's epilogue was not published with the play, but appeared in *A Collection of Poems, Written upon several Occasions* (1672), which Sancroft used as his source.[33] Sackville's epilogue, then, is not a dramatic extract taken from a play, but rather, like the poems about plays in this miscellany, a poetic companion piece to a play. In Sackville's epilogue, the ghost of Jonson haunts the stage and censures the audience for criticizing his great works, notably *Sejanus* and *Catiline*. Jonson's Ghost threatens that, if the critics do not repent, unfashionably boring plays—"All the dull follies of the former Age"—will rise.[34] After the theatres reopened, there was something ghostly and dated about Renaissance plays, but they were embodied and renewed by later performances.

Sancroft chose new prologues and epilogues that glorify pre-1642 playgoing. Sancroft redacted Sackville's epilogue to Jonson's play, cutting a handful of lines. In one instance, Sancroft chose to omit the topical remark, "Here's Mr. *Matthew* [Medbourne], our domestique Wit, / Does promise one of the ten Plays h'as writ."[35] Sancroft's omission removes this reference to a contemporary playwright, keeping the focus on Jonson's play and his ghost. Although Sancroft discarded this direct reference to Medbourne, he included Sackville's epilogue to Medbourne's translation of *Tartuffe*, possibly because it touches on another Jonsonian play. Sackville's epilogue to *Tartuffe* associates the Puritans in Jonson's *Bartholomew Fair* to those who closed the theatres:

> Many have bin the vain Attempts of Witt
> Against the still-prevailing Hypocrit.
> Once, (& but once) a poët gott the Day,
> And vanquish'd Busy in a puppet-play.
> But Busy rallying, arm'd wth Zeal, & Rage,
> Possest the pulpit, & pulld down the Stage.[36]

Sancroft's selection from Sackville rewrites Jonson's famous scene to align with past historical events, imagining a version of the play where Zeal-of-the-Land Busy wins the argument with a puppet, rather than the puppet showing Busy to be a fool. Copied from print into manuscript, these epilogues (like the dramatic extracts) in Sancroft's verse miscellany only gesture to their performed roots.

Sackville's Restoration epilogues show the persisting relevance of Renaissance plays. Renaissance plays offered a cultural touchstone for understanding contemporary theatre and its reception. Contemporary theatre during the Restoration included both new plays and revivals of Renaissance plays, sometimes renewed with new prologues like those Sancroft copied. Furthermore, as Sackville's epilogue to *Every Man in his Humour* argues, the audience's responses to earlier theatre can measure their taste and perspicacity. Sancroft abridged a few lines to clarify Sackville's criticism of those who are not interested in Jonson's plays: as Jonson's ghost puts it, "Can you encourage so much Insolence, / And add new faults still to the great offence, / When you condemn'd these noble Works of mine."[37] Continued allusions to Renaissance plays, such as Sackville's description of *Bartholomew Fair*, further highlight their ongoing importance in gauging cultural literacy. Sancroft's dramatic extracts, as well as his extracts from Restoration prologues (to, in one case, a Renaissance play), show how earlier theatre served as measure of literary engagement and theatrical awareness, as well as, perhaps most important, a known point of comparison.

The two Shakespearean extracts in Bodleian MS Sancroft 53 function similarly to the Restoration epilogues because they are written as poems able to stand as complete pieces, independent from the play. Sancroft's attentive inclusion of page numbers reveal that he took both from the third folio: Iago's speech "She that was ever fair, and never proud" from *Othello* (2.1.148-60), and the song "Hark, hark, the Lark" from *Cymbeline* (2.3.20–26).[38] The song and the speech both look like the rest of the poems in the manuscript, lineated and formatted like poetry. As previous chapters have shown, songs from plays can often be found in verse miscellanies. The Shakespearean extracts in Bodleian MS Sancroft 53 demonstrate that it is not only the self-contained, oral, and easily memorized nature of songs that make them a popular choice for manuscript compilers; in these cases, the way songs are typographically differentiated from the surrounding text in printed plays adds to their appeal to compilers. In printed plays, songs were frequently italicized and/ or indented. In the third folio, Sancroft's source, "Hark, hark, the Lark," was separated from the surrounding dialogue in four ways: lineation, font, title, and spacing (see Figure 5.1).[39] "Hark, hark, the Lark" is written in italic verse in stark contrast to the roman prose above and below. The song is visually separated from the adjacent text by the title, "Song," and blank space. These markers reinforce the perception of the song as one unit and signal to the

> Come on, tune : if you can penetrate here with your fin-
> gering, fo : we'll try with tongue too : if none will do, let
> her remain : but I'le never give o're. Firſt, a very excel-
> lent good conceited thing ; after a wonderfull ſweet aire,
> with admirable rich words to it, and then let her con-
> ſider.
>
> Song.
>
> *Hark, hark, the Lark at Heavens gate ſings,*
> *   and Phœbus 'gins ariſe,*
> *His Steeds to water at thoſe Springs*
> *   on chalic'd Flowers that lies :*
> *And winking Mary-buds begin to ope their Golden eyes*
> *With every thing that pretty is, my Lady ſweet ariſe :*
> *   Ariſe, ariſe.*
>
> So, get you gone : if this penetrate, I will conſider your
> Muſick the better : if it do not, it is a voice in her ears
> which Horſe-hairs, and Calves-guts, nor the voice of
> unpayed Eunuch to boot, can never amend.

Figure 5.1 Shakespeare, Folio 3 (1664 edition), sig. Cccc5, detail. "Hark, hark, the Lark" and surrounding text. HEW 7.11.3, Harry Elkins Widener Collection, Harvard University.

reader that this section can be removed. Although Sancroft may have chosen this song for its poetic or artistic merit, his eyes were likely drawn to "Hark, hark, the Lark" because it was typographically differentiated from the surrounding text.

The page layout in the third folio marks "Hark, hark, the Lark" as separate; Sancroft's extract further distances the song from the context of the play. Sancroft accurately retitled Cloten's song for Imogen a "The Morning. Reveille-Matin," or, morning awakening. In the play's context, Cloten has hired musicians to wake Imogen from her sleep at dawn. Taken separately from the play, however, the song itself reveals the morning context: "Phebus gins to rise."[40] Sancroft's extract removes Cloten's aggressive sexual intent. Both before and after the song, Cloten repeats how he hopes this music will "penetrate" Imogen. He graphically instructs the musicians, "if you can penetrate here with your fingering, so: we'll try with tongue too."[41] In the context of the play, Cloten's "Reveille-Matin" is an aggressive interruption of Imogen's sleep. Conversely, in Bodleian MS Sancroft 53 and bereft of the context of the play, the song could be an innocent love song, a lover gently waking his "Lady sweet."[42]

Like "Hark, hark, the Lark," Sancroft copied one of Iago's speeches that was visually distinguished from the surrounding printed text. Similarly, Sancroft's extract disconnects Iago's speech from the context of the complete play. In the third folio, Iago's speech is entirely italicized (see Figure 5.2). The italics in the printed version demonstrate that this misogynistic speech begins around twenty lines earlier, with his first italicized couplet, "If she be fair, and wise; fairnesse and wit, / The one's for use, the other useth it."[43] Sancroft could have copied all of Iago's bad poetry and omitted all of the women's mocking commentary, but instead chose to copy what was already the most self-contained section of Iago's speech. The independence of Sancroft's selection is doubly demarcated by the extra spaces around the speech (see Figure 5.2). The only other times blank lines appear in the third folio *Othello* is to mark act and scene changes and character entrances and exits: Iago's speech is uniquely laid out. Furthermore, like "Hark, hark, the Lark," this speech stands out as verse surrounded by prose. The lineation, font, and layout emphasize that Iago's speech is a single unit.

The tone of Iago's aggressively misogynistic speech to Desdemona and Emilia changes when read outside the context of the play. In the play, when Iago begins spouting doggerel about how women should behave, Desdemona and Emilia mock him and his "old fond [foolish] Paradoxes" that are suitable only "to make fools laugh ith' Alehouse."[44] In Sancroft's manuscript the dissenting female voices are absent, leaving only the conclusion of Iago's misogynistic rant:

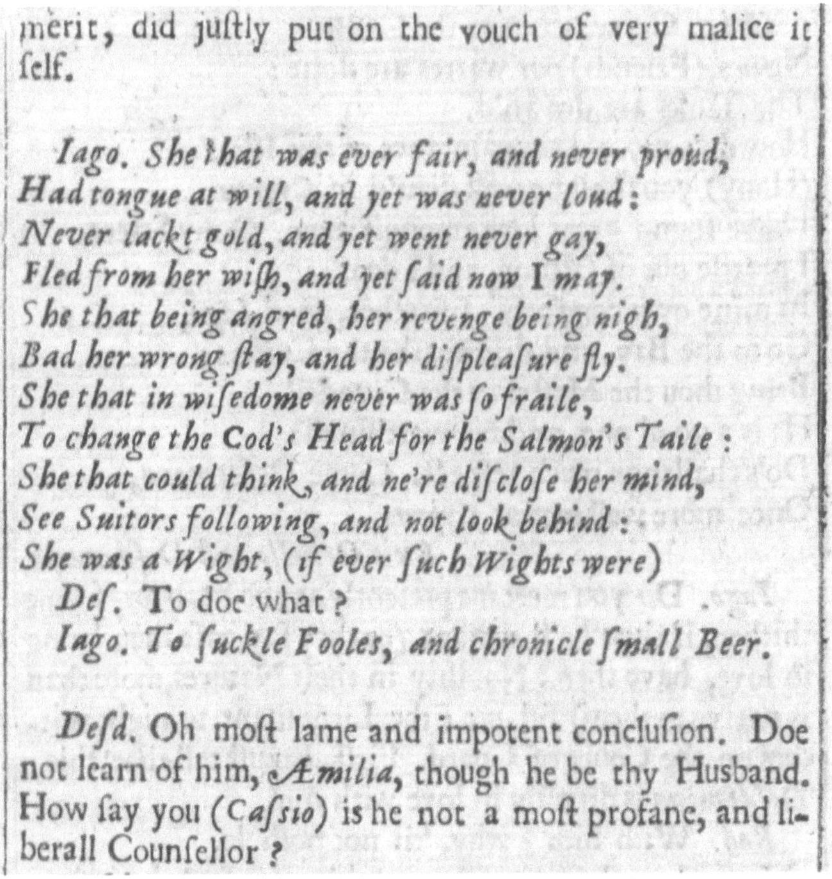

merit, did juftly put on the vouch of very malice it felf.

Iago. *She that was ever fair, and never proud,*
Had tongue at will, and yet was never loud:
Never lackt gold, and yet went never gay,
Fled from her wish, and yet said now I may.
She that being angred, her revenge being nigh,
Bad her wrong stay, and her displeasure fly.
She that in wisedome never was so fraile,
To change the Cod's Head for the Salmon's Taile:
She that could think, and ne're disclose her mind,
See Suitors following, and not look behind:
She was a Wight, (if ever such Wights were)
  Def. To doe what?
  Iago. To fuckle Fooles, and chronicle fmall Beer.

  Defd. Oh moft lame and impotent conclufion. Doe not learn of him, *Æmilia*, though he be thy Husband. How fay you (*Cafsio*) is he not a moft profane, and liberall Counfellor?

Figure 5.2 Shakespeare, Folio 3 (1664 edition), sig. Xxx5, detail. "She that was ever fair" and surrounding text. HEW 7.11.3, Harry Elkins Widener Collection, Harvard University.

> She, that was ever fair, & never proud;
> Had Tongue at Will, & yet was never loud;
> Never lackt Gold, & yet went never gay;
> Fled from her Wish, when she said, Now I may:
> She that being angred, & Revenge being nigh,
> Bad her Wrong, Stay, & her displeasure, Fly:
> She that could think, & ne'r disclose her Mind;
> See Suitours following, & not look behind:
> She were a Wight, (if ever such Wights were,)———
> R———To suckle Fools, & Chronicle small Beer.[45]

In the play, however, Desdemona interrupts Iago:

IAGO. *She was a Wight (if ever such Wights were)*
DESDEMONA. To doe what?
IAGO. *To suckle Fooles, and chronicle small Beer.*[46]

Sancroft omitted Desdemona's interjection and marked its elision with a line and "R" for response. Sancroft's exclusion of Desdemona's words is understandable because the lines are typographically distinct (Iago's in italics, Desdemona's in roman typeface), but this omission nevertheless changes the reception of this speech. By skipping Desdemona's almost-hostile interjection, Sancroft shaped Iago's words into one unit that can be read outside the context of the play. In Bodleian MS Sancroft 53, the female voices are silenced, but their absence is most palpable at the conclusion of Iago's speech. In Shakespeare's play, Desdemona rebuts Iago's speech with an emasculating retort: "Oh most lame and impotent conclusion."[47] In Sancroft's verse miscellany, Desdemona's rejection of Iago's premise, and indeed, the objecting female voices throughout the scene, are excluded.[48] Reformatting this speech as a lyric poem removes the polyvocality inherent in all dialogues, and, by extension, multi-actor plays.

In reconfiguring these lines as a poem, Sancroft added a title, "Womens unknown virtues" (p. 43). This added title can be read in two ways: it could undermine or underscore the sexism of the tirade. If the title is taken seriously, it emphasizes the speech's misogyny by implying that these "virtues" (such as never lacking gold and being silent) represent the pinnacle of femininity, yet no woman can attain them. In Shakespeare's play, Iago's villainy undermines his words: without him as speaker, the interpretation of this poem is more open to the reader. If the title is tongue-in-cheek, it points out the absurd nature of these standards—in this case, mocking the poem in the way that the female listeners mock Iago's speech. Sancroft's decontextualized excerpt leaves the interpretation of this poem more open than it is in the play.

The two Shakespearean extracts in Sancroft's verse miscellany illustrate how a dramatic extract takes on new meaning outside the context of the play, particularly when they are trimmed into poems. Furthermore, these pieces demonstrate how the layout and formatting of a playbook could influence manuscript compilers. Sancroft's verse miscellany shows how poetry and dramatic extracts can converge. As recopied and partial texts, the Restoration epilogues and dramatic extracts are no longer performed pieces, nor are they scripts to be performed; instead, Sancroft copied and adapted them for their poetic merit.

PROSE DRAMATIC EXTRACTS IN BODLEIAN MSS SANCROFT 97 AND 18

Sancroft wrote dramatic extracts as both verse and prose. In his poetic miscellany, Sancroft manipulated the extracts within the generic context of poems. In Bodleian MS Sancroft 97, a prose miscellany, Sancroft processed verse and prose alike into short, choppy prose phrases. In Bodleian MS Sancroft 18, another prose miscellany, Sancroft included only one witty dramatic extract from a recently republished play. These prose dramatic extracts show how Sancroft conceived of drama, to follow Horace's formulation, as a source of both instruction and delight.

The contexts of Sancroft's prose dramatic extracts in Bodleian MS Sancroft 97 establish the potential gravitas of drama. The first fifty pages of this prose miscellany are filled with theological tracts, with titles such as "H. A. his Arrow against Idolatry" (p. 5) and "Mr. Hill's sermon on Prov.[erbs] 23:23" (p. 50).[49] These opening pages include extracts from John Weemes's *The Pourtraiture of the image of God in Man* (1627), *An Exposition of the Ceremoniall Lawes of Moses* (1636), and others. Following this religious material, Sancroft copied extracts from historical and political prose works, including Jean de Serres's account of Henri III's reign, translated into English by Edward Grimestone in 1607 (p. 68), and Richard Butcher's *The Survey and Antiquitie of the Towne of Stamford in the County of Lincolne* (1646; p. 70). After this historical and religious material, Sancroft transcribed four pages of Shakespearean extracts before returning to his overtly religious material with "[John] Gaudens Sermon."[50] This manuscript includes some extracts from other works that might be considered lighter or more jesting, such as the extracts from Shakespearean comedies, A. O. Exquemelin's *Bucaniers of America* (1684) and Tom Fuller's romance *Triana* (1655), although on the whole it is full of dense theological texts. In this prose miscellany, Sancroft positions Shakespearean extracts amid philosophical, religious, and historical texts; scholars today would agree that Shakespeare's plays offer valuable insights on all these fronts, and similarly, these texts can illuminate our understanding of the plays.

The Shakespearean extracts in Sancroft's prose miscellany (Bodleian MS Sancroft 97) contrast with the Shakespearean extracts in his verse miscellany (Bodleian MS Sancroft 53): each manuscript demonstrates a different way of copying dramatic extracts, a different way of reading plays for dramatic extracts, and a different use of dramatic extracts. For Sancroft and other early modern readers, drama was a multipurpose resource that was valuable for its poetry and poetic language, for its engagement with interesting themes, and for its role as a template for discourse. Unlike in his verse miscellany, where the extracts were positioned as poems in a context of poetry, in Bodleian MS Sancroft 97, Sancroft did not copy the extracts with the original verse lineation. The dramatic extracts, often written as verse in their sources, look like prose on Sancroft's page, although he gestured to the original lineation by frequently using a majuscule to mark where lines begin in his source text. When copying extracts as prose, Sancroft took multiple extracts from various scenes from each play, often just one or two lines long, whereas when he copied extracts as poems, he chose to excerpt a single longer portion of each play. In Bodleian MS Sancroft 97, Sancroft offered a title for each play from which he copied, and he copied many short extracts from each play in the order they appear in the play. He formatted extracts to look like prose on the page and did not offer speech prefixes.[51] The dramatic extracts are laid out identically to the extracts from non-dramatic sources, including the theological tracts and romances. Rather than valuing the scansion and poetic conceits of Shakespeare's plays, Sancroft's prose miscellany shows his appreciation for Shakespeare's diction and wit.

Not only do the verse and prose miscellanies show different ways of writing and presenting dramatic extracts, they also highlight different styles of reading, both continuous and discontinuous. In Bodleian MS Sancroft 97, his prose miscellany, Sancroft copied many short extracts from plays in order, so extracts from act one appear before those from act two, and so forth. That Sancroft copied the extracts in order suggests a beginning-to-end reading, or at least skimming, of the plays.[52] This contrasts the single, longer excerpts in his verse miscellany; as discussed above, these extracts were typographically differentiated from the rest of the play-text, so Sancroft could have easily found them without reading the complete play. Sancroft's prose dramatic extracts (in both his prose miscellany and his dramatic miscellany) indicate that he read plays for content and theme, whereas his verse dramatic extracts could have been taken when leafing through the folio. Sancroft's extracts show that our history of reading should not be monolithic. Just as they do today, the practices of continuous and discontinuous reading existed simultaneously and could be applied by the same reader in different circumstances.

The extracts in Bodleian MS Sancroft 97 reveal that Sancroft saw plays as a repository of rhetorically well-phrased ideas. Sancroft excerpted from seemingly incongruous plays that differ in genre and register: *A Midsummer Night's Dream*, *2 & 3 Henry VI*, and *King Lear*. The thematic differences between the plays, however, are inconsequential because Sancroft was interested not in plot but in witty phrases. At times Sancroft copied only a brief phrase, such as Puck's "black browd night" or Edward's "Willingnesse rids way."[53] Along with the extracts, Sancroft included some commentary that would allow him to know what the phrases he copied are about, if their meaning was not self-evident. For instance, he singled out one line from

Helena's speech about Cupid, "Wings, & noe eyes figure unheedy hast," but added the word "Cupid" to make the topic clear.[54] Sancroft copied some witty advice from *King Lear*, "Have more than thou shewest, speake less than thou knowest, lend less than thou owest, ride more than thou goest, learn more than thou trowest, sett less than thou throwest, & thou shall have more than 2 tens to a score," prefacing it with "The fooles lesson to the K."[55] Sancroft's marginal notations ("Cupid"; "The fooles lesson to the K.") clarify the topic of what might otherwise be obscure language, suggesting that he was copying dramatic extracts for the practical reason of borrowing these rhetorical flourishes. Sancroft's prose miscellany is more than a series of jumbled and half-complete thoughts from oddly matched plays; rather, it is a collection of pithy phrases that can be emulated and reused. Instead of admiring Shakespeare's plays from an artistic distance, Sancroft copied both beautiful (delightful) and practical (instructive) extracts.

If Bodleian MS Sancroft 97 demonstrates the usefulness and potentially instructive nature of dramatic extracting, Bodleian MS Sancroft 18 highlights the pleasure of the act and shows how Sancroft's play reading habits were influenced by London revivals and republication of old plays. Bodleian MS Sancroft 18 contains a range of materials, primarily in English and Latin, that include religious letters, selections from the scandalous memoirs of Marguerite de Valois, and extracts from histories, including Sir Thomas More's *Edward V* and *Richard III*. Sancroft's hitherto overlooked selection from Webster's *The White Devil* is the only dramatic extract in this miscellany.

In these particularly miscellaneous contexts, Sancroft chose to copy a trenchant and amusing passage from *The White Devil*. He telescoped and paraphrased two of Flamineo's lines into one cohesive unit: "There are not Jewes enough; for why else do so many Christians turn Usurers? Nor priests enough; else why should one have 6. Benefices? Nor Gentlemen enough; why else one shew so many Mushroms of Gentility, that spring up suddenly every day from a Dunghill? Vittoria Coromb. Act. 3. Sc. 3."[56] Sancroft included a careful table of contents for his manuscript, but for some pages, simply lists "miscellanea" (p. i) as is the case for his extract from Webster's play. Sancroft was not interested in considering Webster's play thoroughly or thematically; rather, he zeroed in on a single extract from *The White Devil* that caught his fancy.

The unrelated items on this page show that Sancroft was not concerned with topical commonplacing in this manuscript. Instead, Sancroft was gathering unrelated material from his day-to-day reading. Sancroft's selection from *The White Devil* appears below a crossed out account for "Linen mony."[57] Below the selection from *The White Devil* are some particularly scathing remarks about Sir Francis Bacon's scholarship copied out of Henry Stubbe's *The Lord Bacons Relation of the sweating-sickness Examined. . .* (1671), followed by some paraphrases from *The Amorous Travellers* (1671), a prose romance translated from Spanish. Unlike some of his other miscellanies, which are organized by commonplace headings, author, or genre, Bodleian MS Sancroft 18 is a heterogeneous collection organized only by the index Sancroft added later. The extracts on page five, including that from *The White Devil*, were all taken from works published in 1671 or 1672, which possibly indicates when Sancroft was using this manuscript to copy notes from his current reading material regardless of genre.

Sancroft's play reading habits were influenced by the availability of plays, which was in turn often dictated by Restoration audience reception. Sancroft's use of the 1672 version of Webster's *White Devil* as a source text is evident from his attribution to "Vittoria Coromb. Act. 3. Sc. 3." The 1672 edition was the first to include scene divisions, and, unlike the other editions, presents *Vittoria Corombona* as the play's primary title.[58] Webster's play was revived in 1661 and 1665 at the Theatre Royal; according to the 1672 title page, it was still being performed there.[59] As John Downes wrote, in 1663 *The White Devil* was one of the "Old Plays . . . Acted but now and then; yet being well Perform'd, were very Satisfactory to the Town."[60] The continued Restoration performances undoubtedly contributed to the play's republication in the late seventeenth century. Even for readers, like Sancroft, who preferred earlier plays, a play's continued appeal and popularity would, through republications, make earlier texts easier to access.

Sancroft's selection from *The White Devil* in some ways mirrors his extract from Elkanah Settle's *Cambyses* in another of his miscellanies, Bodleian MS Sancroft 33 (p. 37). Both the Webster and Settle extracts are found in multilingual manuscripts without other extracts from English plays. Both were recently published. *Cambyses* was a great success when it was staged in 1666 and subsequently republished in 1671, 1672, and 1675. Although *The White Devil* was written decades earlier, Sancroft's extracting from it was not motivated by antiquarian drives; rather, like *Cambyses*, this is an instance of him reading a recent publication. As Sancroft's other extracts will show, he did not always copy from recently published plays. For instance, in his dramatic miscellany (Bodleian MS Sancroft 29), he copied extracts from another Webster play, *The Devil's Law Case*, which was published only once in 1623. Sancroft's engagement with *The Devil's Law Case*, however, was quite different than *The White Devil*. For his dramatic miscellany, he sought out dramatic material and copied multiple extracts from each play (including more than a page of extracts from *The Devil's Law Case*), whereas the single extract from *The White Devil* is found in more miscellaneous contexts and does not even bear mentioning in Sancroft's table of contents.

Sancroft's prose miscellanies show that he read both older and recently published plays. When we turn to Sancroft's dramatic miscellany, much of which is comparable to Bodleian MS Sancroft 97, we learn that Sancroft read both individual play quartos and collected works in folio. Sancroft was an insatiable reader who relished plays, but was by no means limited to reading only plays, poetry, and other fictional works. The dramatic extracts in his prose miscellanies show that he found drama both edifying and pleasurable. Sancroft collected dramatic extracts because they were funny and useful as rhetorical templates, sometimes both at once.

REPRESENTATIONS OF AUTHORSHIP AND CANON IN BODLEIAN MS SANCROFT 29

Like the dramatic miscellanies discussed in Chapters 3 and 4, Bodleian MS Sancroft 29 comprises primarily dramatic extracts. This small volume has been surprisingly neglected by scholars, although in the *Summary Catalogue*, Falconer Madan noted it contained "Extracts from Beaumont and Fletcher, Shakespeare, Sir Philip Sidney, &c."[61] Sancroft's inclusion of drama in his other manuscripts shows that he saw drama as equal to other genres; his focus on dramatic material for this miscellany suggests that he made a concerted effort to collect and read plays specifically. Sancroft's organizational system shows his high hopes for reading multiple plays while also highlighting his commonplacing ideals. Sancroft read plays for short witty phrases, memorable descriptions, and pithy circumlocutions. This dramatic miscellany reveals both how Sancroft read (primarily sequentially) and what he read (both Renaissance and Restoration plays, in folio and quarto editions). Because this manuscript includes so many dramatic extracts, it offers insights into Sancroft's taste in plays and his understanding of authorship and canon, particularly as it relates to Shakespeare, Jonson, and Beaumont and Fletcher.

Sancroft began this manuscript with a specific organizational system in mind, although he abandoned the system when it became unmanageable. The general layout of the manuscript is as follows:

pp. 1–61, dramatic extracts arranged by commonplace heading
pp. 62–112, extracts (primarily dramatic) without headings, arranged by source text[62]
pp. 113–23, extracts from Sir Philip Sidney's *Arcadia*
pp. 124–29, primarily dramatic extracts without headings, arranged by source text
pp. 130–310, blank
pp. 311–12, 315, 317 dramatic extracts arranged by source text[63]
pp. 313–14, 316, 318–541, blank
pp. 542–558 (rev.), notes on etymologies and rhetoric in Latin, Greek, and English.

Sancroft began the manuscript by setting out a numbered list of plays (see Figure 5.3).[64] Sancroft listed the first five plays in the Beaumont and Fletcher folio, attributing them to Fletcher, then changed his mind:

1. The Mad Lover.
2. The Spanish Curate.
3. The Little French Lawyer.
4. The Custom of the Country.
5. ~~The Noble Gentleman.~~
   The Virgin Widow. Quarles.

For the opening section of the manuscript, he copied dramatic extracts under commonplace headings and numbered many of the extracts so it referred to his table of contents. He used only one heading per page, leaving the bottom of the page blank so that further extracts could be added if they were relevant to the topic.

Sancroft's use of commonplace headings shows that he found plays a valuable source of commonplaces, advice and turns of phrase that could, based on their topic, be applied to other scenarios. Although Sancroft began his manuscript attempting to keep a traditional commonplace book organized by headings, he slowly abandoned his organizational intentions. After copying a few dozen pages under commonplace headings with relative success, Sancroft started giving only one extract per heading (pp. 39–51), as if he could not find any material to fill the earlier subject headings in the later plays that he read. Sancroft possibly forgot what headings he had already written, or was unable to find them easily. Some commonplace transcribers attempted to

Figure 5.3 **Bodleian MS Sancroft 29, f. i. Sancroft's list of plays.** Image courtesy of The Bodleian Libraries, The University of Oxford.

avoid memory and organizational problems by alphabetizing their headings. Even alphabetization fails, however, when there are synonymous headings, like Sancroft's "Covetous" (p. 27) and "Jealous" (p. 28); overlapping headings, like Sancroft's "Platonick Love" (p. 12) and "Love & Lovers" (p. 25); or descriptive and therefore hard to alphabetize headings, such as Sancroft's "Profane, & debaucht Atheists" (p. 1; see Figure 5.4). Even though Sancroft did not continue to use commonplace headings in the rest of his manuscript, he still read plays for short, witty, and potentially useful phrases.

The opening pages of Sancroft's manuscript (1–61) show the commonplace value of plays; the rest of the manuscript offers evidence of how Sancroft read each play (see Table 5.1 for a list of the non-Shakespearean plays in Bodleian MS Sancroft 29). After he stopped organizing extracts by topical heading, Sancroft copied extracts generally in the order in which they are found in the play. Even when Sancroft excerpted a significant amount of material from the plays, such as the almost two pages of excerpts from Middleton's *A Game at Chess*, the extracts do not offer a coherent representation of plot. Sancroft did not regularly title or ascribe his extracts. Those extracts he does title are often faintly written in the margin in abbreviated forms, for instance, "M. well lost" for Thomas Heywood's *A Maidenhead Well Lost*.[65] The archbishop omitted speech prefixes that use characters names, but at times offered markers to clarify dialogue, such as "A. Is the Door fast? B. yes, as an Usurers purse."[66] Sancroft's paratextual additions do not offer a uniform guide to the extracts' sources, although he did provide thorough and reliable documentation of his sources in some of his other miscellanies. Rather, in Bodleian MS Sancroft 29, the extracts are presented as valuable because of their inherent merit, regardless of their (often unnamed) source.

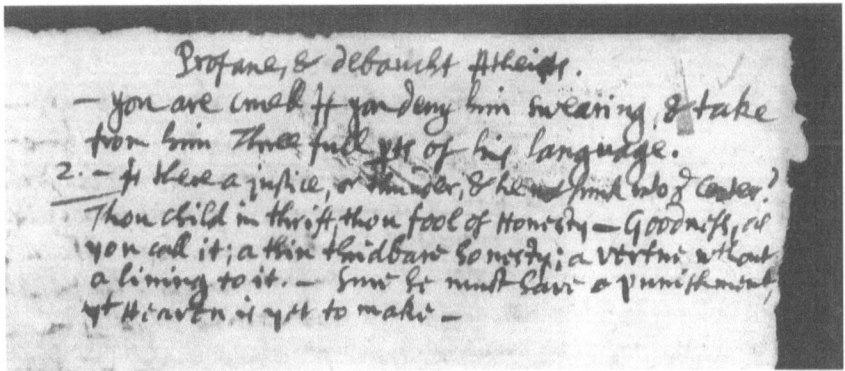

Figure 5.4 Bodleian MS Sancroft 29, p. 1. Sancroft's initial extracts from plays sorted by commonplace heading. Image courtesy of The Bodleian Libraries, The University of Oxford.

Table 5.1 Non-Shakespearean dramatic extracts from Bodleian MS Sancroft 29.

Page(s)	Author	Title (Normalized)
1–57 (by commonplace heading)	Fletcher	The Mad Lover
	Fletcher	The Spanish Curate
	Fletcher	The Little French Lawyer
	Fletcher	The Custom of the Country
	Quarles	The Virgin Widow
	Jonson	Every Man in His Humour
	Ford	The Fancies Chaste & Noble
	Suckling	Aglaura
58–61	Suckling	Aglaura
62		The Mountebanks Masque
68	Jonson	Every Man in His Humour
68	Wilkins	The Miseries of Enforced Marriage
68	Dekker	The Wonder of a Kingdom
68	Chapman	Sir Giles Goosecap
68	Cartwright	The Royal Slave
68–69	Heywood	A Maidenhead Well Lost
69–70	Webster	The Devil's Law Case
70–71	Tomkis	Albumazar
71–73	Middleton	A Game at Chess
106–7	Tate	The Loyal General
107–8	Marmion	The Antiquary
108–9	Davenant	The Platonic Lovers
109–110	Brome	The Jovial Crew
110	Sedley	The Mulberry Garden
110	Dryden	Cleomenes[1]
111	Davenant	The Just Italian
111–12	Suckling	Aglaura
124	Fletcher	The Island Princess
125	Otway	Don Carlos
125	Dryden	Aureng-Zebe
127–28	Jonson	Every Man in His Humour
128–29	Jonson	Every Man out of His Humour
311–12, 315, 317 (by commonplace heading)	Fletcher	The False One
	Fletcher	The Mad Lover
	Fletcher	The Spanish Curate
	Fletcher	The Custom of the Country
	Quarles	The Virgin Widow

[1] The extract from *Cleomenes* is cited from an intermediary source, Charles Blount's *Mr. Dreyden Vindicated* (1673).

Sancroft's extracts reveal that he often (but not exclusively) read plays sequentially, that is, both from beginning to end and in the order they are presented in anthologies. We can tell that Sancroft used multiple anthologies of plays, including Beaumont and Fletcher's 1647 *Comedies and Tragedies*, Jonson's 1616 *Workes*, and Shakespeare's 1664 third folio. Knowing that Sancroft was reading from collections of multiple plays offers insight into his opinions about particular playwrights, as well as his ideas of authorship and canon. Sancroft's use of these three folio anthologies demonstrates his lack of attention to Jonson's works in this manuscript, his hesitation about Beaumont and Fletcher, and his penchant for Shakespeare. Sancroft's manuscripts indicate his awareness of authorial issues as it relates to these three: notably, he pointed out Jonson's classical sources, credited Fletcher (and not Beaumont) with the plays in their folio, and depicted a particular view of Shakespeare's canon.

Although Jonson's plays are underrepresented in Bodleian MS Sancroft 29, his other manuscripts suggest that reading Jonson's works was an integral part of dramatic literacy. Sancroft had access to a folio of Jonson's collected works, yet chose only a few selections from the first two plays in the collection, *Every Man in his Humour* and *Every Man out of his Humour*. We know Sancroft's Jonsonian source because Sancroft copied a phrase that is found only in the folio versions ("un-in-one-breath-utterable") and provided page numbers from the 1616 edition.[67] Sancroft could have selected extracts from a much broader range of Jonson's works, including further plays, masques, and poetry. Instead, he chose to copy only a few lines from the humors plays, as well as selections from a poem "To Esme, Lord Aubigny."[68] Sancroft's other manuscripts suggest that readers would know Jonson's works; for instance, the Sedley epilogues in Sancroft's verse miscellany assume familiarity with *Bartholomew Fair*, *Sejanus*, and *Catiline*. In Bodleian MS Sancroft 27, the archbishop quotes from Cicero's *In Verrem* and links it to Jonson's work: "See how Ben Johnson makes use of this, <u>Silent Woman</u> Act. 2. Sc. 6."[69] Although Sancroft did not copy from many Jonsonian plays in his dramatic miscellany, he demonstrates a familiarity with them elsewhere.

Sancroft copied far more from Beaumont and Fletcher than he did from Jonson; indeed, the archbishop began compiling this manuscript by extracting only from the 1647 Beaumont and Fletcher first folio. Sancroft's use of the 1647 folio is evident because he quoted from the frontispiece with Fletcher's portrait, an element that was not reprinted in the second folio. The first four plays in Sancroft's index are in the same order as the collected works. Although Sancroft intended to continue copying extracts from the Beaumont and Fletcher folio (as the reconsidered *Noble Gentleman* title shows, see Figure 5.3), he instead turned to other plays for extracts (namely, Francis Quarles's *The Virgin Widow*). Sancroft's initial enthusiasm for Beaumont and Fletcher's plays petered out as he found more captivating dramatic material. Sancroft expressed his mixed feelings about Beaumont and Fletcher's complete works, saying that he "took the pains (the pleasure rather) to read it over."[70]

Sancroft's dramatic miscellany conveys not only his ambivalence toward Beaumont and Fletcher's plays but also his hesitance to include Beaumont as a co-author. Sancroft only ascribed the plays to Fletcher. In his source, the frontispiece (see Figure 5.5) conspicuously omits Beaumont, while facing a title page that names both Beaumont and Fletcher.[71] Sancroft's attribution of the plays to Fletcher might indicate that he was swayed by Beaumont's absence from the frontispiece, or that he was aware of the questionable attribution of these pages. If Sancroft believed that Beaumont had little to do with the plays, his would not have been a lone dissenting voice; in his *Small Poems* (1658), Aston Cokayne had reprimanded Humphrey Moseley for false advertising, claiming that Fletcher wrote the majority of each play and that Philip Massinger had a part in some. Sancroft may have purposefully omitted or simply overlooked Beaumont's name. Regardless, the archbishop's manuscript presents a single-author approach to the plays in the Beaumont and Fletcher canon.

Extracts from paratextual material published with plays such as frontispieces can often be as valuable and revealing as the dramatic extracts themselves. Sancroft copied only part of the inscription on the 1647 folio frontispiece: "Fletcher, friend to Beaumont and thus a two-headed Parnassus...your features are depicted here but not your spirit."[72] This excerpt from John Berkenhead's poem about Fletcher takes on an entirely new meaning in Sancroft's commonplace book. In Bodleian MS Sancroft 29, Fletcher is no longer "depicted" by a portrait; rather, Fletcher is now portrayed by portions of the drama he wrote—he is constructed in this manuscript by a collection of dramatic extracts. "Feature" similarly changes meaning: Fletcher is no long formed by facial features but is instead constituted by the parts of plays.[73] Sancroft becomes the artist portraying Fletcher, supplanting William Marshall, the portrait's engraver. Sancroft's extracts present Fletcher as an individual playwright, not a collaborator; other seventeenth-century readers, like Sancroft, could have drawn similar conclusions from the frontispiece of *Comedies and Tragedies* and Cokayne's poem.

Sancroft's marginalia reveals that he was familiar with more Beaumont and Fletcher plays than those from which he gathered extracts, as was the case for Jonson. Following the extract from the frontispiece, Sancroft copied another description of Fletcher from a paratext of the first folio, the final stanza of Waller's "Upon Mr. John Fletcher's playes."[74] Because Sancroft chose to omit the poem's opening lines, "Fletcher, to thee, wee do not only owe / All these good Playes, but all those of others too," he added Fletcher's name to the final stanza. Even though he altered Waller's poem, Sancroft carefully retained its relation to Fletcher. Even more telling, perhaps, is that Sancroft explained the identity of Fletcher's "inimitable Maid," inserting Aspatia's name beside Waller's poetic description of her (p. 63). The addition of Aspatia's name indicates that Sancroft was familiar with more of the Fletcher canon than just those four plays he extracted in his dramatic miscellany.

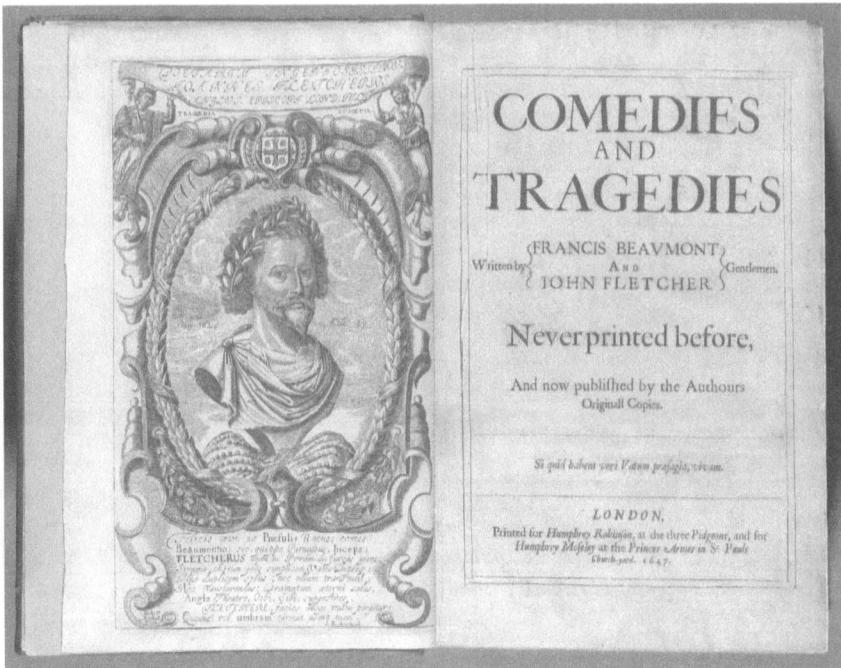

Figure 5.5 Title page and frontispiece of the first Beaumont and Fletcher folio (1647). HEW 7.11.5, Harry Elkins Widener Collection, Harvard University.

Although he did not include any extracts from *The Maid's Tragedy*, he can name its heroine. Sancroft's para-dramatic material and annotations supplement his dramatic extracts as evidence of his extensive play reading habits, particularly in relation to Fletcher and Jonson.

Unlike his selective extracts from Beaumont and Fletcher's and Jonson's works, Sancroft extracted broadly from Shakespeare's folio. Sancroft's treatment of Shakespearean (and apocryphal) plays demonstrates his high estimation of Shakespeare's plays and his understanding of the Shakespearean canon. Sancroft excerpted more than a page of extracts from *Pericles*, a single line from both *Sir John Oldcastle* and *The London Prodigal*, and a handful of extracts from *The Puritan Widow*, *Locrine*, and *A Yorkshire Tragedy* (see Table 5.2). This suggests that he was using the expanded 1664 edition of Shakespeare's works, which announced that it included "seven Playes, never before Printed in Folio."[75] The extracts Sancroft copied from particular apocryphal plays appear in the middle of a twenty-eight-page long section of the manuscript filled entirely with Shakespeare's other works (see Table 5.2), labeled "Shakespear" (p. 75, margin). Sancroft's dramatic

Table 5.2 Shakespearean and apocryphal extracts in Bodleian MS Sancroft 29.

Page(s)	Title
29, 75	The Two Gentlemen of Verona
67, 315	The Two Noble Kinsmen
75, 85–86	Measure for Measure
76–77	Pericles
77	Sir John Oldcastle
77	The London Prodigal
77	The Puritan Widow
77	A Yorkshire Tragedy
77	Locrine
77–79	Troilus and Cressida
79–80	The Winter's Tale
80–81	All's Well that Ends Well
81	The Comedy of Errors
82	King John
82–83	Much Ado About Nothing
83	The Taming of the Shrew
83–84	As You Like It
84	Love's Labour's Lost
85	The Merchant of Venice
86	A Midsummer Night's Dream
86	Merry Wives of Windsor
86	Richard III
86–87	Othello
87–88	Romeo and Juliet
88–89	Cymbeline
89–90	Henry VIII
90–91	Timon of Athens
91	Titus Andronicus
91–92	Antony and Cleopatra
92–94	Hamlet
94–95	Macbeth
95	King Lear
95–96	Julius Caesar
96–99	Coriolanus
99–100	1 Henry IV
100–101	2 Henry IV
101–102	Henry V
102	1 Henry VI
102–103	2 Henry VI
103	3 Henry VI
103–104	The Tempest

miscellany suggests that he believed *Pericles* to be a work of Shakespeare, although he did not put as much faith in the other attributions—or, perhaps, as a reader, he did not find as much worthy material in the other plays included in the 1664 edition. Sancroft's judicious use of source material suggests that while early modern readers valued prestigious and useful folio editions, they did not see the printed text as inherently trustworthy or as an unalterable whole.

Just as it is possible to determine Sancroft's dramatic tastes by what he chose to excerpt, his omissions can be equally telling. Sancroft's dramatic miscellany reveals his preference for Renaissance writers over Restoration writers (see Table 5.1). He selected extracts from only four plays composed after 1660: Sedley's *The Mulberry Garden,* Dryden's *Aureng-Zebe*, Thomas Otway's *Don Carlo*, and the chronologically latest, Nahum Tate's *The Loyal General* (1680). In Sancroft's dramatic miscellany, the Elizabethan and Stuart plays far outnumber the Restoration plays.[76] The Restoration playwrights Sancroft passed over when reading plays for this miscellany include William Wycherley, George Etheridge, and Aphra Behn. Sancroft's omissions do not reflect an active dislike or disdain toward Restoration theatre; indeed, he copied extracts from Charles Blount's *Mr. Dreyden Vindicated*, which praises Dryden as a poet and playwright (p. 110). Sancroft's miscellany implies that the archbishop was not averse to Restoration plays; he simply preferred earlier ones.

Beyond showing Sancroft's broader tastes in plays and playwrights, his dramatic miscellany also reveals his interest in each play. These extracts will surely reward further analysis; here, I touch on just a few plays in depth, focusing on the most prevalent dramatist in this collection, Shakespeare. Approaching Sancroft's Shakespearean extracts (and the other extracts not arranged by commonplace heading) can be disconcerting for a modern reader. Sancroft rarely identified the play from which he copied, and generally separated each play with a small dash between the lines, although at times he does not separate the plays at all. This lack of visual cues leads to some incongruous moments in reading his manuscript. Consider, for instance, these unmarked transitions from *The Merry Wives of Windsor* to *Richard III* and then to *Othello*:

> [*Merry Wives* 4.2.223-24] Come then, to the forge with it, & shape it; I would not have things cool then.
> [5.1.24-25] When I pluckt Geese, plaid truant, whipt the Top
> [*Richard III* 1.1.9] Grim-visag'd War hath smoothd his wrinckled front: [1.1.7] Our bruised Arms hung up for monum[en]ts
> [3.2.38] It is a reeling World. [3.1.37] a tottering State.
> [3.5.27-29]—made him my Book wherein my Soul recorded
> The History of her most secret thoughts: so smooth he
> daub'd his Vice with Shew of Vertue
> [5.3.209-10] the Early Village-cock hath twice done Salutation
> to the Morn—[*Othello* 1.3.256] a Moth of peace
> [1.1.2-3, paraphrase]—commanded my purse, qu. the strings were his—
> [1.1.91]—the Devil will make a Grandsire of you. (p. 86)

Sancroft's extracts juxtapose various genres, themes, topics, and situations. The first unmarked transition, from Falstaff's speech vowing revenge on Ford to Richard III's famous introduction of his villainy, is a jarring move from comedy to tragedy. Falstaff's and Richard's lines are entirely decontextualized. The solemn effect of "Grim visaged War" is undermined when placed next to "pluckt geese." The second unmarked transition to *Othello* comes, even more surprisingly, mid-line. The phrases from *The Merry Wives of Windsor*, *Richard III*, and *Othello* show that here Sancroft was not copying for a theme or plot, but rather for interesting phrases: those that are rhetorically innovative and catching.

The phrases that interested Sancroft are not always beautiful, nor even erudite. For instance, one of Sancroft's interests was copying the most colorful insults from *Timon of Athens*. Sancroft strung the insults together, regardless of who spoke them. In the play, Timon and Apemantius hurl abusive epithets at each other:

> TIMON. Away thou issue of a mangy dog.
>   Choller does kill me,
>   That thou art alive; I swound to see thee.
> APEMANTIUS. Would thou wouldst burst.
> TIMON. Away thou tedious rogue, I am sorry I shall lose
>   a stone by thee.
> APEMANTIUS. Beast.
> TIMON. Slave.
> APEMANTIUS. Toad.
> TIMON. Rogue, rogue, rogue.[77]

Sancroft created his own effective insult from Shakespeare's material: "Slave, Beast, Toad, Issue of a mangie Dog; How do I swoon to see thee!" (p. 91). In his unflattering depiction, Bishop Burnet, one of Sancroft's contemporaries, described Sancroft's "timorous temper," a trait that more favorable descriptions also highlight.[78] It is difficult to envision the meek archbishop using these insults, although it is compelling to picture bookish Sancroft quietly reveling in the rude slurs, imagining a time when he might use them. Sancroft not only copied insults from *Timon*; he also included a page headed "Epithetes" with other choice aspersions, mainly taken from Fletcher's plays, such as "dead peace, this bastard breeding lowzy lazy idlenesse" from *The Mad Lover*.[79] While Sancroft's extracts could be used as a template for actual discourse, they could also have been copied as exercises or flights of fancy that were never intended to leave the page.

Sancroft's interest in insults might explain his choice of extracts from *3 Henry VI*, entirely given here, all of which focus on either Richard or Warwick:

> Of Rich[ar]d 3d| Love did forswear him in his Mothers womb;
> That he might never deal in her soft lawes, He did cor=
> rupt frail N[atu]re with some Bribe, To shrink his Arm
> up like a witherd shrub, To make an Envious-
> Mountain on his back, Where sits Deformity to
> mock his Body, To shape his legs of an unequall size
> To disproportion him in every part, like to a chaos, or
> unlickt Bearswhelp, That carries no Impression
> like the Damm.
> I'd rather chop this Hand off with a blow, And with the other
> fling it at thy face, Than bear so low a sail to strike to ^thee^
> Thus yields the Cedar to the Axes edge, who's arms gave
> shelter to the princely Eagle, Under who's shade the
> ramping Lion slept, Who's top branch overpeerd
> Jove's spreading tree, and kept low shrubs from Winter's
> powerf[ul] wind. (of Warwick's fall
> Lascivious Edw[ard] perjur'd George, misshapen Dick
> Richard 3d| The owl shrik'd at his Birth, the night crow
> cry'd, The Raven croak'd upon the chimney's Top; And
> chattring pies in dismal Discord sung; His Mother
> felt more than a Mothers pain And yet brought forth
> less than a Mothers Hope, A rude, deform'd, & indigested
> Lump, ~~He~~ came into the World with his legs forward:
> the midwife, & the women cry'd O Jesu bless me, he
> is born with teeth,- As he would bite the World[80]

Sancroft's demarcated "Of Richard 3d" marks his interest in the play's subject matter. He changed the first speech he extracts so it is no longer spoken in Richard's first person, but instead in a descriptive third person. Richard's "Love forswore me in my Mothers Womb" became "Love did forswear him in his Mothers womb"[81]: Sancroft, while interested in Richard, distanced himself from Richard's subject position. Similarly, Sancroft took King Henry's second-person description of Richard, "The Owle shriek'd at thy birth," and changed it to "The owl shrik'd at *his* Birth," so it no longer addresses Richard directly, but can be used as a descriptive insult (emphasis mine).[82] The second speech is an amalgam of Henry's and Richard's words, demonstrating Sancroft's main interest in the play: the vicious language used to vilify Richard.[83] Sancroft's interest in Richard's character and the aspersions that describe him is further supported by his extracts from More's *Richard the Third* in Bodleian MS Sancroft 97.

Sancroft's manipulation of multiple speeches is particularly pointed when we consider his selections from *Measure for Measure* in relation to his rocky political situation. Sancroft altered Isabella's soliloquy on her brother's support of her chastity. Shakespeare's original runs, "That had he twenty heads to tender down / On twenty bloody blocks, hee'ld yeeld them up, / Before his sister should her body stoop / To such abhord pollution."[84] Sancroft changed it to first person and gave the speaker more bravery and less reliance on outside sources: "Nay had I 20 Heads to tender down On 20 bloody Blocks, / I'ld yeeld them up, before I'ld do't—Were it but my Life, / I'ld throw it down as frankly as a pin."[85] Sancroft's version generalizes Isabella's lines: the "it" that the speaker would not do is no longer restricted to sexual submission. It is tempting to imagine Sancroft, re-casting himself as a martyr because of his political and religious beliefs, identifying with Shakespeare's words.[86] It seems unlikely that Sancroft considered himself a royalist martyr during the Civil War, as he remained silent and did not serve. In 1688, however, Sancroft (as one of the Seven Bishops) took a stance and refused to announce James II's Declaration of Indulgence, a declaration that would have led to broader freedom of religion in England. Sancroft stood trial rather than announce the declaration from his pulpit, leading to great popular support.[87] In 1689, Sancroft was at the forefront of the nonjurors, refusing to swear the oath of fealty to William and Mary, a refusal that ultimately cost him his position and social standing. Sancroft's generalized extracts personalize Shakespeare's expression of a desire for martyrdom. While not exactly commonplaces, these extracts are part of a collective and common experience. Sancroft's extracts from *Measure for Measure* offer his customized statement of religious martyrdom by using first person to indicate his appropriation of the sentiment; Sancroft's political and religious stance, that is, the evidence of his biography, supports this reading.[88] By changing Shakespeare's words to the first person, Sancroft aligned himself with Isabella's and Claudio's positions: honesty and honor threatened by powerful forces.

Sancroft chose the phrases that he deemed to be the most rhetorically rich. Sancroft's fascination with rhetorical devices is evident in the final section of the commonplace book that contains a list of tropes, such as apocope, anastrophe, pleonasmus, and ellipsis, written in reverse from the back of the manuscript. These short jottings sometimes offer cross-references or examples, such as, "Aphæresis": "—neweth, for reneweth. 1)2. bate for debate. 1)4. Plaine for complain" (p. 557 rev.). Both parts of the manuscript serve similar functions: the dramatic extracts function as rhetorical exemplars, and the list identifies rhetorical devices in other works. Sancroft selected a passage from *Love's Labour's Lost* that reveals what should be rhetorically admired in a speaker: "Sharp, & sententious, pleasant without scurrility. Witty / without affection. Bold without impudence."[89] The excerpts that Sancroft chose are indeed "sharp & sententious": they are sharp in their interesting rhetoric and they are sententious in that they have a degree of universality to them, particularly when Sancroft removed from each extract such particulars as speaker, context, and play. At times, Sancroft even copied interesting words or phrases without making each into a complete thought or without referencing the over-arching ideas in his sources.

The dramatic extracts in Bodleian MS Sancroft 29 reveal Sancroft's reading habits, his interests in certain plays, and his views on particular playwrights. In this one manuscript, Sancroft left evidence of both continuous and discontinuous reading practices. He read for interesting and functional phrases as well as for the knowledge that can be gained from commonplaces, organizing his material accordingly (by commonplace headings or by play). Although some of his extracts (such as those from *Measure for Measure*) lend themselves to an autobiographical reading, we cannot know for certain what attracted him to other extracts (such as those about Richard III) beyond his personal interests. Bodleian MS Sancroft 29 functions like a time capsule, preserving the archbishop's tastes in drama. Sancroft's dramatic extracts offer concrete evidence of the rise of Shakespeare's popularity and the nostalgia for Renaissance drama at the close of the seventeenth century.

Although he will probably always be remembered primarily as a nonjuror and religious figure, Archbishop William Sancroft should also be recognized as an avid reader of plays, a prolific manuscript compiler, and a dramatic extractor, one who appropriated material from plays and masques. As Chapter 4 illustrated, dramatic extracting from Renaissance plays continued unabated after the theatres reopened in 1660. In many cases, we have little or no knowledge of the compilers' identities. With Archbishop Sancroft, we have an abundance of archival evidence about his reading habits and responses to plays. Further close reading of his manuscripts will add to our knowledge of Restoration responses to Renaissance drama.

I have previously argued that Sancroft's extracts (and others') should be taken into consideration by textual editors and literary scholars because of the variant readings they can offer, which show us how early readers understood play-texts.[90] Sancroft's dramatic miscellany, in particular, offers multiple fruitful readings. For instance, in the prologue to the folio version of *Every Man in his Humour*, Sancroft changes "Yorke and, Lancasters long jarres" to a metrically equivalent yet more sensible "Wars."[91] Sancroft changed Thomas Tomkis's "as many eyes as heaven" to add a classical allusion, "as many eyes, as Argus," demonstrating that he read intertextually, bringing other stories (in this case, the myth of Argus Panoptes) to his reading of early modern theatre.[92] Sancroft is both an exceptional and exemplary reader; as the learned Archbishop of Canterbury, he is perhaps the socially highest and best-educated person we know who copied dramatic extracts, but also one who engaged with dramatic texts like many other early modern readers, treating plays as works to be adapted for personal use.

Sancroft's manuscripts show a range of ways and reasons for collecting dramatic extracts, from gathering separates, to copying complete songs or speeches as poems, to excerpting sententious phrases for reuse. Sancroft's choice of source plays reveals his conception of the Shakespearean canon, his reaction to Beaumont and Fletcher's collaborative authorship, and his theatrical tastes. Sancroft's excerpts showcase the malleability of dramatic extracts in manuscript and attest to how one person could adapt dramatic extracts in multiple ways for future use. While we cannot generalize Sancroft's views as representative of the entire population, these manuscripts offer a testament to the theatrical tastes of one educated late seventeenth-century clergyman. There is surely more valuable knowledge to be gained by further investigating Sancroft's vast collection of manuscripts, not just for the study of dramatic extracts but also for understanding his literary coterie, his religious and political views, and the education of clergy in the seventeenth century, to name a scant few. Moreover, further examination of the individual extracts in Sancroft's dramatic miscellany (Bodleian MS Sancroft 29) will undoubtedly lead to a better understanding of early modern theatre and its reception by providing detailed readings of each play, by offering new contexts in which to read the plays, and by showing the longevity of certain printed plays.

NOTES

1. Sancroft may have adapted the first unattributed extract (Bodleian MS Sancroft 29, p. 18) from the prologue to John Ford's *Fancies Chast and Noble*: "The Fancies! that's our Play; in it is showne / Nothing, but what our Author knowes his owne / Without a learned theft; no servant here / To some fair Mistris, borrowes for his eare" (1638, sig. A1v; Prologue 1–4). The second extract is from *The Mountebanks Masque*, Bodleian MS Sancroft 29, p. 62.

2. As present-day historians lament, there is no modern biography of Sancroft. The earliest biographical source is Thomas Wagstaffe's "A Letter out of Suffolk to A Friend in London," about Sancroft's death (1694). Gilbert Burnet, a Whig historian, wrote scathingly of Sancroft in *Bishop Burnet's History of his own Time* (1724, published posthumously). George D'Oyly's biography, *The Life of William Sancroft, Archbishop of Canterbury* (1821, revised 1840) offers a much more generous portrait. The three most useful modern sources are Edward Carpenter, "William Sancroft: Piety and Non-Compliance," in *Cantuar: The Archbishops in their Office*, 3rd ed. (London: Continuum, 1997), 213–22; Patrick Collinson, "William Sancroft, 1617–1693: A Retiring Disposition in a Revolutionary Age," in *From Cranmer to Sancroft* (London: Continuum, 2006), 173–200; and R. A. P. J. Beddard, "Sancroft, William (1617–1693)," *ODNB*.

3. Wagstaffe, "Letter" (1694), sig. C; Collinson, "Sancroft," 173; Craig Rose, *England in the 1690s: Revolution, Religion and War* (Malden, MA: Blackwell, 1999), 156; Carpenter, "Sancroft," 213.

4. Helen Carron, "William Sancroft: A Seventeenth-Century Collector and his Library," *The Library*, 7th ser., 1 (2000): 290–307.

5. Two popular tracts from the early 1650s, *Fur Prædestinatus* (1651) and *Modern Policies, taken from Machiavel, Borgia, and other choice Authors by an eyewitnesse* (1652) are sometimes attributed to Sancroft. *Fur Prædestinatus* is a dialogue between a preacher and a thief who is sentenced to death. *Fur Prædestinatus* refutes the Calvinist notion of the elect and the reprobate: for, as the thief argues, if he is one of the elect then it is inevitable that he will reform and find salvation. *Modern Policies* is a satirical work that was republished seven times in less than seven years. D'Oyly and Carpenter attribute these two works to Sancroft, although Beddard (*ODNB*) disagrees. Collinson suggests that the author of *Fur Prædestinatus* was Dutch.

6. Sancroft tried to restore Inigo Jones's work on St. Paul's Cathedral, although after the great fire of 1666, he realized that the cathedral would have to be entirely re-built and began a new design with the architect Christopher Wren. The first stone was laid in 1675 and the entire project was completed after he died in 1710.

7. Together, the group was known as "the seven bishops." The other bishops were Thomas Ken, Bishop of Bath and Wells; John Lake, Bishop of Chichester; William Lloyd, Bishop of St. Asaph; Jonathan Trelawny, Bishop of Bristol; Francis Turner, Bishop of Ely; and Thomas White, Bishop of Peterborough.

8. Beddard, "Sancroft," *ODNB*.

9. Sancroft et al, *A Vindication of the Arch-Bishop And Several other Bishops* (1690), 2. This tract was mostly to defend themselves against the accusations made in *A Modest Enquiry Into The Causes Of The Present Disasters In England* (1690). Sancroft and his co-authors (Thomas Ken, Bishop of Bath and Wells; Francis Turner, Bishop of Ely; and Thomas White, Bishop of Peterborough) wrote, "We are so far from being the *Authors or Abbettors of* England's *Miseries*, (whatever the Spirit of Lying and Calumny may vent against us) that We do, and shall to our dying Hour, heartily, and incessantly pray for the Peace, Prosperity, and Glory of *England*" (2).

10. Collinson, "Sancroft," 194.

11. Although he remained out of the spotlight for his later years, Sancroft was accused of treason in 1692. In the "flowerpot plot," Stephen Blackhead and Robert Young added Sancroft's name (and others, including Sprat, the Bishop of Rochester) to a document calling for the restoration of King James (D'Oyly, *Life of William Sancroft*, 1840, 290–91). Collinson points out that Sancroft's correspondence on the flowerpot plot was acquired in 2004 by Lambeth Palace ("Sancroft," 200). Some of Sancroft's and Rochester's correspondence survives at Lambeth Palace. Rochester printed his response to this plot in *A Relation Of the Late Wicked Contrivance Of Stephen Blackhead, and Robert Young, against the Lives of several Persons by Forging an Association under their Hands* (1692).

12. Carron, "Sancroft," 307.

13. Ibid., 306.

14. Collinson, "Sancroft,"197.

15. Carron, "Sancroft," 306.

16. Sancroft's manuscripts include the 145 Sancroft shelfmarks at the Bodleian Library, as well as a number of Tanner manuscripts. More can be found in the British Library in the Harleian and Additional Collections and yet others are now located

in the Lambeth Palace Library. See Richard Sharpe, "Thomas Tanner (1674–1735), the 1697 Catalogue, and *Bibliotheca Britannica*," *The Library*, 7th ser., 6 (2005): 381–421, esp. 384–85, for a brief discussion of Sancroft's bibliographical catalogues, which include Bodleian MSS Tanner 268–75.

17. D'Oyly, *Life of William Sancroft* (1840), 316.

18. For more the physical quality and content of manuscript separates, see Harold Love, *Scribal Publication in Seventeenth-Century England* (Oxford: Oxford University Press, 1993), esp. 13.

19. The contents of Bodleian MS Tanner 306 have been catalogued in the Bodleian Library Quarto Catalogue (part 4, Tanner MSS), 713–25.

20. See for instance, *CELM*, the Bodleian Library Quarto Catalogue, and Hilton Kelliher, *Andrew Marvell: Poet & Politician, 1621–1678* (London: British Library, 1978). The items that post-date Sancroft's death all come at the end of the second volume (ff. 435 onwards) in roughly chronological order: two possibly unique elegies by Peter Glean on Sancroft's death (1693, f. 435v), letters to Charles Trimnell when he was bishop of Norwich (1708–1721, from ff. 454–65v), poems mainly about the events of the 1710s (ff. 473–79), and finally some poems dated in the 1720s (ff. 484 and 492).

21. Printed works bound in this manuscript (though outnumbered by handwritten documents) include "The Speech of Her Majesty the Queen Mother's Palace, Upon the Reparation and Enlargement of it, by Her Majesty" (1665, ff. 369–370v) and "Carmen Proseuticon Basiliphili" (1689, f. 124–25v). One ballad begins "The churches darling son your self" (f. 369); a sheet of manuscript music on paper lined with staves opens, "True Englishmen drinke a good health to the mitre" (f. 399).

22. Bodleian MS Tanner 306, ff. 1–41. The two copies of *Ignoramus* differ slightly: the first (ff. 1–21), includes an extra scene that the copyist notes is not in the 1630 print version of the play (2.2). The second copy (ff. 22–41) omits the character of Pyropus and abridges the play, possibly for a revival. For more information on these versions of the play, see Dana Sutton, introduction to *Ignoramus*, by George Ruggle, *The Philological Museum*, http://www.philological.bham.ac.uk/ruggle/. Sancroft's interest in *Ignoramus* is further evident in Bodleian MS Tanner 465, where the archbishop copied two poems about the performance of Ruggle's play: "Faith gentlemen, I doe not blame your wit" and "Reverend John Stile, for stile wee will not jarre" (ff. 79–79v). Sancroft titled the first poem "Unto the Comœdians in Camb. who in their Acts before the King abused the lawyer with an imposed ignorance by Ignoramus the Laywer & Dulman his Clerke, John Stiles student of the common lawes wisheth a sounder judgement, & a more reverent opinion of their betters" (f. 79) and labeled it, "From Graies Inne" (f. 79v).

23. Bodleian MS Tanner 306, f. 42. E. K. Chambers notes that the date of 1582 was probably added later and is probably erroneous; the generally accepted date of performance is 1579. Chambers, *The Elizabethan Stage* Vol. 3 (Oxford: Clarendon, 1953), 408.

24. Bodleian MS Tanner 306, ff. 252–53v. For a discussion of other excerpts from *The Gypsies Metamorphosed*, see Chapter 2 and James Knowles, "'Songs of baser

alloy': Jonson's *Gypsies Metamorphosed* and the Circulation of Manuscript Libels," *Huntington Library Quarterly* 69 (2006): 153–76.

25. For more on the circulation of these two poems both together and separately, see Steven W. May, "The Circulation in Manuscript of Poems by King James VI and I," in *Renaissance Historicisms: Essays in Honor of Arthur F. Kinney*, ed. James M. Dutcher and Anne Lake Prescott (Cranbury, NJ: Associated UPs, 2008), 206–24.

26. Bodleian MS Tanner 306, f. 246. This poem's title is strikingly similar to that found in Bodleian MS Rawl. poet. 26, "Verses made by the Kinge, when hee was entertaynd at Burly in Rutland-shire, by my L. Marquesse of Buckingham. August: 1621." (f. 4).

27. Bodleian MS Tanner 306, f. 266. For a complete transcription of this speech, see Marion Colthorpe, "An Entertainment for Queen Elizabeth I at Wimbledon in 1599," *Records of Early English Drama Newsletter* 10 (1985): 1–2.

28. These plays were published together in Cavendish's *Plays, Never before Printed* (1668).

29. Stern touches on the *Masque of Queens* argument in *Documents of Performance in Early Modern England* (Cambridge: Cambridge University Press, 2009), 79.

30. A complete first-line index for Bodleian MS Sancroft 53 is available from Meredith Sherlock, Felicity Henderson, and Harold Love's *Source Index to English Clandestine Satire*, Monash University, http://www.arts.monash.edu.au/english/resources/clandestine-satire/introduction.php.

31. The print sources that Sancroft copied from have publication dates as late as 1690. Sancroft dated two poems 1691 and 1692 (Bodleian MS Sancroft 53, p. 68).

32. Bodleian MS Sancroft 53, pp. 7–8; Waller, *The Second Part of Mr. Waller's Poems* (1690), sig. F4v.

33. Sancroft's source is evident from the page numbers he provides.

34. Bodleian MS Sancroft 53, p. 53; Charles Sackville, "Epilogue To every Man in his Humour," *A Collection of Poems*, 32.

35. Sackville, "Epilogue To every Man in his Humour," *A Collection of Poems Written upon several Occasions* (1672), sig. C7v.

36. Bodleian MS Sancroft 53, pp. 5–6. Sackville's epilogue to *Tartuffe* was published with the play (1670) and, like his epilogue for *Every Man in His Humour*, in *A Collection of Poems* (1672, republished 1673), sigs. E7–8v.

37. Bodleian MS Sancroft 53, p. 7; Sackville, "Epilogue To every Man in his Humour," *A Collection of Poems, Written upon several Occasions* (1672), sig. C8r-v.

38. "Harke Harke the Larke" is also found in Bodleian MS Don. c. 57 (f. 40v) with music. For a facsimile of this manuscript, see Elise Bickford Jorgens, ed., *English Song 1600–1675: Facsimiles of Twenty-six Manuscripts and an Edition of the Texts* (New York: Garland, 1987), vol. 6, for a facsimile of this manuscript. See also Willa McClung Evans's article discussing the significance of the song and music found in Bodleian MS Don. c. 57, "Shakespeare's 'Harke Harke Ye Larke,'" *PMLA* 60 (1945): 95–101.

39. In the third folio, the same conventions were used for the printing of the second song in *Cymbeline*, "Fear no more the heat o' the sun" (4.2.268-81).

40. Bodleian MS Sancroft 53, p. 43; Shakespeare, *Cymbeline* 2.3.21 (1664 folio), sig. Cccc5.
41. Shakespeare, *Cymbeline* 2.3.14–15 (1664 folio), sig. Cccc5.
42. Bodleian MS Sancroft 53, p. 43; Shakespeare, 2.3.26. *Cymbeline* (1664 folio), sig. Cccc5.
43. Shakespeare, *Othello* 2.1.129–30 (1664 folio), sig. Xxx5.
44. Ibid., 2.1.137-38.
45. Bodleian MS Sancroft 53, f. 43; Shakespeare, *Othello*, 2.1.148–53, 56–58, 60 (1664 folio), sig. Xxx5.
46. Shakespeare, *Othello* 2.1.158–60 (1664 folio), sig. Xxx5.
47. Ibid., 2.1.161.
48. Sancroft also cut one couplet from the speech, "She that in wisedom never was so frail / To change the Cod's Head for the Salmon's Taile" (1664 folio, sig. Xxx5, 2.1.154–55). Perhaps Sancroft omitted this couplet because he was unsure of its meaning: modern scholars remain hesitant on the exact sense. Sancroft, as a pious man, might also have omitted this couplet because of the sexual innuendo, another aspect not easily explicated.
49. These are, respectively, Henry Ainsworth's *An Arrow against Idolatry Taken out of the Quiver of the Lord of Hosts* (1640) and Thomas Hill's "A sermon preached at the fast before the Honourable House of Commons," published in *The Trade of Truth Advanced* (1642).
50. Bodleian MS Sancroft 97, pp. 79–82. "Gaudens sermon bef[ore] the Parl[iament]" (p. 82) is John Gauden's *The Love of Truth and Peace. A Sermon Preached Before the Honourable House of Commons Assembled in Parliament* (1641).
51. The style of copying from plays in Bodleian MS Sancroft 97 mirrors Folger MS V.a.87 (discussed in Chapter 3) in many ways: titles, multiple short extracts, prose layout, no speech prefixes.
52. Sancroft may also have marked the passages he wanted to copy in the printed text and then returned to copy the extracts. Note that Sancroft's dramatic miscellany (when not sorted by commonplace heading) is also generally organized this way.
53. Bodleian MS Sancroft 97, p. 79; Shakespeare, *Midsummer Night's Dream*, 3.2.387 (1664 folio), sig. N6v. Bodleian MS Sancroft 97, p. 81; Shakespeare, *3 Henry VI*, 5.2.21 (1664 folio), sig. tt5.
54. Bodleian MS Sancroft 97, p. 79; Shakespeare, *Midsummer Night's Dream*, 1.2.37 (1664 folio), sig. N2.
55. Bodleian MS Sancroft 97, p. 81; Shakespeare, *King Lear*, 1.4.118-27 (1664 folio), sig. Ttt2v.
56. Bodleian MS Sancroft 18, p. 5. The original in *The White Devil* runs,

> FLAMINEO. There are not Jew enough, Priests enough, nor gentlemen enough.
> MARCELLO. How?
> FLAMINEO. Ile prove it: For if there were Jews enough, so many Christians would not turn Usurers; if priests enough, one should not have six Benefices; and if gentlemen enough, so many early Mushrooms, whose best

growth sprang from a Dunghil, should not aspire to Gentility. (3.3.42-49; 1672, sig. E5)

57. Bodleian MS Sancroft 18, p. 5. One of the dates that is now blotted may have read Apr. 23 1664. "Oct. 16 1662" and "the year ending march. 25. 1661/2" are clearly visible.

58. As the other selections on this page show, Sancroft offered the page number where possible. The 1672 edition does not have page numbers and only occasional signatures. The extract, however, is from a page without a signature, which likely accounts for his use of act/scene instead.

59. For more information on the play's performance history, see John Russell Brown, ed., *The White Devil*, by John Webster (London: Methuen, 1960), lvii–lix.

60. John Downes, *Roscius Anglicanus* (1708), sig. B5.

61. Falconer Madan, et al., Bodleian Library Summary Catalogue, entry 10330. Beal's printed *Index* catalogued excerpts from works by Ben Jonson and Sir Philip Sidney, but overlooks the vast majority of dramatic material. My research led to the inclusion of extracts by additional canonical authors (including Beaumont and Fletcher, Thomas Dekker, Sir John Suckling, and Shakespeare) in *CELM*.

62. The non-dramatic excerpts in this manuscript include (but are not limited to) poems by Edmund Waller (p. 63) and Francis Quarles (pp. 63–64 and 315); selections from Giacomo Affinati, *The Dumb Divine Speaker* (1605), p. 39; *The Loyall Sacrifice* (1648), p. 55; and Robert Codrington, *The Life and Death of the Illustrious Robert, Earl of Essex* (1646); p. 57, Gilbert Saulnier Duverdier, *The love and armes of the Greeke princes* (1640), pp. 65–67; Luca Assarino's *La Stratonica Or The Unfortunate Queen* (1651), p. 67; James Howell's ΔΕΝΔΡΟΛΟΓΙΑ *Dodona's Grove* (1640), p. 67 and *Lustra Ludovici* (1646), p. 67; and Thomas Fuller's *A Pigsah-sight of Palestine* (1650), pp. 67–68. The latest extracts from published works in this manuscript are from *The Amours of Messalina* (1689), p. 129. There are a number of extracts from translations into English, including works by Cervantes (p. 74), Balzac (p. 105), Pierre Le Moyne (p. 112) and others.

63. As is later discussed, one of these pages (315) has a heading: "Epithetes."

64. Bodleian MS Sancroft 29, f. i. Note that Sancroft replaced *The Noble Gentlemen* with *The Virgin Widow* for number five: later extracts he marked with the number five are indeed from *The Virgin Widow*. Sancroft uses this numbering system from pp. 1–57 and 311–12, 315, and 317.

65. The play titles that Sancroft includes in his margins are: "2 Noble Kinsmen" (p. 67), "M[aidenhead] well lost" (p. 68), "Divels Lawcase" (p. 69), "Album[azar]" (p. 70), "Game at Chess" (p. 71), "P[er]icles" (p. 76), "Tr[oilus] & Cress[ida]" (p. 77), "Platon[ic] Lovers" (p. 108), and "Mulb[erry]. Gard.[en]" (p. 110); Sancroft sometimes includes playwright's names in the margin: "Shakespear" (p. 75), "Sr Jo. Sucklg" (p. 111). The "loial General" (p. 106) is attributed in-line; "The Antiquary. Shack[erly] Marm[ion]" (p. 107) and "The Merry Beggars" (p. 109) are titled mid-column. Every other play in the miscellany is untitled, although Sancroft identifies some with numbers (see Tables 5.1 and 5.2 for a complete list; see Figure 5.3 for Sancroft's numbering system).

66. Bodleian MS Sancroft 29 p. 71; Thomas Tomkis, *Albumazar* (1615), sig. H2v.

67. Bodleian MS Sancroft 29, p. 68 and 127; *Every Man in his Humour* (1616 folio), sig. B3, 1.5.121.

68. Extracts from Jonson's poem can be found in Bodleian MS Sancroft 29, p. 105. The poem was, like the humors plays, published in the 1616 folio, where Jonson also dedicated *Sejanus* to Lord Aubigny (sig. Gg5).

69. Cicero, *In Verrem*, II.4.42. Bodleian MS Sancroft 27, p. 286. Sancroft's ascription might read "Act. 2. Sc. 6.4."—there is a blotted character after the 6.

70. Bodleian MS Sancroft 29, p. 63. This formulation is also perhaps borrowed: John Bachiler's epistle to the reader in *The Soules Own evidence* runs, "if thou wilt take the pains, (I might say, the pleasure rather) to gaine the knowledge. . ." (1646), sig. A3v.

71. For a reading of this portrait that suggests Beaumont's influence on Fletcher, see Lois Potter, "The Portrait-Frontispiece of John Fletcher, 1647" in *Two Noble Kinsmen,* by William Shakespeare (Surrey: Cengage, 1997), 337–39.

72. Bodleian MS Sancroft 29, f. 63. Sancroft copied the original Latin. The translation is from Potter, "Portrait-Frontispiece," 337–38.

73. According to the *OED*, in the late seventeenth century "feature" could mean both "part of the face" and "A distinctive and characteristic part of a thing."

74. Bodleian MS Sancroft 29, p. 63; Beaumont and Fletcher, *Comedies and Tragedies* (1647), sig. B2. For a reading of this poem as it relates to Fletcher's influence on Restoration theatre, see Nancy Klein Maguire's "The Commercial Market: Genre as Commodity" in *Regicide and Restoration: English Tragicomedy 1660–1671* (Cambridge: Cambridge University Press, 1992), esp. 65–68. This poem was republished in Waller's *Poems &c., Written Upon Several Occasions, and to Several Persons* (1686).

75. Shakespeare (1664 folio), title page. Sancroft certainly used the third folio (he gives a page number from *Antony and Cleopatra*): the extracts suggest he used the 1664 imprint rather than the 1663 imprint that appeared without the apocrypha.

76. Sancroft's dramatic tastes leaned toward the pre-Restoration, although he did not hold Caroline theatre in a lower esteem than Elizabethan or Jacobean plays. William Cartwright's *The Noble Slave*, Shackerly Marmion's *The Antiquary*, William Davenant's *Platonic Lovers*, and Richard Brome's *The Jovial Crew*, among others, were all written in the Caroline period.

77. Shakespeare, *Timon of Athens* (1664 folio), sig. Mmmv; 4.3.365–74.

78. Gilbert Burnet, *Bishop Burnet's History of his own Time*, 2 vols. (London: Thomas Ward, 1724), 1.675. Collinson characterized the Archbishop as having "a retiring disposition in a revolutionary age" ("Sancroft," 173). See Collinson for a discussion of Sancroft's reception.

79. Bodleian MS Sancroft 29, p. 315. Other gems from this page include "a raw untutor'd youth" from *The Spanish Curate* and "Squint eyd Suspition" from Quarles's (non-dramatic) *Divine Fancies*. Perhaps oddly given his personality, Sancroft included "a retir'd life, private & close, & still" from *The Spanish Curate* under this heading.

80. Bodleian MS Sancroft 29, p. 103; *3 Henry VI*, 3.2.153–63, 5.1.50–52, 5.3.11–15, 5.4.34–35 (phrases from), 5.6.45-51 (including paraphrases), 5.6.71, 5.6.74–78, 5.6.54. The deletion three lines from the bottom is unclear.

81. Shakespeare, *3 Henry VI* (1664 folio), sig. Ss6v.

82. Shakespeare, *3 Henry VI* (1664 folio), sig. Tt6. In a similar thematic vein, Sancroft copied "the slanderous cuckow. & the boding Raven" from *Two Noble Kinsmen* (Bodleian MS Sancroft 29, p. 315).

83. For a reading of "the Raven croak'd," see Estill, "Archbishop William Sancroft's Emendation of *3 Henry VI*: Rereading 'rook'd,'" *ANQ* 25 (2012): 86–90.

84. Shakespeare, *Measure for Measure* (1664 folio), sig. F5v; 2.4.180-83.

85. Bodleian MS Sancroft 29, p. 85; Shakespeare, *Measure for Measure*, 2.4.180–181, 3.1.103–5.

86. The exact date of compilation of Bodleian MS Sancroft 29 is unknown. The latest published work Sancroft includes in this collection is Nahum Tate's *The Loyal General* (1680). Sancroft's predilection for copying older plays, however, does not mean that Tate's play was recently published, which leaves open the possibility of a later date. The opening section of the manuscript (including this selection from *Measure for Measure*) might have been compiled before 1680.

87. Collinson notes that while the Seven Bishops have often been depicted as "passive martyrs," the heart of the matter was actually a struggle between church and state for dominance (190).

88. New Critics argue that we can never know an author's intentions by analyzing their works through literary biography, and that reasoning might also hold true for compilers. While it would be foolhardy to read all extracts as relating directly to the life experiences of the compiler, in some rare cases where there is ample information about a compiler's biography (as is the case with Archbishop Sancroft), it would seem equally foolhardy to jettison that information as irrelevant.

89. Bodleian MS Sancroft 29, p. 84; Shakespeare, *Love's Labour's Lost*, 5.1.3–5. In the play, these lines are spoken by Nathaniel, a man without much taste, to Holofernes, a pedant without rhetorical skill, but in the commonplace book, this context is removed. In the play, the next line is Moth's biting aside, "he hath been at a great Feast of language & stole the scraps" (5.1.35–37). Without the context of speaker or rebuttal, however, this description can be taken at face value in the manuscript.

90. Estill, "Archbishop William Sancroft's Emendation," 86–90.

91. Bodleian MS Sancroft 29, p. 68; Jonson, *Every Man in his Humour* Prologue.11 (1616 folio), sig. A3. Note that the second time Sancroft copied the same selection into this manuscript, he left it as "long jars" (p. 127).

92. Bodleian MS Sancroft 29, p. 70; Tomkis, *Albumazar* (1615), sig. B1v.

Chapter 6

Proverbial Shakespeare

The Print and Manuscript Circulation of Extracts from Love's Labour's Lost

> [H]as it not been noted by the best Observers, and the ablest Judges, both of Things and Persons, that the Wisdom of any People or Nation has been most seen in the Proverbs and short Sayings commonly received amongst them? And what is a Proverb, but the Experience and Observation of several Ages, gathered and summ'd up into one Expression?
>
> —Robert South's *Twelve Sermons Preached upon Several Occasions* (1694)[1]

Shakespeare is regularly credited with coining more than a thousand English words (sometimes as many as ten thousand!) including such gems as *eyeball* and *radiance*. Merriam-Webster has published an entire book of words and phrases that were allegedly invented by Shakespeare: the authors, Jeffrey McQuain and Stanley Malless, estimate that Shakespeare added 1500 words to the English language.[2] Lexicographers, however, recognize that these words often existed before Shakespeare included them in his plays or poems. The *Oxford English Dictionary* (like the Philological Society's *New English Dictionary* and Samuel Johnson's *A Dictionary of the English Language* that predated it) privileges Shakespeare's language over his contemporaries' and cannot be relied on for the earliest usage of each word.[3] Many of the words that Shakespeare allegedly coined are borrowed from other languages and other sources. Shakespeare is also occasionally credited with inventing sayings or proverbs that we use today, such as "all that glisters is not gold" (*The Merchant of Venice* 2.7.65) and "brevity is the soul of wit" (*Hamlet* 2.2.91).[4] One couplet that Shakespeare wrote, "Fat paunches have lean pates, and dainty bits / Make rich the ribs, but bankrupt quite the wits" (*Love's Labour's Lost* 1.1.26–27), continued to circulate throughout the seventeenth century, although it is not still in popular use.⁵ The "fat paunches" couplet mirrors what we know about the overstated reputation of Shakespeare's immense vocabulary: he is often not the ultimate source of a so-called new word or proverb, but a rather extraordinary borrower.

While the other chapters in this book have taken a synchronic approach and considered dramatic extracts as they relate to particular moments in the seventeenth century, or, in the case of Chapter 5, examined those extracts copied by one reader, this chapter uses a diachronic approach and considers the circulation of one extract over the course of the entire century. This in-depth research reminds us that we cannot assume the source of any given quotation. Most important, focusing on a single extract shows how much more work there is to be done on the circulation of dramatic extracts and para-dramatic texts like prologues and songs.

The circulation of proverbs is both like and unlike the circulation of dramatic extracts—and can often overlap. As this chapter demonstrates, playwrights included existing proverbs in their work, which could later be extracted from their plays. The slip of paper that once served as a bookmark (BL MS Add. 41063), for instance, includes Richard III's "Soe wise soe young, they say never live long."⁶ Shakespeare's use of "they say" highlighted for his readers that Richard was offering proverbial wisdom, which, as the bookmark demonstrates, a later reader chose to copy. On the bookmark, however, Richard's words change from a sinister threat to an innocuous adage; one that continues to be used to this day, perhaps most memorably in Billy Joel's formulation "only the good die young." Both extracts and proverbs are manipulable texts that can be changed and pass from person to person. Unlike proverbs as many of the examples discussed in this book show, extracts could be taken from larger texts and refer back to particular circumstances.

Shakespeare's work has been described as proverbial in two main ways: his work both used existing proverbs and created new ones. This analysis combines these two approaches by focusing on a classical proverb that Shakespeare rephrased and that continued to circulate in Shakespeare's phrasing. The proverb "Fat paunches have lean pates, and dainty bits / Make rich the ribs, but bankrupt quite the wits" is found in the opening scene of *Love's Labour's Lost* when the gentlemen are considering their three years of scholarly asceticism. The King of Navarre and his friends, Longaville, Berowne and Dumaine, swear that they will live an austere life. The four men promise not to see women, to fast for an entire day each week, to eat only one meal on other days, to sleep only three hours a night, and to devote themselves to study—goals that are as untenable over the course of the play as they seem to be ridiculous at the beginning of the play. In this opening scene, Longaville shows his determination to uphold their oaths and offers this quasi-logical reason behind the men's chosen austere lifestyle: "I am resolved: 'tis but a three years' fast. / The mind shall banquet though the body pine. / Fat paunches have lean pates, and dainty bits / Make rich the ribs, but bankrupt quite the wits" (1.1.24–27). The last two lines of Longaville's speech were copied and recopied in multiple seventeenth-century print and manuscript sources. The "fat paunches" couplet gained popularity because it was excerpted in two influential print sources: Robert Allott's *Englands Parnassus* (1600) and Thomas Walkington's *Optick Glasse of Humors* (1607). The circulation of the "fat paunches" proverb, however, is not a sign of the popularity of Shakespeare's play. As Charles Whitney observes, allusions to plays "often include no certification either that they really refer to a play rather than to some other source."[7] Archival evidence demonstrates that in the case of the "fat paunches" proverb, although we are faced with what looks like a direct quotation from a play, the people copying this couplet might never have seen or read *Love's Labour's Lost*: they took the couplet from these intermediary sources. It was the process of dramatic excerpting itself that led to the dissemination of the "fat paunches" couplet as a proverb.

Investigating the circulation of the "fat paunches" dramatic extract ultimately reveals that what might seem at first glance to be a quotation from a play may in fact be copied from an intermediary source. The "fat paunches" couplet offers an example of the inter-related effects of print, manuscript, and oral transmission. The popularity of these lines is due to a snowball effect: the more a phrase or poem appears in print and manuscript, the more possibilities there are to read and memorize it, the more sources there are to copy from and (in the case of this extract) the more likely it is to be spoken, repeated, and become a proverb. Conversely, when dramatic extracts appear in fewer sources, the chance that they were copied from the complete masque (either performed or written) increases, as there are fewer intermediary sources that it could be copied from.

As discussed in earlier chapters, the majority of dramatic extracts from early modern plays found in seventeenth-century manuscripts are songs, possibly because songs are more easily memorized and songs can carry a meaning without the larger context of the play. The "fat paunches" extract from *Love's Labour's Lost* appears to be the most popular non-song excerpt from all of Shakespeare's plays,[8] possibly because it shares song-like attributes. As a rhyming couplet, it would be easy to memorize, and as an old saw, it does not need a specific theatrical or narrative context. The "fat paunches" proverb traces a generically circular route: it began as a proverb that Shakespeare included in *Love's Labour's Lost* and later continued to circulate as a proverb without the larger context of the play.

PRINT HISTORY OF THE "FAT PAUNCHES" PROVERB

Although "proverb" is a notoriously hard word to define,[9] its close relative, the commonplace, is easier to pin down: commonplaces are sayings that express an insight and are rhetorically well-phrased. Some commonplaces are proverbial, but not all. As early as the nineteenth century, scholars recognized Shakespeare's "Fat paunches have lean pates, and dainty bits / Make rich the ribs, but bankrupt quite the wits" as a translation of St. Jerome, who was himself translating from the Greek.[10] St. Jerome wrote, "pinguis venter non gignit sensum tenuem" (a fat belly does not produce fine sense).[11] Shakespeare probably encountered Jerome's saying during his early education. As Chapter 1 outlines, Tudor schoolboys were given collections of sayings and asked to translate them from Latin to English or from English to Latin. The fat paunches proverb appears in two texts known to have influenced Shakespeare: Erasmus's *Adages* and Leonard Culman's *Sententiae Pueriles*.[12] The early modern transmission of this proverb demonstrates that it was a well-known saying in the sixteenth and seventeenth centuries, even though it is no longer a common saying today.

Other writers, like Shakespeare, similarly borrowed and rephrased this proverb: see Table 6.1 for a chart with some examples of other versions of this proverb found in print texts.[13] The idea of fat bodies betokening lean brains was not only repeated in print sources, but variations on the theme also appeared multiple times on the English stage, in plays such as Richard Edwards's *Damon and Pithias*, John Lyly's *Campaspe*, Thomas Dekker's *Old Fortunatus*, and Francis Beaumont and John Fletcher's *Loves Cure*, the latter of which contains an even pithier version of the saying: "fat bodies, lean braines."[14] However, there are no known early modern extracts or quotations of Beaumont and Fletcher's "fat bodies, lean braines,"[15] just as there are no known dramatic extracts of Edwards's, Lyly's, or Dekker's versions of Jerome's proverb. Variations of this proverb continued to circulate after the seventeenth century; Benjamin Franklin, for instance, is often credited with "a full belly makes a dull brain," which he included in *Poor Richard's Almanack* (1758).[16]

It is precisely because there were so many other versions of Jerome's proverb that the seventeenth-century circulation of Shakespeare's proverb deserves note. These other phrasings, even those spoken aloud on the stage, did not have the cultural currency of Shakespeare's translation because they were not excerpted in print sources. This proverb, in all its variations, was popular because of the early modern English inclination toward physiognomy, and, as this investigation demonstrates, an early modern text on physiognomy increased the circulation of Shakespeare's wording of this proverb.[17]

Table 6.1 Some Non-Shakespearean print versions of Jerome's proverb.

Author	Source	Date	Wording	Page
Richard Edwards	*Damon and Pithias*	1571	"small diet maketh a fine memorie"	sig. C2
John Lyly	*Campaspe*	1584	"The belly is the heads greve [grave]"	sig. A3v
Stefano Guazzo, trans. Barth. Young	*The Civil Conversation*	1586	"a fat bellie doth not engender a subtill witte"	sig. Bb6
Thomas Dekker	*Old Fortunatus*	1600	"a leane dyet makes a fat wit"	sig. B4
Leonard Culman	*Sententiae Pueriles*	1612	"A fat belly doth not beget a fine wit"	sig. E6v
John Leycester	*Enchiridion*	1623	"*Pinguis venter non gignit sensum tenuem*"; "A fat belly hath not a thin sense"	sig. C8
John Withals	*A Dictionary in English and Latine*	1634	"*Pinguis venter non gignit sensum tenuem*"; "A ful-fed-belly must have his bones at rest"	sig. Oo8
John Fletcher and Francis Beaumont	*Loves Cure* [in *Comedies and Tragedies*]	1647	"Fat bodies, lean braines"	sig. Rrrrr1
John Rogers	*A Godly & Fruitful Exposition*	1650	Gluttons "have fat Bodies, but lean Souls"	sig. L2
Giovanni Torriano	*Common Place of Italian Proverbs*	1666	"*Corpo* grasso, sovente ha'l cervello magro"; "A *fat* body *hath a lean brain*"	sig. Ov

Robert Allott printed the earliest known extract of the "fat paunches" proverb from *Love's Labour's Lost* in *Englands Parnassus* (1600), a print commonplace book where he intended to collect "the choysest Flowers of our Moderne Poets."[18] He followed Shakespeare's words from *Love's Labour's Lost* exactly: "Fat paunches have leane pates, and daintie bits / Make rich the ribs, but bankrout quite the wits."[19] Allott published this saying under the heading "Gluttonie" and attributed it to "W. Shakespeare." In *Englands Parnassus*, Allott collected many extracts from Shakespeare's works, including *Venus and Adonis*, *The Rape of Lucrece*, *Richard II*, *Romeo and Juliet*, and others.[20]

After this couplet was printed in *Love's Labour's Lost* and *Englands Parnassus*, it was reproduced in multiple print sources throughout the seventeenth century (see Table 6.2). In 1607, Thomas Walkington used Shakespeare's phrase to illustrate his discussion of diet in *The Optick Glasse of Humors*, a treatise on melancholy and physiognomy often compared to

Table 6.2 Transmission of the "Fat Paunches" couplet in print sources. Solid arrows show definite sources. Dashed arrows indicate two possible sources. *A Helpe to Discourse* is asterisked because it used Walkington as a source, but also includes the phrasing found in the play and *Englands Parnassus*.

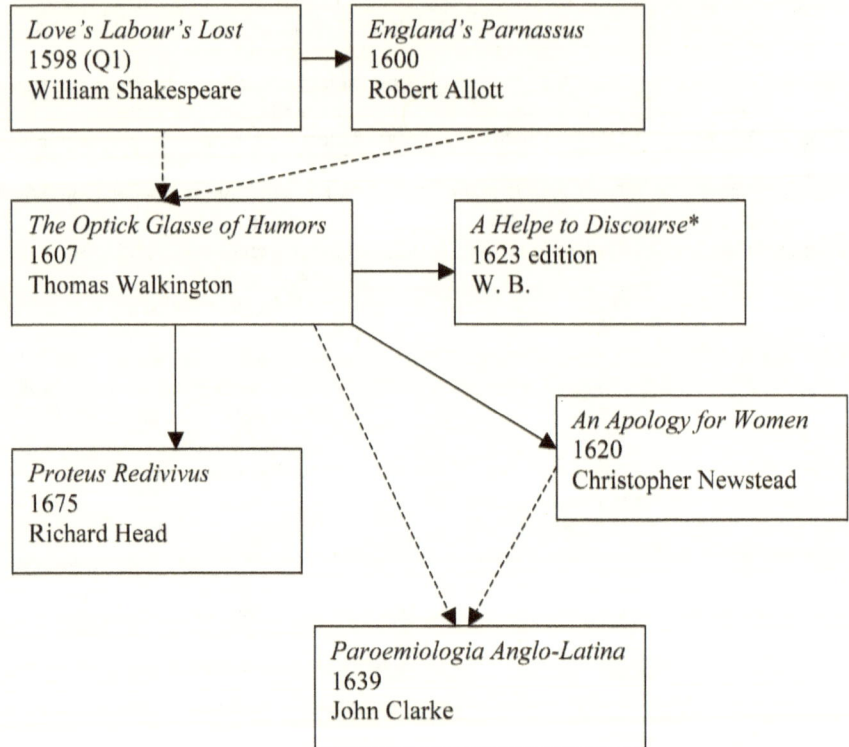

Robert Burton's *The Anatomy of Melancholy* (1621).[21] Walkington asked, "Who is not acquainted with this of the philosopher... a fat belly has a leane ingenie," and continues, "this is sett downe by a moderne english poet of good note pithyly in two verses" before giving Shakespeare's phrase. According to Walkington's introduction, Shakespeare's couplet qualifies as the ideal *sententia*: it is a well-phrased ("pithy") universal idea ("who is not acquainted with this"?). Walkington's quotation of Shakespeare, however, is not verbatim. He wrote, "Fat paunches *make* lean pates, and *grosser bitts / Enrich the ribs but bankrout quite the witts.*"[22] Walkington might have copied the phrase from the play directly, or he might have used *Englands Parnassus*. Even if he did not turn to the play as his source, he would have been aware of Shakespeare's authorship because Allott attributed this couplet. For Walkington, Shakespeare is a "poet of good note" whose phrase is worth borrowing. Although I trace Walkington's source to Shakespeare's play or *Englands*

Parnassus (see Table 6.2), the transmission that I outline is based on extant textual evidence. Walkington may, of course, have been copying the line from a yet-to-be determined or now-lost intermediary source. Intermediary sources may have been present at any point in this imagined transmission, but the chart is constructed from extant instances. There does not seem to be any point in this transmission that necessitates imagined intermediary texts, although that does not rule out their possible existence.

Christopher Newstead copied the phrase from Walkington in his *An Apology for Women* (1620). Both Newstead's and Walkington's quotations describe fat paunches *making* lean pates rather than *having* lean pates and discuss "grosser bits" rather than "dainty bits."[23] Newstead's use of Walkington is shown by his introduction to the proverb: Newstead's "as a modern Poet pithyly Englisheth" echoes Walkington's "sett downe by a moderne english poet."[24] Both Walkington and Newstead give the original Greek version of the proverb and present Shakespeare's couplet as a translation to be admired.

Shakespeare's couplet is often found alongside Walkington's memorable discussion of physiognomy. Walkington presents physiognomic interpretations as widely accepted facts: "Who is ignorant, that men of greater size are seldome i' the right cue, i' the witty vaine; who knowes not that little eyes denotate a large cheuerill conscience? a great head a little portion of wit?"[25] Richard Head, like W. B., copied the "fat paunches" phrase from Walkington in his *Proteus Redivivus* (1675), subtitled *The Art of Wheedling, or Insinuation*. Head's quotation of the couplet follows a discussion of outward appearances from Walkington. Head writes that "goggle eyes" betoken "a stark staring fool"; he discusses "great ears," "thick nails, harsh hair and a gross hard skin" among other traits.[26]

A Helpe to Discourse gives Shakespeare's quotation as part of the answer to the question "Who were the most lascivious belly-gods that stories make mention of?"[27] The question that follows is "What are the outward signes of the body to judge of the inward disposition of the minde?" This answer is clearly taken from Walkington's *Optick Glasse*: "little eyes [denote] a large conscience; a great head and goggle eyes, a starke staring foole; great eares, to be akin to *Midas* Asse" and so on.[28] *A Helpe to Discourse* is another early seventeenth-century print source that takes Walkington's *Optick Glasse* as a source for Shakespeare's couplet, although with a different phrasing. Possibly written by William Basse, Shakespeare's famed eulogist, *A Helpe to Discourse* was originally printed in 1619 and went through dozens of reprints in the seventeenth century. The Shakespearean extract first appeared in the 1623 edition.[29] The frequently republished *A Helpe to Discourse* is a guide for social graces that includes talking points for discussing classical authors and philosophers, the Bible, science, and history, among other things.

Though *A Helpe to Discourse* borrowed material from Walkington's *Optick Glasse*, the conduct guide did not use Walkington's exact phrasing. *A Helpe to Discourse* included the phrase as it is found in Shakespeare's play: "Fat paunches have leane pates, and dainty bits; / Make rich the ribs, but banckrupt quite the wits."[30] Someone—perhaps W. B., perhaps a publisher, perhaps the compositor—corrected the quotation to its original phrasing, from knowledge of Shakespeare's play, or from oral tradition.[31] Here, the return to Shakespeare's wording complicates what would otherwise be straightforward textual transmission. The inherent orality of proverbs makes it challenging to trace their origins and circulation, as the only evidence that remains is necessarily written.

John Norton's *The Scholar's Vade Mecum* (1675) offers Walkington's version of the couplet (see Table 6.3) as a translation of Jerome's couplet. Norton's usage, however, is not definitively from Walkington, as it gives no contextual material (unlike *Proteus Redivivus*). Rather, Norton offered Walkington's couplet as a translation of the Latin in a series of proverbs about making. While Norton could have taken the couplet from Walkington, Walkington's phrasing ("Fat paunches make lean pates, and grosser bits / Enrich the ribs but bankrout quite the wits") could also have been well known by the 1670s: that is to say, proverbial.

Poor Robin's Almanack (1697) includes a late instance of the proverb in a seventeenth-century text.[32] *Poor Robin* almanacs were parodies of the traditional almanac form that were published from the mid-1660s and throughout the eighteenth century.[33] In the 1697 almanac, amid astrological prognostications are tucked poems and many couplets containing commonplace wisdom, such as "That those who spend their Wealth on Dice, on Drink, and Whores, / Will quickly turn themselves out of Doors."[34] The "fat paunches" couplet comes after a song from Cartwright's play *The Ordinary* (perf. 1635?; pub. 1651), that claims that "He that's full, doth Verse compose; / Hunger deals in sullen Prose."[35] To counter the song, according to Poor Robin, "the Shoemakers . . . to prove that great Eaters are for the most part meer Dunces, produce these Verses of the Comedian: / *Fat Paunches make lean Pates, and dainty Bits / Make fat the Ribs, but banckrupt the Wits*."[36] This couplet combines the two main variations found in print and manuscript sources, combining *make* lean pates with *dainty* bits, suggesting that this was written from memory or an oral source. The most notable change in the second line is the omission of "quite," so that the line no longer scans. Whether Shakespeare is "the Comedian" to whom Poor Robin refers is similarly unknown: although Shakespeare was listed as one of the "principall Comœdians" in Jonson's *Every Man in his Humour*, this almanac dates from almost a century later.[37]

The two most common versions of the couplet (fat paunches *make* lean pates or *have* lean pates; *grosser* bits or *dainty* bits) have caused some speculation about whether or not this wording of the couplet was proverbial before Shakespeare included it in *Love's Labour's Lost*. Although there is no print or manuscript evidence of this couplet predating the 1598 play quarto,[38] this does not preclude the possibility that this version of the proverb was spoken before Shakespeare wrote it down. There are three schools of thought on whether or not Shakespeare invented this couplet: some believe that Shakespeare included a preexisting proverbial couplet in his play, others believe that he added the conclusion to the couplet, and still others believe that Shakespeare's own diction became proverbial. The evidence for Shakespeare including a proverbial couplet in his play is thin: the earliest printed collection of proverbs that includes this couplet is John Clarke's *Paroemiologia Anglo-Latina* (1639).[39] Since Clarke uses Walkington's phrasing, and Walkington says that a "modern English poet" wrote the phrase, it seems that Shakespeare deserves at least part of the credit.

Horace Howard Furness claims that the first part of the phrase, "fat paunches make lean pates" was proverbial before Shakespeare's time, but that the rest of the phrase is Shakespeare's own.[40] This theory is possibly supported by later books of proverbs (see Table 6.3), such as John Ray's *A Collection of English Proverbs* (1670) and William Robertson's *Phraseologia Generalis* (1681). Ray notes the Greek source text translated by Jerome, and gives the English version as "Fat *paunches* make lean pates, &c."[41] Ray's

Table 6.3 Print sources that contain the "Fat Paunches" couplet arranged by variants.

"Fat paunches **have** lean pates, and **dainty** bits/**Make rich** the ribs, but bankrupt quite the wits"	"Fat paunches **make** lean pates, and **grosser** bits/ **Enrich** the ribs but bankrout quite the witts"	"Fat paunches **make** lean pates" (without concluding line)	"Fat paunches **make** lean Pates, and **dainty** bits/**Make fat** the Ribs, but banckrupt the Wits"
Love's Labour's Lost Q1: 1598 F1: 1623 Q2: 1631	*The Optick Glasse of Humors* (1607)	*A Collection of English Proverbs* (1670)	*Poor Robin's Almanack* (1697)
Englands Parnassus (1600)	*An Apology for Women* (1620)	*Phraseologia Generalis* (1681)	
A Helpe to Discourse (1623 and later editions)	*Paroemiologia Anglo-Latina* (1639)		
	The Scholar's Vade Mecum (1674)		
	Proteus Redivivus (1675)		

off-hand "&c" indicates that the kernel of the proverb is "fat paunches make lean pates" but that there is also more to the proverb—perhaps Shakespeare's addition?—with which readers would be familiar. Robertson only includes "Fat paunches make lean pates." Most of Robertson's Latin translations tend to be short; often, he translates only a word or a phrase.[42] Although these examples suggest that the first part of the couplet circulated alone, they do not preclude Shakespeare's authorship of the entire couplet: these print sources come decades after *Love's Labour's Lost*. The notion that Shakespeare built his couplet on an original phrase ("fat paunches *make* lean pates") perhaps accounts for Walkington's slight modification of Shakespeare's line. The return to "*have* lean pates" in *A Helpe to Discourse* suggests that the phrase was popular as it was published in the play (see Table 6.3).

"Proverbs, by definition, are oral expressions,"[43] although what we can conjecture about the oral tradition must be reconstructed from extant print and manuscript evidence. The oral transmission of this proverb, however, possibly explains the two versions of this proverb evident in print. If the wording originated with Shakespeare, it would have been first performed on the stage. Adam Fox asserts that theatre popularized proverbial sayings and led proverbs into circulation and every day discourse.[44] Fox's claim can be construed in two ways with regards to the "fat paunches" proverb: either Shakespeare popularized an existing oral phrasing of a proverb, or Walkington (or his source), taking brief notes while reading or attending the play, later misremembered Shakespeare's line.[45] Walkington's attribution of the phrase to "a modern English poet" shows that he believed that Shakespeare wrote at least part of the proverb. Walkington also noted the poet's genius in "pithyly" capturing the meaning in "two verses" (21). Shakespeare's contribution could have been expanding an existing English proverb into two verses, or it could be inventing both lines.

To sum up, the print circulation of "Fat paunches make lean pates" is as follows: Shakespeare's play was first printed around 1597. In 1600, Allott quoted directly from the play in *Englands Parnassus*. In 1607, Walkington adapted the quotation from either Shakespeare's work or *Englands Parnassus*. Walkington changed the couplet so "fat paunches *make* lean pates" (instead of *have* lean pates) and "dainty bits" (instead of "grosser bits") enrich the ribs. From these changes and further similarities, we can tell that Newstead (1620), Head (1675), and Norton (1675) copied from Walkington—not Shakespeare. In 1623, *A Helpe to Discourse* used Shakespeare's phrasing yet also contained source material from Walkington. Clarke (1639) used Walkington's phrasing, but could have copied from Newstead. The proverb in *Poor Robin* (1697) does not map neatly into this transmission, although it was not taken directly from the play. In the case of "Fat paunches make lean pates," Shakespeare's play launched this saying into circulation, but it is Walkington's quotation of Shakespeare that garnered the most imitation in print and manuscript.

In Walkington's *Optick Glasse*, Newstead's *Apology*, and Head's *Proteus Redivivus*, Shakespeare's words are visually emphasized for the reader with italics and indentation.[46] Although Shakespeare's couplet is not typographically emphasized in the print editions of the play (Q1, Q2, F1), later writers italicize Shakespeare's couplet to bring attention to its proverbial or commonplace nature. In the case of the *Love's Labour's Lost* couplet, Shakespeare's words are not extracted because of the commonplace markers, but earn their commonplace markers because they were extracted. That is to say, Allott (and perhaps Walkington) copied the couplet from a print version of the play where the couplet was not signaled as a commonplace, but in their works, they chose to mark the phrase as a commonplace; Shakespeare's wording became proverbial because of Allott's and Walkington's extracts, their use of italics, and their prefatory remarks about Shakespeare's rephrasing of the proverb.

MANUSCRIPT HISTORY OF THE "FAT PAUNCHES" PROVERB

There are four manuscripts that contain the "fat paunches" excerpt from *Love's Labour's Lost*: Bodleian MS Rawl. poet. 117, Bodleian MS Rawl. D. 954, and BL MSS Add. 18044 and Add. 63075.[47] None of the "fat paunches" excerpts in these three manuscripts is taken directly from the play (either in performance or in print). These manuscripts demonstrate that the circulation of dramatic extracts in print affected the circulation of dramatic extracts in manuscript. Three of the four manuscript compilers used Walkington's *The Optick Glasse of Humors* and W. B.'s *A Helpe to Discourse* as their sources. Once this couplet was extracted in one print source, it was copied multiple times in manuscript. The manuscript evidence mirrors the print evidence: in this case, a Shakespearean proverb is not born from the play, but from a dramatic excerpt. Rather than being a part of a whole (a couplet from a play, or lines that build a character), the "fat paunches" lines become complete when considered as a proverb. The print and manuscript circulation of this couplet demonstrates that for early modern readers (and writers), a quotation by Shakespeare was not always a quotation from Shakespeare, nor was it always meant to bring up associations with a particular play.

The compiler of Bodleian MS Rawl poet. 117 used Walkington's *Optick Glasse* for at least one of his sources. Bodleian MS Rawl. poet. 117 is a mid-seventeenth-century commonplace book compiled partly by Christopher Wase (1627–1690), the scholar and prolific translator.[48] Bodleian MS Rawl. poet. 117 is a quarto-sized miscellany. A large part of this manuscript is a verse anthology, although it also contains anagrams, notes, leases, and grants, as well as a list of books. Many items were written upside down at the back of the manuscript; as with many commonplace books, it was intended to be turned over and read from the back as well. When reading the manuscript from the back (upside down and backwards), the first page begins with a book-list that includes Erasmus's *Adages*.[49] A few pages later, the compiler began copying, although not verbatim, from the epistle of Walkington's *Optick Glasse* (f. 267v rev.). He copied out three longer passages from Walkington's *Optick Glasse* above a series of couplets and one prose selection from other sources. Here, as Sasha Roberts points out, the compiler included a couplet from *Venus and Adonis*: "Love is a Spiritte all compact of fyre / Not dull to sinke, but light, and will aspyre."[50] The following page holds further selections from *The Optick Glasse*, including the proverb: "Fat paunches make lean witts, and grosser bitts / Inrich the ribs, but bankrout quite the witts" (f. 267v rev.). Wase attributed this selection to "Humo:" that is, *The Optick Glasse of Humors*. Following the Shakespearean quotation from *The Optick Glasse*, the rest of the page is filled with excerpts from Walkington about physiognomy, such as "goggle ies [denote] a staringe foole."

When Wase copied the "Fat paunches" couplet, he used Walkington as a source. It is tempting to read the material surrounding the "fat paunches" proverb as an indication that the compiler knew of the proverb's Shakespearean source. This instance of the "fat paunches" is surrounded by the theatrical, the literary, and even the Shakespearean. For instance, the page with the "fat paunches" proverb begins with five quotations from Thomas Middleton's *The Phoenix*.[51] In the same section of the manuscript (written by the same hand), there are further dramatic extracts from Samuel Daniel's *Philotas* and *Cleopatra*,[52] as well as literary extracts from Sir Philip Sidney's *Arcadia* and John Harington's translation of *Orlando Furioso* (f. 265v rev., 274v rev.). Excerpts from Walkington share a page with the Shakespearean excerpt from *Venus and Adonis*. In this case, however, the arrangement of the miscellany might be (as the name implies) miscellaneous: these pages are also filled with unrelated materials, including Latin epigrams and episodes from prose histories.

The second instance of the couplet in Bodleian MS Rawl. poet. 117 could be in the same hand as the first. This second couplet reads, "Fatt paunches have leane pates, and danty bitts / make rich the ribs, but bankerout the witts" (f. 156 rev.). The couplet is not the only repeated extract in the manuscript. In the same hand are further quotations (including some repetitions) from Walkington's *Optick Glasse*, titled "Walkinton" (f. 154 rev.). Unlike the first versions of this couplet, the second is not attributed to Walkington, nor does it use Walkington's phrasing; it reads "*have* lean pates" and "*danty* [dainty] bits" instead of Walkington's "*make* lean pates" and "*grosser* bits" (emphasis added). This couplet was probably either copied from memory or from another handwritten source.[53]

Even though Wase ascribed the first "fat paunches" couplet to Walkington, the context of the second couplet also suggests that he may have known of Shakespeare's authorship. Following the couplet from *Love's Labour's Lost* is another Shakespearean couplet: "The Auntient saying is no Herisye / Hanginge and wivinge goes by destinye."[54] The lack of attribution on either Shakespearean couplet, however, means that we cannot know if the compiler believed this couplet to be the work of Shakespeare. Although we do not know the compiler's source, the change in wording suggests that this extract was not taken from a print text, but perhaps from another manuscript, from hastily written notes, or from memory. Perhaps *The Merchant of Venice* extract was later added to this page because it relates to the material above it. Both are by Shakespeare (other Shakespearean extracts in this manuscript are also grouped together), and both offer Shakespeare's pithy rephrasing of an ancient couplet. The other dramatic extracts in this manuscript (which are also frequently unattributed) are possibly in the same hand as the "fat paunches" couplet, which suggests that the writer was familiar with Shakespeare's work, although this does not definitively prove he knew the "fat paunches" extract was from the play.[55]

Two other manuscript compilers, Marmaduke Rawdon and John Abbott, both used *A Helpe to Discourse* as their sources for the "fat paunches" couplet. Marmaduke Rawdon of York (1610–1669) was a traveller and an antiquary who compiled BL MS Add. 18044, a small miscellany with the title *Collections out of severall Authors by Marmaduke Raudon Eboriencis 1662 Hodsden.*[56] This manuscript is mostly devotional verse, including twelve poems by Richard Crashaw (ff. 7v–22). Rawdon's manuscript looks like a small, modern, spiral-bound notebook, because it is octavo-sized, rectangular, and bound on the short edge at the top of the page. John Abbott of St. John's College, Oxford (b. 1653/4) owned and probably compiled Bodleian MS Rawl. D. 954 (a duodecimo manuscript containing 60 leaves) in the 1670s.[57] Chapter 4 considers the other dramatic extracts in Abbott's manuscript.

Above the "fat paunches" extract, both Rawdon and Abbott included this extract from Robert Southwell's poem "Content and Rich": "My wishes are but few, all easie to fulfill / I make the limits of my power the bounds unto my will."[58] Both Rawdon and Abbott copied other proverbs along with "fat paunches." Abbott excerpted liberally from *A Helpe to Discourse* and credited his source multiple times (ff. 40, 44v, 45). Along with Shakespeare's couplet, which warns against overeating, and Southwell's couplet, which praises self-discipline, Abbott included a third couplet, also from *A Helpe to Discourse*, on the theme of self-control: "If thou a long & healthfull age require / Put bounds unto thy glottonous desire" (f. 45). Rawdon included an alphabetical index at the end of his manuscript. He listed "fat paunches" (and, presumably, Southwell's couplet) under the heading "Proverbs" (f. 185v).

Although Rawdon and Abbott copied extracts from other full-text plays,[59] neither Rawdon nor Abbott used *Love's Labour's Lost* as their direct source for the "fat paunches" proverb. *Love's Labour's Lost* is still the ultimate source; that is to say, we can trace the transmission of this couplet through print and manuscript sources to the play without conjecturing about oral transmission. The trajectory is as follows: these two manuscript compilers used *A Helpe to Discourse* as their source, *A Helpe to Discourse* was influenced by Walkington's *Optick Glasse*, and Walkington quoted from Shakespeare's play (either directly, or from Allott's extract). Rawdon and Abbott did not only include this quotation because it was a popular oral proverb—they each had a print source. Because they each copied more than one selection from *A Helpe to Discourse*, their sources can be definitively identified.[60]

Bodleian MS Rawl. D. 954, BL MS Add. 18044, and Bodleian MS Rawl. poet. 117 all contain the same Shakespearean extract and they all use intermediary source texts. The transmission of the "fat paunches" couplet in manuscript sources (Table 6.4) mirrors the transmission in print sources (Table 6.2): they both show that *The Optick Glasse of Humors* was

Table 6.4 Transmission of the "Fat Paunches" couplet in manuscript sources.

```
Love's Labour's Lost          England's Parnassus
1598 (Q1)             ──▶     1600
William Shakespeare           Robert Allott
        │
        ▼
The Optick Glasse of Humors   A Helpe to Discourse*
1607                  ──▶     1623 edition
Thomas Walkington             W. B.
        │                           │
        │                           ▼
        │                     Bodleian MS Rawl. D. 954
        │                     ca. 1670s
        │                     John Abbott of St. John's College (?)
        ▼
Bodleian MS Rawl. poet 117
(first instance of couplet)
mid-seventeenth century
Christopher Wase et al

                      BL Add. MS 18044
                      ca. 1662
                      Marmaduke Rawdon of York
```

instrumental in disseminating Shakespeare's couplet. Unlike many the other instances of dramatic excerpting (even other examples from the manuscripts themselves), this is not a case of manuscript compilers copying from printed versions of the play or taking notes while attending a performance.

The chronologically latest seventeenth-century manuscript that is known to contain the "fat paunches" proverb is Henry Sturmy's commonplace book, BL MS Add. 63075. The British Library catalogue describes this manuscript as a "commonplace book of prayers and moral and religious extracts in prose and verse, c.1696. Many of the verses are taken from Francis Quarles's *Divine Fancies* and the prose extracts largely from Owen Felltham's *Resolves*." The "fat paunches" couplet, found on a page with multiple selections from Quarles's work, reads "Fatt panches make leane pates & grosser Bits / Enrich th'Ribs but Bankrupt quite the wits."[61] Sturmy's phrasing shows that he used Walkington or another intermediate text that used Walkington, although his exact source is not known. From Quarles, Sturmy similarly chose couplets warning against over-indulgence, for instance, "Of drunkenness": "It is a thief; that oft be/fore his face, / Steales man away and/Layes a beast in place" (f. 64v). Sturmy places the "fat paunches" commonplace in a context of devotional material and Protestant guidelines. Sturmy's recontextualization is logical because this couplet, like many of the texts from which he extracts, lauds self-control. Shakespeare's play engages with the theme of abstinence, but he could never have foreseen that this line would be appropriated in one man's personal religious miscellany. As Sturmy himself wrote in his dedication, "I writ for my own devotions . . . Notwithstanding I hope it may have good effect and use" (f. 2). Sturmy's book positions his excerpts as useful, just as they show the value of his source texts.

A century after he included it in *Love's Labour's Lost*, Shakespeare's rephrasing of an old proverb was still circulating in print (*Poor Robin*) and manuscript (BL MS Add. 63075); it was still useful and worth copying. This proverb continued to circulate throughout the eighteenth century.[62] Shakespeare's couplet appeared, credited to him, in multiple sources: in 1797, it was even included in a seller's book-list of medical texts.[63] By the late eighteenth century, Shakespeare's name was again associated with these words. One satirist even brought Shakespeare, "the great physician of the mind," and this couplet to criticize another's bad writing in order to suggest that abstinence from both food and writing might be best solution for this poor fellow.[64]

Abbott's manuscript includes a quotation from *A Helpe to Discourse* that discusses the oral and written circulation of texts, and unwittingly comments on the tangled transmission of the "fat paunches" couplet. The excerpt directly preceding the "fat paunches" couplet is a translation of a Latin epigram from John Owen's *Epigrammatum*: "Although the speaking word have life, / The written word be dead; / The written word shall last & be / When th' spoken word is fled" (Bodleian MS Rawl D. 954, f. 44v). The truth of Owen's poem, that "The written word shall last & be," is borne out by this investigation of written words—we have only traces of the oral transmission of this adage, but we do have written evidence that shows a clear textual heritage. Calling written words "dead," however, denies the changeability of dramatic extracts as they circulate in early modern print and manuscript. The "fat paunches" couplet exemplifies the malleability of dramatic extracts: Shakespeare's words circulated in multiple versions in print, manuscript, and oral culture.

The "fat paunches" couplet shows how Shakespeare reworked one preexisting proverb, one proverb, as R. W. Dent's *Shakespeare's Proverbial Language* shows, among the hundreds that Shakespeare used. Carefully tracing the circulation of more of Shakespeare's proverbs in print and manuscript will lead to a better understanding of the playwright's sources and his readership, as well as print and manuscript culture.

The prevalence of the "fat paunches" couplet in print and manuscript texts does not demonstrate the popularity of *Love's Labour's Lost*, although perhaps it does reflect on Shakespeare's popularity. In *Englands Parnassus*, Allott chose multiple extracts from Shakespeare's works, particularly his poetry. Walkington credited "a moderne english poet of good note" and Newstead recognized "a modern Poet" for the proverb. Later extractors, however, do not attribute the couplet at all, or sometimes credit the intermediary sources. Shakespeare's rephrasing of the proverb continued to circulate throughout the seventeenth century when dozens of other translations and wordings did not achieve the same popularity. The continued circulation of this couplet points to the popularity of Shakespeare's words (even when circulating anonymously), although not, perhaps, to his status as revered playwright.

Even including the circulation of this couplet from *Love's Labour's Lost* (that this analysis has proven was not extracted directly from the play), extant early to mid-seventeenth-century manuscripts contain fewer extracts from Shakespeare's plays than from plays by Ben Jonson, John Fletcher, or James Shirley—Shakespeare was not revered above these other writers. Shakespeare's legacy in seventeenth-century manuscripts developed most notably after the 1642 closure of the theatres. Our contemporary inheritance of Shakespeare as a cultural commodity began in the eighteenth century with the rise of bardolatry and grew with the acceptance of the Romantic notion that presented authors as inspired and individual geniuses. A quotation *by* Shakespeare is not always a quotation *from* Shakespeare, although in early modern culture, it still sounded as sweet.

NOTES

1. South, *Twelve Sermons* (1694), sig. M7.
2. Jeffrey McQuain and Stanley Malless, *Coined by Shakespeare: Words and Meanings first used by the Bard* (Springfield, MA: Merriam-Webster, 1998), viii.
3. Charlotte Brewer, "*OED* sources," in *Lexicography and the OED: Pioneers in the Untrodden Forest*, ed. Linda Mugglestone (Oxford: Oxford University Press, 2000), 40–58; John Willinksy, *Empire of Words: The Reign of the* OED (Princeton, NJ: Princeton University Press, 1994), 57–75.
4. "All that glisters is not gold" (Tilley A146) offers a clear example of Shakespeare using a preexisting proverb; "brevity is the soul of wit" (Tilley B652) may or may not have been a preexisting proverb. Morris Palmer Tilley, *A Dictionary of the Proverbs in England in the Sixteenth and Seventeenth Centuries: A Collection of Proverbs found in English Literature and the Dictionaries of the Period* (Ann Arbor, MI: University of Michigan Press, 1950).
5. A note on methodology: I relied on print proverb books to find these variations, including Tilley, *A Dictionary of the Proverbs*; G. L. Apperson, *English Proverbs and Proverbial Phrases: A Historical Dictionary* (1929; repr., Detroit: Gale, 1969); R. W. Dent, *Shakespeare's Proverbial Language: An Index* (Berkeley: University of California Presses, 1981); and Dent, *Proverbial Language in English Drama Exclusive of Shakespeare, 1495–1616: An Index* (Berkeley: University of California Presses, 1984). Online, I consulted *CELM*; *EEBO*; *Literature Online*, ProQuest; the Folger Shakespeare Library's *Union First Line Index of English Verse: 13th-19th Century (bulk 1500–1800)*, firstlines.folger.edu; GoogleBooks, books.google.com; and the Internet Archive, www.archive.org.
6. BL MS Add. 41063; Shakespeare, *Richard III* 3.1.79 (1623 folio), sig. r5v.
7. Charles Whitney, *Early Responses to Renaissance Drama* (Cambridge: Cambridge University Press, 2006), 6.
8. See Chapter 5 for a discussion of some of the more popular songs from Shakespeare's plays, notably those from *The Tempest* and *The Winter's Tale*.
9. While a proverb can be roughly defined as a traditional saying that pithily expresses a piece of conventional wisdom, scholars continue to debate what qualifies as a proverb. Tilley writes that "there is no agreement on what constitutes a proverb" (*A Dictionary of the Proverbs*, v). In *Shakespeare's Proverbial Language*, R. W. Dent admits that although it is paradoxical, he will not attempt to define what makes a proverb. Dent even disagrees with Tilley on what is proverbial, which underscores the difficulty of defining a proverb.
10. Jerome translated this proverb from Greek ("Παχεία γαστήρ λεπτόν ού τίκτει νόον") to Latin in epistle 52.11. W.H. Fremantle, G. Lewis, and W. G. Martley, who translated Jerome's epistles, give the English as "Fat bellies have no sentiments refined" (52.11). Although we do not know Jerome's direct source, he notes that he is translating "an excellent saying" from the Greek. Erasmus claims the saying was "well known among the Greeks" (*Adages* III.6.18); Denis Drysdall points out two Greek sources: Gregory of Nazianzus's *Carmina* ("De virtute" 1.10.589 PG 37 723A) and Antonius Melissa's later, medieval work *Loci Communes* (1.29 PG 136 911D).

See Jerome's "Letter 52: To Nepotian," trans. W. H. Fremantle, G. Lewis, and W. G. Martley, *From Nicene and Post-Nicene Fathers*, 2nd ser., vol. 6., ed. Philip Schaff and Henry Wace (Buffalo, NY: Christian Literature Publishing, 1893) and Dennis Drysdall, trans. and annotator, *Collected Works of Erasmus*, vol. 35: Adages III iv 1 to IV ii 100, ed. John N. Grant (Toronto, Canada: University of Toronto Press, 2005).

11. Jon R. Stone, *The Routledge Dictionary of Latin Quotations: The Illiterati's Guide to Latin Maxims, Mottoes, Proverbs, and Sayings* (New York: Routledge, 2005), 88.

12. Erasmus originally published *Adagiorum Collectanea* in 1500. He continued to revise and augment the work, changing the title to *Adagiorum Chiliades* (1508). The discussion of Jerome's saying (III.6.18) was augmented in the 1526 edition. Culman's (also known as Leonhardus Culmannus) *Sententiae Pueriles* was first published in 1540 and went through multiple editions in the early modern period (see Smith, 5–6). Both T. W. Baldwin and Kenneth Muir argue that echoes from Erasmus's *Adages* are found throughout Shakespeare's works. Charles G. Smith traces more than two hundred parallels between Culman's text and Shakespeare's plays, including the "fat paunches" couplet. T. W. Baldwin, *William Shakspere's Small Latine and Lesse Greeke* (Urbana, IL: University of Illinois Press, 1944); Kenneth Muir, "Shakespeare among the Commonplaces," *Review of English Studies* 10 (1959): 283–89; Charles G. Smith, *Shakespeare's Proverb Lore: His Use of the* Sententiae *of Leonard Culman and Publilius Syrus* (Cambridge, MA: Harvard University Press, 1963).

13. Many of these sources are listed by Tilley, *A Dictionary of the Proverbs*, and/or Apperson, *English Proverbs*. Tilley lists these further variants of Shakespeare's couplet: "A belly full of gluttony will never study willingly"; "When the belly is full the bones would be at rest"; and "The sparing diet is the spirit's feast" (526). Note that the earliest editions of *Sententiae Pueriles* were Latin only, but included Jerome's proverb in Latin (for instance, 1544, sig. B6v). There are multiple editions that contain this proverb; this is the earliest facsimile on *EEBO*. Later editions include both Latin and English and translate the phrase differently: consider, "A fat belly doth not beget a fine wit" (1658, sig. C6v-C7). Withals's dictionary was first published in 1553 and went through various editions. The proverb appears in the 1634 version of the dictionary. Shakespeare might have been exposed to earlier versions of Withals's dictionary as a schoolboy, although none that contained this proverb. See Werner Hüllen, "John Withals' dictionary for young boys (1553)," *English Dictionaries, 800–1700: The Topical Tradition* (Oxford: Oxford University Press, 1999), 168–201.

14. Francis Beaumont and John Fletcher, *Loves Cure*, in *Comedies and Tragedies* (1647), sig. Rrrrr1. In *Campaspe* (1584), sig. A3v, John Lyly attributes his version of the "old saw" to Socrates.

15. The only known pre-twentieth-century usage of "fat bodies, lean braines" is Charles Coffey's appropriation in *The Merry Cobler* (1735). Even though Beaumont and Fletcher's phrasing did not circulate in the early modern period, it is frequently recopied in twentieth-century proverb books.

16. Ormond Seavey, ed., *Benjamin Franklin Autobiography and Other Writings* (Oxford: Oxford University Press, 1993), 258.

17. For an overview of the importance of physiognomy to early modern Europe, see Martin Porter's *Windows of the Soul: Physiognomy in European Culture, 1470–1780* (Oxford: Oxford University Press, 2005); for a more specific look at English uses of physiognomy, see Sibylle Baumbach's "Physiognomy," in *A New Companion to English Renaissance Literature and Culture*, vol. 1, ed. Michael Hattaway (Malden, MA: Blackwell, 2010), 82–97.

18. Allott, *Englands Parnassus* (1600), title page.

19. Ibid., sig. H8.

20. For a complete listing of the Shakespearean extracts in *Englands Parnassus*, see C. M. Ingleby et al., eds.,*The Shakspere Allusion-Book: A Collection of Allusions to Shakspere From 1591 to 1700*, 2 vols. (London: Chatto & Windus and Duffield & Company, 1909). 2.470–79.

21. Thomas Walkington, *The Optick Glasse of Humors* (1607), sig. D5v. For a summary and discussion of *The Optick Glasse of Humors*, see Charles F. Mullett, "Thomas Walkington and his 'Optick Glasse,'" *Isis* 36 (1946): 96–105.

22. Walkington, *Optick Glasse* (1607), sig. D5v, emphasis mine. John Pitcher argues that just as Walkington read Shakespeare, Shakespeare read Walkington before writing *The Winter's Tale*, in "Some Call him Autolycus," in *In Arden: Editing Shakespeare: Essays in Honour of Richard Proudfoot*, ed. Ann Thompson and Gordon McMullan (London: Arden Shakespeare, 2003), 252–68.

23. In her edition of *An Apology for Women*, Susan Gushee O'Malley points out that Newstead's version of the quotation parallels Walkington's, although her chronology is reversed (156 n.177). It is not Walkington who cites Newstead, but Newstead (1620) who cites Walkington (1607). O'Malley, *Custome is an Idiot: Jacobean Pamphlet Literature on Women* (Urbana: University of Illinois Press, 2004).

24. Newstead, *An Apology for Women* (1620), sig. C8v; Walkington, *Optick Glasse* (1607), sig. D5v.

25. Walkington, *Optick Glasse* (1607), sig. D5.

26. Richard Head, *Proteus Redivivus: The Art of Wheedling or Insinuation* (1675), sig. E4; Walkington, *Optick Glasse* (1607), sig. D5r-v.

27. *A Helpe to Discourse* (1623), p. 116. This gathering in the 1623 *Helpe* is irregular, so I offer page numbers instead of signature numbers. *A Helpe to Discourse* was republished frequently over the seventeenth century. Eighteenth-century works like *Brett's Miscellany* (1748) take sections wholesale from *Helpe*, including the "fat paunches" couplet (p. 93).

28. *A Helpe to Discourse* (1623), pp. 116–18; from Walkington, *Optick Glasse* (1607), sig. D5v.

29. Although this is the same year as the publication of Shakespeare's first folio, the folio was not completed until early November 1623, making it unlikely that the first folio influenced the selection of Shakespeare's couplet. Charlton Hinman, ed., *The Norton Facsimile of the First Folio of Shakespeare*, 2nd ed. (New York and London: Norton, 1996), xx.

30. *A Helpe to Discourse* (1623), p. 117.

31. *A Helpe to Discourse* contains Shakespearean excerpts at other points: *The Shakespere Allusion-Book* notes an excerpt from *Hamlet* in the 1640 edition (1.464);

in "A Shakespearean Quotation in 1628," *Notes & Queries* 22 (1975): 175–76, John Feather discusses excerpts from *2 Henry IV* in the 1628 edition. These later Shakespearean extracts demonstrate that someone involved in the revision and republication of this conduct guide was familiar with Shakespeare's plays and perhaps explains why they would emend Walkington's misrepresentation of Shakespeare's lines.

32. The title page reads: *Poor Robin 1697. An Almanack Of the Old and New Fashion* (1697).

33. Frank Palmeri, *Satire, History, Novel: Narrative Forms, 1665–1815* (Newark: University of Delaware Press, 2003), 44.

34. *Poor Robin's Almanack* (1697), sig. C2v.

35. *Poor Robin's Almanack* (1697), sig. C3v; William Cartwright, *The Ordinary* 3.5, TLN 1548–1549 (in *Comedies, Tragi-Comedies*, 1651), sig. D6; p. 55.

36. *Poor Robin's Almanack* (1697), sig. C3v. Italics in the original.

37. Ben Jonson, *Every Man in his Humour* (1616 folio), sig. F6v.

38. *Love's Labour's Lost* was likely performed c. 1597, although we do not have an exact date of performance. The earliest extant quarto was published in 1598 and is generally known as Q1. There may have been an earlier 1597 quarto. See H. R. Woudhuysen, ed., *Love's Labour's Lost* (London: Arden Shakespeare, 1998), Appendix A. I give the date of Q1 as 1598 with 1597 offered as an earlier possibility.

39. Clarke includes the Latin with Shakespeare's translation under the heading "Gula" (appetite), along with two other English quotations, "His brains are in 's belly—" and "His belly is too strong for 's purse" (1607, sig I4). Clarke does not attribute the couplet to Shakespeare, although he does not attribute any of his sayings in the text.

40. Horace Howard Furness, *A New Variorum Edition of Shakespeare*, vol. 14: *Love's Labour's Lost* (Philadelphia: J. B. Lippincott, 1904), 15.

41. John Ray, *A Collection of English Proverbs* (1670), sig. K, emphasis in original.

42. William Robertson, *Phraseologia Generalis* (1681), sig. Pp6. Robertson also includes the proverb, "Fat men are of dull understanding; Pingues hebetis ingenii" (sig. Pp5v).

43. Charles Clay Doyle, "Collections of proverbs and proverb dictionaries: Some historical observations on what's in them and what's not (with a note on current gendered proverbs)," in *Topics in English Linguistics: Phraseology and Culture in English*, ed. Paul Skandera (Berlin and New York: Mouton de Gruyter, 2007), 182.

44. Adam Fox, *Oral and Literate Culture in England 1500–1700* (Oxford: Clarendon, 2000), 132.

45. It is possible that Walkington saw the play performed and copied notes during a performance. *Love's Labour's Lost* was performed at court in the Christmas season of 1604/5; Woudhuysen (*Love's Labour's Lost*) conjectures further public and private performances at the opening of the century. If Walkington saw the play performed, it is perhaps the actor's line that he recorded, or he perhaps took notes in shorthand, which would explain the slight difference.

46. In Guazzo's *Civil Conversation*, the typeface changes from blackletter to Roman to emphasize the presence of this proverb, although not Shakespeare's particular phrasing. In the edition at the Huntington Library (call number 61245), a reader has further underlined the proverb. Richard Head, *Proteus Redivivus* (1675), sig. E4; Newstead, *An Apology for Women* (1620), sig. C8v; Walkington, *Optick Glasse* (1607), sig. D5v.

47. The only other seventeenth-century manuscripts known to contain different excerpts from *Love's Labour's Lost* are BL MS Lansdowne 1185, Bodleian MS Sancroft 29, and Bodleian MS Eng. poet e. 97, discussed in Chapters 4, 5, and 1, respectively.

48. Wase (or Wace, or Wasse) translated Sophocles's *Electra* (1649) and later one of Cicero's orations against Catiline (1671). In 1671, Wase became a printer to Oxford University (Stringer 2.lxxxii). There are multiple hands in the manuscript, but I will follow scholarly convention in assigning the literary sections of the manuscript to Wase. See Richard E. Hodges, "Wase, Christopher (1627–1690)," *ODNB* and Gary Stringer, *The Variorum Edition of the Poetry of John Donne*, Vol. 2: The Elegies. (Indiana: Indiana University Press, 2000), 432 (see Chapter 1, n. 143).

49. Bodleian MS Rawl. poet. 117, f. 279v. There are three sets of foliation in this manuscript, including one from back-to-front. I follow the archivist's foliation in pencil that runs from front-to-back.

50. Bodleian MS Rawl. poet. 117, f. 276v rev.; Sasha Roberts, *Reading Shakespeare's Poems in Early Modern England* (Basingstoke: Palgrave, 2003), 90.

51. The quotations from *The Phoenix* are: 8.20–21 (paraphrased); 15.339–40; 6.103–4; 4.228–29; 13.199–200. Line numbers are taken from Gary Taylor and John Lavagnino, eds., *Thomas Middleton: The Collected Works* (Oxford: Clarendon Press, 2007).

52. Bodleian MS Rawl. poet. 117, f. 275v rev. The excerpts from Daniel's *Philotas* are as follows: epistle ll. 13–14; ll. 60–61, 154–55, 967–68, 1085–86, 1717–18, 2121–22. There are only two excerpts from Daniel's *Cleopatra*: the final lines in the revision of 1.2 (ll. 163–64).

53. The Folger *Union First Line Index* suggests that this manuscript reads "full paunches"; although it is likely "fatt paunches," the handwriting is unclear. A change from "fat paunches" to "full paunches" could also be explained by copying from a manuscript source: "fatt" could easily be mistaken for "full" depending on handwriting. A person remembering the couplet might easily change "fatt" to "full," as they share the same meaning, syllabic length, and even the same first letter. Roberts suggests that the slight error in the couplet from *Venus and Adonis* "perhaps represents a memorial construction" in *Reading Shakespeare's Poems*, 219, n. 56. Laurie Maguire lists paraphrase as a common way that texts change when they are remembered in *Shakespearean Suspect Texts: The 'Bad' Quartos and Their Contexts* (Cambridge: Cambridge University Press, 1996), 173.

54. Bodleian MS Rawl. poet. 117, f. 156 rev.; *The Merchant of Venice* 2.9.82. The proverb "Weddyng is destiny, And hanging lykewise" (Tilley W232) is found in John Heywood's *Dialogue of Proverbs* (1546) and various other fifteenth- and sixteenth-century sources. The last four items on the page include two passages, translated,

from the story of Clitophon and Leucippe, a Greek romance that was translated into English and published in 1597 and 1638 (the translation in Rawl. poet. 117 might be original), followed by the "paunches" couplet and the proverb found in *Merchant*.

55. Bodleian MS Rawl. poet. 117 contains extracts from multiple plays, including the song "If I freely may discover" from Jonson's *Poetaster* (f. 30v; note ff. 31 and 32 have been torn out), selections from Jonson's *Sejanus* (f. 149v), and Shakespeare's *Troilus and Cressida, Much Ado About Nothing, A Midsummer Night's Dream* (f. 156v), *Twelfth Night* and *The Winter's Tale* (f. 162), John Marston's *The Malcontent* (f. 164), Jonson's *Volpone* (f. 164), Shakespeare's *Hamlet* (f. 164r-v), Thomas Middleton's *A Mad World, My Masters* (f. 164v), Marston's *Parasitaster* (f. 164v), Daniel's *Philotas* and *Cleopatra* (f. 275v), and Middleton's *The Phoenix* (f. 276). These extracts were most likely taken from the plays themselves: the compiler copies multiple selections from many of these plays.

56. BL MS Add. 18044, f. 1v. Rawdon composed this manuscript when he lived with his cousin (most of 1656–1669), also named Marmaduke Rawdon, at Hoddesdon, Hertfordshire. In this manuscript, Rawdon includes verses for Sir Marmaduke Rawdon (1582–1646), who was his uncle and adoptive father, a wine merchant and Governor of Basing House. See Natasha Glaisyer, "Rawdon, Marmaduke (*bap.* 1610, *d.* 1669)," *ODNB*.

57. At least part of this manuscript was compiled after 1672, when Sparrow's *Rationale upon the Book of England* was published. The cover (f. 60) reads "John Abbot Hart Hull" and is dated February 21, 1671. Abbott's name appears again on f. 2, linking him to "John Bapt. Oxon."

58. *A Helpe to Discourse* (1627), sig. F12v. Although the *Love's Labour's Lost* extract can be found in editions of *A Helpe to Discourse* dating from 1623, the Southwell extract was only added in 1627 and is found in subsequent editions. BL MS Add. 18044, ff. 71 (Southwell) and ff. 71v ("Fatt Panches"); Bodleian MS Rawl. 954, f. 45v (Southwell and "Fatt Panches").

59. Rawdon copied lines 151–52 and 154–55 of *Philotas* (BL MS Add. 18044, f. 142r-v) from Daniel's *Whole Works* (1623). Rawdon altered the print source of *Philotas* from "Now good my Lord, conforme you to the rest / Let not your wings be greater than your nest" to "Lett all wise men conforme them to thir rest / Lett noe mans wings be bigger then his nest," in order to make it proverbial. For more on Abbott's dramatic extracts, see Chapter 4.

60. Rawdon's manuscript (c.1662) is not the source for Abbott's quotations (c.1670s) from *A Helpe to Discourse*. Abbott directly attributes the quotations to the print source, whereas Rawdon does not.

61. BL MS Add. 63075, f 64v. This transcription and analysis corrects my article in *Shakespeare* on this point, where I relied on the Folger *Union First Line Index* for the phrasing.

62. One eighteenth-century text, James Kelly's *A Complete Collection of Scotish Proverbs* (1721), gives "Fat paunches bode lean Pates" (sig. H5v) as a Scottish proverb, but he admits found it "impossible strictly to distinguish the *Scotish* from the *English*" (sig. A4). Kelly comments that this proverb is "A groundless Reflection upon fat Men, of whom I have known many ingenious, and but few ill-natur'd or malicious" (sig. H5v). Other eighteenth-century examples offer only "fat paunches make

lean pates" without the concluding line of the couplet (Thomas Fuller's *Gnomologia,* 1832, p. 57; Elisha Coles's *A Dictionary, English-Latin, and Latin-English,* under "Fat"; and others).

63. "Medical Books published by J. Callow," bound with Robert Couper, *Speculations on the Mode and Appeareances of Impregnation in the Human Female* 2nd ed. (1797), John Rylands University Library of Manchester (available through *Eighteenth-Century Collections Online*).

64. *Pindarics; or an Ode of Lamentation Addressed to Peter Pindar* [John Wolcot] (1800), sigs. Fv-F2.

Conclusion

In the mid-nineteenth century, John Payne Collier claimed that "not a single written fragment of any of the Plays of Shakespeare has come down to us, with the exception of a few passages in some unprinted poetical miscellanies."[1] A hundred years later, James C. McManaway argued, "Any literate person with a little industry can copy lines out of a play. The results will reveal something of the interests and the taste of the compiler, but may be without general or enduring worth."[2] Separated by a century, Collier and McManaway both expressed skepticism about the value of dramatic extracts.

As this book demonstrates, there are more than "a few passages in some unprinted poetical miscellanies"; we know of thousands of extracts from plays by Shakespeare and his contemporaries found in hundreds of manuscripts, and more are yet to be discovered. The "general and enduring worth" of dramatic extracts is that they offer tangible evidence about how readers and playgoers approached plays as malleable and divisible texts. Furthermore, as McManaway notes even when dismissing many of these texts, extracts "reveal something of the interests and the taste of the compiler." And, as this analysis shows, extracts also reveal early tastes in plays, motivations for extracting, and varying attitudes toward drama, which is perhaps a natural product of the heterogeneous readers and audiences.

The narrative of dramatic extracts is not just one of disconnected readers and audiences: indeed, patterns do emerge over the course of the century. Early readers and audiences did not spontaneously begin copying parts of plays; rather, dramatic extracting builds on the commonplacing tradition. Furthermore, dramatic extracting did not occur in a vacuum, as increased play publication and commonplace markers in plays gave readers opportunity and encouragement to write and memorize passages. The boom in miscellaneous manuscripts at the universities in the 1620s and 1630s similarly stimulated extracting. Indeed, catalogued and extant archival evidence suggests that it is only after the closure of the theatres that readers began creating dramatic miscellanies and choosing a particular book to hold play selections. Dramatic extracts provide a rare glimpse into the mind of a reader in a particular historic moment.

The continued history of dramatic extracts, both from later plays and in print and manuscript after 1700, will surely improve our understanding of theatrical reception. Eighteenth-century print miscellanies and commonplace books offer continued evidence of dramatic extracting. The eighteenth century saw not only continued print and manuscript commonplacing from plays but also the publication of collections of longer passages, or "beauties." The title page of one dramatic miscellany, *Thesaurus Dramaticus* (1724), announced that it contained "all the Celebrated Passages, Soliloquies, Similies, Descriptions, and other Poetical Beauties in the Body of English Plays, Antient and Modern," and highlighted that it was arranged by heading, "Digested under Proper Topics." *Thesaurus Dramaticus* was adapted for republication as *The Beauties of the English Stage*, which was republished multiple times over the eighteenth century.[3] The eighteenth century also saw the publication of a number of print dramatic miscellanies devoted entirely to prologues and epilogues, such as *A Second and Last Collection Of the most Celebrated Prologues and Epilogues* (1727) and *The Court of Thespis* (1769). General miscellanies also continued to include selections from early works, such as Henry Headley's *Select Beauties of Ancient English Poetry* (1787), which contains "Cleopatra with the Asps before her debating on her own Destruction."[4] Over the eighteenth and nineteenth centuries, a renewed turn to antiquarianism contributed to the continued and changing interest in pre-1642 plays, championed by antiquarians of varying repute such as Robert Dodsley, John Payne Collier, William Hazlitt, and Charles and Mary Lamb, the last of whom were known for their children's adaptation, *Tales from Shakespeare* (1807). Increasing bardolatry led to greater interest in Shakespeare's plays over those by his contemporaries. Indeed, Mary Cowden Clarke's *Shakespeare Proverbs* (1848) is a Shakespearean miscellany and Thomas Price's *The Wisdom and Genius of Shakspeare* (1838) is a Shakespearean commonplace book. Just as changing circumstances altered the reception of plays throughout the seventeenth century, dramatic extracting continued to change in relation to current events, predilections and publications, from David Garrick's 1769 Shakespeare Jubilee to Thomas Bowdler's *The Family Shakspeare* (1807) and beyond.

Dramatic extracts not only allow us to understand readers and audiences; they also build on what we know about playwrights and play writing. We have long known that playwrights included existing proverbs in their plays, but these extracts, like the use of commonplace markers, suggest that playwrights might have done so with the hope that readers and audiences would recognize sententious and therefore useful or applicable material. Knowing that people would take parts of their plays (for both print and manuscript commonplace books and miscellanies), playwrights designed their works as texts to be mined in multiple ways: they could be read for extracts; they were meant to be minded, that is, noted; and they were meant to be "mined," as in, made mine, taken, and personalized.

Increasingly available digital facsimiles and ever-improving cataloguing will no doubt facilitate further study of these hitherto overlooked archival texts. This book is not intended to be the final word on dramatic extracts and the culture of extracting; it stands as an invitation for further work in this field. The manuscripts analyzed here offer a range of frameworks for approaching dramatic extracts: by examining the transmission of one extract over time, by considering the works of one compiler, by investigating a single manuscript or related group of manuscripts, or by tracing the meaning of an excerpt in relation to changing historical events. These approaches can be both synchronic and diachronic. Dramatic extracts impel us to consider the original performed and published contexts of a given work, how that work was received, and how parts of it came to be decontextualized and recontextualized.

Examining dramatic extracts allows us to find polysemous and variable meanings instead of narrowing the text to one possible reading. The study of dramatic extracts is one way that scholars can, as Leah Marcus suggests, "un-edit the Renaissance." "Un-editing" involves opening the text to multiple meanings and interpretations; with their variant readings and new contexts, dramatic extracts insist on multiple interpretations.[5] Indeed, as this book has shown, early modern manuscript compilers changed the words they copied, adapting their meaning and phrasing for new situations. Extracting from plays was part of a culture that prized repetition and imitation and deliberate alteration in a way that improved or personalized the source.[6] Bibliographers and editors have established early modern plays as what John Bryant would call "fluid texts." For Bryant, changes in a text reveal the energy of the culture interacting with that text.[7] Dramatic extracts add to our understanding of a text's fluidity: it is not just in authorial revisions, performance, publication, and adaptation that plays change. Early modern plays change meaning when readers and audiences experience and interpret them. And while we may not be able to directly access these early readers and audiences, at least we can turn to the traces they left—their dramatic extracts. Dramatic extracts are material evidence of the individual, contingent, and personalized relationships of seventeenth-century playgoers and readers to the plays.

In this book, I have sought to express some of the new implications that dramatic extracts gain in manuscript contexts, which requires an attention to the plays, the extracts, and the print and manuscript source texts, as well as to the historical circumstances in which they were excerpted. Other approaches to early modern drama have demonstrated its performative nature, its religious symbolism, and its revolutionary aspects, to name just a few; the study of dramatic excerpts reveals that for a seventeenth-century audience, drama was, above all, multifunctional and useful. As fragmented, altered, reconstructed, and recontextualized selections from plays, dramatic extracts demonstrate the educational, moral, ameliorating, political, aesthetic, entertaining, and ultimately personal uses of early modern drama.

NOTES

1. John Payne Collier, *Reasons for a New Edition of Shakespeare's Work* (London: Whittaker, 1841), 6.

2. James C. McManaway, "Excerpta Quaedam per A.W. Adolescentem," in *Studies in Honor of DeWitt T. Starnes*, ed. Thomas P. Harrison et al. (Austin: University of Texas Press, 1967), 122.

3. *The Beauties of the English Stage* was first published in 1737, expanded in 1756, and, as *The Beauties of the English Drama*, expanded again in 1777.

4. Henry Headley, *Select Beauties of Ancient English Poetry* (1787), 71.

5. Even in "Confessions of a Reformed Uneditor (II)," Leah Marcus practices and advocates "scrupulous . . . evaluation of manuscript and printed materials" (1072) See Marcus, *Unediting the Renaissance: Shakespeare, Marlowe, Milton* (London: Routledge, 1996); "Confessions of a Reformed Uneditor," in *The Renaissance Text: Theory, Editing, Textuality*, ed. Andrew Murphy (Manchester: Manchester University Press, 2000); and "Confessions of a Reformed Uneditor (II)," *PMLA* 115 (2000): 1072–77.

6. See, for instance, Julie Maxwell, "How the Renaissance (Mis)Used Sources: The Art of Misquotation," in *How To Do Things with Shakespeare* ed. Laurie Maguire (Oxford: Blackwell, 2008), 54–76.

7. John Bryant, *The Fluid Text: A Theory of Revision and Editing for Book and Screen* (Ann Arbor: University of Michigan Press, 2002), esp. 62–63.

Bibliography

SELECTED BIBLIOGRAPHY OF SECONDARY SOURCES

Alexander, Gavin, ed. *The Model of Poesy.* By William Scott. Cambridge: Cambridge University Press, 2013.
Apperson, G. L. *English Proverbs and Proverbial Phrases: A Historical Dictionary.* 1929. Reprint, Detroit: Gale, 1969.
Archer, Jayne Elizabeth, Elizabeth Goldring, and Sarah Knight. *The Progresses, Pageants, and Entertainments of Queen Elizabeth I.* Oxford: Oxford University Press, 2007.
Beal, Peter. *A Dictionary of English Manuscript Terminology.* Oxford: Oxford University Press, 2010.
———. "Notions in Garrison: The Seventeenth-Century Commonplace Book." In *New Ways of Looking at Old Texts: Papers of the Renaissance English Text Society, 1985–1991*, edited by W. Speed Hill, 131–47. Binghamton: Renaissance English Text Society, 1993.
Beaurline, L. A., and Thomas Clayton, eds. *The Works of Sir John Suckling.* 2 vols. Oxford: Oxford University Press, 1971.
Bentley, Gerard Eades. "John Cotgrave's *English Treasury of Wit and Language* and the Elizabethan Drama." *Studies in Philology* 40 (1943): 186–203.
Bevington, David, Martin Butler, and Ian Donaldson, et al., eds. *The Cambridge Edition of the Works of Ben Jonson.* 7 vols. Cambridge: Cambridge University Press, 2012.
Carpenter, Edward. *Cantuar: The Archbishops in their Office,* 3rd ed. London: Continuum, 1997.
Chan, Mary. *Music in the Theatre of Ben Jonson.* Oxford: Oxford University Press, 2002.
Collinson, Patrick. *From Cranmer to Sancroft.* London: Continuum, 2006.
Crane, Mary Thomas. *Framing Authority: Sayings, Self, and Society in Sixteenth-Century England.* Princeton: Princeton University Press, 1997.

Dent, R. W. *Shakespeare's Proverbial Language: An Index.* Berkeley: University of California Presses, 1981.

Evans, G. Blakemore. "A Seventeenth-Century Reader of Shakespeare." *Review of English Studies* 21 (1945): 271–79.

———, ed. *The Riverside Shakespeare*, 2nd ed. Boston: Houghton Mifflin, 1997.

Goldring, Elizabeth, Faith Eales, Elizabeth Clarke, and Jayne Elisabeth Archer, eds. *John Nichols's The Progresses and Public Processions of Queen Elizabeth I: A New Edition of Early Modern Sources.* 5 vols. Oxford: Oxford University Press, 2014.

Gowan, Juliet. "An Edition of Edward Pudsey's Commonplace Book (c. 1600–1615) from the Manuscript in the Bodleian Library." MPhil thesis, University of London, 1967.

Greg, W. W. *Jonson's Masque of the Gipsies in the Burley, Belvoir, and Windsor Editions.* London: Oxford University Press, 1952.

Hao, Tianhu. "*Hesperides, or the Muses' Garden* and its Manuscript History." *The Library*, 7th ser. 10 (2009): 372–404.

Havens, Earle, ed. *"Of Common Places, or Memorial Books": A Seventeenth-Century Manuscript from the James Marshall and Marie-Louise Osborn Collection.* New Haven, CT: Beinecke Rare Book and Manuscript Library, 2001.

Heaton, Gabriel. *Writing and Reading Royal Entertainments: From George Gascoigne to Ben Jonson.* Oxford: Oxford University Press, 2010.

Hunter, G. K. "The Marking of *Sententiae* in Elizabethan Printed Plays, Poems, and Romances." *The Library*, 5th ser. 6 (1951): 171–88.

Ioppolo, Grace. *Dramatists and Their Manuscripts in the Age of Shakespeare, Jonson, and Middleton.* New York: Routledge, 2002.

Jorgens, Elise Bickford, ed. *English Song 1600–1675: Facsimiles of Twenty-six Manuscripts and an Edition of the Texts.* 12 vols. New York: Garland, 1987.

Kelliher, Hilton. "Contemporary Manuscript Extracts from Shakespeare's *Henry IV, Part 1*." *English Manuscript Studies 1100–1700* 1 (1989): 160.

———. "Donne, Jonson, Richard Andrews and The Newcastle Manuscript." *English Manuscript Studies 1100–1700* 4 (1993): 134–73.

Kirsch, Arthur C. "A Caroline Commentary on the Drama." *Modern Philology* 66 (1968): 256–61.

Knowles, James. "'Songs of baser alloy': Jonson's *Gypsies Metamorphosed* and the Circulation of Manuscript Libels." *Huntington Library Quarterly* 69 (2006): 153–76.

Lesser, Zachary, and Peter Stallybrass. "The First Literary *Hamlet* and the Commonplacing of Professional Plays." *Shakespeare Quarterly* 59 (2008): 371–420.

Love, Harold. *Scribal Publication in Seventeenth-Century England.* Oxford: Oxford University Press, 1993.

MacDonald, Robert H., ed. *The Library of Drummond of Hawthornden.* Edinburgh: Edinburgh University Press, 1971.

Marotti, Arthur F. *Manuscript, Print, and the English Renaissance Lyric.* Ithaca: Cornell University Press, 1993.

McGee, C. E., and John C. Meagher. "Preliminary Checklist of Tudor and Stuart Entertainments: 1588–1603." *Research Opportunities in Renaissance Drama* 26 (1981): 51–155.

---. "Preliminary Checklist of Tudor and Stuart Entertainments: 1603–1613." *Research Opportunities in Renaissance Drama* 27 (1984): 47–126.
---. "Preliminary Checklist of Tudor and Stuart Entertainments: 1614–1625." *Research Opportunities in Renaissance Drama* 30 (1982): 17–128.
---. "Preliminary Checklist of Tudor and Stuart Entertainments: 1625–1634." *Research Opportunities in Renaissance Drama* 36 (1997): 23–95.
---. "Preliminary Checklist of Tudor and Stuart Entertainments: 1634–1642." *Research Opportunities in Renaissance Drama* 38 (1999): 23–86.
McManaway, James C. "Excerpta Quaedam per A.W. Adolescentem." In *Studies in Honor of DeWitt T. Starnes*, edited by Thomas P. Harrison et al., 117–29. Austin: University of Texas Press, 1967.
Moss, Ann. *Printed Commonplace-Books and the Structuring of Renaissance Thought*. Oxford: Clarendon, 1996.
Moulton, Ian Frederick. *Before Pornography: Erotic Writing in Early Modern England*. Oxford: Oxford University Press, 2000.
Palfrey, Simon, and Tiffany Stern. *Shakespeare in Parts*. Oxford: Oxford University Press, 2007.
Randall, Dale B. J. *Winter Fruit: English Drama 1642–1660*. Lexington, KY: University Press of Kentucky, 1995.
Roberts, Sasha. *Reading Shakespeare's Poems in Early Modern England*. Basingstoke: Palgrave, 2003.
---. "Reading Shakespeare's Tragedies of Love: *Romeo and Juliet*, *Othello*, and *Antony and Cleopatra* in Early Modern England." In *A Companion to Shakespeare's Works: The Tragedies*, edited by Richard Dutton and Jean Elizabeth Howard, 108–33. Malden, MA: Blackwell, 2003.
Smyth, Adam. *"Profit and Delight": Printed Miscellanies in England, 1640–1682*. Detroit: Wayne State University Press, 2004.
Stallybrass, Peter, and Roger Chartier. "Reading and Authorship: The Circulation of Shakespeare 1590–1619." In *A Concise Companion to Shakespeare and the Text*, edited by Andrew Murphy, 35–56. Oxford: Blackwell, 2007.
Stallybrass, Peter, Roger Chartier, J. Franklin Mowery, and Heather Wolfe. "Hamlet's Tables and the Technologies of Writing in Renaissance England." *Shakespeare Quarterly* 55 (2004): 379–419.
Stern, Tiffany. *Documents of Performance in Early Modern England*. Cambridge: Cambridge University Press, 2009.
Taylor, Gary, and John Lavagnino, eds. *Thomas Middleton and Early Modern Textual Culture*. Oxford: Clarendon, 2007.
Tilley, Morris Palmer. *A Dictionary of the Proverbs in England in the Sixteenth and Seventeenth Centuries: A Collection of Proverbs found in English Literature and the Dictionaries of the Period*. Ann Arbor, MI: University of Michigan Press, 1950.
Werstine, Paul. *Early Modern Playhouse Manuscripts and the Editing of Shakespeare*. Cambridge: Cambridge University Press, 2012.
Whitney, Charles. *Early Responses to Renaissance Drama*. Cambridge: Cambridge University Press, 2006.
Wiseman, Susan. *Drama and Politics in the English Civil War*. Cambridge: Cambridge University Press, 1998.

Woudhuysen, Henry. *Sir Philip Sidney and the Circulation of Manuscripts 1558–1640*. Oxford: Clarendon, 1996.

SELECTED BIBLIOGRAPHY OF ONLINE SOURCES

Please note that sources with no URL given are subscription access.

British Literary Manuscripts Online. Medieval and Renaissance; c. 1660–1900. Gale Cengage Learning.
Catalogue of English Literary Manuscripts 1450–1700 (*CELM*). Compiled by Peter Beal. King's College London. celm2.dighum.kcl.ac.uk
Database of Early English Playbooks. Edited by Alan B. Farmer and Zachary Lesser. University of Pennsylvania. deep.sas.upenn.edu
Dictionary of Literary Biography Complete Online (*DLB*). Gale Literature Collections.
Early English Books Online (*EEBO*). Chadwyck-Healey.
Eighteenth-Century Collections Online (*ECCO*). Gale Cengage Learning.
English Short Title Catalogue (*ESTC*). British Library. estc.bl.uk
The Internet Archive. www.archive.org
Literature Online. ProQuest.
Oxford Dictionary of National Biography (*ODNB*). Oxford University Press.
Oxford English Dictionary (*OED*). Oxford University Press.
Union First Line Index of English Verse: 13th–19th Century (bulk 1500–1800). Folger Shakespeare Library. firstlines.folger.edu

Manuscript Index

Alnwick Castle, Northumberland, 525, 55, 56
Arbury Hall, Nuneaton, Warwickshire, A414, xxvin5, 70n44

Birmingham Central Library, 57316, 125, 153nn37–38, 154nn41–42
  See also Edinburgh University Library, Edinburgh, Dc 1.69
Bodleian Library, Oxford
  Ashmole 36/37, 73n82
  Ashmole 38, 38n111, 41n134, 42n147
  Ashmole 420, xxvin1
  Ashmole 750, 31n26
  Donation c. 57, 68n19, 195n38
  Donation d. 58, 42n147, 104, 114nn134–137
  Donation e. 6, 104, 114nn139–140
  English miscellaneous c. 34, 117, 136–142, 156–57nn74–78, 157nn80–87, 157n91, 160n123
  English poetry c. 50, 69nn30–31
  English poetry d. 3, 16–17, 35nn69–70. *See also* Shakespeare Birthplace Trust Record Office ER 81/1/21. *See also* Bodleian English poetry d. 3
  English poetry e. 14, 22, 38n110, 42n144, 42n147

  English poetry e. 97, 22–23, 39nn113–115, 39n117, 221n47
  English poetry f. 2, 31n26
  Firth e. 4, 42n144
  Malone 19, 22, 42n147
  Music b. 1, 39–40n119
  Music d. 238, 68n20, 125, 153nn33–34. *See also* Edinburgh University Library, Edinburgh, Dc 1.69
  Music School B. 2, 67n9
  Music School F. 575, 114n132
  Rawlinson D. 951, xxvin1
  Rawlinson D. 954, 119–121, 151n10, 152nn11–12, 152nn14–15, 211, 213–14, 216
  Rawlinson D. 1361, 166
  Rawlinson poetry 26, 8, 32n31, 195n26
  Rawlinson poetry 31, 42n144, 42n147
  Rawlinson poetry 65, 122, 123, 152n23
  Rawlinson poetry 85, 46–47, 68n26
  Rawlinson poetry 117, 211–13, 214, 221nn49–52, 221–22nn54–55
  Rawlinson poetry 172, 42n144, 73nn90–91, 152n13
  Sancroft 18, 165, 175, 177–78, 196–97nn56–58

Sancroft 27, 183, 198n69
Sancroft 29, 80, 164, 165, 178,
    179–191, *180–82*, *186*, 192,
    192n1, 197–98nn61–70,
    198n72, 198nn74–76, 198n79,
    199n80, 199n82, 199nn85–86,
    199nn89–92, 221n47
Sancroft 33, 178
Sancroft 53, 165, 168–174, 175,
    195nn30–34, 195nn36–37,
    196n40, 196n42, 196n45
Sancroft 97, 165, 175–77, 179, 189,
    196nn49–55
Tanner 168, 38n99
Tanner 169, 21
Tanner 207, 166
Tanner 306, 73nn90–91, 165,
    166–68, 194n19, 194nn22–24,
    195nn26–27
Tanner 407, 7
Tanner 465, 194n22
Wood 397, 152n16
British Library, London (BL)
  Additional 6038, 71n60
  Additional 10309, 25–28, 41n131,
      41nn134–136, 42n141, 42n144
  Additional 11518, 70n47
  Additional 11608, 103, 106n5
  Additional 12497, 71n61
  Additional 17797, 54–55, 68n17
  Additional 18044, 211, 213–14,
      222nn56–59
  Additional 22601, 49, 50, 70n41
  Additional 22608, xxiii, xxvin12,
      78, 80, 81–88, *82*, *83*, 108n46,
      109nn52–54, 110n55
  Additional 24655, 40n126
  Additional 29369, 153nn30–31
  Additional 30982, 22, 38n110
  Additional 31432, 67n9
  Additional 34064, 46, 68nn24–25
  Additional 40838, 71–72n65
  Additional 41063, 19, 37n86, 202,
      217n6
  Additional 42518, xix

  Additional 48023, 34n56
  Additional 52585, 68n21
  Additional 53723, 70n47, 103
  Additional 61822 (also known as
      Houghton), 8, 12–14, *15*, 33n51,
      33n53, 34n54, 34nn58–64
  Additional 63075, 211, 215, 222n61
  Additional 64078, 8, 11–12, 16
  Additional 81083, xxii, 8, 10–11,
      33nn43–45
  Additional Charter 19491, 31n28
  Additional Roll 63481, 31n26
  Egerton 923, 39n119
  Egerton 1994, 80
  Egerton 2013, 114n132
  Egerton 2421, 22
  Egerton 2877, 42n147, 48–49
  Harley 944, 103
  Harley 3889, 104, 114n138
  Harley 4955 (also known as
      Newcastle), 56–59, 61,
      72nn72–75
  Harley 5353, 50, 70n42
  Harley 6057, 38n111
  Harley 6797, 55
  Harley 6947, 167
  Lansdowne 1185, 80, 107n20,
      117, 142–150, *144–46*,
      158–59nn104–105, 159nn107–110,
      159nn114–120, 221n47
  Music Books and Manuscripts
      R.M.24 d. 2, 67n16
  Royal 18 C.XXV, 114n138
  Sloane 161, xxiv, 40n125, 66n1,
      117, 127–135, *129*, 154nn48–49,
      154nn51–52, 155nn55–56,
      155nn58–60, 155nn63, 156n67
  Sloane 542, 38n111
  Sloane 1487, 151n3
  Sloane 1792, 38n110
  Stowe 961, 24, 40n126

Cambridge University Library,
    Cambridge, Mm I.18, 31n27
Christ Church Library, Oxford

Music 87, 40n127
Music 350, 114n132

Durham Cathedral Library, Durham,
　Durham Dean Chapter 1.2
　Archidiac, Dunelm, 31n27

Edinburgh University Library,
　Edinburgh
　Dc 1.69, 68n19, 125, 153nn37–38,
　　154nn41–42
　Halliwell-Phillipps Collection 401,
　　42n144
　See also Birmingham Central
　　Library, 57316; Bodleian Library,
　　Oxford, Music d. 238

Folger Shakespeare Library,
　Washington, D.C.
　J.b.8, xviii
　V.a.75, 112n97
　V.a.79, 112n97
　V.a.80, 112n97
　V.a.87, xxvin12, 78, 80,
　　98–102, *100*, *102*, 106n11,
　　113nn114–128, 148, 196n51
　V.a.96, 39–40n119, 64, 75n115
　V.a.162, 42n147
　V.a.169, 123, 152n26
　V.a.219, 38n104
　V.a.226, 80, 117, 140–42,
　　158nn93–94, 158nn96–101
　V.a.262, 42n144
　V.a.308, 68n23
　V.a.339, 42n144
　V.a.345, 38n110, 42n144
　V.a.409, 127, 154nn45–47
　V.a.411, 153n33
　V.b.34, xxvin4
　V.b.93 (*Hesperides, or the Muses'
　　Garden*), 94–97, 112nn96–99,
　　113n107, 113nn109–111
　V.b.110, xix
　V.b.213, 56, 72n66
　V.b.214, 56

V.b.222, 106n14
X.d.177, 32n32

Gray's Inn Library, London, 29, 50

Harvard University Library, Cambridge,
　Massachusetts
　English 686, 22
　French 487, 51–54, *52*, 70–71n52,
　　71n54
Houghton manuscript. *See* British
　Library, London (BL), Additional
　61822
Huntington Museum Library, San
　Marino, California, HM 172, 64,
　75n115

Inner Temple Library, London, Petyt
　538, volume 36, 71–72n65

Killigrew Miscellany. *See* University
　of Texas at Austin, Killigrew,
　T Misc B Commonplace Book

Lambeth Palace Library, London, 933,
　71–72n65
Longleat House, Somerset, Harley
　Papers, vol. I, xxii, 8–10, 11,
　32nn33–34, 32n37

National Archives (United Kingdom),
　Kew, State Papers 14/122/58,
　73nn90–91
National Library of Scotland,
　Edinburgh (NLS)
　1692, 20
　2059, xxvin1, 19–21, 37nn90–91
　2060, 19, 37n94
　Advocates 1.1.6, xxvin4
　Advocates 19.3.4, 68n22
National Library of Wales,
　Aberystwyth, 5308E, 48
Newcastle Manuscript. *See* British
　Library, London (BL), Harley
　4955

New York Public Library, New York
  Drexel 4041, 39n119, 42n149
  Drexel 4175, 24, 40n128
  Drexel 4257, 24, 40n128, 42n149

Queen's College Library
  121, 56, 71–72n65
  130, 71–72n65

Rosenbach Museum and Library,
  239/23, 62–63

Shakespeare Birthplace Trust Record
  Office, ER 81/1/21, 16, 35n69,
  35n71
Shrewsbury School VI, 31n26

University College Library,
  Ogden 42, 103
University of Chicago, 824, 118–19,
  121, 124, 151n4, 151n6

University of Glasgow Library, Euing
  R.d.58-61, 68n17
University of Leeds Library, Brotherton
  Lt. 25, 38n106
University of Texas at Austin,
  Killigrew, T Misc B
  Commonplace Book (Killigrew
  Miscellany), 121–22, 122, 123,
  152nn18–22

Warwickshire County Record Office,
  Warwick, CR 136/B690, 107n20
Westminster Abbey, 41, 38n110
Winchester College Library, 33, 31n28

Yale University Library
  Osborn b 114, 40n126
  Osborn b 148, 40n126
  Osborn b 356, 42n144
Yelverton MS 26. *See* British Library,
  London (BL), Additional 48023

Subject Index

Abbott, John, 119–121, 151n9, 213–14, 215
    See also Bodleian MS Rawl. D. 954
abridgements/adaptations, xviii
Adams, J. Q., 32–33n39
Adams, Thomas, 25
adultery
    in Bellasys's miscellany, 28
    and Purbeck scandal, 62
aggregate volumes. *See* "separates"
album amicorum, 52–54, *52*
Allott, Robert, *Englands Parnassus*, 5–6, 95, 203, 205, 206–7, 210, 216
allusions, xviii–xix
anthologies, 80, 106n14
appearances, in "Still to be neat" extract, 27–28
Aristotle, 2
Astington, John H., 90
autograph book. *See album amicorum*

Bacon, Francis, 6, 54, 61, 63
    A Device to Entertain the Queen at Essex House, 55–56
    Of Tribute, 55
    works by, extracted, 55–56
Bacon, Nicholas, 56
Baldwin, John, 45
Bannatyne, George, xviii

Basse, William, *A Helpe to Discourse*, 120, 207–8, 210, 211, 213, 215
Bate, Jonathan, 32n37
Bateman, James, 123
    See also Folger MS V.a.169
Batty, Edmund, 53–54
Beal, Peter, 32–33n39, 48, 79, 106n10
    Catalogue of English Literary Manuscripts (CELM), xix, 65, 124
Beale, Robert, 13
Beaumont, Francis, 47–48, 84
    first folio frontispiece, 185
    works by, extracted in Bodleian MS Sancroft 29, 183–84
"beauties," 226
Behn, Aphra, *The Emperor of the Moon* extracted in Bodleian MS Eng. misc. c. 34, 137–38
Bell, Ilona, 40–41n130
Bellasys, Margaret
    extracts compiled by, 25–28, 41n134
    identification of, 40–41n130
    See also British Library, Additional 10309 in Manuscript Index
Benson, John, 61
Berkenhead, John, 184
Berry, Herbert, 32n36
Blackhead, Stephen, 193n11
Blague, Thomas, 4

Subject Index

Blayney, Peter, 18, 36n80, 36n84
Bodenham, John, 5
  Belvédere, 6
Bodleian MS Eng. misc. c. 34
  commentaries in, 137–140, 157n76
  compiler's preference for
    Restoration plays, 136–140
  The Conquest of Granada (Dryden)
    extracted in, 139–140
  Cynthia's Revels (Jonson) extracted
    in, 137
  The Emperor of the Moon (Behn)
    extracted in, 137–38
  The Goblins (Suckling) extracted
    in, 137
  The Northern Lasse (Brome)
    extracted in, 137
  "PD" as compiler of, 157n75,
    160n123
  Shakespeare's works extracted
    in, 137, 138–39, 157n85
  Suckling vs. Shakespeare in, 136–37
  Wycherley's work extracted in, 137
Bodleian MS Rawl. D. 954
  decontextualization of extracts
    in, 119
  extracts included in, 213
  "fat paunches" proverb extracted in,
    213–15, 216
Bodleian MS Rawl. poet. 117
  extracts included in, 212, 222n55
  "fat paunches" proverb extracted in,
    211–13, 214–15
Bodleian MS Tanner 306, 167–68
  See also Sancroft, William
book-lists, xviii–xix
bookmarks, extracts written on, 19,
  22, 202
Boyle, Roger (Earl of Orrery), 141–42
Breton, Nicholas
  as circulated separately from source,
    46, 47
  from masque for Elizabeth I, 45
  popularity of, 45–47
  wide circulation of, 48

Bridgewater, Earl of. *See* Egerton, John
  (Earl of Bridgewater)
Brinsley, John, 119–120, 151n9
British Library (BL) MS Add. 18044
  extracts included in, 213
  "fat paunches" proverb extracted in,
    213–15
British Library (BL) MS Add. 63075,
  215
British Library (BL) MS Harley 6947,
  167–68
British Library (BL) MS Lansdowne
  1185, 158–59n104
  and *Caractères* (Bruyère), 149
  commentaries in, 11, 143, 149–150
  compiler's preference for
    Renaissance plays, 142–150
  Shakespeare's works extracted
    in, 142–150, *144–46*,
    159n107
Briton, William
  extracts compiled by, 8, 12–14, *15*,
    16, 33n53, 34n57, 34n66
  See also British Library, Additional
    61822 in Manuscript Index
Brome, Richard, 77
  The Northern Lasse extracted in
    Bodleian MS Eng. misc.
    c. 34, 137
  works by, extracted by Sancroft, 169
Brooke, Nathaniel, 90
Brooke, Ralph, 63
Bruyère, Jean de la, *Caractères*, 149
Bryant, John, 227
Buckingham, Earl of. *See* Villiers,
  George (Earl of Buckingham)
Burke, Victoria, 32n32
Burton, Robert, *Anatomy of*
  Melancholy, 97, 206

Caesar, Julius, 54–55
Carron, Helen, 162
Cartwright, William, xvii, 119
  The Ordinary, 208
  The Royall Slave, 120

Subject Index 239

The Siedge: Or, Love's Convert, 120–21
Catalogue of English Literary Manuscripts (CELM) (Beal). See Beal, Peter
Catholicism, 163
Cavendish, Margaret, 167
Cavendish, William, 57–58, 59
See also British Library, Harley 4955, in Manuscript Index
CELM (Catalogue of English Literary Manuscripts) (Beal). See Beal, Peter
Cerdagni, Camillo, 52–53
See also Harvard University Library, French 487
Chan, Mary, 42n146, 124
Chapman, George
Caesar and Pompey, 101
Revenge of Bussy D'Ambois, 90–91, 96
Sir Gyles Goosecappe, 101
Charles I, 59, 62
Eikon Basilike, 87, 109n47
Charles II, 163
Chartier, Roger, 3
Christ Church (Oxford University), 22–23
Cicero, 2, 183
Clapham, John, 21
Clarke, John, *Paroemiologia Anglo-Latina*, 209, 210
Cleyton, Elizabeth, 128, 130
Cockayne, Aston, 77, 184
code, 17
 used by Muddyclift, 154n48, 154–55n52
 used by Peacham, 9
 used by Wright, 109n53
Coffey, Charles, *The Merry Cobbler*, 218n15
Coke, Edward, 61, 64, 74n94
Coke, Frances (Viscountess Purbeck), 60, 61, 62–64, 75n118
Collier, John Payne, 32n36, 225

Collinson, Patrick, 193n11
Colthorpe, Marion, 167
commentaries on plays in early modern manuscripts
 in BL MS Lansdowne 1185, 11, 143, 149–150
 in Bodleian MS Eng. misc. c. 34, 137–140, 157n76
 as early of literary criticism, 117
 in Scott's dramatic extracts, 11, 16
 in Wright's miscellany, 81–83, 107n20
See also marginalia
commonplace books
 criticisms of, 94
 in education, 2, 3–4, 117, 119–120, 204
 in manuscript form, 6
 and Moseley, 95–96
 printed, 6
 and Sancroft, 180
 and status of drama, 16
 as type of miscellany, 79
See also specific texts
commonplace markers
 in Deedes's dramatic miscellany, 142
 emergence of, 18–19, 36n84
 and "fat paunches" proverb, 211, 221n46
 in *Gorboduc* (Sackville and Norton), 18, 33n53
See also typographical elements
commonplaces
 and "bee" metaphor, 2–3
 Bodleian MS Sancroft 29, 180–81
 Brinsley on, 151n9
 compiled by Deedes, 141
 criticism of, 93–94
 definition of, 2, 106n10, 204
 dramatic extracts as, 103
 and educational practices, 2, 3–4, 117, 119–120, 204
 and extracts, 5–6, 22
 Foxe's publication of, 4–5
 in *Hamlet* (Shakespeare), 118–19

240   Subject Index

Hesperides (Evans) as, 94–95
history of, 2–6
Moseley as publisher of, 95–96
printed vs. manuscript versions, 6
in Restoration era, 117–127
self-improvement as function of, 3,
    4, 87
sententiae, xx
as trans-historical, 78
value of, 94
Wright on, 87
compilers, of extracts
  extracts as reflective of tastes,
    xvii–xviii, xix, xxv, 20, 101,
    136–140, 225
  women as, 25, 40–41n130
  See also readers
composite volumes, 55, 80
  See also Bodleian MS Tanner 306;
    "separates"
Comus (Milton)
  decontextualized meaning of, 43
  and Milton's self-extracting, 51–54
  music for, 70n47
  overview of, 51–52
The Conquest of Granada (Dryden)
  extracted in Bodleian MS Eng. misc.
    c. 34, 139–140
  Muddyclift's reading of, 128, 130
contextualization, of Abbott's
    commonplace, 119, 120–21
  See also decontextualization;
    historical contexts
Cotgrave, John
  and pro-Parliament newsletters,
    110n68
  republican politics of, 88, 89, 90
  and theatre closures, 89, 90,
    92–93, 94
  Wits Interpreter, 89
  See also *English Treasury of Wit and
    Language*
Cotgrave, Randle, 91, 110n68
Cotterell, Charles, 125–26
court culture, 54–59

Cromwell, Oliver, 91
Cromwell, Richard, 126
cross-dressing
  in *Epicoene* (Jonson), 27–28
  of Lady Purbeck, 62, 64
  in *The Widow* (Middleton), 27
Culman, Leonard, 204
Cutts, John P., 37n92

Daniel, Samuel
  Philotas, 91
  Rosamund, 10
Daniell, Peter, extracts compiled by, 47
Davenant, Elizabeth, 24
Davenant, William, 84
  The History of Sir Francis Drake, 89
  The Siege of Rhodes, 89
decontextualization
  of *The Gypsies Metamorphosed*
    (Jonson) extract, 60
  of lots, 49–50
  of masque extracts, xxiii, 44, 51, 65
  of *Othello* (Shakespeare) extract, 174
  of "peace and silence be the guyde"
    (song), 47
  of *Pericles* (Shakespeare) extract, 92
  of songs, 47–48, 117, 123
  of speeches, 48
Deedes, William, 117, 158n92
  extracts compiled by, 140–42,
    158n94
  Orrery's works extracted by, 141–42
  preference for Restoration over
    Renaissance plays, 140
  and printed plays, 141–42
  The Sophy (Denham) extracted by,
    140–41
Denham, John, *The Sophy*, 140–41
Dent, R. W., 216, 217n9
de Ricci, Seymour, 32n32
Dering, Edward, xviii
Diemerbroeck, Isbrand van, 131
Dorset, Earl of. See Sackville, Charles
    (Earl of Dorset)
Downes, John, 178

Subject Index

D'Oyly, George, 165
drama as genre
   Sancroft's conception of, 175
   as valued, 93, 105
dramatic extracts. *See* extracts, dramatic
dramatic miscellanies
   and anthologies, 106n14
   BL MS Lansdowne 1185, 142–150
   Bodleian MS Sancroft 29, 179
   Deedes's (Folger MS V.A.226), 140–42
   definition of, 79–80
   development of, 78, 80
   English Treasury of Wit and Language (Cotgrave), 79–80, 88–94
   and *flores poetarum*, 80
   Folger MS V.a.87, 98–102
   post-17th century, 226
   and printed plays, 141–42
   as reflective of compiler's reactions to plays, 101
   and theatrical nostalgia, 80
   Wright's (British library MS Additional 22608), 81–88, 106–7n19
   See also specific miscellanies
drawings, in Peacham's extracts from *Titus Andronicus* (Shakespeare), 8–10, 16, 32n34
drolls, 78–79
Drummond, William, xvii
   extracts compiled by, 19–21, 22, 37n92
   playwrights missing from extracts of, 19–20
Dryden, John
   "Defense of the Epilogue," 139–140
   Essay of Dramatick Poesie, 11, 116
   popularity of, 116
   See also The Conquest of Granada
Dudley, Robert (Earl of Leicester), 134
Duncan-Jones, Katherine, 9, 134

Earle, Giles, 24
East, Michael, 45
"EC." *See* Folger MS V.a.87
Eckhardt, Joshua, 59
education, commonplace books in, 2, 3–4, 117, 119–120, 204
Egerton, John (Earl of Bridgewater), 51
Eglesfield, Francis, 87, 109n49
Elizabeth I, 13–14, 45, 49, 50, 54, 134, 167
Elizabeth of Bohemia, 47
Elson, John James, 79
English Treasury of Wit and Language (Cotgrave)
   as commonplace book, 79–80
   historical contexts of, 90–93
   Moseley as publisher of, 90, 95
   and plays in manuscript form, 18
   politics of, 78, 88–92
   theatre in, 92–93
   and value of commonplaces, 94
   war in, 92
Erasmus, Desiderius, 4, 204, 218n12
Evans, G. Blakemore, 160n123
Evans, John. *See Hesperides, or The Muses Garden*
excerpts. *See* extracts
extracting, practice of
   Brinsley on, 120
   as common activity, xix, 120
   definition of, xviii
   methods of, 1–2
   origins of, 2–6
extracts, dramatic
   before 1600, 7, 7–16, 8
   in bound volumes, xx
   circulation of, 103
   during closure of theatres, 77–114
   commentaries in, 11, 16, 81–83, 107n20, 137–140, 143, 149–150, 157n76
   and commonplaces, 5–6, 22
   as commonplaces, 103
   criticism of, 93–94

decontextualization of, in Bodleian
MS Rawl. D. 954, 119
as destabilizing source texts, 49
and development of dramatic
miscellany, 78
vs. drolls, 79
earliest documented, 1
early 17th century, 16–22, 22–29
and English literary canon, 31n21,
101
ephemeral nature of, xix–xx
function of, xxv, 79, 226–27
generic status of, 168–69
historical contexts of, 13, 63,
65, 90
identification of, xxi
from lost source texts, 48
vs. masque extracts, 43
and Moseley, 95
music history approach to, xxi,
xxvii–xxviiin17
versus other types of excerpts,
xviii–xix, 79, 166
poetic, 5
popularity of, 1, 5–6
and printed texts, 18–19
profitability of, 4–5
and proverbs, 202, 203
as reflective of compiler's reactions
to plays, xvii–xviii, xix, xxv,
20, 136–140, 225
Restoration period, 115–151
scholarly contexts of, xxi
as "separates," 165
and textual fluidity, 227
transmission of, 167, 168
value of, 225
women as compilers of, 25,
40–41n130
See also commonplaces; dramatic
miscellanies; songs; specific
extracts; specific manuscripts;
specific plays
extracts, from masques
by Bacon, 55–56

as circulated separately from source,
44, 49–51
courtly motivations for, 54–59
decontextualization of, xxiii, 44,
51, 65
vs. extracts from plays, 43
by Jonson, 57–66, 75n118
from *The Queen's Entertainment at
Harefield*, 49–50
as representative of source, 48–49, 51
songs, 45–47, 45–51, 47, 48
See also songs

Fanshawe, Richard, *Il Pastor Fido (The
Faithfull Shepherd)*, 142
Farmer, Alan B., 36n80
"fat paunches" proverb
circulation of, via extracts, 203
and commonplace markers, 211,
221n46
debate over Shakespeare's coinage
of, 209
extracted in *England's Parnassus*
(Allott), 205–7
Jerome as source of, 204, 209,
217–18n10
in *Love's Labour's Lost*
(Shakespeare), 201–3, 210–11
manuscript history and transmission
of, 211–16, *214*
non-Shakespearean print versions
of, 204, *205*
origins of, 204
popularity of, 203
print history and transmission of,
204–11, *206*
variants of, 208–9, *209*
Ferrabosco, Alfonso, 27
Fitzgerald, Edward, *Polonius:
A Collection of Wise Saws and
Modern Instances*, 119
Fletcher, John, 84
extracts from works by, 30n20,
183–84
first folio frontispiece, *185*

Subject Index

The Mad Lover, 188
The Nice Valour, 22
Valentinian, 24, 91–92
flores poetarum, 5, 6, 80
florilegia, 3
   See also commonplaces
"flowerpot plot," 193n11
Flynn, Dennis, 86
Folger MS V.a.87
   canonical and non-canonical works extracted in, 101
   as dramatic miscellany, 98
   "EC" as compiler of, 98
   extracts included in, *100*, 101–2, *102*
   as generalized, 98
   language modernization in, 99
   marginalia, 99
   narrative voice in, 98–99
Folger MS V.a.169, 123
Ford, John, *Fancies, Chast and Noble*, 101
formatting
   of Bodleian MS Sancroft 29, 187–88
   of Bodleian MS Sancroft 97, 176
Fox, Adam, 210
Foxe, John
   Locorum Communium Tituli, 4
   Pandectae Locorum Communium, 4–5
fragments, xviii, 2, 7, 166
Franklin, Benjamin, 204
Frederick V, 47
Frevile, Gilbert
   on *The entertainment of the two Kings* . . . (Jonson), 49
   extracts compiled by, 48–49
Fuller, Tom, *Holy Wars*, 81, 106–7n19
Furness, Horace Howard, 209

Gastoldi, Giovanni Giaocomo, 45–46
gender
   in Bellasys's miscellany, 26–28
   in *Epicoene* (Jonson), 27–28
   in *The Widow* (Middleton), 26, 27

Goffe, Thomas, *The Courageous Turke*, 24
Gorboduc (Sackville and Norton)
   commonplace markers in, 18, 33n53
   extracted by Briton, 8, 11, 12–14, *15*, 16, 33n53, 34n57, 34n66
Grazia, Margreta De, 18
Green, Richard, 56
Greville, Fulke
   "Mishchiefe is like the Cockatrices eyes," 21–22, 38n103, 38n105
   Mustapha, 90
The Gypsies Metamorphosed (Jonson), 22, 43, 56–66, 73–74n91, 166–68
   circulation of extract from, 60–66
   decontextualization of extract from, 60
   extracted by Sancroft, 166–68
   extracted in Christ Church manuscripts, 22
   extracted in Newcastle manuscript, 56–59
   fortunes in, 73–74n91
   performances of, 61
   and Purbeck scandal, 60–65
   topics of, 43

Habington, William, *The Queene of Arragon*, 123
Hall, Joseph, 25
Halliwell-Phillipps, James Orchard, 95
Hannay, Margaret, 40–41n130
Harbage, Alfred, 85
Harriot, Thomas, 12
Harvey, Gabriel, xix
Hathway, R., 6
Hatton, Elizabeth, 61, 63, 64, 74n94
Hausted, Peter, xix
   Rivall Friends, 101
Head, Richard, *Proteus Redivivus*, 207, 210–11
Hesperides, or The Muses Garden (Evans)
   audience of, 78

as commonplace, 94–95
death in, 97
historical contexts of, 97
and Moseley, 95, 96
Heywood, Thomas, 17
A Maidenhood Well Lost, 181
Hilton, John, 103, 114nn133
Catch that Catch can, 127
historical contexts
  of Briton's extracts of *Gorboduc*
    (Sackville and Norton),
    13–14, 34n57, 34n66
  of *English Treasury* (Cotgrave),
    90–93
  of *Hesperides* (Evans), 97
  of *The Lady of May* (Sidney),
    156nn67–68
  of Muddyclift's extracts, 133
  of Sancroft's life, 162–64
  of "Where the bee sucks"
    (Shakespeare), 126
  See also decontextualization
*The Honorable Entertainment at
  Elvetham*, 45
Horace, 52
Houghton manuscript, 8, 12
  See also British Library, Additional
    61822 in Manuscript Index
How, William, 98
Howard, Robert, 62
Howard-Hill, T. H., 17
Howell, James, 62
Hughes, Alan, 9
humor, in Muddyclift's extracts,
  134–35
Hunter, G. K., 18

insults, Shakespearean, 188–89
interregnum period, and Cotgrave's
  dramatic extracts, 90–91

James I, 166–67
James II, 163–64, 190
Jerome, 204, 209, 217n10
Joel, Billy, 202

Johnson, Robert, 125
Jones, Inigo, 193n6
Jonson, Ben
  "Beauties, have you seene a toy,"
    122
  Catiline extracted by Muddyclift,
    130, 132
  and Cavendish, 57–58, 59
  Christmas His Masque, 57, 58, 59
  "Cock Lorell," 47, 48, 60
  "Come, my Celia," 26–27,
    42nn144–145
  "Come Noble Nymphs," 59, 73n82
  Cynthia's Revels extracted in
    Bodleian Eng. misc. c. 34, 137
  The Devil is an Ass, 24, 104
  and Drummond, 19
  *The entertainment of the two
    Kings...*, 48–49
  Epicoene, 22, 25, 27–28, 104
  extracts, from masques by, 57–66,
    75n118
  The Fortunate Isles, 57, 58, 59
  "Have you seene the white lillye
    grow," 104
  "If I freely may discover," 24, 104,
    122
  *The King and Queen's
    Entertainment at Bolsover*,
    57, 59
  *The King's Entertainment at
    Welbeck*, 57, 59
  "Kisse me sweet, the wary lover,"
    27
  Neptune's Triumph, 59
  poetry of, and royalism, 84
  The Sad Shepherd, 23
  Sejanus, 132–33
  songs extracted from works by, 24
  "Still to be neat," 27–28, 42n146,
    42n149, 104
  "Though I am young and cannot
    tell," 23, 121
  The Vision of Delight, 57, 58, 59
  Volpone, 25, 93

works by, extracted in Bodleian MS
    Sancroft 29, 183
works by, extracted in Newcastle
    manuscript, 56–59
See also *The Gypsies
    Metamorphosed*; *Poetaster*

Kastan, David Scott, 95
Kathman, David, 109n46
Keenan, Siobhan, 107n20
Kelliher, Hilton, 11–12
Kelly, James, 222–23n62
Kempe, William, *The Education of
    Children in Learning* (1588), 3
Killigrew Miscellany, 121–22
Kirsch, Arthur C., 107–8n29

Lacy, John, *Sir Hercules Buffoon*,
    157n76
Lansdowne manuscript. *See* British
    Library (BL) MS Lansdowne
    1185
Laud, William, 165
Lawes, Henry, 53, 103
Lawes, William, 42n140
Lee, Nathaniel
    "Blush not reder then the morning,"
    122
    The Princess of Cleve, 157n76
Leicester, Earl of. *See* Dudley, Robert
    (Earl of Leicester)
Lesser, Zachary, 18, 36n80, 36n84
Levin, Richard, 9, 32n34
Lilly, William, xvii
Limon, Jerzy, 67n7
Lindsay, David, *Ane Satyre of the Thrie
    Estaits*, xviii
literary appropriations, xviii, 79
literary criticism. *See* commentaries
    on plays in early modern
    manuscripts
Longleat manuscript, 8–10
Love, Harold, 107n22
Lowe, Edward, 124, 125
Lyly, John, 55

MacDonald, Robert, 19, 20
Madan, Falconer, 179
Malless, Stanley, 201
Manningham, John, 50
manuscripts
    commonplaces, 6
    full-text plays, 17–18
    and print culture, 19, 35–36n77
Marcus, Leah, 57, 227
marginalia
    in BL MS Lansdowne 1185, 143, 149
    Bodleian MS Sancroft 29, 184
    in Bodleian MS Sancroft 97, 177
    in Folger MS V.a.87, 99
    in Muddyclift's diary/miscellany,
        130–31
    in *Poetaster* (Jonson), 1
    See also commentaries
Marlowe, Christopher, *The Massacre at
    Paris*, xviii
Marotti, Arthur F., 63
Marsh, Henry, *The Wits, or Sport upon
    Sport*, 79
Marshall, William, 184
Marston, John, 80, 93
    Antonio's Revenge, 101
    The Dutch Courtezan, 98–99
    Parasitaster, or the Fawne, 20–21, 99
    The Masque of Mountebanks, 50
    *The Masque of the Inner Temple and
        Grayes Inne*, 47
masques
    as malleable/divisible, 44–45
    for marriage of Elizabeth of
        Bohemia to Frederick V, 47
    political readings of, 43–44
    use of term, 66n2
    See also extracts, from masques;
        specific masques
Massinger, Philip, 184
    The Great Duke of Florence, 91,
        99, 101
    The Maid of Honour, 101
    A New Way to Pay Old Debts, 83
May, Steven, xxviin13

Mayne, Jasper, 81
  The Amorous Warre, 84, 85–86, 108n40
  The Citye Match, 86
  Ochlo-machia, or, The Peoples War, 86
  as royalist, 85–86
McKenzie, D. F., xvii
McManaway, James C., 107–8n29, 225
McQuain, Jeffrey, 201
memorization, 3, 6
Merchant Adventurers, 48
A Mery P[rog]nosticacion, 23, 39n113
Middleton, Thomas
  A Game at Chess, 181
  "Hence all you vain delights," 103
  Hengist, King of Kent, 18
  "I keep my horse," 25–26, 41n134, 42n140
  Mad World My Masters, 92–93
  The Widow, 25–26, 27, 41n134, 42n140
  The Witch, extracted in Christ Church manuscripts, 22
Milton, John
  autograph of, 52–53, *52*, 71n55
  self-extracting of, 51–54
  on Shakespeare, 54
  See also Comus
Mirandula, Octavianus, *Illustrium Poetarum Flores*, 5
miscellanies, 38n99, 123
  See also dramatic miscellanies; extracts; verse miscellanies
More, Thomas, 177
Moseley, Humphrey, 78, 184
  and *English Treasury* (Cotgrave), 90, 95
  and *Hesperides* (Evans), 95, 96
  as "inventor of English literature," 95
  as publisher of commonplaces, 95–96
Moss, Ann, 29n4, 31n21
Moulton, Ian, 26, 40–41n130

Muddyclift, John, 117
  Catiline (Jonson) extracted by, 130, 132
  coded language used by, 154–55n52, 154n48
  diary of, 128, *129*, 130
  extracts compiled by, 128, 130–36
  humor in extracts, 134–35
  The Lady of May (Sidney) extracted by, 133–35
  The Miser (Shadwell) extracted by, 131–32
  and political contexts of extracts, 133–35
  Sejanus (Jonson) extracted by, 132–33
  and social reading practices, 128, 130

narrative voice, 98–99
The New Academy of Complements, 47
Newcastle manuscript, 56–59
New Criticism, 199n88
Newdigate, John, 107n20
Newstead, Christopher, *An Apology for Women*, 207, 210–11, 216
The Nice Wanton, 23, 39n114
Nicholson, Richard, 45
Norton, John, *The Scholar's Vade Mecum*, 208, 210
Norton, Thomas. *See* Gorboduc.
nostalgia
  in BL MS Lansdowne 1185, for Renaissance, 142
  and dramatic miscellanies, 80
  in *English Treasury* (Cotgrave), 89, 94
  of Restoration readers, 116
  royalist, in Wright's miscellany, 81
  Sancroft's, for Renaissance theatre, 163

Oldham, John, 123
  See also Folger MS V.a.169
Orgel, Stephen, 61
Orrery, Earl of. *See* Boyle, Roger (Earl of Orrery)

Owen, John, *Epigrammatum*, 216
Oxinden, Henry, xix

paradoxes, 70n46
  modularity of, 50
paratextual materials, 169–170
  frontispieces, 184–85
pastoral, 108n32
Patterson, Annabel, 85, 108n32
Paynell, Thomas, 4
"PD." *See* Bodleian MS Eng. misc. c. 34
Peacham, Henry (the younger)
  The Compleat Gentleman, 8
  date of manuscript, 32–33n39, 32nn36–37
  Titus Andronicus (Shakespeare) extracted by, 8–10, 16, 32n34
Peaps, William, xix, 81
  Love In it's Extasie, 84, 85
  as royalist, 85
Peele, George
  The Hunting of Cupid, 37n92
  The Old Wives Tale, 32n32
Percy, Thomas, 46
performances
  during closure of theatres, 77, 79
  drolls, 79
  See also masques
Philips, Katherine, 122, 125–26
Phillips, Edward, *The Mysteries of Love Eloquence*, 96
Pierrepont, Robert, 123
  See also Folger MS V.a.169
Playford, John, 42n140
  Select Musicall Ayres and Dialogues, 121, 123
playgoers, as compilers of extracts, xvii
  See also compilers; readers
plays (early modern)
  and commonplace markers, 36n84
  Dryden's praise of, 116
  as malleable/divisible, xx, xxv, 2, 115, 116–17, 127, 150, 192, 216, 225

  in manuscript (complete plays), 17–18
  paratextual materials extracted from, 169–170
  as printed texts, 18–19, 36n80, 141–42
  printed vs. manuscript versions, 17–18, 35–36n77
  Restoration adaptations of Renaissance plays, 115
  See also drama as genre; extracts, dramatic; specific plays
playwrights
  as "play patchers," xxi
  use of existing proverbs, 226–27
  See also specific playwrights
Poetaster (Jonson), 1, 22, 24, 104, 122
  marginalia in, 1
  songs extracted from, 24, 122
politics
  of *English Treasury* (Cotgrave), 78, 88–92
  of extracts during theatre closure, 78
  of *The Lady of May* (Sidney), 134
  and Muddyclift's extracts, 133
  See also royalism
Poole, Walton, "Why should passion," 26, 41n135
Poor Robin's Almanack, 208, 210
Potter, Lois, 85
Powle, Stephen, 2
  extracts compiled by, 21, 22
  See also Bodleian Library, Tanner 169 in Manuscript Index
Pricket, Robert, *Times Anotomie*, 21
printed texts
  and manuscript culture, 19, 35–36n77
  plays as, 18–19, 36n80, 141–42
  rise of, and increase in extracting, 18–19
  typography of, 18–19, 142
profitability, of extracts, 4
prologues, 7, 25

prose miscellanies
   Bodleian MS Sancroft 18, 177–79
   Bodleian MS Sancroft 97, 175–78
   vs. verse miscellanies, 175–76
proverbs
   circulation of, 202, 203
   definition of, 217n9
   as oral expressions, 210
   theatre's popularization of, 210
   See also "fat paunches" proverb
Prynne, William, 90, 110n57
Pudsey, Edward, 2, 108n42
   extracts compiled by, 16–17, 22
   use of table-book, 17, 35n72
Purbeck, Viscount. *See* Villiers, John (Viscount Purbeck)
Purbeck, Viscountess. *See* Coke, Frances (Viscountess Purbeck)

The Queen's Entertainment at Harefield, 49–50
The Queen's Entertainment at Mitcham, 54–55
quotation marks. *See* commonplace markers

Randall, Dale B. J., 85
Rawdon, Marmaduke, 213–14, 222n56, 222n59
Ray, John, *A Collection of English Proverbs*, 209–10
readers
   of commonplaces, 96
   as compilers of extracts, xvii
   nostalgia of, 116
   view of early modern plays, as malleable/divisible, xx, xxv, 2, 115, 150, 192, 225
   See also compilers
reading practices
   paradoxical, 78
   Sancroft's, 176, 177–78, 182, 191
   as seduction, 128, 130
   social, 127–136

Renaissance drama
   Lansdowne compiler's preference for, 142–150
   Restoration revivals of, 169, 170
   Sancroft's preference for, 161, 187
   See also specific plays
Restoration period
   Bodleian MS Eng. misc. c. 34, 136–140
   commonplaces of, 117–121
   Deedes's preference for plays of, 140
   extracting during, 115–16
   Muddyclift's extracts, 128–136
   PD's preference for plays of, 136–38
   revivals of Renaissance plays during, 169, 170
   songs, 121–27
   See also specific works
Reynes, Robert, 7–8, 16
rhetorical devices, in Bodleian MS Sancroft 29, 190–91
Ringler, William, 34n57
Roberts, Sasha, 26, 159n107, 212
Robertson, William, *Phraseologia Generalis*, 209–10
Roe, John, "Come Fates, I feare thee not," 41n136
Rogers, Benjamin, 45–46
Rolleston, John, 57–59
royalism
   of Brooke, 90
   of Eglesfield, 87
   and Jonson's poetry, 84
   of Mayne, 85–86
   of Moseley, 90
   of Peaps, 85
   of Sancroft, 162–63
   Sauer on, 109n47
   and songs, 103
   of Wright (Abraham), 87
   of Wright (James), 86
   in Wright's miscellany, 81, 84, 85, 88

Subject Index 249

Sackville, Charles (Earl of Dorset),
   Every Man in his Humour
   extracted by Sancroft,
   169–170, 191
Sackville, Thomas. *See Gorboduc.*
sammelbände, 80
Sancroft, William
   Bodleian MS Sancroft 18
      extracts included in, 177
      as prose miscellany, 177–79
      The White Devil (Webster)
         extracted in, 177–78
   Bodleian MS Sancroft 29
      authorship in, 183–84
      Beaumont and Fletcher's works
         extracted in, 183–84
      dating of, 199n86
      decontextualization of extracts
         in, 188
      The Devil's Law Case (Webster)
         extracted in, 178
      as dramatic miscellany, 179
      extracts included in, 180, *180,*
         181, 182, 187
      formatting of, 187–88
      Jonson's works extracted in, 183
      The Mad Lover (Fletcher)
         extracted in, 188
      marginalia, 183–84
      organization of, 179–181
      rhetorical devices in, 190–91
      Shakespearean insults in,
         188–89
      Shakespeare's works extracted in,
         185–191, *186*
   Bodleian MS Sancroft 33, *Cambyses*
      (Settle) extracted in, 178
   Bodleian MS Sancroft 53
      decontextualization of extracts
         in, 174
      Every Man in his Humour
         (Sackville) extracted in,
         169–170, 191
      extracts included in, 168–69
      paratextual materials in, 169–170

      Shakespeare's works extracted
         in, 170–72
      as verse miscellany, 168
   Bodleian MS Sancroft 97
      extracts included in, 175
      formatting of, 176
      marginalia, 177
      as prose miscellany, 175–78
      Shakespeare's works extracted
         in, 175–76
   Bodleian MS Tanner 306
      extracts included in, 166
      "separates" in, 166–68
   as compiler of extracts, 161
   library of, 162, 164–65
   life of, 162–64
   overview of extracts compiled
      by, 165
   preference for Renaissance over
      Restoration plays, 161, 187
   reading practices of, 176,
      177–78, 182, 191
   and rebuilding of St. Paul's
      Cathedral, 193n6
   refusal to swear fealty to William
      and Mary, 164, 190, 191
   as royalist, 162–63
   and Seven Bishops, 163, 190,
      193n7, 199n8
Sarcerius, Erasmus, 4
Sauer, Elizabeth, 109n47
Savage, Richard, 17
Schlueter, June, 32n34
Scott, William
   extracts compiled by, 8, 10–11, 16
   "The Modell of Poesye," 10–11, 16
   See also British Library, Additional
      81083 in Manuscript Index
Scott-Warren, Jason, 38n99
scribal publication
   definition of, 107n22
   and Scott's dramatic extracts, 11
   Wright's dramatic miscellany, 84
sealing wax, 20–21
seduction, play reading as, 128, 130

self-extracting, 51–54
self-improvement, as motive for
　　commonplacing, 3, 4, 87
Seneca, 2–3, 29n4
sententiae. See commonplaces
"separates," 165, 166–68
　See also Bodleian MS Tanner 306
Settle, Elkanah, *Cambyses*, 178
Seven Bishops, 163, 190, 193n7,
　　199n87
Shadwell, Thomas, *The Miser*, 131–32
Shakespeare, William
　As You Like It
　　extracted in Bodleian Eng. misc.
　　　c. 34, 138
　　"What shall he have that kild the
　　　deere," 127
　All's Well that Ends Well, extracted
　　in BL MS Lansdowne
　　1185, 147
　Antony and Cleopatra, extracted
　　in BL MS Lansdowne 1185,
　　159n107
　Cymbeline, extracted in Bodleian
　　MS Sancroft 53, 170,
　　171–72, *171*
　"fat paunches" proverb, 201–16
　Hamlet
　　Polonius's speech as extract,
　　　118–19, 151n6
　　Wright's commentary on, 81–82
　1 Henry IV
　　adaptations of, xviii
　　extracted in BL MS Add. 64078,
　　　8, 11–12, 16
　　extracted in BL MS Lansdowne
　　　1185, 143, 149
　3 Henry VI, extracted in Bodleian
　　MS Sancroft 29, 188–89
　King Lear, extracted in Bodleian
　　MS Sancroft 97, 177
　Love's Labour's Lost
　　and Drummond, 20–21
　　extracted in BL MS Lansdowne
　　　1185, 147–48

　　extracted in Bodleian MS
　　　English poetry e.97, 22–23
　　extracted in Bodleian MS
　　　Sancroft 29, 190
　　"fat paunches" proverb, 201–16
　　See also "fat paunches" proverb
　Macbeth
　　extracted in BL MS Lansdowne
　　　1185, 143
　　extracted in *Hesperides*
　　　(Evans), 97
　Measure for Measure
　　extracted in Bodleian Eng. misc.
　　　c. 34, 138
　　extracted in Bodleian MS
　　　Sancroft 29, 189–190
　The Merchant of Venice
　　extracted in BL MS Lansdowne
　　　1185, 148–49
　　extracted in Folger MS V.a.87,
　　　101
　The Merry Wives of Windsor
　　extracted in Bodleian Eng. misc.
　　　c. 34, 137, 138
　　extracted in Bodleian MS
　　　Sancroft 29, 187–88
　Midsummer Night's Dream
　　droll from, 79
　　and Drummond, 20–21
　　extracted in Bodleian MS
　　　Sancroft 97, 176–77
　　Milton on, 54
　Much Ado About Nothing
　　extracted in BL MS Lansdowne
　　　1185, 147–48
　　extracted in Bodleian Eng. misc.
　　　c. 34, 138
　Othello
　　decontextualization of extract
　　　from, 174
　　extracted by Pudsey, 16–17
　　extracted in Bodleian Eng. misc.
　　　c. 34, 137, 139, 157n85
　　extracted in Bodleian MS
　　　Sancroft 29, 187–88

extracted in Bodleian MS
Sancroft 53, 170, 172–74, *173*
Wright's commentary on, 81
Pericles
"bookmark" extract of, 19
decontextualization of extract from, 92
extracted in *English Treasury* (Cotgrave), 92
proverbial nature of works, 202
The Rape of Lucrece, 5, 10, 46, 206
Richard II
extracted by Scott, 8, 10–11, 16
extracted in BL MS Lansdowne 1185, 143
Richard III
"bookmark" extract of, 19, 202
extracted in BL MS Lansdowne 1185, 143, 146–47
extracted in Bodleian MS Sancroft 29, 187–88
scholarly focus on, xx, xxi
songs, 125–26, 127
The Tempest
extracted in Christ Church manuscripts, 22
songs extracted from, 125–26
"Where the bee sucks," 125–26
Timon of Athens, extracted in Bodleian MS Sancroft 29, 188
Titus Andronicus, Peacham's drawing, 8–10, 16, 32n34
Venus and Adonis, 5, 205, 212, 221n53
The Winter's Tale, 127
words and phrases coined by, 201, 217n4
works by, extracted in BL MS Lansdowne 1185, 142–150
works by, extracted in Bodleian MS Eng. misc. c. 34, 137–39
works by, extracted in Bodleian MS Sancroft 29, 185–191, *186*
works by, extracted in Bodleian MS Sancroft 53, 170–72

works by, extracted in Bodleian MS Sancroft 97, 175–76
See also specific works
Shakespearean insults, 188–89
The Shakspere Allusion-Book, xix
Sheldon, Gilbert, 126, 163
Shirley, Henry, *The Martyr'd Soldier*, 83, 84, 108–9n46
Shirley, James, 84
"Come, my Daphne, come away," 103, 122, 124
The Gamester, 101
"The Glories of our Blood and State," 47, 103
The Gratefull Servant, 91
The Lady of Pleasure, 83, 87
The Royall Master, 84
The Traytor, 53
Sidney, Philip
The Arcadia, 10, 179
Astrophil and Stella, 14, *15*, 34n65
The Defense of Poesie, 10
The Lady of May, 43, 117, 133–35, 156nn67–68
Smith, Miles, 126–27
Smuts, R. Malcolm, 67n8
Smyth, Adam, 30n20
songbooks, 103, 114nn133, 123–24
See also verse miscellanies
songs
from *As You Like It* (Shakespeare), 127
"Beauties, have you seene a toy" (Jonson), 122
in Bellasys's miscellany, 25–27
as circulated separately from source, 47, 48, 117, 122–23, 124, 127
"Cock Lorell" (Jonson), 47, 48, 60
"Come, my Celia" (Jonson), 26–27, 42nn144–145
"Come, my Daphne, come away" (Shirley), 103, 122, 124
"Come Noble Nymphs," 59, 73n82
decontextualization of, 47–48, 117, 123

252   Subject Index

from *Epicoene* (Jonson), 25, 27–28
extracted, from masques, 45–51
extracted, from plays, 23–27, 103–5, 117, 121–27
"The Glories of our Blood and State" (Shirley), 47, 103
"Have you seene the white lillye grow" (Jonson), 104
"Hence all you vain delights" (Middleton), 103
"If I freely may discover" (Jonson), 24, 104, 122
"I keep my horse" (Middleton), 25–26, 41n134, 42n140
Killigrew Miscellany, 121–22
"Kisse me sweet, the wary lover" (Jonson), 27
Lowe's compilation of, 124–25
as malleable/divisible, 127
"peace and silence be the guyde," 47, 48
"The Plowman's Song (In the Merry Month of May)" (Breton), 45–47, 48
vs. speeches, 48
"Still to be neat" (Jonson), 104
from *The Tempest* (Shakespeare), 125
"Though I am yong & Cannot tell" (Jonson), 23
typography of, 171–72
in verse miscellanies, 104, 121–23
from *Volpone* (Jonson), 25
"Where the bee sucks" (Shakespeare), 125–26
"Why should passion," 26, 41n135
"Why so pale and wan fond lover?" (Suckling), 23, 39–40nn119, 39n118, 40n120, 46, 121, 122
from *The Widow* (Middleton), 25–26
from *The Winter's Tale* (Shakespeare), 127
source texts, instability of, 49

speeches
decontextualization of, 48
vs. songs, 48
Speght, Thomas, xix
Spenser, Edmund, *The Faerie Queene*, 10
Stafford, Anthony, *Niobe*, 81
Stallybrass, Peter, 3, 18, 36n84
stenography, 17
Stephens, John, 93
Stern, Tiffany, 24, 25, 123–24*Documents of Performance in Early Modern England*, xxi
St. Paul's Cathedral, 193n6
Stubbe, Henry, 177–78
Sturmy, Henry, 215
    See also British Library (BL) MS Add. 63075
Suckling, John
    Aglaura, 104
    The Goblins extracted in Bodleian Eng. misc. c. 34, 137
    "Why so pale and wan fond lover?," 23, 39–40nn119, 39n118, 40n120, 46, 121, 122
Symonds, Richard, 103

table-books, 17, 35n72
Taverner, Richard, 4
Taylor, Gary, 40–41n130, 41n134
Terence, 5, 80
T. G., *The Rich Cabinet . . .*, 21–22
theatre, and proverbial sayings, 210
theatres, closure of
    commonplacing during, 103
    and *English Treasury* (Cotgrave), 89, 90, 92–93, 94
    and Folger MS V.a.87, 97–102
    and *Hesperides* (Evans), 94–97
    song extracts circulated during, 103–5
    theatrical activity during, 77
    and Wright's dramatic miscellany, 81–88

Tilley, Morris Palmer, 217n9, 218n13
Tillotson, John, 164
Tomkis, Thomas, 191*Albumazar*, 93–94
Tompkins, William, 123
Tragedy of Nero, 93
Trumbull, Katherine, 125
Trumbull, William, 125
Tudor England, commonplace books in, 3–4
typographical elements
  commonplace markers, 18–19, 33n53, 36n84, 142
  in extract from *Othello* (Shakespeare), 172–74, *173*
  and rise of printed texts, 18–19
  of songs, 171–72
  See also commonplace markers

Van Strien, Kees, 154n48
verse miscellanies
  Bodleian MS Sancroft 53, 168–174
  definition of, 106n10
  Killigrew Miscellany, 121–22
  vs. prose miscellanies, 175–76
  in Restoration era, 117–127
  songs in, 104, 121–23
Villiers, George (Earl of Buckingham), 60
Villiers, John (Viscount Purbeck), 60, 61, 62, 63
Virgil, 29n4

Wagstaffe, Thomas, 162
Walker, Obadiah, *Of Education*, 120
Walkington, Thomas
  and *Love's Labour's Lost* (Shakespeare), 220n45
  Optick Glasse of Humors, 203, 205–8, 209, 210–11, 212–13, 214–15, 216
Waller, Edmund, "Upon Mr. John Fletcher's playes," 184
Wanley, Humfrey, 167
  See also British Library (BL) MS Harley 6947

war, in *English Treasury* (Cotgrave), 92
Warton, Thomas, 87
Wase, Christopher, 211–13, 221n48
W. B. *See* Basse, William
Webster, John
  The Devil's Law Case, 83, 178
  The White Devil extracted in Bodleian MS Sancroft 18, 177–78
Wells, Stanley, 10
Wentworth, Thomas, 62
West, William N., xix
W. H., 3
Whitney, Charles, 203
  Early Responses to Renaissance Drama, xix
William of Orange, 163–64
Wilson, John, 45, 46
Wolfe, Heather, xxviin13
women
  as compilers of extracts, 25, 40–41n130
  female voices as silenced in Sancroft's extract of *Othello* (Shakespeare), 172–74
Wren, Christopher, 193n6
Wright, Abraham, 11, 78
  aesthetic motivation of, 84
  on commonplacing, 87–88
  dramatic miscellany of (BL MS Add. 22608), 106–7n19
  as coded, 109n53
  commentaries in, 81–83, 107n20
  dating of, 84–85, 107–8n29, 108n30
  dedicatory epistles of, 87–88
  extracts from *Love In it's Extasie* (Peaps) in, 85
  royalist nostalgia in, 81, 84, 85, 88
  table of contents in, 81, *82*, *83*, 84
  influence on son (James), 86–87
  Parnassus Biceps, 84
  as royalist, 87

Wright, James
　Abraham's influence on, 86–87
　Country Conversations, 86
　*Historia Histrionica: An Historical
　　Account of the English
　　Stage*, 86

Wycherley, William
　works by, extracted in Bodleian MS
　　Eng. misc. c. 34, 137

Young, Robert, 193n11

About the Author

Laura Estill is assistant professor of English at Texas A&M University, where she specializes in early modern drama, print and manuscript culture, and digital humanities. She is editor of the World Shakespeare Bibliography (www.worldshakesbib.org). Her work has appeared in journals and collections such as *Huntington Library Quarterly*, *Shakespeare*, *Early Theatre* and, with Arthur F. Marotti, *The Oxford Handbook of Shakespeare*. She has articles and chapters forthcoming in *Shakespeare Quarterly*, *Shakespeare's Language in Digital Media: Old Words, New Tools*, and *Shakespeare and Textual Studies: A Handbook*.

www.ingramcontent.com/pod-product-compliance
Lightning Source LLC
Chambersburg PA
CBHW020609300426
44113CB00007B/574